W9-BYH-973

Praise for A GUEST IN MY OWN COUNTRY

"An East European might say that George Konrád's adventures through two terror regimes and a major revolution have been what one would expect from someone unfortunate enough to have been born in that part of Europe. In reality, Konrád's autobiography reveals much more than that: great tragedies, fabulous escapes, a complex personality, a great writer and beyond that, dignity and courage in the worst of circumstances." —ISTVÁN DEÁK, Professor Emeritus of history at Columbia University; author of *The Lawful Revolution: Louis Kossuth and the Hungarians, 1848-1849*

"Konrád takes you into another country. Another world. His words allow you to feel his world. In intimate and luxuriant detail. The world of childhood, the world of war, of politics, of hatreds. The world of words and of longing. In illuminating his country, his world, Konrád illuminates our world." —LILY BRETT, author of *Too Many Men*

"Konrád's prose was never so luminous as in these moving yet clear-eyed and forthright recollections of his wartime childhood, his youth and early manhood under Communism, and of his life as a writer in the 'soft dictatorship' and after." —IVAN SANDERS, translator, literary critic, and Adjunct Professor at Columbia University

"Emerging from the pen of a premier Hungarian intellectual, and spanning several turbulent decades, this vivid, unsentimental, candidly intimate memoir gives us an invaluable view of a complex history, and of a very Eastern European fate. Konrád's affectionate recollections of his childhood; his astonishing account of growing up precociously at war; and his sharply etched vignettes of repression and dissidence, poverty and pleasures thereafter, are marked by grace amidst turbulence, honesty without bitterness, and by an admirable balance between skepticism and deep attachments. An important, illuminating, and ultimately hopeful book." —EVA HOFFMAN, author of *Lost in Translation* and *After Such Knowledge*

A GUEST IN MY OWN COUNTRY

A Hungarian Life

George Konrád

Translated from the Hungarian by Jim Tucker
Edited by Michael Henry Heim

Other Press · New York

Production Editor: Mira S. Park
Text design: Kaoru Tamura

This book was set in 11 pt. ACaslon Regular by Alpha Graphics in Pittsfield, NH.

10 9 8 7 6 5 4 3 2 1

Library of Congress Cataloging-in-Publication Data

Konrád, György.
[Elutazás és Hazatérés. English]
A guest in my own country : a Hungarian life / by George Konrád ; translated by Jim Tucker ; edited by Michael Henry Heim.
p. cm.
Pt. 1. Originally published in 2001 as Elutazás és Hazatérés. Pt. 2. Originally published in 2003 as Fenn a hegyen napfogyatkozáskor.
ISBN-13: 978-1-59051-139-8
ISBN-10: 1-59051-139-5
1. Konrád, György. 2. Authors, Hungarian–20th century–Biography. I. Konrád, György. Fenn a hegyen napfogyatkozáskor. English. II. Tucker, Jim. III. Heim, Michael Henry. IV. Title.
PH3281.K7558Z46 2007
894'.51133—dc22
[B]   2006024280

I

Departure and Return

FEBRUARY 1945. WE ARE SITTING ON a bench in a motionless cattle car. I can't pull myself away from the open door and the wind whipping in off the snowy plains. I didn't want to be a constant guest in Budapest; I wanted to go home—a weeklong trip— to Berettyóújfalu, the town our parents had been abducted from, the town we had managed to leave a day before the deportations. Had we stayed one more day we would have ended up in Auschwitz. My sister, who was fourteen, might have survived, but I was eleven, and Dr. Mengele sent all my classmates, every last one, to the gas chambers.

Of our parents we knew nothing. I had given up on the idea of going from the staircase to the vestibule to the light-blue living room and finding everything as it had been. I had a feeling I would find nothing there at all. But if I closed my eyes, I could go through the old motions: walk downstairs, step through the iron gate, painted yellow, and see my father next to the tile oven, rubbing his hands, smiling, chatting, turning his blue eyes to everyone with a trusting but impish gaze, as if to ask, "We understand each other, don't we?" In a postprandial mood he would have gone onto the balcony and stretched out on his deck chair, lighting up a long Memphis cigarette in its gold mouthpiece, looking over the papers, then nodding off.

For as long as I can remember, I had a secret suspicion that everyone around me acted like children. I realized it applied to my parents as well when, not suspecting us of eavesdropping, they would banter playfully in the family bed: they were exactly like my sister and me.

From the age of five I knew I would be killed if Hitler won. One morning in my mother's lap I asked who Hitler was and why he said so many terrible things about the Jews. She replied that she herself didn't know. Maybe he was insane, maybe just cruel. Here was a man who said the Jews should disappear. But why should we disappear from our own house, and even if we did, where would we go? Just because this Hitler, whom my nanny followed with such enthusiasm, came up with crazy ideas like packing us off to somewhere else.

And how did Hilda feel about all this? How could she possibly be happy about my disappearing, yet go on bathing me with such kindness every morning, playing with me, letting me snuggle up to her, and even occasionally slipping into the tub with me? How could Hilda, who was so good to me, wish me ill? She was pretty, Hilda was, but obviously stupid. I decided quite early that anything threatening me was idiotic, since I was a threat to no one. I was unwilling to allow that anything bad for me could possibly be an intelligent idea.

For as long as I can remember, I have felt like the five-year-old who ventured all the way out to the Berettyó Bridge on his bicycle and stared into the river, a mere eight or ten meters wide in summer, twisting yellow and muddy through its grassy channel, pretending to be docile but in fact riddled with whirlpools. That boy was no different, no more or less a child than I am today. In spring I watched from the bridge as the swollen river swept away entire houses and uprooted large trees, watched it washing over the dike, watched animal carcasses floating by. You could row a boat between the houses: all the streets near the bank were under water.

I felt that you could not count on anything entirely, that danger was lurking everywhere. The air inside the Broken Tower was cool, moldy, bat-infested. I was frightened by the rats. The Turks had once laid siege to it and finally taken it. This is a wild region, a region of occupations: myriad armies have passed through it; myriad outlaws, marauders, haiduks, and bounty hunters have galloped over its plains. The townspeople take refuge in the swamps.

My childhood recollection is that people had a slow way of talking that was expansive and quite cordial. They took their time about communicating and expected no haste in return. The herdsmen cracked the whip every afternoon as they brought the cows home. Then there were the Bihar knifemen: cutting in on a Saturday-night dance could mean a stabbing.

With my long hair curling at the sides and suspenders holding up my trousers, I step into the living room. The upholstery is blue, blue the tablecloth. The living room opens onto a sunlit balcony, where cheese pastries and hot cocoa stand waiting. I am well disposed to everyone and aware of the many who have been working for me that day, making my entrance possible. The bathroom heater and the living-room tile stove have been lit, the cleaning done. Sounds of food being prepared travel in from the kitchen.

I cock an ear: it might be the diminutive Mr. Tóth, bringing buffalo milk and buffalo butter. On my way to Várad in summer I would see his herd from the train window lolling in a big puddle, barely lifting their heads above water. Mr. Tóth wasn't much larger than I. He was very graceful when he unrolled the bordered handkerchief he used for carrying money, including our monthly payment for the milk, curd cheese, and sour cream he brought, all as white as the buffalo were black.

I would have liked to be big and strong and gave our driver's biceps a hopeful squeeze. They had a nice bulge to them, and I wanted mine to be just as tan and thick. András and his horse Gyurka would bring water from the artesian well in the gray tank-cart. Women waited their turn with two pitchers apiece. I remember András and Gyula, and Vilma, Irma, Juliska, and Regina from the kitchen, and Annie, Hilda, and Lívia from the nursery.

The fire is still crackling in the tile oven. There is no need to close the oven door until the embers start crumbling. I rub its side and take my seat at the table, where a booster pillow rests on the chair. It is nine o'clock. My father went down to the store at eight; his assistants and errand boys awaited him at the door. I will have to eat breakfast without him in the company of my sister Éva and my nanny. Mother will join us later if she can spare the time. She will set her keys down on the blue tablecloth. Opening and closing the various doors and drawers takes a long time.

This is perhaps my third birthday, a Saturday. The play of bright light off the synagogue's yellow wall behind our house is dazzling. The chestnut and sour cherry trees in the garden are already in bud. The living room is quiet, but I hear rustlings coming from the dining room. I'm not looking forward to the door opening, because as soon as it does I will have to express my happiness openly. Once you have your gifts, you must play with them. How long can you sit on a rocking horse?

The big news is that the storks have taken their place on the tower next to the Tablets of the Covenant on the synagogue: the winter has not destroyed their nest. One tower is the family home, the other the sanctum of the paterfamilias, where, towards evening, having supplied his charges with treasures from the hunt, he would retire for meditation, leg up, bill tucked in.

A special smell emanates from the chest where the logs for the fire are kept. It mingles with the aroma of burning oak. From here we may proceed to my parents' bedroom, where the scent of Mother's dresser predominates, the ever-present scent of lavender, a moth repellent. Another exciting symphony of scents calls me to the kitchen, but can't we put off eating for the moment (well, maybe just a cheese pastry to go with my café au lait): the smell of onions and bloody meat is just too much, nor am I ready for the sight of a fowl lying on a stone, the blood spurting from its neck onto a white enameled plate. (The servants let it coagulate, then cook it with fried onions for their morning snack.)

The breakfast is splendid. Now let's make some serious plans for the day. We'll go down to my father's hardware store, a space ten meters by twenty, with a cellar below that serves as a warehouse. If it was made of iron, you could find it there—anything the people of Csonka-Bihar County could need. The reason it was called Csonka-Bihar, "Rum Bihar," was that neighboring Transylvania, including its capital Nagyvárad (together with most of my family, Hungarian-speaking middle-class Jews), had been uncoupled from Hungary after the First World War and Berettyóújfalu had become the seat of what was left of Bihar County. Everyone came here to do the weekly shopping on market Thursdays, even from outlying villages.

On that day things would bustle starting early in the morning: bells chiming on horses' necks, carts on runners in winter. Even closed windows in the children's room could not seal out the beating of hoofs, the whinnying, the rumble of carts, the mooing. My father's hardware store was filled with customers bargaining for goods, punctuated by bouts of hearty conviviality. His assistants, who knew most of them, followed suit, and old Aunt Mari and Uncle János held up their end as well. My father's employees had all started out with him; they were trained by him from the age of thirteen. Before opening they would sweep the greasy floor and sprinkle it down in figure-eights. The assistants wore blue smocks, the bookkeeper a black silk jacket, my father a dark gray suit. The smell of iron and wood shavings wafted over me, then the oil used to grease the cart axles, then the oily paper used to wrap hunting arms. I could have told nails from wire with my eyes shut, by smell alone. The room smelled of men, of boots, of the mid-morning snack: bread, raw bacon, and chunks of onion inserted under mustaches on the tip of a knife.

Lajos Üveges can wait on three customers at a time, tossing pleasantries and encouragement this way and that, yet find time to ask me "How's tricks?" He knows exactly what you need for your cart; there is no artisan in Berettyóújfalu whose craft is a mystery to Lajos Üveges. "Just watch how it's done," is his advice to me in life. I watch him rolling a cigarette with one hand, building a seesaw, repairing a bicycle. So that's how you do it. He loves to work: smelting iron, fixing circuits, extracting honey from a beehive—for Lajos it is all sheer entertainment. He jokes with the old peasants in a way that does not exclude respect. His mustache exudes a pleasant smell of pomade, like my grandfather's, the old man having given him some of his. If there is such a thing as an ideal mustache wax scent, this is it.

When my father's business was taken over by the state in 1950, Lajos Üveges was named manager. By then it had twenty-two employees, had expanded into the second-floor apartment, and used the neighboring synagogue as a warehouse. Among the assistants he was the best man for the job, though not quite so good as my father.

The town crier shouts out public announcements to the festive sound of a drumbeat. A military band marches past. The drum major, generally fat, swings his long, striped staff in the ritual manner. Bringing up the rear, a diminutive Gypsy boy pounds his drum. The lyrics grow ever more unpleasant: "Jew, Jew, dirty Jew!" is how one begins. My father simply closes the door.

The smell of horse and cow manure fills the streets. No matter how much the main street is swept, the horse- and ox-carts leave their muck clinging to the cobblestones. Herds too file by, morning and evening, resourcefully splitting up to fill the small side streets. Cows and geese find their way home as skillfully as people.

To this day I can smell the pool, filled by slow bubblings from the artesian spring. Every Sunday night it was drained; only after it had been cleaned did the refilling, which lasted until Wednesday evening, begin. The well-water, with its aroma of iron and sulfur, surged up several hundred meters to lend the walls of the pool a rust-brown hue. It was our drinking water, arriving at the house in an enameled can and at the table in a glass pitcher. Water for washing was hauled from the well on a horse-drawn tank cart, poured into the cellar, then pumped to the attic. From there it came through the tap to the bathtub. It took the work of many to keep a middle-class household going. I can still hear the servant girls singing. We had an old woman cook, Regina, a gentle soul. When she lost her temper, her curse was, "May a quiet rain fall on him!"

I can hear the congregation singing "The Lord Is One." The synagogue had a sour smell from the prayer shawls, and voices at prayer sometimes melted into a background of rumbling and muttering. I might have a scuffle with a goat in the temple courtyard, grabbing it by the horns and trying to push it back. It would yield to a point, then butt, and down I would fall on my behind.

My family was rural, mainly from Bihar County; some came from Nagyvárad, others from Berettyóújfalu, Debrecen, Miskolc, Brassó, and Kolozsvár. They were Hungarian-speaking Jews. Almost all are dead today. Five of my cousins were killed at Auschwitz and Mauthausen. My father's three older sisters and both of my mother's met the same end. One of my maternal uncles was shot in the head in the street by the Arrow Cross, the Hungarian Fascist party.

My father's generation had a *gimnázium* education, while my own—including a textile engineer, a biologist, a chemist, an economist, a mathematician, and a writer—graduated from the university. The previous generation had been businessmen, factory owners, a doctor, a banker, a pharmacist, and an optician, all respectable members of the middle class until they were deported; my generation became intellectuals and critical spirits: a leftist engineer who organized a strike against his father, a medic expelled from school who organized a group of partisans, and rebellious humanists.

My mother's family was more well-to-do, a result of the practicality and business sense not so much of my grandfather as of my grandmother. My maternal grandfather was more reader than businessman, but he had a son-in-law with a great flair for commerce, and through him the family was involved in a furniture factory, a bitumen and lime plant, and logging tracts. He was a religious man, if not strictly Orthodox, and read widely in Judaica. He belonged to the boards of both the Reform and Orthodox congregations in Nagyvárad. He had a taste for elaborate rituals, but also for the good life: working from nine to twelve was enough for him. Then came the family lunch, the afternoon café session, and, after dinner, reading—this in his own separate apartment, since by then he had had enough of the children and the commotion of family life.

For the Passover Seder dinner he would come to Berettyóújfalu from Nagyvárad. He was the one who read the answers to the Haggadah questions that I, as the youngest present, asked. Our Haggadah—the book containing the readings for the holiday, the memorial of exile—was bound in cedar and ornamented with mosaics. It had drawings as well, four in particular: the wise son, the wicked son, the merchant son, and the son so simple he does not know how to ask. I was particularly delighted by the one who does not know how to ask, but my grandfather said the role did not suit me as I was constantly pestering him with questions.

During the evening ceremony a glass of wine was set out between the two windows for the prophet Elijah. By morning it was gone. I was intrigued by the prospect of the prophet Elijah's visit. Once, in the nursery, I heard rustlings from the adjoining dining room. I darted from my bed and peeped out through the door. I saw my grandfather in a full-length white nightshirt take the glass and drink it. He remarried ten years after my grandmother's death. He was eighty.

We also had a Christmas tree with gifts beneath it, and my sister would play "Silent Night," which we knew as "Stille Nacht, heilige Nacht," on the piano. My parents did not mention Jesus, but my nanny said he came bringing gifts and even decorating the tree. I pictured him as a flying, birdlike creature in contrast to Elijah, who thundered across the sky in a chariot of fire. But in the end I suspected that neither came at all.

My great-grandfather Salamon Gottfried was the first Jew to settle in Berettyóújfalu. He arrived at the end of the eighteenth century and opened a pub, which he left to his son Sámuel. Sámuel, who eventually held seventy acres, was a strong man who commanded respect and kept order, brooking neither crude speech nor boisterousness in an establishment whose clientele included the local toughs. His photograph shows a man with focused and probably blue eyes wearing a wide-brimmed black hat and a white shirt buttoned to the neck—a determined, strong-boned man, browned by the sun, full of endurance, and sporting a bifurcated beard. He too remarried as a widower, at seventy-seven. The only letters on their waist-high marble tombstones in the Jewish cemetery at Berettyóújfalu are Hebrew.

My paternal grandmother Karolina Gottfried was by all reports a kindly, good-humored, plump old woman. She had three girls, then a boy, my father József. She spoiled her only son, and when she looked in on her father in the pub at Szentmárton across the river, she would dress little Józsi up in a sailor suit and patent leather shoes and take him in a fiacre, which inspired sarcastic remarks. It was the same when Karolina took Józsi in a hired carriage to his grandfather. She wore the trousers in that house, at least at table, where the helpers and servants ate together with the master.

The master, my grandfather Ignác Kohn, was a tinsmith, and he and his men produced the buckets, cans, tubs, and other goods of galvanized sheet-iron for the local artisans. He was not happy when factory-produced goods swamped the market, and had no choice but to switch to retailing. By the turn of the century his hardware business, established in 1878, was the largest in the region.

My grandmother was somewhat embarrassed to find herself pregnant again at the age of forty-three. (Apparently in those days it would have been fitting to conceal the fact that Karolina and Ignác were still making love at such an advanced age.) The outcome was my father's youngest and favorite sister, the pretty Mariska, the most spoiled of all the siblings.

Both of their black-granite, life-size gravestones are still standing in the abandoned, weed-infested Jewish cemetery at Berettyóújfalu, where no one has been interred for decades, that is, since the entire Jewish community, some one thousand people, disappeared from the village, which has since become a small city. Ignác, who outlived his wife Karolina, had the following carved on her gravestone: "You were my happiness, my pride." Despite heavy battles in the cemetery at the end of the Second World War their granite pillars were not so much as scratched by the bullets, and they will long continue to stand—if no one sees fit to knock them down, that is.

When I read out my father's particulars to the officials in charge of granting gravesites at the Síp Street congregation in Budapest, the old gentleman who kept the enormous register slapped his forehead and said, "I remember him. Fine reputation. Solid, solvent." Apparently he had once visited us as a traveling salesman. My father tended to buy from factories and had reservations about these wanderers with samples in their bags, but he also had a feeling for people and a sense of humor that made his company quite pleasant. He was a guileless man who never thought his debtors might run off on him, as they generally did not. To his poorer customers he granted credit if they could not pay, certain as he was that sooner or later they would come up with what they owed him. He never bought or sold wares that were less than reliable. Everything associated with him was thoroughly sturdy, be it a kettle, a bicycle, or his word.

My father read several newspapers and started listening to the BBC's Hungarian-language broadcasts at the beginning of the war. I was intimately familiar with the BBC's four knocks, since I would crouch behind my father as he tried to hear the news amidst all the jamming. From the middle of the war he listened to Moscow as well. We had to close the doors and windows: by turning the knob this way and that with great concentration over the forty-nine, forty-one, thirty-one, and twenty-five meter bands of the shortwave we were committing a subversive act.

An old photo from the family album (lost at the end of the war) comes to mind: my grandfather, my aunts, and my father are leaning over a white-enameled basin, their heads cocked to one side, which would be rather odd were it not for the wire hanging out of the basin: it signaled they were gathered around a single headphone to hear the first radio broadcast in the twenties. An uncomfortable setup, yet worth the trouble.

I was not yet in a position to take part in the scene, but by the time of the war I would perch behind my father on the couch every day at a quarter to two listening to the news, the real news, amidst the static. The sound would come and go; you really had to keep your ears pricked. My nine-year-old ears filled the intermittent gaps in my father's hearing. I became so attached to "This Is London" that when the Gestapo arrested my father in May

1944 on the charge of sending news to the BBC from his secret radio transmitter in the attic I was proud he was the object of such a noble accusation. Not a word of it was true.

My Bavarian nanny, the beautiful blonde Hilda, left us for Hitler: her father forbade her to work for Jews no matter how comfortable she felt with us. Then came the warm-hearted Hungarian Lívia, who not only spoke German and French well but played the piano. She wore her waist-length blonde hair braided; I never tired of watching her comb it. The Catholic Lívia fell in love with my father's accountant, Ernő Vashegyi, a quiet, lanky, well-read man, and center on the local soccer team. Ernő Vashegyi was handsome, but a Jew, which gave Lívia some pause. We often went to the soccer field with our nanny and sat in the small, wooden riser; everyone else either stood on the hill or perched on the fence. Whenever Ernő Vashegyi kicked a goal, Lívia and I would squeeze hands. Once in a while the earnest fellow would join us at the family table for lunch, but before long he was called up for forced labor and never returned.

Every Monday the local tradesmen would gather in my father's store to evaluate the previous day's performance of our team, the county champions. Other topics of long conversations included rain (precious), drought (worrisome), the price of wheat, and what that lunatic was after anyway. Politics was a theme to be discussed mainly with other Jews; otherwise it was prudent to hold one's tongue: fascism had crept into the heads of some intelligent people, for whom regaining the Hungarian-speaking territories lost after World War I at the Trianon Conference was conceivable only with Hitler's support.

My ancestors lived out their lives as Jewish middle-class Hungarians. My father was the primary taxpayer in the town's ambit of some twelve thousand people. As such, he was given membership at the gentleman's club, the "casino," though he never went there. Nailed to the right side of the street entrance to his business was a mezuzah, a parchment roll in a mother-of-pearl case containing a handwritten text of the "Sh'ma," the central Sabbath prayer: "Hear O Israel, the Lord our God, the Lord is one." Only He, and no other: no pagan godhead in animal or human form.

On the doorpost below the mezuzah was a small metal plaque showing the outline of the historical borders of Hungary in 1914 and within it, painted in solid black, the 1920 territory, chopped to thirty percent of its original size and the slogan "No, no, never!"—meaning that we would never accept the loss. The members of my family thought of themselves as good Hungarians and good Jews. The two did not come to be viewed as separate until World War II.

The Hungarian government took up arms on the German side with the aim of recovering part of the lost territories, and it was willing to send half a million Jews to German camps in exchange. It was a bad bargain, because in the end they lost not only the Jews but the territory as well, and were left with the shame of it all. True, not everyone feels this way: there are those who feel that while many Hungarian Jews were killed in Auschwitz the number was too small.

The Hungarian flag in the middle of the village flew at half mast, and as one piece of territory or another rejoined Hungary it was raised a bit higher. On 15 March, the holiday of the 1848 War of Independence, the children of the Jewish elementary school would march before it in ceremonial step sporting white shirts and dark blue shorts.

My father took part in the reoccupation of Ruthenia and its principal cities, Ungvár and Munkács. He had an artilleryman's uniform with a single white star on it, signifying the rank of private first class, but with the red arm braid that marked those who had graduated from the *gimnázium*. On weekends he would don his uniform and boots and meet my mother at the hotel in Ungvár.

I advanced one rank higher in the military order, becoming a corporal. (My son Miklós did not carry on the tradition, never advancing past private in the French Army; in fact, they tossed him in the clink for talking back to his commander.) I was interested in military events from the age of seven and prayed for General Montgomery to defeat General Rommel in Africa and for the Allies to take Tunis and Bizerta. I was a patriot who could be moved to tears for Hungary, but at the same time I was for an Allied victory. Based on what I heard and saw in the newsreels, I tried to imagine the battles of Stalingrad, Smolensk, and Kursk as well. Lying prone in the dark under the net of my brass bed, I would press my thumbs lightly to my eyes and on would come the newsreels, my own versions of the Hungarian and German products, all tanks and heavy artillery and air battles fading into the starry night.

The sky is bigger beyond the Tisza, the roads muddier than west of the Danube. This is the eastern end of the country, where you would once have found the highest concentration of people going barefoot and old men standing before their house doors in dark blue burlap aprons. It was a picture as constant as the buffaloes grazing in their lake.

Coming to Berettyóújfalu by train, I make my way over red slag between the tracks, then pass the green iron-tube railing onto the platform with its yellow-brick paving. The red-hatted signalman salutes me with his signal disk, the telegraph machine jingling away behind him. It is some time in the seventies, and I am lying in a room at the Bihar Hotel, a few steps from my childhood home. There is no hot water, and the door to the W.C. does not close: you have to hold the handle. Even though the flies land all over me, I do not swipe at them. I have drunk a lot of *pálinka* in the heat. The bus motors at the station produce a constant rumble. In the cinema across the road the Gypsy kids make the same smacking sound when kissing as they did before the war, but nowadays it is no longer permitted to spit pumpkin and sunflower husks onto the floor.

I take a close look at our house, ambling over the cracked sidewalk by the hapless shacks that seem to survive all events. A couple emerges from the courtyard that was one of my old haunts. The little girls who used to play with dolls are old now; they look like their mothers, the boys like their fathers. Faces peering through the fence. The indifference of the stares.

I go to the marketplace too. Nearly everything is different there now: trucks and tractors stirring up dust, the young scooting around on motorcycles. What has not changed is the rumpus of the women, the clamor of geese and ducks, the long baying of the oxen, the fresh scent of horse manure, the mounds of apricots and new potatoes. The merry-go-round is still there, as are the cotton-candy vendor and the table covered with jackknives. You can still get a little wooden rooster that clacks its wings. All but gone by now, though, is the bench in front of a house where one or two old men would pass the hours smoking a pipe, and the bright light unwrapping all the objects to reveal their slow decay.

I think I wanted to make up my mind about something. One hot afternoon, after lolling for a while on a sweaty bed in a hotel room the size of a coffin, I wandered down the main street and through the soccer field. No one said a word to me. Sometimes I had the feeling I was being watched. In a side-street bar, smelly and raucous, a drunkard launched into a song, then gave up and stared out of the window.

An old man, wearing nothing but a jacket over his bronze, tattooed torso, told me of a time when I liked to sit with him on the coach-box and he would pass me the whip. It was András, our former coachman, he of the large, reverie-inspiring biceps. András was the one who polished the linoleum in my room by skating on waxed brushes, the one who brought the firewood upstairs, who lit the fire in the cast-iron stove in the bathroom so I could have warm water for my bath when I got up. His horse Gyurka pulled the water tank, and András filled it, bucket by bucket, at the slow-gurgling artesian well in front of the post office and behind the national flag in the park. As likely as not, András had never had the experience of lounging in a bathtub. The servants bathed once a week in the galvanized tin tub in the laundry room. Just so I could step in the tub, the servant girl would have to keep the fire going while my nanny set out my ironed whites. The washing-soap smell was part of a larger picture: the servant girl had a servant smell, the valet a valet smell.

The servant girl would not simply take her pay from my mother's hand; she would seize her hand and kiss it. My father would shake hands with his employees when handing them their pay envelopes. I don't remember the coachman or the woman who was our cook ever sitting down in any of our rooms—in the kitchen, yes: András would sit there on the stool, stirring the thick soup the cook ladled straight from the kettle into his bowl with an enameled spoon. No kettle was ever put on the dining table, only a porcelain soup server and a silver spoon for serving. The servants would spend whole afternoons polishing the silverware.

Was I religious? Since I prayed, I was religious. But children are hedonists and enjoy some aspects of a religion while rejecting those that deprive them of pleasure. The wine I enjoyed, though I got it only on Seder evening, when I was allowed to dip my little finger into the wineglass and lick it. The horseradish on the table represented bitterness, the bread dipped in honey good fortune. After presiding over the ritual, my grandfather would listen to my doubts and say that there are many images of God, but that He is greater than any image, for God always transcends what is portrayed.

We were Cohanites, Cohens, that is, descendants of Aaron and the priests who guarded the Ark of the Covenant. My maternal grandfather was also a Cohen, though the designation passed from father to son. Only Cohanites are entitled to remove the Torah scrolls from the tabernacle and carry them around the temple, blessing the congregation. Special regulations of cleanliness forbid them to marry a divorced woman or enter a cemetery: whoever touches Holy Scripture may have no contact with the dead. For my part, I have married two divorcées and enjoy strolling through cemeteries.

My father was comfortable with the positions of responsibility he held, and had no desire to take a leading role in either the town or the congregation. He was who he was. My parents were no more assimilated than other Jews; they simply went a little further into the world at large, where all religions and nationalities learn new ways of life, with mixed feelings perhaps, but slowly and surely, where Jews and Christians alike are assimilants, adapting to the age and to life beyond national borders. But my cousin István and I were the only ones at the Jewish school who did not attend afternoon Talmud lessons in the whitewashed one-story building where one day half a brick tumbled through the dusty courtyard's fence and landed on my head. The others would arrive home from school at one, but had to go to the *cheder*, the religious school, at three, where they would immerse themselves in the study of Jewish law and its interpretation. Since they stayed in the classroom until six, they tended to be sickly. I was stronger. Ugly fights were the fashion. All the kids would stand around the enemies and spur them on. We fought on a floor regularly sprinkled with oil. The winner was the one who pinned the other's shoulders to the ground and held him there. Success was sweeter if a little blood flowed from the loser's nose and mouth.

Even in childhood the pen was my favorite tool, though I also assembled model airplanes and even soldered one from steel wire. Fixing the hubs on my bike or patching an inner tube was no trickier for me than scratching the tip of my nose. The screwdriver and the saw took gladly to my hand. There was nothing I enjoyed more than observing master craftsmen: I loved watching the locksmith, the blacksmith, the radio repairman at work—

my father's customers all. Nagy, the hospital's chief engineer, I considered a superior being, and the fact that he never could wash the oil entirely from his hands met with my reverential approval. Actually I was preparing an enterprise similar to his, an airplane factory, which was to be located just behind the lake where we skated (and bathed the geese in the summertime). All it would take was a little land from the pasture. Obviously I would first have to study at the English *gimnázium* in Sárospatak, then at Oxford or Cambridge. Having returned with my diploma, I would inherit—or simply run—my father's hardware business and thence take the step into production. Though why not manufacture planes from the outset? Start small but quickly move on to passenger planes, so one day all of Berettyóújfalu would ride out to the airport in their oxcarts and take a pleasure flight free of charge, experience Derecske, Mikepércs, Zsáka, Furta, Csökmő, and maybe even Bakonszeg from the air. Such was the plan.

My cousin István Zádor was a month younger then I: He was a Taurus, I an Aries. We entered the world in the same birthing room. He was a nice pink color and quiet, while I (a breech birth, with the umbilical cord wrapped around my neck) came out red, bald, and in agony. My mother, ashamed of my pointed head, kept it a secret by covering it with a crocheted cap before my father came to visit. To this day I have to laugh when I think of my father's face as I plagued him with questions about our first meeting. "You were quite an ugly little runt," he would say, and then add reassuringly, "but you managed to outgrow it."

Both István and I were born at the university clinic in Debrecen, though we lived in Berettyóújfalu. Ours were the two most affluent Jewish families in the Alföld region. József Konrád, my father, was generally considered wealthier, since he had a multistory house on the main street, but actually his cousin Béla Zádor had more money and a college degree to boot.

My father had only a commercial high school education, which he received in Késmárk, an ancient town in the Tatra Mountains, home to a significant Saxon—that is, German—community. Although our family's native tongue was Hungarian, it made sense at the time of the Austro-Hungarian Monarchy to board the boys with a family where German was spoken at table. My father ended up in the house of a mathematics teacher. He would take the young lady of the family walking on the castle walls or skating in the Dobsina ice cave, where the snow lingered into summer. This cave occupied my imagination intensely. Several times I asked my father about it as he reclined on a chaise longue on the balcony after dinner and his words flowed freely. All I learned was that the young lady had a red skating outfit and that my father also turned a few figures with the girl on his arm.

István and I took our first steps with a walker while our mothers chatted. They were sisters-in-law and friends. István's mother was my father's younger sister, his father my father's cousin. Mariska, the young beauty, was noticed early by Béla Zádor, her cousin.

During my first days at school my governess Lívia sat with me at my desk. Whenever she stood, I sobbed at the thought of her leaving me there alone. On the fourth day she managed to tear herself from my side. I cried, and the others made fun of me, so I got angry and beat up every single one of them. At home I announced that I did not want to go to school, and repeated this regularly over the course of a month. My parents finally accepted the situation, and I became a home student. So did István. As our instructor did not come until the afternoon, we were free all morning out in their large garden among the sour-cherry trees on the banks of Kálló Creek. We would finish the lesson quickly and go back to playing soccer or cutting cattails or catching frogs.

When Aunt Mariska allowed it, little István would watch his mother stretch out in the tub. He would feel her clothes and smell her colognes. The governess, who answered to the name of Nene, would shout for him to come out immediately and stop bothering his mother, but István would just stand there, watching through fogged-up glasses as his mother turned her beautiful legs.

We sat together in school and were reluctant to part company. István would walk me home and come up the stairs. "You understand, Gyuri, don't you?" he would ask at intervals, standing in the front doorway. "I understand, I understand," I would answer after a considered pause. No one was as good to talk to as István, and I never talked to anyone else as much. With our arms on each other's shoulders we would walk round and round the courtyard at school. Having failed to shut us up, they tried to separate us, but ended up leaving us in the same row. István was not beyond a few pranks, but was bored by childish rowdiness. I know a number of people who admit that István was smarter than they; I am one.

István Zádor's brother Pál was three years younger than he and followed in his footsteps. A mathematician, he has been living in Washington for about forty years now. Pali could beat both of us in ping-pong: he was bent on making up for those three years. He had no tolerance for an affront. If a salesman happened to say anything out of line, Pali would answer with a single compound noun: "Curcowstupidpig!" In the time it would have taken for his father to come out of the house and set him straight, we were all down on the bank of the creek amid the sour-cherry trees and raspberry bushes.

They lived in a spacious house just opposite ours. It incorporated a large clothing and shoe store. The salesmen cut fine figures in well-tailored suits of English cloth and liked to wave fabrics in the air with a flourish. They had a pleasant way about them, complimenting the women as they pivoted in front of the mirror.

Stepping into my father's hardware store, you inhaled the reliable iron smell of nails, wire, cart-axles, ploughs, harrows, stoves, pots, bicycles, and hunting weapons. You could check the sharpness of a scythe with the tip of a finger, and should you wish to verify whether it was made of well-tempered steel, you would use a twenty-kilo iron weight that had done service since the beginning of human memory: you would knock the head of the scythe (without the handle) hard against the weight a few times and raise it to your ear to hear it ring.

It was an event for me whenever a load of goods arrived at the Berettyóújfalu station, the fruit of one of Father's Budapest trips. András and Gyurka would cart the crates home, and I would sit up on the box, where I had permission to give Gyurka the commands to go (*Ne!*) and stop (*Ho!*). It was exciting to help unload the large crates of flame-red enameled pots nested amid thick beds of fragrant wood shavings.

These pleasures were alien to István, who paid little attention to his father's business and rarely set foot in the store. He was none too comfortable playing the little son, hearing how much he had grown, suffering a pinch on the cheek. After one or two hellos he would retire to the innards of the house. Aunt Mariska, too, observed the store's activity from a distance, leaving things to Aunt Etelka, her untiring mother-in-law, who—small, thin, and deeply wrinkled—kept an eye on everything from the most natural place, her perch at the cash register.

Uncle Béla would pace the store, dealing personally with a few preferred customers, but bilious and impatient as he was he soon retreated into the apartment, which opened onto the garden, and settled into his heavy leather armchair in the half-darkness of the study next to Aunt Mariska's room. There he would read the ever-worsening news, later to discuss it with my father in our living room with concern, though not without hope.

Most ladies from the town's upper stratum found items to their liking in Uncle Béla's store. Aunt Mariska, though, did not—meaning that my mother, her friend, was under no obligation to buy her wardrobe from him either. The two would occasionally travel to Budapest.

Such a trip was inconceivable without a trunk and a hatbox, and they would be dutifully installed in a first-class compartment by András and the fiacre driver and the red-capped railway porter. At the Nyugati Station in Budapest the process was repeated in reverse, except that a taxi took my mother and Aunt Mariska to the Hotel Hungária on the Danube. They spent mornings at the finest tailors and evenings at the theater. When they returned, I would interrogate my mother about the best places to buy fabrics, whites, and shoes, just as I interrogated my father about the strengths and weaknesses of Budapest ironworks and Budapest wholesalers: everything in life had its place.

We all knew who the prettiest girl in the classroom was, who the biggest shrew. I will take this occasion to reveal that it was a true pleasure to grab the thick braids of Baba Blau, who sat in front of me, and give them a tug. Baba would laugh in a deep voice, then squeal on me. I would have to leave the room with the lid to my pen-case, which the teacher would use to slap my hand a few times. Once I had come back, Baba would stroke my hand and gaze up at the ceiling with a little sneer on her large, dark mouth. Then she would position her braids back within reach.

Aunt Mariska prepared all her life for something that never came. She loved clothes and dressed with originality and at great cost. She bought a great many books: modern novels for herself, Indian stories for the boys. But one day she went into the garden to rest under a camel-hair blanket in the whitewashed, rose-covered arbor and emerged all yellow, and yellow she remained. Only her gravestone is white, white marble.

István was left on his own at the age of five: after his mother died, his father grew melancholic. When Aunt Etelka died as well, Nene took over the household. Nene was unshakable in her knowledge of what constituted a proper diet: she was committed to whole-grain bread, creamed spinach, and boiled breast of chicken. Anyone who so much as cleared his throat at this fare was put to bed on the spot. She was a conscientious woman and a devout Catholic, but neither pretty nor happy. There were few signs of joy in István's house.

We would walk up and down the main street wearing jackets, caps, and gloves. We needed to ask permission to take off our gloves or open the top button of the jacket. We were watched by peasant boys wearing poor-quality boots.

When we cranked the arm of the telephone, a young lady answered, "Operator." "Give me 11," I would say. "Give me 60," said István. We did this many times a day. "Why don't you just walk across the street?" the girl would ask. "Just connect me, please," we said coolly, even at the age of seven.

Our fathers would hold onto our shoulders at the edge of the sidewalk until they felt we were old enough to cross the street on our own. An automobile was a rare and wondrous event, but there was no end of horse-drawn carriages.

We received one another in jackets, shook hands, showed our guests to their seats, and proceeded to speak of important issues. If we didn't want others to hear us, we left the house for the autumn garden. It was a pleasure to feel the leaf-bed crunching under our feet.

István never uttered a word lightly, and his face would show irritation at any idle remark; I was interested in all sorts of things that seemed to bore the often distant István, and I tried to amuse him with my clowning. Coming from him, a *yes* or *no* had a real edge to it. He liked to draw the most extreme conclusions from his observations; I followed the path of his logic guardedly: I might see it differently tomorrow, by which time the now devastating train of his thought would have lost some of its force.

When the Germans occupied Hungary on 19 March 1944, I was eleven years old. What around the table we had merely feared had now come to pass: our island of exception was no more; something new was afoot. How simple it had all been! How comical everything that had happened now seemed! I thought back on the evenings I had spent listening to the men's dinner-table strategizing about how the English would move in from

Italy and Greece and initiate the western invasion, thereby giving our leader, Admiral Horthy, more room to maneuver and enabling him to jump ship and Hungary to begin its evolution into a neutral, Anglo-Saxon form of democracy. Until then our fathers could still run their businesses, medical practices, and law offices in peace. Jewish children could attend school in that sad, little one-story building with its dusty courtyard and beautiful prayer room without being humiliated by their teacher for being Jewish. On Friday evenings we could hear the shuffle of footsteps on the walkway by our house, where men dressed in black would make their way to temple under their broad-brimmed black hats accompanied by my wide-eyed schoolmates holding their fathers' hands.

On the day of the occupation I sat with my father at the radio in his bedroom. There was no news of resistance: the Hungarian troops did not put up a fight. The regent, the government, and the country as a whole simply lay down before the mighty Germans. I did not much trust Horthy. I had had a lead soldier of him from my earliest boyhood. I surrounded him with officers and an entire leaden infantry. They were all in green, while Horthy sported a cornflower-blue admiral's coat with gold tassels. I had a cannon as well. It could shoot miniature cannonballs a meter or so. The battlefield was the large, brown linoleum surface, where I would divide the armies and materiel in two. In the early days the winning army was always the one led by His Excellency the Regent. After we entered the war, cannonballs started knocking His Highness over, and from that point on, Horthy's army was the loser. I would shoot him with the cannon; he would fall on his back.

That evening all my uncles and cousins sat around the radio. According to a piece of stray news a local garrison commander had exhibited displeasure at the German invasion, and I immediately decided it would be the Újfalu regiment, under the command of Lieutenant Colonel Egyed, that would push the Germans back. After all, we had a large barracks on the edge of town, a powerful garrison with cannons drawn by giant artillery horses. If the Regent called on the people to fight for their freedom, he would find a foothold here in Bihar County.

"Him, of all people? Here?" István's smile was more than acerbic. Yes, the Lieutenant Colonel was a good man and no friend to the Germans. For years I had been formulating political prayers in bed after the lights were out. At school I discussed the war only with István, between classes, out in the corridors. We looked around to make sure others could not hear us. We soon learned we were individuals to be avoided. On the very eve of the occupation we had to concede that not only Horthy but also the commander of the local garrison had offered no resistance. The next day German tanks stood before the town hall and the Calvinist church manned by soldiers in pike-gray uniforms. Civilians avoided contact with them, avoided even looking in their direction. To the strains of a vigorous march, in rows so tight they practically touched, the Germans demonstrated how a military review was meant to look. They put our cockeyed Hungarian sad sacks to shame.

Before long there were patrols moving through the town commandeering living quarters. As my uncle's house was occupied in its entirety, my cousins moved in with us. Friends and relatives visited my parents to exchange news and share their bewilderment. My father sat out in the sunshine of the balcony with his eyes shut. He had had to close down the business, it being no longer his: there was a lock with a seal on the door. All valuables had to be turned in, the radio included. We three boys slept in the living room or, rather, pretended to sleep, then turned on a low lamp and availed ourselves of the walnut brandy in the sideboard to keep us awake through a night of talking politics.

New decrees appeared daily, so we knew that each day would be worse than the one before. We played ping-pong until dusk and fortunately did not have to part in the evening. Lacking the patience for board games, we discussed the chaotic current events. István thought the Russians would get here first and we would have communism. We did not know much about that. People returning from Ukraine said it was quite poor: goats slept in houses in the countryside; many families shared one apartment in the city. In our high-backed leather chairs we opined that poverty was tolerable as long as there was justice.

Ukraine held dark associations for the Jews of Berettyóújfalu. The younger men had been taken off to forced labor there in 1942. They had been forced to run naked through the halls of a Ukrainian school strewn with boot-nails. Hungarian police standing along the walls would hit them with the butts of their rifles. Something had got them worked up: they must have been drinking rum. Once the men's bundles had been inspected, they were allowed to dress outside in the snow. Watches, rings, and other valuables were confiscated. If they had concealed something, they were sent back to dance in the hall.

As the army retreated, they were moved westward. The sick were delivered to infirmary barracks; those who could not walk were carried on their comrades' backs. One night tongues of flame shot into the sky beyond the field of snow: soldiers had doused the infirmary in gasoline and set it afire, burning the sick Jews of the forced-labor patrol to death. Bandi Svéd rushed back through the snow, hallucinating that his brother at the barracks was walking towards him. His comrades ran after him and brought him back before the guards could shoot. The survivors were released in 1943, went back to Újfalu, and took up their previous lives. Everything was as in the old days, except they didn't talk much.

Our classmates were not particularly hostile to us, nor did they rejoice in our situation. They were uninformed and indifferent. They would look at the tanks and say nothing. "Now you're gonna have a peck of trouble," scornfully remarked a scraggly little boy, the poorest of us all and the worst pupil. His father had joined the Arrow Cross as a road worker. There were only two Jews at the school: István and myself. The poorer ones were not accepted.

István liked to establish bitter truths, the kind that got you absolutely nowhere. "We are the richest in our class and the best pupils: of course they don't like us. How many people are free of envy? Some like one or two Jews but not the rest. There are few good people and few truly bad ones; the rest are neither one nor the other. If they let the Jews live, all well and good; if they kill them, that's fine too. Everyone agrees to everything."

We were still heating the living room, and the atmosphere was familial: my mother was sewing yellow stars onto everyone's coats and jackets. Homemade stars were acceptable, though private industry was flexible in responding to the new needs. Everyone knew the specifications: canary yellow, machine-hemmed, six-by-six centimeters. You had to sew it on tightly enough to keep a pencil from going under the threads: those clever Jews were capable of putting it on just for show and taking it off whenever they felt like it. The Jewish newspaper encouraged its readers to follow the authorities' instructions to the letter.

One day István and I decided that the yellow star was nothing to be ashamed of, and walked all over town. It was spring, and since the school year had ended in April we had time on our hands. We stomped through the mud-covered unpaved side streets in heavy boots. Women stared down at us from tile-roofed, white-colonnaded porticoes.

I took to drinking from the lids of water barrels like a peasant boy. I went to the artesian well in front of the post office, where my good suit and shoes provoked pleasure at our misfortune from the constant semicircle of its users. But even with the yellow star I made new acquaintances: women occasionally greeted me warmly on the street; I would exchange a few words while waiting for the well. The village idiot, who once managed to eat an entire bucket of cooked beans on a bet, asked me for my yellow star. The onlookers laughed: still crazy as ever.

Then one morning they came, a loud pounding at the garden gate. I looked down from the balcony and saw five German officers, as many Hungarian gendarmes, and the ridiculous policeman Csontos, who had previously threatened to inform on everyone, but would let it slide for a few pengős. There were black caps too, but we did not yet know that they were the Gestapo. My father donned his tweed jacket, regulation yellow star and all, and went down to open the gate.

The Gestapo officer informed him in German that he had received a report accusing him of being an English spy and keeping a radio transmitter hidden in the attic. The house was searched from cellar to roof. I knew he had no transmitter, but it felt good to think he had been accused of having one. I very much wanted to look up to him. Had they searched him for a weapon I would have respected him even more.

My father was rather fearful and sensitive to pain, so my mother, the stronger of the two, led the Germans and gendarmes through the house, moving among them without any show of nerves and providing succinct information. They collected a few things—money, jewelry, a camera—but made no major finds. They appeared dissatisfied and ordered my father and uncle to go with them to the gendarmerie barracks and divulge where they had hidden the radio transmitter and, in general, what was hidden where. "Or, madam, would you *truly* have us believe that you are hiding nothing?"

Starting 15 May my father was no longer mine but the Gestapo's. He departed through the garden gate accompanied by gendarmes and German officers. I watched his slightly bent back from the upstairs balcony. I had never seen him escorted by bayonets before. After he and my uncle had been led off, we went to the dining room, where we could follow them through the window facing the street. In front were the Gestapo officers, behind them a couple of gendarmes in their sickle-feathered caps, then my father and uncle, then more gendarmes with bayonets at the ready, and the ridiculous Csontos policeman drawing up the rear. Everything else was as it always was: the cow pats drying in threes on the hot cobblestones, it being mid-May, the yellow light falling on the thick spire of the Calvinist church, the indifferent row of locust trees lining the main street.

My father looked neither right nor left: he greeted no one, nor did anyone greet him. It is instructive to observe the faces of acquaintances approaching from the opposite direction when one is being escorted by armed men. Although my father knew everyone he passed, he walked like an actor making an entrance on stage. The scene was not outrageous, just unusual. At first the faces showed puzzlement; then, slowly, things fell into place: Well, of course, it's the next step, they're taking the Jews. Only my mother and we children remained in the house.

Mother felt something had to be done. How could Hungarian gendarmes take her husband away at the command of some Germans in black uniforms? And what of the Hungarian leadership in the local administration? Had those gentlemen, whom we knew, contributed to the situation?

Mother put on a good dress and went to report the incident to the chief constable and lodge a complaint. As she was leaving the constable's office, a black car pulled up alongside her and a voice in German called out, "Step in, Mrs. Konrád, or do you want me to lock you up with your husband?" He was the chief Gestapo officer. My mother nodded. They did her the favor of putting her in the same jail as my father, though in another section. The gendarmes had rounded up a number of wealthier and better known Jews as hostages. Their wives had stayed at home. Only my mother went with her husband.

That saved our lives. I later found out it was an Arrow Cross pastry-maker who had turned us in. I have him to thank that I am alive today. Perhaps he bore us a grudge for avoiding his shop, though the entrance was pretty spectacular: polar bears—cut from planks with jigsaws and painted in oils—licking raspberry and vanilla ice cream. But the fare was worse than at Petrik's, where two little bird-faced old ladies with buns of gray hair served cream pastries and ice cream against a backdrop of butter-colored tile walls. They used eggs, sugar, vanilla—the proper ingredients— and eschewed experimentation. They were not Arrow Cross, and they went to church every Sunday morning, arm in arm, in white silk blouses and dark gray veiled hats. They opened their shop only after Mass, still redolent of church, selling cream pastries still warm from having been baked at dawn.

But they did not determine history. Providence had placed my fate in the hands of their rival, the one who compensated for poor quality with painted icebergs and seals. By finding an appropriate outlet for his flights of fancy in the genre of the denunciation letter and thereby landing my parents in a Gestapo internment camp, he bestowed a great fortune upon us, for the result was that we all, each in his own way, avoided the common fate of the Jews of Újfalu: Auschwitz.

Four of us children were left: myself, my sister, and my two cousins. They still had their Jewish governess Ibi, who, what with the fear and uncertain prospects of the times, exuded a less than pleasant smell. She was an awkward, weak-spined girl who had trouble with the cooking and cleaning: everything ended up jumbled and more or less dirty.

It was disturbing to see a way of life disintegrate, and I watched it crumble day by day. The absence of our parents and the worry were bad enough, but the nausea of helplessness was worse. István and I decided that our parents had made a mistake: we should have abandoned everything and departed earlier, because now we would have to abandon the house and garden anyway.

It was hot, a beautiful early summer, the cranes occupying their usual spot by the Tables of the Covenant. We played ping-pong like maniacs. The small market on Mondays, the large one on Thursdays, and on Friday afternoons, yellow stars on their jackets, a prayer shawl under their arms, the Jewish men plying their usual route past our house to the synagogue. Every evening we followed the regulations for the blackout, putting slat frames covered with black paper in the windows.

Though no longer allowed into the pool, we would peek through the fence and watch the boys imitating Stukas, the German dive-bombers, as they dived screeching from the trampoline into the twenty-five meter basin fed by the lazy, quiet flow of the artesian water. As usual it was drained on Sunday and would refill by Wednesday afternoon. The previous year István, Pali, and I had swum eighty lengths and were given money for chicken paprikás and noodles at the pool restaurant.

Taking walks with the yellow star gradually grew less pleasant. The message in the faces of the passersby did not generally leave a good feeling. The crudest would communicate, "Well, now you'll get what's been coming to you!"; the majority, "Aha. So that's how it is. So they're taking you away. Well, let them!" Even the warm looks, looks of sympathy, were combined with a quickened pace: solidarity in a hurry. We preferred to stay in the garden. I would swing for hours, until my head spun.

One day at noon a squadron of English and American bombers flashed their silver over the town. They dropped nothing on us, just sparkled in the light on the way to bomb the Debrecen railway station. The church bells tolled; a siren bleated. Gendarmes checked to see that everyone was down in the cellar. But we did not hide; we put our heads back and scoured the sky: Good. Up there at least *they* are in charge.

We got a postcard from my parents in Debrecen saying they were well, nothing more. Although the radio had been confiscated, we had other things to conceal: a sack of flour obtained without a permit, a few sides of bacon. They were in the cellar in a very clever spot that the house's architect (Mr. Berger, who ended up in the same transport and same camp as my parents) had shown my father in 1933, saying that a hiding place might come in handy some day. It was a tiny nook in total darkness on the far side of the concrete water tank and under the basement stair, a place only the most meticulous searcher would find. Our searchers were not so meticulous as all that.

There was also some money concealed behind the drawer in my father's desk: three packs of hundreds, thirty thousand pengős, the price of a large house. Even more serious was a cache of two iron boxes buried in the pipe shed and containing gold jewelry, for which my father had regularly traded a portion of his inventory. One box was buried in the corner and was later discovered, but they never found the other one because it was in the asymmetrical center of the area, where a gray-enamel kettle holding oats for the angora rabbits hung from a ceiling beam.

In those days we kept a dozen rabbits in a warren in the yard. Along the sides of the uppermost two cages were little wooden birthing-boxes, their doors open to the mother's large compartment. Bunnies are pink and hairless at birth and cuddle together, shivering, under their mother's belly. I would have liked to stroke them with at least the tip of my finger, but was told that the mother smells the scent of the human hand on her young and either pushes the human-scented young away or eats it. We were allowed to touch them only after their fur began to grow. Then we could take a few bunnies on our beds and play with them.

It was a joy to spin the soft, white shearings into yarn on a wheel. The line tended to break unless I was careful, in which case the foot-powered spinning wheel, jerry-built from bicycle wheels, could turn it unbroken for minutes on end, gently winding the line onto the spindle. The line that was unwinding from the ball of wool I held in my left hand, regulating its thickness between my right thumb and index finger. On winter afternoons, when the stove gave off more than enough heat even with its doors closed, we would transfer the yarn onto reels. We would listen to war news and classical music over the radio while my mother knitted us warm hats and skating sweaters from a Norwegian pattern.

Anyway, the kettle in the pipe shed hung there to keep the mice from fouling the oats for the rabbits. Though it was suspended from a wire attached to a hook on the ceiling, the mice managed to reach the oats by climbing along the ceiling beams and plopping down into Canaan, which turned out to be their vale of tears, because they were unable to clamber up the enameled walls of the kettle with their little claws and would scramble round and round, just above the endless bounty until a gruesome hand grabbed them by the tail and slammed them down on the cornerstone.

Night after night with admirable foresight Mother showed us exactly what she and Father had buried. "In case we are separated or never meet again, you children need to know what we have." Both my sister and I noted everything precisely. We spoke to no one about it. Even children can keep a secret. Our mother also sewed a few thin gold chains into our overcoats in case we needed them wherever we ended up. We had to prepare to be parted. The tone of the conversation was quite objective.

In May 1944 it was rumored that Jews outside the capital would be resettled in a work camp in what had been Polish territory. Cities were being built for them amidst lakes and forests. They would be set off from the population at large, but their lot would otherwise be decent. From this point on, Jews and Christians could not live together or even have contact with one another. The source of the problem—we, that is—had to be isolated.

The authorities relied on our understanding: Of course we can't live together; how could we ever think such a thing? The Hungarian Jewish newspaper was still exhorting everyone to respect the laws and follow regulations to the letter: Now, in this difficult hour, in this time of trial we must hold our own and show we are good Hungarians; only then can we hope for relief.

The national solidarity behind segregation was all well and good, but how complicated the process was to organize and execute, how much meticulous work was required on the authorities' part, how many Interior Ministry functionaries, high and low, had to curtail their hard-earned sleep and beg their wives' forgiveness. And this deportation took a great deal of work. Every bureau had to play its part, from the gendarmerie to the Commissioner for Abandoned Possessions. Worthy of special praise was the railway workers' model cooperation during enemy bombing: in a matter of weeks they had packed the Jews into freight trains and rolled them out of the country. Collecting six hundred thousand Jews, fencing them in, then transporting them with an armed patrol to freight cars—now *that* was something to drink to. The daily papers of the provincial cities announced with a sigh of relief that the air was clear, the region *judenfrei*, Jew-free.

We received a letter from relatives in Budapest inviting us to stay with them. We needed to decide quickly whether to go. Jews were no longer allowed to travel on trains, and papers were checked constantly: denunciation was a responsibility generally accepted. To travel to our relatives' in Budapest would require special permission from the gendarmerie, an exception, a one-time suspension of the regulations. And why go, anyway? Why not stay behind with the others? We had aunts and uncles and cousins here in town; we were still in our own house. Maybe they wouldn't come for us. Maybe some higher power would intervene. Swinging on my swing, I felt the joy of our ever-present swallows unalloyed. I was an Újfalu boy to the marrow of my bones. I would live here and die here.

But if they did come? It was easier to hide in Budapest, harder to find a needle in that haystack. I cast spells on the garden gate, still foolishly hoping my parents would simply return. I'd hear a knock, open the gate, and there they'd be, smiling in the gateway. I heard a knock. Jumping off the swing, I ran to the gate and slid back the bolt. There was no one standing there. Only German soldiers sauntering along the street with local girls.

I gave myself a good shake: we must leave the house after all. I went up to the apartment to make sure the cache of thirty thousand pengős was in its place. It was. I crossed the street to the house of a Christian lawyer, a good customer of my father's, rightist, yes, but not excessively anti-Semitic. I asked him to arrange transit permits for us. "It will cost a lot," he said. "Do you have money?" I said we did. "How much?" I told him. He said it was enough and I should give him half in advance. I went home and took him the fifteen thousand. He said he would let us know the next day what he had arranged. The whole matter was to remain between ourselves. Not a word about the money.

All of us discussed the issue. I was the most intent on going. That the others were hesitant was understandable: none of us relished the idea of being lodgers. Besides, we still had enough to eat and could curl up in our own armchairs. Our nearest relatives came and told us not to leave: they might deport only the residents of Nagyvárad, not us. Hungarian Jews had long since been reassuring themselves that what had happened to the Polish Jews could never happen to them.

By now every Jew had been registered. Under orders from the county registrar the congregation itself drew up the list, organizing it by street and number. As a result the gendarmes had no trouble rounding everyone up in the wee hours. Absolutely no one in town would risk hiding us. Since it would be harder to round up the Budapest Jews—they outnumbered us by far—they would go last. At least we could gain time.

The lawyer came the next day for the other fifteen thousand and told me I could pick up the papers. But first, he said, I should go to see Somody, the headmaster at the Civic Boys' School, a good man who had a high opinion of my abilities. I should thank him for being receptive to our petition. I went to the headmaster, thanked him for his kindness, and clicked my heels. He smiled at me, stroked my head, and said that I should continue to study hard and be a good Magyar. Now I could go to the gendarmerie for the transit papers.

A staff sergeant at the gendarmerie formulated the permit and knocked it out on a typewriter with his large hands. It took him some time to extract the information from the birth records and police registration papers and integrate it into the text. Rifles in the corner stand, hats with sickle-feathers on the hat stand, the smell of boots, an old desk, a green table lamp, an ink pad, separate permits for each of us four, eight thumps with the seal. A corporal eating bacon at the other desk looked over at me.

"So you're leaving?"

"Yes we are."

The staff sergeant handed me the four sheets of paper. He had worked hard and was satisfied with himself. And with me because I smiled at him deferentially. He wished me a pleasant journey, for which I thanked him. The papers fit into the inner pocket of my linen suit jacket. I had something in my pocket that other Jews lacked. The town leadership had given its blessing to our departure.

Laló Kádár offered to accompany us to our relatives' in Budapest. We were glad: Christians would no longer set foot in our garden; segregation was practically total. He was an assistant in my uncle's textile factory, a tall and elegant young man, center-half on the town's soccer team. His younger sister Katalin was my sister's classmate and friend and often came to our place to play board games. She had a black ponytail, very white teeth, and large brown eyes. I used to stare at her when she visited, and when it was time to say hello or goodbye I never neglected to kiss her on the cheek. She was three years older than I and therefore taller as well. She would come up to me to say goodbye. We would stand in silence before she let me kiss her.

My cousin Vera, who was my age, also came to see us. She wanted to know if I would write to her and where. It was still unclear which of us should feel sorry for the other. I kissed her on the cheek too, at dusk on 5 June 1944. We then set to packing. The question was how much to take and for what? What should we leave behind? Come to think of it, we wouldn't need this, we wouldn't need that either. Beyond the weight limit prescribed by railway regulations we had to keep in mind that once we arrived we could keep only what we could carry.

The next morning we got up at three-thirty. Standing in the bathtub, the cold water having gushed over my head, I opened my eyes and saw myself in the mirror. Laló Kádár came for us at five in a light, gray suit. He had bought the tickets the previous day. The stork couple stood motionless in the growing light by the Tablets of the Covenant.

Our parents' house closed behind us. Whoever comes may have whatever remains. We took a fiacre to the station. There was little traffic. Whoever looked at us looked at us with indifference. No one said anything. We were shadows, irregular shadows at that, on a road of our own, without bayonet escort for the time being. We waited at the station for the Budapest express from Nagyvárad. We leaned against the platform's green railing. It was growing warm. People stared at the yellow stars on our chests. How could *we* be *there*?

I was glad to see the train come. By the time I began looking back from the train window, I could make out only the steam mill and the Calvinist church tower. Soon nothing at all. Something had ended. Today I would say it was childhood. I saw that István too was clenching his teeth: we both felt the finality of it. We stood wordlessly by the window: German military trains with cannons and tanks on flatbed cars, someone playing a harmonica, gray uniforms, rubber mackintoshes.

There were people at work in the fields. The wheat was high and turning yellow in spots: a good harvest. The previous day the Szolnok railway station had been bombed. The control tower had toppled, the overpass been struck. Burned out, blackened ruins. We stood there for some time, giving priority to German military trains. Another train also went by. Women's eyes behind a cattle-car window screened with barbed wire, Jewish women's eyes most likely.

People on the platforms looked serious and frightened. The train made long stops. Everything was slow, but ordinary. Announcements often spoke of track repairs. Inspectors came twice during the journey to examine papers. The first time the chief inspector, a chubby, red-faced mustachioed man, wearing a small round feathered cap, snarled at Laló Kádár and said, "How come you're meddling in Jew business if you're a real Hungarian? How come you're escorting Jew brats?" Laló paled and did not respond.

There was no problem with the papers themselves, but I had a feeling that this inspector had the power to kick us off the train under some pretense or other. He looked us over, not yet sure whether he felt like it; we looked back, unsmiling, serious. We were children of privilege, and he was clearly not a member of the gentry, but I could not tell whether this would tip the scales in our favor or vice versa. He moved on.

Our stars and this little incident made us unusual passengers. Our fellow passengers said not a word either to us or to Laló. At times like this it is better to say nothing. The second inspection was almost lackadaisical and went more smoothly. The papers were in order, the inspector nodded coolly.

I was afraid of Budapest though I had traveled there with my mother for a week the previous year to partake of its pleasures. In the glass gallery of Nyugati Station we had entrusted ourselves to the care of a pink-capped porter, then taken a cab to the Hungária Hotel, where a bellboy opened the door to our anteroom and pulled back the floor-length cambric lace curtain so I could step out onto the balcony and view the Danube, the bridges, the green row of chestnut trees on the far bank, and the Royal Castle in all their radiance. I could hardly breathe I was so happy; I grew weak, as one does when the curtain rises at the opera and a fabulous ballroom emerges from the darkness. Then my mother stood behind me; now she might have been in that cattle car. Then we had a porter; now we carried our own bags. Yet now as then the glassed-in gallery was beautiful, untouched by bombs. "The invasion has begun!" shouted the newspaper hawker. "British and American troops land on the beaches of Normandy!" People pressed around the leather bag holding the papers, but made no comment. István and I set down our bags and shook hands. Then we looked around at the people. They were just like the people back in Újfalu: they acted as if nothing had happened.

We bade Laló Kádár a heavy-hearted farewell. He could return home now. How I would have liked to go back with him.

We later found out that the next day all Berettyóújfalu Jews were rounded up. Accompanied by gendarmes, they dragged their bags through the streets. The rest of the population watched them from the sidelines, some with greetings, others with insults, but most were silent. Thus just one day after our departure the Újfalu Jews were taken in cattle cars to the ghetto in Nagyvárad and from there to Auschwitz.

Two weeks later I was strolling along the Danube, and Vera had been gassed and burned. I did not know at the time that of the two hundred Jewish children in the town the only ones still alive were the four of us who had left, two quiet twins with freckles, who became the subjects of testicular experiments, and my cousin Zsófi, fourteen at the time, who was waved by Doctor Mengele's baton into the group of those capable of work. She endured the ordeal and came home. All the others ended up as ashes.

I spent the summer of 1944 mainly on the balcony of my Aunt Gizella's Budapest apartment on the fourth floor of 36 Ernő Hollán Street. I could see the corner from there and would wait for my parents to appear, coming up from Saint Stephen Ring. They never did.

Aunt Gizu's husband, Uncle Andor, had served his country as a first lieutenant in the First World War. A glass case housing porcelain and silver knickknacks also contained a small burgundy cushion for his war decorations: a *signum laudis*, iron crosses, and various other medals of honor. Having failed to gain special status in light of his war record, he would haunt the Budapest Jewish Council during the hours Jews were permitted to circulate, and bring back reassuring news.

Uncle Andor was far from the pride of the family, but he did save our lives: when the Gestapo took our parents off, it was Uncle Andor who sent the letter of invitation. That he would later abandon us was the result of duress, but rescue us he did. Not a handsome man, he carried himself as dashingly as he could, holding his chin high and pulling his shoulders back. Always the "gentleman," he ate corn on the cob and peaches with a knife and fork. There was something cloyingly condescending in his manner: he would give me encouraging pats on the back. But he also indulged in surprising and graceless outbursts of emotion.

Back in the twenties Andor had sent twenty-one red roses to Gizella, my mother's older sister, to win her dowry and settle his debts. After they said their vows, he asked my grandfather—proudly at first, though ultimately on his knees—to keep his money in his, Andor's, bank, because how would it look for the young man if even his wife's father had no faith in his institution. Grandfather acceded and transferred his accounts. The next day Andor's bank declared bankruptcy and my grandfather went broke through the good offices of his son-in-law. With the family's support Andor rented an apartment in Budapest, opening a glove shop nearby and securing them a comfortable bourgeois existence.

Uncle Andor was the air-raid captain in his five-story building and would make his way with a squeaky lamp up and down between the shelter and the ground floor. He wore a shiny helmet that barely revealed his prideful, jutting chin and pink dewlap. By September the Jews were required to squeeze together into a smaller space, and we had to move, because he, Aunt Gizi, and our two cousins Ági and Jancsi got so small a room that it barely held their four cots. I remember the heavy smell of the friendly but unfamiliar woman and children. There was no place for us.

Aunt Zsófi lived in the next building. She was not a blood relative but the wife of Dr. Gyula Zádor, my father's cousin. By then my two cousins, István and Pál Zádor, were living there, along with Aunt Zsófi's son, Péter Polonyi, who was nearly our age. The face of a man with close-cropped graying hair emerges from the fog of memory. I liked his family name: Mandula, "Almond." I also recall a child a little older than me. Since we were forbidden to go out into the street, we played in the hallway. Aunt Zsófi was willing to let us live there as long as Uncle Andor's family took care of feeding us. For the first few days we still went back to our relatives' room for lunch.

Then came 15 October, the day Regent Horthy announced on the radio that he had requested a cease-fire. It was a bright autumn Sunday morning. People flowed out into the street. We too were giddy with the news. Everyone in the building—women and children, old and young—was Jewish. The old men climbed a ladder to take down the yellow paper star on the plank over the entrance. Some ripped off the yellow stars from their coats right there in the street. We might go on living after all, go home, find our parents; everything might again be as it had been in the days of a peacetime that perhaps never was. We waited for news of confirmation; the radio broadcast nothing but some incomprehensible public announcements: the Regent's address was not followed up by official substantiation.

We walked around our block. Not everyone in the neighborhood had dared to remove the emblem from the doorways of Jewish buildings, but one of the children had set fire to the yellow cardboard star and we stood around watching it burn. A couple not wearing yellow stars strolled past arm in arm. "See how insolent they've become," said a man in a hat to the woman in a hat. The new armed command was nowhere in evidence, but German military vehicles and trucks full of green-shirted men with Arrow Cross armbands raced along the Ring wearing looks of agitated determination.

A Jew asked a policeman whether there were any new regulations, whether we could now go outside after curfew. Officially we had the right to be in public areas only from eleven in the morning until five in the afternoon. Uncertainty was everywhere. What were we to do now that things had taken a 180-degree turn and official talk was of peace, not heroic battle, when the old rules seemed no longer to apply and Jews were not partitioned off from the Aryan "national organism"? What should we Jews be doing once the law no longer permitted persecution? That day we had no idea what to do on our own behalf.

By that night we had: the cease-fire had merely been a clumsy move by a clumsy regent, who had informed the German ambassador of his intention before telling his own troops! Szálasi, the leader of the Arrow Cross, announced the regent's removal, declaring that we would now fight even more resolutely at the side of our great German allies to win the war and cleanse our fatherland —of me. Extermination was next. Vermin, cockroach, Jew—you're done for! The will of steel was there; the rest was merely a matter of execution. It was important to remain discreet, since there were still about one hundred thousand Jews in Budapest and the open murder of so many people might create a mood of defeatism among the Christian population, but slaughter was on the way, a St. Bartholomew's night. Stay away from your home, hide if you can, or blend into the crowd, fade into the background, don't be conspicuous or you'll get yourself popped off.

We looked down through the open roof at the cinema screen: the Jew-baiting propaganda film *I Came from Tarnopol* was still playing. We trotted up and down the hallways of our building and even dared to go outside, where we excitedly discussed developments. We were wild game and fearful of the hunters, who, though little people like us, had been supplied by politics with weapons and the authorization to kill even children and the aged for as long as the yellow star was legal.

My view was that since I was innocent the laws that ordered my extermination were themselves illegal. I had seen little snots go around killing as easily as one shoots a hare or swats a fly, all in the name of our state, our fatherland. We were dealing with the ultimate enemy, the one who claims your life, and for want of a better method he was prepared to shoot you into the Danube and let the water carry you off.

We *took a powder*, as people used to say. Uncle Andor laid out his plan to us with sober self-confidence: we were to hide in the basement workshop they called the glove factory, three blocks away. We couldn't take much, as the Arrow Cross was patrolling the area and we had to be inconspicuous. We could sleep on the cutting table and wash at the basin in the toilet. We couldn't turn on the lights, but when the sun was shining enough light came into the room at midday to read by. Not hearing any shooting outside, we hoped the worst would not come. By the second day certain comforts made their absence felt in the dark workshop, particularly to Uncle Andor, who noticed in the morning that he had left his shaving brush at home. A painful loss. Though you could rub up a little rudimentary foam with the tip of your finger after wetting the skin and applying soap, neither the operation nor its result was aesthetically satisfactory. Uncle Andor felt it was inadvisable to return home (though the St.

Bartholomew's night had not materialized), but he did want that shaving brush. The simplest solution in Uncle Andor's eyes (after excluding the draconian options of brushless shaving and not shaving at all) was for me to fetch the brush.

I set off. There were soldiers wearing armbands standing at the gate of the third building down. It was drizzling. Perhaps they didn't know what they were supposed to be doing. They called me over.

"Hey kid, come over here. Are you a Jew?"

"What makes you ask?"

"Well, you could be," they said.

"I could," said I.

"Well, are you?"

"What makes you ask?" I said, returning to my original question.

"Hey, that's the way Jews talk."

"Are *you* a Jew?" I asked.

"What makes you ask?" he said.

"You know how they talk."

"Drop your pants."

I didn't move. We stared at each other.

"Well?"

"It's raining."

"All right. Get going."

He and I both knew the score. He just didn't feel like killing me.

The rest of the way was incident-free. When I got to the apartment, the elderly ladies asked me excitedly where the family had spent the night. I no longer remember what I came up with— something about being guests somewhere—but they got a peek of me slipping the shaving brush into my pocket from the shelf below the bathroom mirror. "You came for *that*?" asked one of the ladies.

"Good-bye," I said.

On the corner I saw Arrow Cross men coming up Hollán Street at a run. I took a quick turn to the left, hoping to get back to my family via a Pozsonyi Avenue detour, but I didn't realize they would be making parallel runs, and in large numbers, and that they would not only be coming down Pozsonyi Avenue in a row that spanned the entire street, but also from behind, from the Saint Stephen Ring, to sweep up everyone in sight. In those days it was not unusual to find Jews at midday in the New Leopold Town district. Those they detained were dispatched to a brick factory in Old Buda, and from there they would be sent westward, on foot. There were still a few spots where Jews could be packed off onto railroad cars. It would be a few weeks before the authorities adopted the simplified procedure of fencing in an area and shooting people into the Danube.

I saw a thin man wearing glasses and a white armband trying to explain his exceptional status: he had once risked his life fighting Béla Kun's commune. The Arrow Cross man was silent for a moment, then spit a cigarette butt into his face and led him off to the side. People stood in line to have their papers checked. It wasn't enough to have a document with an official seal; you had to answer questions.

I picked a line where a man in a leather coat and a hat with a flipped-up visor, hands on hips, was putting people through the questions. When there were only two people in front of me, I slipped down on my hands and knees and crawled off past his brown hunting boots: there was no way he could keep track of what was going on with all the people milling around. I was careful to amble my way back to the workshop, going around the block and making sure no one saw me enter.

"So you're back," said Uncle Andor, kindly patting my head. He immediately had a shave using plenty of cologne, then paced up and down stroking his chin. The lunch hour was approaching. Uncle Andor said the workshop was not a good hiding place, so one by one we should all go back to where we had been staying. As for my sister and me, we could go to his place for lunch after four, until which time we were to wait "with that woman," meaning Aunt Zsófi. He liked to speak disparagingly of her. But when we rang the bell at 9 Hollán Street at four o'clock, the door was opened by the same elderly lady who had noticed my little maneuver with the shaving brush that morning. When I asked where the family was, she said that my uncle, his wife, and their two children had departed with their luggage. Where they had gone she did not know.

There we stood, Éva and I, at a loss what to do. It took a little time for us to grasp that our relatives had left for a hiding place, that Uncle Andor had procured them false papers with which they would register as a Christian family of Transylvanian refugees under a new name and stay with acquaintances who had agreed to take them in for money. We went back the next day and the day after, but there was no news.

Half a year later, in April of 1945, I caught a glimpse of Aunt Gizu on a street corner in Nagyvárad. I did a double take, but she went her way on the other side of the street. A week later we met face to face. She invited me to walk with her, but I demurred. She told me their new address. It was the address of relatives from Várad who had disappeared into thin air and whose apartment she and her family had taken over. I quickly took my leave with a shaky promise to visit.

On that night, 15 October, Aunt Zsófi also went into hiding with the boys, Péter, István, and Pali. They took very few bags and went to the Margaret Ring, where an acquaintance had given them his apartment. They entered without yellow stars. They had only just set down their bags when a resident phoned and told them to make a quick getaway because the concierge had reported them as possible Jews. Rushing down the stairs, they saw the elevator moving up with armed Arrow Cross men inside. They heard the pounding on the door upstairs and scurried back to their wonted place of fear.

Aunt Zsófi not only gave us lodging; she gave us food and care as well. After taking in my sister and me, she had five children in the two rooms of a good-sized temporary apartment. She sold her things to feed us. Meanwhile, we children thought up ways to escape—climbing down a rope from the bathroom window onto a garage roof—should the Arrow Cross come to take us away.

Every morning, when we were permitted outside, Aunt Zsófi set out to procure papers. One or another neutral embassy took apartment buildings under its wing, hanging signs over the main entrance indicating that a given house was under the protection of the Swiss, Swedish, Spanish, or Vatican mission. Papal protection was said to be the best. If you couldn't make it into a safe house, you went to the ghetto, where they had started dismantling the high fence and gates. Owing to Aunt Zsófi's secret morning trips we had a good chance of getting letters of protection from the Swiss.

I did not grieve over the loss of Uncle Andor's supervision, as I felt more at home with Aunt Zsófi and my cousins from Berettyóújfalu. We were a natural "we" again, a branch of my father's family. Dr. Gyula Zádor, Zsófia's husband and István and Pali's paternal uncle, was interned in a work camp. A neurologist and psychiatrist, he had studied in Heidelberg and practiced in Zurich, and returned home in 1938. He had been the personification of irony in my childhood mythology. For some inner reason a chilly element would infiltrate his otherwise warm, heartfelt smile. It gave me pause: he seemed to be making fun at my expense.

Here is an example. When I was five, I had a hernia operation, after which I screamed at the top of my lungs for them to remove my bonds: I had just come around from the anesthesia and could not tolerate being tied down. It was outrageous not to be trusted with my own decisions, as if my five-year-old self lacked the brains to lie motionless and rest after the operation without being humiliatingly strapped to the bed. Besides, the white gauze they used, the white bed, the staff all in white, the white room—it offended my sense of color.

My governess Lívia's camel-hair housecoat was of a warm beige. Whenever she touched me—to give me a spoonful of medicine or hold my left arm down and take my temperature—she did so with kindness. But the nurse —that unfamiliar, middle-aged excuse for a woman—had no right to lay a hand on me just because she happened to be disguised in a white shell. I wanted her out of there, her and her energetic, aggressive benevolence! I had stiffened my body into a girder and was screaming bloody murder—No! I won't give in! Unbind me!—when a familiar face appeared at the foot of my bed. Thick, graying hair, a high forehead, and that cheeky smile, incredulous at my rage, certain I was playacting. Where did that white-gowned figure get off looking into my soul? Even if he was Uncle Gyula behind the white mask.

Our family doctor, Dr. Spernáth, would come and see us in civilian clothes, a gray suit. Éva and I would hide behind the dining-room curtains so he wouldn't be able to "stick us" or so we wouldn't have to take that disgusting cod liver oil or just for the sake of hiding, so we could later appear, forcing back giggles of complicity. Uncle Spinach (for that was what we called him) would talk politics with my father even as he listened to our chests. This tickled unpleasantly, because Dr. Spernáth was bald and his cold pate had a medicinal smell that turned our stomachs. We shuddered when that head pressed against our bare skin. Yet despite his white gown Uncle Gyula said he would recommend that they untie my straps if I stopped squirming. The pact was made and kept.

Some thirty years later I asked another ironist, the psychologist Ferenc Mérei, whether he had known Uncle Gyula. He said something to the effect that he had been considered half-crazy. In 1941 Dr. Gyula Zádor had rented a large apartment in the middle of town, at 5 Szép Street, furnished it in his wife's Bauhaus taste, and opened a private practice with his Heidelberg and Zurich diplomas and his reputation as chief neurologist at the Jewish Hospital. There might have been no Second World War; he had simply followed the logical path for a man of his standing. His beautiful wife, whom he wooed away from a respected and successful journalist, was a friend to poets, painters, and all kinds of revolutionaries.

Uncle Gyula himself came from a more modest background. His family in Berettyóújfalu gave him his portion of the inheritance early to get him started. Their house served as both shop and workshop. They were their own bosses and enjoyed looking in on the warm, private side of life whenever they felt so inclined. The shop and workshop gave onto the street, the world, while the back and upstairs room belonged to the Biedermeier zone, the realm of passions, quick successions of joy and despair, passion and resentment. Their life was beautiful one moment, unbearable the next.

So this Berettyóújfalu citizen of the world, who had the temerity to look down on us, natives of the same town, had taken up residence in the capital as if everything were perfectly normal, as if the number one business of the day were to build his patient base and publish his findings in domestic and international professional journals. As he sat under the arbor in his Újfalu garden I would stare at his white cord trousers, yellow shoes, and bluish-pink silk shirt. He would let us villagers turn our finest phrases, but even as he listened he was forming his own big-city opinions about us. We were naive; irony was something we had no experience of; we did not realize that existence is ambiguous and even love jaundiced. Uncle Gyula's village optimism was tainted with the city-dweller's ability to see through things. The city slicker pokes his nose into everything and always seems to know what cards you've got. As if people didn't reveal their true selves the very first time they shake hands! When Uncle Gyula first gave me that look of his, he was not yet forty. Now that I could be his father, I feel that had he not been killed his true, naive nature would have won out. (Actually, it did win out, though in a self-destructive way: through his village burgher's respect for the law he voluntarily returned to a labor camp, leaving his wife behind.)

Aunt Zsófi was a delicate, thin figure of a woman. Everything about her was silvery: her voice, her eyes, and the few graying locks in her thick, black hair. I often had the feeling that we little wild creatures amused her. She had a son, Péter Polonyi, and acted as guardian for my two cousins, István and Pál Zádor. And by the good graces of fate and Uncle Andor my sister Éva and I added two more to her charge. Four boys make a lot of noise, and Aunt Zsófi would occasionally get a headache and ask us to disappear—for a while at least.

In the fall of 1944 Aunt Zsófi must have been thirty. She sometimes had a sardonic glint in her eye, but her voice had a delicacy to it that came from a distant shore. Never one to hesitate about doing what her taste dictated, she treated us as her very own, a single mother to five children. She even managed to see to it that we got through those abominable times with our souls intact.

Her husband would have been able to skip out on the forced-labor camp: he was granted a day's leave to visit his family at Christmas of 1944. Despite Zsófi's entreaties the doctor returned to the camp: he had no desire to get his family into trouble, he had his sick comrades to treat, and what is more he had promised his charitable commander to return. But while he was away, the charitable commander had been replaced, and the honest Doctor Zádor and his patients—poets and scholars all—ended up in a mass grave.

Jews were still being deported to Auschwitz from Budapest's outer districts of Újpest and Kispest as late as the summer. They could have come into the city on foot or by tram, but they followed orders and went to the railway station. The communists among them—the Zionists, the resistors, the bold—got hold of false papers and went into hiding. The more resigned and perhaps fearful middle class tried to ride out the dangerous times in safe houses. The safe houses were inhabited by better-off, secular Jews who had managed to contact one of the neutral diplomatic embassies. The poorer, orthodox Jews, who had black beards and hats, wives wrapped in shawls, sons with side-locks, and daughters with big eyes, went to the ghetto. That was their place: it had the greatest concentration of synagogues. Both they and the neutral diplomats must have felt this. But it was open season in the ghetto: drunken Arrow Cross men would go in and shoot at will.

Swiss letters of protection, *Schützpässe*, were distributed in an operation organized by the Swiss consul, Carl Lutz. His name comes up less often than that of his Swedish colleague Raoul Wallenberg, though Lutz saved as many people as Wallenberg. Under the protection of the Helvetic Confederation we moved to 49 Pozsonyi Avenue, a building where my greatest respect went to three or four young men hiding out in the cellar, about whom people whispered that they were resistors and had defected from the military. There were perhaps eighty of us living in a three-room apartment on the fourth floor. At night we would stack up any furniture that could not be slept on. Not everyone got a bed or mattress, but everyone had at least a rug. The four of us boys slept on mattresses on the floor by the window behind a pile of furniture. It was like an ongoing house party. There was always someone to talk to. For two hours every morning we could leave the building, five children clinging to a beautiful young woman. Aunt Zsófi protected us, as perhaps we did her. Whoever asked for her papers was astounded. "Are they all yours?" The crush diminished as time passed: some people moved down to hiding places, while others were abducted during spur-of-the-moment raids and shot into the Danube.

In the winter of 1944–45 I saw any number of dead bodies. I could picture myself among them, but the tasks of day-to-day existence obscured most of my imaginings. Danger makes you practical. Only at isolated moments do you face the possibility of death—when someone holds a pistol to your head, for example. Then you feel: yes, it could happen. You become an adult from the moment you face your own death, which means I have been an adult from the age of eleven. For some people it happens earlier, for others later, and there are those for whom the moment never comes.

Death is hardly pleasant, nor is mortal danger. But you can be standing on a rooftop terrace with fighter planes machine-gunning above and feel the whole scene is not all that serious. So let's just slide around in our hobnailed boots on the ice rink we have made with a few buckets of water. *Not all that serious* later saved me from succumbing to melodramatic moods.

I owe my life to a benevolent chain of coincidences. It has proved an enduring gift to recognize, at the age of eleven, the bald fact that I could be killed at any time, and to have learned how to act in such a situation. In the winter of 1944–45 I thought of death as I might have thought of, say, firewood: there was nothing unusual about it. It was outside my control, like drawing the wrong card.

Beautiful young women in ski boots and Norwegian sweaters were smoking cigarettes, their abundant hair combed smooth into a bun, their long legs crossed in ski pants. They laughed at all kinds of things I did not understand. They were different from the small-town beauties I had known: more malicious, more enigmatic, radical yet refined. They spoke of the French surrealists, German expressionists, and Russian abstractionists like old friends. They were artists, dancers, left-wingers—and they stretched so beautifully. They would sing for us children, sing the "Internationale" and "Dubinushka" in Hungarian.

But none amazed me more than Aunt Zsófi. I would have loved to perform some heroic act for her and did not dare to so much as scratch myself in her sight. Her slightly indolent voice would ask, "My knight in shining armor, will you accompany me?" I would have accompanied her to the gates of hell. For Aunt Zsófi's sake I was willing to hold thick novels under my arms to keep my elbows in while eating. The more fearful moved down into the cellar, but Aunt Zsófi was unable to separate cleanliness from human dignity. She would have found it repulsive for us to hide from the explosive and incendiary bombs, the cannonballs and artillery mines, down in the bomb shelter, the putrid darkness, the chaotically congested company of so many illwashed bodies. What if it did raise the level of risk a notch.

"Dignity means more than security," she would say. "We are not going to let the lice take us over." We did not go down to the cellar even when the sirens started. The most sensible choice was the rooftop terrace, where the winter sun shone brightly every morning even in January, though at temperatures of twenty degrees below freezing. We would pour out a few buckets of water and make a fabulous skating rink for ourselves. With a running start you could slide from one end to the other. Machine-gun rounds from Ratas, Soviet fighter planes, landed on the ice with a pop. We always looked up to see where the bombs pouring from their bellies would fall. A cloud of dust or smoke indicated whether the bomb was explosive or incendiary.

From the street below came the rumble of trams carrying trunks of ammunition to the front, now just a few blocks away, and the voices of Germans shouting to one another. The Russians were getting close, but the Arrow Cross was still goring Jews and Christian defectors in the neighborhood. The word "gore" was on every public poster; it meant kill on the spot and leave the body behind. With weapons exploding in the street, documents meant nothing: only drunkenness and fear had meaning—and the sympathy or antipathy of the moment. The armed men in armbands had plenty of people to shoot, though they had begun to sense they couldn't execute every single Jew. They may even have had trouble getting into the man-hunting mood day in and day out. Filling the ice-flow-congested Danube with old ladies and young girls was an art whose charm was intermittent. Even the defenseless people they killed—and they could have killed as many as they pleased—even they expressed a modicum of resistance in their eyes, reinforced by the gaze of passersby, who watched the quiet winter coats being led down to the riverbank with some degree of empathy. Of course you needed to make time for other things too, like drinking and getting warm. It must also have occurred to the men in armbands that if the Russians were at the outskirts of the city—and with plenty of artillery too, judging from the din—they would hardly stop but forge on into the center. If they occupied the entire city, Arrow Cross troops could expect anything but decorations, not a pleasant thought by any means. The mood for murder flared up and flagged by turns.

Shooting at Russians was dangerous; Jews were fish in a barrel. Life is a matter of luck, and death bad luck. You can do something for yourself, but not much, and sometimes pride keeps you from doing even that. Several people had been taken from the apartment the previous night. From the next room, not ours.

I watch the Germans. Can they really believe they will drive back the Russians, just five blocks away? Intelligent as they are, they have no idea what they are and are not allowed to do. The Arrow Cross, on the other hand, are the bottom of the barrel, the school dropouts. Their only talent is for torturing cats. A child has to grow up to understand just how underdeveloped adults can be. A fourteen-year-old kid with a gun accompanies unarmed people down to the bank of the Danube. Instead of grabbing the gun from his hand, they go where he orders them. Most victims call it fate, but fate should cause fear and stir them to self-defense whether the threat be sleet falling on their garden or death at the hands of an enemy. Yet people much like pets get used to seeing their companions cut down around them. You can't feel outrage and empathy every half hour. Standing out on the roof terrace, we hear the occasional sputter of shots. Someone (armed) checks the papers of someone else (unarmed). The former doesn't like the latter's face or papers, stands him against the wall, and shoots him dead. The people taken down to the Danube have to stand in a row, their faces to the river. The shots come from behind.

Even so abundant a variety of violent deaths could not obscure the beauty of those dazzling winter mornings. In the shadow of our mortality bread became more like bread, jam more like jam. I gladly chopped all kinds of furniture into firewood. We even ventured down to the riverbank, where we chopped up a small pier. It was good dry pine that burned wonderfully with its white paint.

We knew that the Russians had come in great numbers with tanks and heavy artillery. They had relatively fewer planes than the English and Americans, whose bombers arrived mostly later, in the summer of 1944; in the winter it was still the Ratas that thundered though the sky.

Klára often stood out on the roof terrace, adjusting her black ponytail, tying and untying it. I would give it an occasional yank. She had a little birthmark at the base of her nose and a mole at the tip. In exchange for my services I was granted permission on that very terrace to plant a quick kiss on that mole. It was forbidden to tarry on the nose. Klára liked to speak of parts of her body without possessive pronouns, as if they were independent beings: "The nose has had enough," she informed me. We spent a lot of time wrestling. It was no easy task to pin Klára down: one of us, then the other would end up on top. Once in a while I managed to pin her shoulders to the horsehair mattress on the floor and lie on her belly, but I would get such a bite on the wrist that the rows of teeth left a lasting mark. "Do you have what it takes to hold your hand over the candle?" asked Klára. I did, and got a burn mark on my palm. Klára kissed it. I carefully slid my fist into my pocket, as if holding a sparrow.

Klára could not stand being shut in and was incapable of spending the entire day in the safe house. The curfew for Jews did not apply to her. I would try to detain her. I was worried, but did not dog her heels. She would make the rounds of the neighborhood, then boast of what she had seen. When an officer asked for her papers, she lacked the nerve to answer his skeptical questions; she merely held her peace. They led Klára down to the Danube together with a long line of Jews. There she recognized one of her aunts and squeezed in next to her. The were all told to empty their pockets and stand with their hands up, facing the bare trees of Margaret Island, the freestanding piers of the bombed-out Margaret Bridge. Her aunt pitched forward into the river, but Klára was not hit. "You're lucky my magazine ran out," said the machine-gunner with a friendly laugh. "Now move it—and be good at home!" Thus did the junior (though no longer all that young) officer send her on her way.

I opened the street door for Klára, having recognized the sound of her footsteps through the planked-up door. "Let's stand here a minute," she said. "Hold my hand. And don't let me out tomorrow. Stay with me all day. Don't tell Mother they shot Sári dead right at my side."

The next morning I squatted in the courtyard in front of a stove—three bricks and an iron grill—on which bean soup was cooking painfully slowly. My duty was to keep it well stirred, taste it from time to time to see if it was softening up, and stoke the embers with pieces of sawed-up chair legs. Klára stood next to me and talked about her first two years in school, when she couldn't bring herself to say a word. She would do her work, but not utter a single syllable. She would have liked to say at least hello to the other children, but could not open her mouth. I was more interested in whether the soup was ready. I lifted the cover and stuck in a wooden spoon.

The roar of a Russian fighter plane. Klára pressed against the wall. When she screamed "Come here!" there was such rage in her voice that I spun around in astonishment. The fighter sprinkled the interior flagstone courtyards of the block with machine-gun rounds, hitting no one. The reason Klára was so angry was that I was always playing the hero, which was a decided exaggeration. Suddenly I heard the embers sizzling and looked down to see soup pouring out of a hole in the pot: a bullet had passed through the bottom of the large red enameled vessel. Had I not turned around, it would also have passed through my head, which had been bent over the soup. Finding another pot was no easy task.

"Why did you scream at me?" I asked Klára that evening.

"I don't know," she answered, unsure of herself by then.

We stood on the rooftop and heard a famous actress singing. Coming from the Russian military's speakers, her voice took on a deep, threatening thrum. The goal was to plant fear in the faltering hearts of the Hungarian soldiers pointlessly defending themselves alongside the Germans: "You cannot run, you cannot hide. Your fate, it cannot be denied." The Russians had entered the city and advanced all the way to the Angyalföld district. The speakers were just a few blocks away. A Stalin-candle shot up, illuminating the rooftops. Hand in hand, we watched, squinting. "It's beautiful," whispered Klára. We both laughed at her whisper.

We had an unexpected visitor at the safe house: Nene. She brought a small aluminum medallion of Mary on a chain. Nene asked us to wear it around our necks. She wanted us to convert to Catholicism. If we did—or merely declared our willingness to do—she would take us to a convent where they protected and hid converted Jewish children. We thanked Nene for her offer, but told her we would rather not.

We children had agreed on a plan in case we were driven out in a large group, which would most likely end with our being shot into the Danube: we would drop our knapsacks at the corner of the park and run off in different directions. Even if they shot at us—and plenty of guards would be on hand if hundreds of Jews were turned out of their building—some might make it.

The next morning four or five Arrow Cross men and gendarmes burst into the room, screaming at us to get dressed and turn over all weapons, including kitchen knives and pocketknives, plus anything of value, and then line up obediently and quietly on the sidewalk in front of the building. They had a rabbi with them, who gently counseled us to obey and specifically recommended that we hand over all necklaces, mementoes, and engagement rings. I took my time putting my socks on.

Down in front of the building Rebenyák's red hat stood out. Rebenyák was the house's bad boy. He would have liked to belong to our gang, but we never let him in. He speculated that the rabbi would get his cut of the items, assuming they didn't shoot him. We looked at one another inquisitively, wondering whether this was the time to implement the plan and whether we should let Rebenyák in on it, when two loud-voiced men came along, one wearing a gendarme's uniform, the other a German officer's. They were shouting—not at us but at the Arrow Cross men and the two gendarmes with us—and ordered us back into the building. They might have been communists in disguise or two Jewish actors. The better actor played his role less effectively; the worse actor was more convincing. Soon we were back in our room again, still in our overcoats, clueless.

The lobby was our clubhouse. Kids would alternate looking out while the rest of us slid down the marble ramp along the bottom flight of stairs. Rebenyák showed up in his red cap. He was fourteen or so and was always pestering me with his stamps, knowing I had brought my stamp album from Újfalu. I always traded smaller, more valuable stamps for larger, nicer-looking ones. I had trouble understanding him: his language was full of city-tough words. Instead of "piss" he would say "drimple," or "wankle," or "slash." He spoke obscurely of some pussy or other, by which I finally realized he meant the sexual organ of one of the older girls. He would punctuate his sentences with "You dig, buddy? No? Then suck my dick!" Klára said he was just throwing his weight around; she had more brains in her shoelaces than Rebenyák under that red hat of his. He liked to boast he could no longer even look at the broads, the tomatoes, the merchandise—in short, at women—who were supposedly all over him down in the cellar. Klára reviewed my trades, checking the stamps' value in a catalogue. "That lying bastard is constantly getting the better of you. Don't you mind?" I didn't really. Ultimately I gave Rebenyák my entire stamp album for a hunk of bacon which, when roasted with onion atop a dish of peas, became the envy of the apartment house. Rebenyák had pinched the bacon from under his mother's bed in the cellar and crept back with it, weasel-like. He slept in the same bed as his mother, a strong-smelling corpulent woman with hair sprouting from her chin.

I ran into Rebenyák decades later. He was lame and living in a cellar again: he had ceded three apartments to three wives, who would come home with lovers more muscular than he and announce that for the time being Rebenyák would be sleeping in the next room. In his basement flat Rebenyák bought and sold girls from orphanages to rich tourists, instructing the former to steal the latter's passports. Rebenyák delighted in the possibilities: Swedish, Brazilian, Australian . . .

In the safe house Rebenyák would venture upstairs despite his mother's warning that fire was more likely to hit the building there: he was attracted by our cosmopolitan ways. Longingly, he would study the Rosenthal soup cups we ate beans from at the long black table, holding them up to the light: translucent. He stole one.

"Don't be a creep," I said. "They might shoot you tomorrow."

Rebenyák was superstitious, and my remark got to him. "Know who they're going to shoot tomorrow? *You*, you wooden-dicked Újfalu crybaby!"

Klára twisted his arm. "You take that back!" She was superstitious herself.

"Just see if your wooden pussy ever gets my jism!" But after whimpering a while in his agony, he brought it back.

More shots penetrated the apartment. Shards of glass made the beans in the Rosenthal cups inedible. The iron stove, whose exhaust pipe we had aimed out of the window, was buckled over like a man kicked in the stomach. Machine gun fire ricocheted off the outside wall. Klára suddenly turned childlike, sitting underneath the table and directing a sumptuous wedding of a clay lamb and a wooden mouse. Rebenyák crouched under the table next to her. I made him nervous.

"Are you really in love with that dodo? I mean, he doesn't even know the difference between allegory and paregoric."

"What's . . . allegory?" I asked suspiciously.

Rebenyák changed the subject to the pot with the hole: "You saved that hick's life. Isn't that enough? Now fall in love with me."

A depraved smile appeared on Klára's face.

"Fine. Just give me your stamp collection and fill my hat with sugar cubes."

Rebenyák blushed, but did not reach for the hat, whose wheat-blue tassel had dangled before my eyes from morning to night.

That night a young fellow named Mário, who lived in the next room, came back from the Danube. The shot had hit him in the arm, and he'd managed to swim out. The only hard part was to free himself from his father, to whom he had been tied. His father had been hit in the chest and held him fast for a while, but finally let go. Clinging to a block of ice, Mário had drifted down the Danube under the bridges. He was afraid of being crushed between blocks of ice. Ultimately he had climbed out onto the stairs at the foot of the Elisabeth Bridge and made his way home, wet and bloody. He was stopped on the way, but was by then indifferent to everything.

"Shoot me into the Danube again if you want."

"Jews are like cats," said an old Arrow Cross man. "They keep coming back to life." He sees it all the time. That's why they're so dangerous. Here he's hardly out of the river and he gets cheeky. When it's all over, they'll have the nerve to blame it all on us. "Hey, weren't you our guest once?"

Yes, he had been—he and his father. They had grilled him about his younger brother, who had taken part in a weapons heist. His father didn't know anything. They said that if he didn't tell them they would take care of his other son, Mário. The father gave a false address. The Arrow Cross men came back enraged, then shot someone else instead of the brother they were after. As long as they had him there, they subjected Mário's testicles to their boot heels. Finally a gendarme officer came into the Arrow Cross building and dragged them off. A good thing.

Dr. Erdős and a group of other elderly Jews had been pulled out of 49 Pozsonyi Avenue to build a cobblestone barricade on the corner: the younger Jews had long since been taken away. Six stones high and four deep, the wall was impenetrable. The T-34 tanks that had made it all the way from Stalingrad would certainly be stopped dead here.

We children watched from the entrance as the old men, stooping against the cold, hacked at the stones with pokers and hammers, separating the blocks stuck together with pitch, then lifting them into their laps and lugging them over to the roadblock. Young men in hunting boots, black trousers, and green shirts watched over the work, prodding the old men on. One of them cracked a whip, once used by a cabby on his horses, over the old Jews' necks. They could in fact have worked with more vigor.

It was probably the fellow with the whip who outraged an older gentleman from the next building, a building inhabited by Christians. Sometimes old men stick together, even if it means crossing congregational boundaries. In any case the old gentleman pulled out his hunting rifle and wounded the young whip-cracker. The Arrow Cross men thought that one of the Jews had taken the shot, and started shooting back blindly. The twenty barricade builders ran for cover and fell. Dr. Erdős himself made for the main door of the building, though taking his time so as not to draw attention to himself. I was the only one still standing in the doorway: the other children and the door-keeper, an even older Jew, had dashed up the steps upon hearing the shots. I opened the boarded-up entrance door. Dr. Erdős darted inside. I wanted to shut and lock it before the tall young man pursuing him could shove his way in, and the two of us, child and graybeard, pushed from the inside, but our besieger, who was twenty-five or so, took a running start and rammed us back enough to make a crack for the tip of his boot. The game was his. There he stood, pistol in hand.

He was taller than Dr. Erdős, and his lip was quivering from wounded pride: Jews slamming the door in my face just like that? A slight smile, the smile of the vanquished, flashed over Dr. Erdős' face. The young man held up the pistol and fired into the doctor's temple. Dr. Kálmán Erdős fell, his blood flowing over the muddy, pink imitation marble. Then the young man took aim at my forehead. I looked at him more in amazement than in fear. He lowered his pistol and headed out of the door.

By this time the trams were delivering ammunition crates ever more desperately to the front, that is, the immediate vicinity, yet courageous women would leave the building and still manage to forage bread. On the night of 17–18 January 1945 we moved to the inner room to sleep, since the outer one, damaged by a bomb, lacked a windowpane. Instead of going to bed, however, we crouched by the window, where we could watch the fighting. By the light of the Stalin-candles whizzing into the sky we saw a newsreel scene in all its glory, unbounded by the screen: a tank rumbling through the barricade, sweeping aside the basalt blocks, with more tanks and infantry in its wake; German soldiers, who had been on their bellies with machine guns behind the stone-piles, dashing for the park as the front moved on toward the Saint Stephen Ring.

As dawn came up on 18 January I watched the historical turning point of the war (liberation for me, defeat for others) with my own eyes. A few excited young women—teachers, fashion designers, dancers—hummed the "Internationale." Magda, a tall, strawberry-blonde dancer, taught us to sing with them. She was a communist and said we should be communists too, because they were the only party in the underground; the others were collaborating with the government. At four o'clock on that morning we gave ourselves over to the spirit of liberation.

In time Magda lost her enthusiasm. She tried to slip over the border in 1949, wearing the same ski boots she had worn during the winter of the siege. The border guards shot her dead.

At ten in the morning on 18 January 1945 I stepped out of the front door of 49 Pozsonyi Avenue. Two Russian soldiers were standing on the sidewalk in their torn coats, slightly scruffy and more indifferent than cordial. People spoke to them. They did not understand, but nodded. It was obvious they were not much interested in us. They asked whether Hitler was in the building. I had no information suggesting that Hitler was living with Budapest Jews under Swiss protection at 49 Pozsonyi Avenue. Then they asked about Szálasi, head of the Arrow Cross: no, he wasn't living there either. After a moment we caught on that "Hitler" meant Germans and "Szálasi" meant Arrow Cross. They were fairly simple boys. They went down into the shelter with a flashlight, prodding people with the barrels of their machine guns and shining their light into every nook. They found some military defectors in civilian dress, whom they let be. They did not particularly care that the building was inhabited by Jews: if you tried to explain to them you were a Jew and expected to get some kindness out of them, you didn't get very far. But they were friendly enough to us boys, and we got used to their poking around in the basement looking for Hitler. There was a man down there who spoke Slovak and could understand them a little. He immediately offered to interpret for them, and as they went through a passageway, which had been opened with a pickaxe, to the shelter next door, this Slovak-speaking Jew started barking out instructions like a commander in mufti, newly appointed from the ranks of the blanket-clad. Eventually, having conquered his last vestige of hesitation, he bade farewell to his family and ran off after the Russians.

The soldiers broke into a pharmacy and drank a bottle of Chat Noir cologne. They reached for it confidently, as if familiar with the brand. It was the closest thing to liquor there. We—soldiers in mufti, locals, Jews and Christians alike—flocked after them. The more resourceful took along knapsacks. I picked up a harmonica, which I later traded to Rebenyák for a bag of sugar cubes.

We could now leave the building at will, the building whose neutral status had protected us, though it had not been enough to keep the other half of its residents alive. A few markings in Cyrillic had begun to appear. The yellow star had come down from the front entrance and lay on a snow heap. As I stepped out as a free man for the first time, I was perhaps also stepping out of my childhood, the years when prohibitions of all sorts hemmed me in. The shooting and bombing were over, and it was safe to come out of the cellar. There were still the occasional stray shots, but now it was the Germans shooting from the Buda side.

At times an entire round of machine-gun fire showered the street, and I learned just how flat I could press myself against a wall.

Given that the apartment had been hit by gunfire and we were sharing it with thirty others, thought it best to leave for Aunt Zsófi and Uncle Gyula's apartment in Szép Street, which might be empty or at least not so crowded. We felt a sudden urge to take leave of the people in the cellar and break free of the seven-story Bauhaus ghetto into which we had been squeezed.

The hard-trampled snow had iced over the asphalt. We all wore knapsacks, clutched quilts, and pulled the rest of our meager belongings on a sled behind us. The wind was kicking up snow-dust. It was well below freezing, and as we had no gloves our fingers were purplish-red. We passed burning buildings in the darkening evening. Through black windows we saw dying flames painting the ceilings a rusty red. They were like a cross-section revealing the building's naked innards after a bomb had torn its façade off: a bathtub dangling, but the sink still in place; a heavy mahogany cupboard on the wall, but the dining table three flights down. It was the shameless, twisted humor of destruction.

Exhausted, but reviving, people were carting their belongings from place to place, going home, going in search of their loved ones, going just to go: after all, someone might be baking bread somewhere. People trudged through the streets weighed down with their goods and chattels while soldiers sat around on tanks or moved around in squads. Tongues of flame soared out of windows; people and horses lay scattered on the ground. Survivors did not carve meat from people, though they did from horses:

elderly gentlemen crouched inside horse corpses scraping frozen shreds of meat off bones with their pocketknives.

Our bundles of bedding were falling apart; we hung onto the quilts in desperation. I would have liked to earn Aunt Zsófi's praise. Once she called me her "little mainstay," but my joy at this mingled with the disappointment of being called "my little hypocrite" again for another of my attempts at pleasing her. That slightly chilly but still flirtatious irony was in Aunt Zsófi's face now too, curious to see how I would manage a bundle that was threatening to disintegrate.

The building on the corner had been razed to the ground, but 5/a Szép Street was miraculously still standing. It had taken a few cannon shots here and there, but they were patchable holes. The marble fountain in the courtyard, untouched, had icicles hanging from the stone-rumped nymph's jug.

The brass nameplate had disappeared from the front door of Dr. Gyula Zádor's apartment, and Aunt Zsófi's key would not turn the lock. The buzzer would not ring. She had to pound on the door. Out of the darkness of the long foyer a little circle of light emanated, and as the tiny grille-protected window in the door opened we saw a gray-haired woman sizing us up in a manner less than friendly.

Zsófi was wearing a light-colored fur coat, and her black hair was bound in a light-gray silk kerchief. The five of us children were standing behind her. We were curious and determined to reclaim the apartment.

"Good day, madam. I am Zsófia Vágó, the wife of Dr. Gyula Zádor, owner of this apartment and the possessions therein."

The gray-haired lady answered as follows from behind the grille: "I am Mrs. Kázmér Dravida, rightful tenant of this apartment. Your apartment, madam—inasmuch as it was in fact yours—has been officially granted to us as refugees from Transylvania." To which Zsófi said: "Madam, the legality of your procedure is subject to several objections."

To which Mrs. Dravida replied, "I trust, Madam, that you wish to impugn neither our good faith nor our patriotic obligation to observe the spirit of our thousand-year-old state as it is embodied by the authorities in power at any given time."

Zsófia: "You might, however, let us in, Madam."

Mrs. Dravida: "My conscientious observation of recent developments leads me, Madam, to do so. I note that you have of your own initiative removed the distinguishing emblem from your overcoats, trusting that the days of discrimination are over. Well, I do not discriminate against you, Madam, and out of patriotic sympathy do hereby bestow the use of two of the apartment's five rooms to you and yours."

Zsófia: "Madam, I have no wish to deceive you into thinking that I would not have been happier to find my apartment uninhabited, but then, of course, you yourselves must find refuge of a winter's day. How else might I put it? Kindly make yourselves at home in my rooms and with my furniture to the extent that propriety allows."

We watched motionless as these two elderly people, Dr. Kázmér Dravida and his wife, deftly salvaged their vital reserves—several bags of potatoes, beans, flour, bacon and sausage on spits, sugar in a large paper bag, pork lard in a red-enameled pot, and crackling in a large pickle jar—from pantry to bedroom, lest the invading horde make short work of them.

Not until then could they bring themselves to ask, panting, whether we had brought any food with us. Well, no, we had brought nothing at all. Good will moved the Dravidas to give us enough potatoes, flour, and bacon to hold us for dinner and the next day. For the third day we got nothing, but they did not hide the news—the most useful item of all—that there was a German storehouse in the basement of the Reáltanoda Street school perpendicular to Szép Street, and though the locals had carried off most of the inventory on that day, 18 January, there might still be something left.

We boys set out with empty knapsacks to see what we could find. We heard a machine gun ratatatatting from the direction of the Danube. There would be trouble if the Germans came back: the Dravidas would have us removed from Aunt Zsófi's apartment and our feet would never again cross the copperplate but long unpolished threshold.

A well-worn path led from the front gate of the school across the snow-covered courtyard to the back staircase and down into the cellar. We saw German corpses sticking out of the snow and shone our flashlight in their faces. I had always thought the dead grimaced, but every one of the faces was peaceful, including the one lying on his back on a wooden crate in the cellar next to a depleted bag of beans, his head hanging in a rather uncomfortable position. The only possible explanation was that there had been another crate under his head. And if they didn't leave it there, it must have been worth taking.

We filled our knapsacks with beans, peas, wheat, and dried onions, which was all that remained by then, but were still interested in the crate lying under the young German. He was a tall, handsome young man with a powerful brow and a light-colored stubble on his narrow face. His deep-set large eyes were open, and he observed us with interest.

"Forgive us," we said to him as we tried rolling him off the crate.

"I will *not* forgive you," the soldier responded coolly. "I have no idea why I had to die on this crate after taking a bullet on the basement staircase and dragging myself over here. In fact, I have no idea what I am doing here. You will find this crate to contain fairly high-quality sausage, and though it has turned white on the outside with mold, after a bit of scraping you will find it perfectly edible. I have turned stiff, and you will take the crate out from under me and steal away with the goods, but I will remain here in the dark, in this cellar of death, until the corpse-removers take me to an even darker place. No, I will not forgive you."

But we persevered. "O unknown German soldier, we understand your sense of injury, since, to put it bluntly, we are not allowing your earthly remains to rest (however uncomfortably) in peace, though it might be said in our favor that by removing the crate of sausage from under you we may actually straighten you out. Still, we hasten to observe that you have come a great distance from your permanent place of residence, by command to be sure, but not by invitation. Moreover, it is probable that when the bullet hit you you were engaging in activities of which we do not approve. May we point out that it would not have occurred to us to shoot at you, but the issue of whether or not you shot at us was a function purely of the random circumstances of the commands you received. From your perspective there would have been no obstacle. You shot your innocence dead, whereas we are still innocent—though understandably cynical— young boys."

The moment we lifted the crate, we were filled with disappointment: it proved mournfully light. And what remained of the ten scrawny sausages once we had scraped off the white and chopped it into the beans on the little utility stove would not hold us for very long. Two weeks later we were resigned to the wheat, grinding it up and boiling it for hours to soften it. While it cooked, we stood around it to keep warm, dipping dried onions in mustard to trick our hunger in the meantime.

Mr. Dravida, a fur cap on his head, sat in a rocking chair wrapped in a blanket up to his waist, squeezing a tennis ball in each hand. "It works the muscles, very soothing, and helps you think." He wore a winter coat with tassels and hiking boots with gaiters. His mouth, thin but sharply delineated and outlined by an equally thin mustache, had the sour twist of scorn and pride. From Uncle Gyula's high-backed reading chair he cast an occasional glance at us noisy ghosts. "Just because you've won, you've no right to come snooping around." Next to him sat his old dog, slapping its tail back and forth. Now and then Mr. Dravida touched the tennis ball to the dog's head. "I brought Bella's food inside because you ate her baked potatoes. There are a lot of you, and you make noise, and you eat my dog's potatoes. Don't stand in the door! Either come in or get out! What's this? Garlic sausage? You've got it good. You people always have it good."

We were hungry. We ate the dog's food and stole garlic from Mr. Dravida's kitchen cabinet. Nibbling away on a clove was almost like eating. Outside, the popping of a machine gun. We exchanged glances, then looked over at Mr. Dravida, who seemed encouraged: "The game isn't over yet. If things turn around and our troops come back, you'll need my protection. You might get it, but that depends on you. If you're nice and quiet and don't eat up Bella's food, I'll put in a word or two on your behalf. Though to tell the truth you are a bother. I keep finding the bathroom door closed. Have you so much to eat that you're constantly on the toilet, you locusts?"

We boys, the four of us, lay side by side on the double couch, talking about what was to come. Once the lights were out, I imagined myself at home with my parents as if nothing had changed. I would have been ashamed to speak of this to the others, though I was curious to know what they were imagining. It was cold and dark in the large apartment, and we wore socks in bed. The fire in the utility stove died early.

Once some Russians came. They checked Aunt Zsófi's papers and eyed her and my sister like cats eyeing sour cream. My sister pulled her clothes under the covers and got dressed. Aunt Zsófi went into the bathroom. One of the soldiers followed her in, but a minute later tiptoed out, as if signaling that no youth on earth was as tactful as he. After shining his flashlight on our four deeply attentive young faces, they praised Zsófi. "Good Mama, nice Mama, many children. Good!" They growled at us not to make a racket, though we had been quiet anyway. They took a can of meat and three eggs out of their pockets and put them on the table.

"It's cold," said the Soviet soldiers, whose faces were of various shapes. They got the fire going, one of them pulled a bottle of brandy out of his pocket. They bit off pieces of bacon, red onions, and black bread to go with it and even gave us a piece or two while they regaled themselves. On their way out they offered everyone their hands. I took hold of the magazine on one of the soldiers' machine guns. "And what do *you* want?" He pressed his fur cap down on my head, then set it back on his own. They took nothing and left a smell of warmth, onions, and boots. They also left us with an uneasy feeling, since Dravida muttered something to them in the front room in Slovak.

The next day I waited in line outside the baker's, if only for the smell wafting out. The quicker ones had taken their place early in the morning, though bread didn't go on sale until ten. It was not often I managed to get there early enough to avoid coming away empty-handed. But at least I didn't have to drop down onto my belly or press against the wall as machine gun fire strafed the street. At this point the real fighting was over, even in Buda. Newsboys shouted out the name of the newspaper: *Szabadság! Freedom!* In the parks graves surged up in mounds, and in the streets people went around in search of their loved ones.

Aunt Zsófi kept expecting her husband. One day she went down to Nyugati Station in a light fur because she had dreamed he was lying in a field, his still-open eyes staring at her. She had also dreamed of a village, which she now sought. She turned to a Russian officer for help, explaining that she wanted to travel west. At first the officer didn't follow what she was saying, but when Zsófia continued in French he gave her a seat on his train and told her that no one would bother her there and she should let him know when she wanted to get off, because he would be in the next compartment. And in fact she did find the village she had seen in her dream. She inquired whether there was a mass grave within the town limits. There was. They opened it. She found her husband.

Aunt Zsófi and Uncle Gyula had last spoken on the sixth floor of 49 Pozsonyi Avenue on the balcony facing the courtyard used for carpet-beating. It was there they had kissed for the last time. In 1953 Zsófia jumped from that balcony onto the cobblestones below.

The day after our liberation I went with Aunt Zsófi to the Wesselényi Street ghetto hospital, where we found her mother, still alive, on the third floor. Her head had been shot through, the bullet entering the right side of her face and exiting the left side of her skull under the ear. She was a slight woman, still in late middle age, and even in her state could manage a bit of a smile upon seeing her daughter. A few sugar cubes were all we could take her, though we couldn't bring ourselves to put one on her lips. The ghetto hospital had once been a school and is now a school again. On that day in January 1945 I looked out onto the school courtyard and saw a hill of bodies rising to the level of the second floor. Zsófi sat next to her mother. They were holding hands. Neither asked the other what had happened since they had last seen each other. When I accompanied Zsófi there again the next day, her mother was on her way to the pile in the yard. Aunt Zsófi sent me home and tried to arrange for her mother's body to be identified and removed from the mass grave.

I didn't much feel like wandering around Budapest, as I found the city inhospitable and yearned for the familiarity of home, for our house in Újfalu. It felt miserable to come back from the baker's empty-handed and stand around stirring the wheat in the pot, the fire almost out. Even dazzling winter days can be miserable when you look out from a dark room with nothing to hope for. Nor was there anything left to steal. Those elegant gentlemen who three weeks earlier had sat in their galoshes on the ribs of a dead horse lying in the snow had now acquired the status of a comical memory: there was nothing left to hack.

By now we were just a nuisance, extra mouths to feed, and there was no immediate danger to save us from. The smartest thing would be to go where we belonged. There would certainly be something to eat there. So my sister Éva and I decided to return to Újfalu and wait for our parents. István and Pali were heading for Kolozsvár: their paternal great aunt had survived the barely survivable year and invited them there. We would go home to the village and manage somehow. Homesickness for Berettyóújfalu and our house was hard at work inside me. If my parents didn't return, then we, the inheritors, would open the business. I would invite all the old shop assistants back and behave exactly like my father, free of all Budapest arrogance and scorn. But if my parents did return, I would give my father the keys and the cash books and accept his handshake and thanks for what I had done to keep the business going.

The role of guest was not to my liking; I felt much more at home in the role of host. Once I had grown up, I would bring a woman into my father's house and make lots of babies using the method described to me by the Gypsy Buckó one day on the way to Herpály. I had once gone to visit him to see how Gypsy children of my age lived. A boy came up to me, only slightly smaller than I, wearing absolutely nothing but a cap. You need a woman in the house, with a nice-smelling wardrobe and a nice-smelling muff. And you need children for the swings and ping-pong tables.

If during abnormal times you act according to notions born in normal ones, you owe the Devil a trip. This requires a train ticket.

The news in the bakery line, which the Dravidas had also heard, was that tickets were available only at the Rákosrendező Station, a good couple of hours on foot from the center. It was a long trip, with Russian and Romanian soldiers everywhere. At times I was a bit afraid. My sister couldn't accompany me, as the city was dangerous for young girls. I had no gloves and tried to protect my hands from the cold with—heaven knows why—a hair net. The thought that I was now truly hungry and truly cold gave me a certain pride, but I also kept my eyes open, there being plenty to see.

What I saw were second-line troops, the front line having moved on from Budapest toward Vienna. These young men had collected all kinds of clothing and were not beyond wearing skirts over their trouser and women's turbans on their heads to keep warm. They were a wild bunch, making derisive remarks from their trucks. We didn't understand them, but they were always laughing. When they urinated from the trucks, they enjoyed seeing the women turn their heads, which of course made them shake their cocks with all the more gusto. I saw one of them jump down from the vehicle and offer a woman a square loaf of black bread cut in half. The woman stepped back, but the soldier sidled up to her, stuffed it into her pocket, and left the woman trembling.

I took an interest in these round-headed boys, wondering at their rag parades, their antics, their sudden impulses. As natural as it all was, it struck me as strange. Yet they did have a sense of humor. Watching the rouge-lipped Romanian officers in white gloves swinging their cameras like proper gentlemen, they hunched over and laughed up their sleeves like village girls looking at polished city ladies.

Then there were soldiers with machine guns who escorted men to do a little work, just over to the neighboring town, or country, or continent, or the other side of the Urals— *"Davai, davai!"* (Come on, come on!). Promised a *bumazhka*—an identity document—the men obediently followed them out of town to the Tisza, there to continue by rail to camps and the distant cold, and all for the illusory security of those papers. A mirage.

The number of escapees per thousand was quite small, among Jewish and Christian Hungarians alike. Many more could have escaped than did; many more could have remained alive. As for their freshly arrived solider escorts, whether ruthless, indifferent, or humane, they were always unfathomable, unsusceptible to understanding. They were not as natty, disciplined, or angular in their movements as the Germans; they were less soldierly and more relaxed. Nor were they predictable: one would give the locals gifts; another would rob them. The same man often did both. There was no particular need to fear that the Germans would rape a woman, whereas these boys couldn't wait to unbutton their flies. Yet they did not kill on principle, and even if they looked glum while spooning out their mess tins, they also were happy to smile at someone, just like that, for no reason. What they would have liked more than anything was clear: a warm room, a woman, and a meal. They would have pulled the moon from the sky for the woman who could give them that. *Davai*, moon, *davai!*

The railway station on the outskirts of town was a pile of rubble. A long line toward a temporary ticket window snaked its way under an overpass that had remained intact. Well, well, it turns out we weren't the only ones who knew this was the place to get a train ticket! Word had got out that the window would eventually be opening up. Long hours passed and darkness was falling when a railway employee announced there were no tickets—nor were tickets necessary. Whoever fit into the train would go, and whoever did not would not. A train would be heading east from Nyugati Station the following afternoon at three. All aboard who's going aboard.

We were there at noon, standing petrified, my sister and I, amidst the crowd elbowing its way up and down the train. We let ourselves be swept up by the flow. There seemed to be no way for us to get on. People were sitting on the roof, standing in the entryways, clambering onto the couplings. Some had even curled up into the luggage nets above the seats. We couldn't get our feet onto the steps; we were just not good enough at shoving. Our situation seemed hopeless.

And suddenly who did we see but Zolti Varga, the Újfalu photographer, wearing a fur-lined overcoat and pelt hat with earflaps. Varga had taken pictures of us from the time I had entered the world. I had to lie prone on a platform at three months, practically without hair and clothed with only an angry look, my ankles the rolls of fat of the well-nourished infant. Then there is the picture from perhaps three years later in which I am sitting on my father's knee in a sailor shirt, my hair long; my sister is sitting in my mother's lap, her head flirtatiously cocked.

Once Zolti Varga had stuck his head into that black, harmonica-pleated, waxed-canvas cone—the jaws of darkness, almost—we would wait (who could tell if the master's head was even in there still?) for the promised birdie to pop out. We imagined it as a canary of sorts, but then all there was was a click and no bird at all, just Zolti Varga pulling his head from out of his glass-eyed box, like a magician who, slightly flushed and perspiring, rightfully expects applause for his trick.

And now Zolti Varga stood before us. He gave us a hug and said how glad he was to see us safe and sound: How splendid. His wife and two children were with him, and he invited us to join them. I was pleased at Zolti's kindness, though I seemed to recollect he had been expecting a German victory the previous year. After fleeing Újfalu for Budapest and sitting out the siege there—they did not go further west, as they wished to avoid the war—he and his family were homesick for the old house, no matter what shape it was in. My sister and I knew we would not find our mother and father at home, but we too looked forward to seeing our house and somehow beginning our old lives again.

Our voluntary travel companion managed to squeeze my sister through a window into the baggage net of one of the passenger cars. He pressed me into a cattle car, where we were packed so tightly that an old man gave me a piece of his mind: "Stand on one leg, boy. You're a kid, you can do it. There's no room for both. Switch off."

That was my first long trip: it took a week. But it was no departure; it was a return. We were not fleeing; we were returning, returning to the scene of a questionable paradise lost. A house is always unfaithful: either it goes before you do or it survives you and offers shelter to anyone or anything. Who was living there now? Who had the key? I dared not imagine we would find things as they had been. Maybe the furniture had been rearranged; maybe the clothes would be gone; maybe it would be completely empty. There was one possibility that had not occurred to me, however: the filth. In my thoughts the house had always been so attractive it never entered my mind that my first view of it might be repulsive.

Standing there on one leg in a cattle car with eighty others, shoved in not by guards' rifle stocks but by my own free will, pressed among those bodies, I shut my eyes and conjured up images full of longing: How would I find my sister? How was Éva managing in the baggage net? How long would our beans keep or the two rolls we had bought from a young man squatting in a broken, empty shop window for an astronomical price? What would happen if the trip dragged on? Could Zolti Varga give us something to eat? Could he—and would he?

Supposedly the Russians had commandeered our locomotive, but would provide another. The train was still standing at the Nyugati Station in Budapest, but I was a little more comfortable now, because a few people had grown tired of waiting and abandoned their travel plans. From the narrow window I could see the moon shining through the station hall's now glassless ribs. The self-appointed big shots who got on and off and shoved their way through the crowd spread the word that we would leave at one in the morning, at five, at ten—yes, certainly by ten.

I slipped down and peed between the wheels. The urine froze instantly. People were still sitting on the roof, back to back, but fewer than before. The more determined cattle-car passengers were putting up with each other now, and I managed to squat down behind a fat old woman. Though we had moved not an inch closer to our destination, it felt good to have had one long night on the train now behind us.

Ultimately we set off at about two in the afternoon. It was stop and go all the way. Locomotives came and went (if we had the better locomotive, we would lose it), tracks needed repairing, military trains had right-of-way. After a while Éva and I were sitting on benches in the cattle car and getting bread and bacon from Zolti Varga to assuage our hunger. At one point we heard a round of machine-gun fire: stray soldiers frightening civilians. The usual heralds said they were going from car to car seeking women. The women got lumps of coal from somewhere and smeared their faces to make themselves look wrinkled and ugly. Even aging ladies rubbed coal under their eyes my sister and I noticed, smiling to each other. I put Éva in a corner and stood in front of her. The other women pulled their kerchiefs down to their eyes and sat hunchbacked. In came the five or six soldiers on their rounds. One of the soldiers must have been attracted to a woman even through the pitch, but when he moistened his finger and rubbed and the black came off he grew angry and spat in the woman's face. The soldiers left the train in a ruckus of dissatisfaction.

We came to a jerry-built bridge spanning the Tisza where the Allies had hit the old bridge with a bomb and what was left had been blown up by the Germans. The temporary stilts between the pylons would not have borne the train, so we crossed on foot to where another train was waiting, though without a locomotive. Eventually we were moving again, and eventually we stopped again, sitting out a February snowstorm at night in the snowed-over bins of an open coal car. The wind off the Great Plain, unimpeded in its mad rush, pounded us mercilessly. We could no longer feel our hands and had ice crystals hanging from our eyelashes. Glued shut, our eyes transported us to a happy place, and the cold came close to rapture. We stood out on the open track surrounded by darkness.

We decided to strike out on a dirt road and ask for shelter at the first house we found. The wind practically knocked us on our backs as we made our way, dragging our clumsy bags, until at last a faint light flickered on the edge of the blue-white plain. I was frozen to an anesthetic purple by the time my legs had taken me there, stumbling through clods of ice. Obediently I stretched out on the straw covering the dirt floor, and my good will was restored when a young servant girl lay down at my side and told me to snuggle up, pulling my hand onto her belly to stave off my shivering. I pressed against her from behind and buried my face in her back to fit her bottom into my lap. We were entirely one. I realized that you can love someone whose face you have never seen and respond to a stranger as you would to your closest loved one. I held onto her as if I had long since chosen her as my one and only. In the morning I thanked the residents of the house for their kindness and expressed special gratitude to my sleeping companion.

Given that the train was still standing the next day, I set out on a reconnaissance foray and came upon a flat, black, cube-shaped solid amid the tire tracks on an icy hillock not far from some horse manure. Detailed inspection revealed it to be a piece of Soviet military-issue bread, albeit hard as a rock. But as long as it was indeed bread, it could soak up the steady stream of luke-warm water from the bronze pipe of an artesian well to become soft enough to eat. My supposition was borne out, and I chewed contentedly on my find.

A woman walked past, briskly tossing lumps of goat manure from a breadbasket over the snow, as if sowing seeds, left and right, making sure to cover the entire width of the street. Watching me paw at that wet bread, she held out her basket and said, laughing hilariously, "Have some meat with it. These last few I won't sow. You'll get a nice bleating in your belly."

"Where am I?" I asked her.

"In Törökszentmiklós."

"What shall I do with the bread?"
"Leave it here for the birds."

On 28 February 1945, the seventh day of our journey, we reached the Újfalu station. It had hardly changed over the year, as there had been no serious battles in the vicinity. We fumbled our way with our bags out of the first car, which had assumed the noble rank of passenger car since Püspökladány. It would have been natural for Father to pick us up, as when we arrived with Mother and after a few words of greeting he hugged us on the yellow-brick platform and we told him our news: Just imagine, we skated on the lake in the park in Pest and fed the baboons apples in that terribly smelly monkey house and then saw a performance of *Latyi Matyi* at the Operetta (Latyi could hardly get a word in edgewise what with all the children laughing) and then touched the very rope the Regent would as he walked through the rooms of the Royal Castle and then there was an air-raid siren when we were still in the Castle district and we went down with everybody else into a deep stone cavern, a cave under the Castle, where a teacher standing next to us explained that there was a lake in the belly of the hill and, just imagine, he said you could row a boat on it. But when we alighted on the platform looking straight ahead, it was clear our father was not waiting for us. Nor was anyone else.

Where fiacres had once offered their services to travelers coming from Budapest, there were now a few ox-drawn carts. The first acquaintance we saw was my former teacher at the Jewish school, Sándor Kreisler. Everyone in our class had been killed, as had all the pupils in our school, so our teacher was naturally deeply moved to see us. There he stood, a short, plucky man with a mustache. Seeing him was almost as unbelievable as it would have been to see my father.

Sándor Kreisler had been a good teacher: reserved, but kind and fair. In addition to primary school science he gave me a few slaps with the cover of my pen-case, generally because of Baba Blau. Mr. Kreisler had been my teacher as early as the first grade, when I still had private instruction: he would come to the house and teach István and me in our living room afternoons from three till four, which was all we needed of book learning. The rest of the time was our own. Sometimes he came down into the garden with us, and once in a while he gave the ball a kick, but he never got involved in the game, being a young man and mindful of his dignity.

His father was a fine tinsmith and went in for politics. He was a friend of my father's. He came into our store every day in his work clothes, and they would stand at the oven and crack jokes. Yet I cannot recall his father ever coming to our living quarters, and where the father was not admitted the son could not feel at home. He told my father to send me to school: it would do me good to be together with other children. I got top marks but, as I have said, not a few raps on the knuckles as well. For rhythmically grabbing the bottom of the girl hopping in front of me when we squatted for the circle-dance that begins "The hare called his son out onto the green meadow." Or for the usual reason: fighting. I gave as well as I got. We were three classes in one classroom. While the teacher was busy with the first graders, the second and third graders worked on a quiet assignment. I still find it a good idea to avoid focusing constantly on one group activity: we could lose ourselves in reading, drawing, or writing.

Mr. Kreisler had returned from forced labor. His parents and siblings had been taken to Auschwitz, and all his pupils had perished there. He was as surprised to see us as we were to see him. He hugged us and kissed us, which he had never done before. He listened to Zolti Varga's story, thanked him for bringing his two pupils home, and promised to testify to Zolti's valor should he ever need it. Eight months earlier the act of taking us to Budapest had been a political scandal; now the act of bringing us back conferred political credit, which was not particularly pleasant either.

Soon thereafter we encountered a leather-jacketed young man with a holster on his belt. "Sanyi," he said, "make these kids into good communists."

"Fine," said Sándor Kreisler, and the three of us walked on.

After the war he had a distinguished career: he began as a primary school teacher in Debrecen and entered retirement as a commissioner of schools. On the day we arrived, he was primarily concerned with practical questions: where we would sleep that night and who would feed us. We were stubbornly drawn to our house. Our teacher recommended we wait until the next day. But why shouldn't we sleep in our own home, move back in and wait for our parents?

In a little main-street shop we were met by three friendly faces: Imre Székely, Márton Glück, and András Svéd. The first two were my father's cousins. They had returned together from forced labor, each having lost a wife and two children. The three of them had united forces to open a small shop where you could get everything you might need, from brown sugar to a black woolen kerchief. The merchandise—for which they traded flour, smoked sausage, and wine—was brought from Várad and Debrecen by cart. There was jubilation when we entered. Then all three of those muscular men retreated, each to a different corner, and shed tears. When they returned, they did their best to put on smiles. Then they accompanied us to our house.

There was filth everywhere, from the attic to the cellar: trampled books and photographs lay all over the floor; the bathtub, which had served as a latrine for the soldiers who had quartered there, was full of dried excrement. The only furniture left was a large, white rococo wardrobe with three doors, decorated with angels, its mirror still intact. It was probably too heavy for them to have carried off. At my feet lay a story I had written in school about a young fir tree that became the mast of a seagoing ship and engaged in conversation with the wind, an old friend from the mountaintop. There was a photo album scattered about in loose pages, the vanished faces, ourselves among them, stained and muddy. I turned to see the three men standing behind me. We were beginning to understand that what had been would never be again.

"Let's go to my place, then," said Uncle Imre. His housekeeper cut thick slices of bread from an enormous round loaf, buttered and salted them, and set them down next to cups of tea. I rubbed my eyes. Only then did we realize what had happened. The men already knew, of course, though they themselves had been in forced labor digging entrenchments near the front, not in Auschwitz or the deportation camps. Their commander, a local landowner, had led them home when the Russians passed through the village. Most of the Jews left in the town were young men. Before the war approximately one thousand of Újfalu's twelve thousand citizens had been Jews. About two hundred of them survived. They had been lucky in their commander, who had known them all from peacetime, having bought from their businesses and commissioned items from their workshops. He wanted nothing more than to return to peace, to his own house, together with his men and therefore with a clear conscience. The Soviet troops passed through after a big tank battle on the edge of the village on 20 October, and by November even the forced laborers had gone home. By the time we arrived, they knew what had become of their families and had read about the gas chambers in the Nagyvárad paper. The only question was whether their wives had been sent to the gas chamber or to work camps: they were strong young women, so their husbands could still hope that only their children had been lost. What they did not consider was that the Germans in charge wanted everything to run as smoothly as possible. Children were less likely to create noisy scenes and more likely to step naked into the showers if their mothers were at their sides. To keep the children from crying, they preferred to gas the young women along with them.

It was not easy to accept the affection of those men, those hundred-odd widowers around us who had lost their children. They were kind to us, glad to see us alive, but I could not help thinking that my survival reminded them of the death of their own. One of them said to me, "You realize, don't you, that you are living for the others, not only for yourself?"

Uncle Imre, who looked after us and was actually my father's second cousin, was a warm-hearted, frank, quiet man, with broad shoulders and a sense of humor. He waited in vain for his wife, Aunt Lenke, his daughter Panni, and his son Gyuri to return from Auschwitz, whereas I still had hope, knowing that my parents had gone to Austria, where the war was not yet over. Imre lived in just two rooms of his former house, sleeping in the old bedroom. I slept in the bed next to his—his wife's.

My sister and the housekeeper occupied the other room. Imre did not sleep much and smoked a lot. His lighter, made from a cartridge shell, would flame up now and again. From the corner of my eye I would look at his face, illuminated by the cigarette's glow. One time he cried, the way men do, the sobs welling up from his chest, through his throat, and he turned onto his stomach and pressed his face into the pillow, his shoulders shuddering, biting the pillow so I would not hear. I pretended to be asleep.

I returned to the public school to which István and I had transferred from the Jewish school the previous autumn. The teachers and pupils were the same, except that István, who had remained in Budapest, was not sitting next to me. There was no military education, from which we had been excluded the previous year, so I was a full-fledged member of the class community. Neither the teachers nor the pupils knew quite how to deal with me. The homeroom teacher asked me where I would like to sit. No one was sitting next to little Bárczi, so I asked to sit there. He was the one who little less than a year earlier had said that now we Jews would get ours, in spades. Our Hungarian-geography-gymnastics teacher had once pulled his hair while slapping his face to make the slaps more effective. We pitched buttons together and shared our larded bread.

"Where's your father?" asked my classmates, but all I knew was that my parents had been deported. There was a boy in the class whose father had fallen at the front and one whose father was a prisoner of war and still missing. Rumor had it that there, abroad, civilians and prisoners alike were starving and the weak had frozen to death. I was not alone in my orphaned state. We came to accept one another again and avoided speaking of our families.

We slid over icy paths on our boot heels and looted tanks that had been shot up. We collected cartridge shells. Once in a while we found a helmet or a belt or a cartridge bag with dum-dum bullets that explode inside your body, throwing their brass shrapnel everywhere. We would drill a hole in a plank of wood, force the brass shells in, and plant a sharp-tipped bullet in the tapered tube. Then we would hold a nail to the cap and hit it with a hammer to make it explode. A plank with a dozen or so bullets in it looked like a multi-barrel mortar. We used to say we were going out to fire the *katyusha*. There was plenty to shoot at, especially ravens, since the harvest had been bountiful in forty-four and there was plenty for them to pick at under the snow. It is a miracle we never hurt ourselves.

A year before, one of our teachers had plied us with anti-Bolshevik admonitions. He no longer did so now, though he said nothing against the Germans either. Privately he let one of his good pupils know that given their miracle weapons they might stage a comeback yet. Once the Russians had occupied Vienna, though, the teacher applied to be admitted into the Hungarian Communist Party. The previous summer the children still fantasized about those German miracle weapons, wailing like German dive bombers. One of the big kids was called Tiger, after the German tank. But by the spring of 1945 Germans had gone out of fashion, and the children's imagination was taken over by the Cossacks and their red cloth caps with fur along the sides and gold crosses on top.

The Cossacks could not sit still for a minute: they were like bad boys. They would burst in with eggs, onions, and a big hunk of bacon and ask us to fry them up. They would gobble it all up, wash it down with a tumbler-full of vodka, and munch on a whole red onion. They would get drunk and cry. We had to smuggle my sister out of the house through a side door.

Once Duci Mozsár, a pretty, buxom girl of barely fifteen, was standing in front of her gate when a motorcycle with a sidecar came screaming by. The Cossack in the sidecar reached out for her, whisked her off the ground, sat her down in front of him, and shot off. They were next seen a year later, when the motorcycle came screaming back into town, and the soldier in the side car set down Duci Mozsár with a baby and a suitcase, then shot off again as if he had never been there.

A whole squad of sharpshooters had their way with a peasant woman while two marksmen held machine guns to her husband on the porch to keep him quiet. There were times when they shot the woman and her husband if they resisted too strongly. They would drive up in trucks, bringing things, taking things. You could trade with them if you could make out what on earth they wanted. One of them just wanted us to look at a photo album he had found in the frozen mud. He had carried it with him ever since, gazing at the stranger grandparents in its pages.

I had brought back a wounded patriotism from Budapest. There were things you could not speak of. That one year had become like a bell jar of silence between me and my Christian friends, since they had been normal children even during that year.

"Why I Love My Fatherland." Such was the title of a composition we were assigned in March 1945. What was I supposed to write? Things were far from simple. I believed my fatherland wanted to kill me. There have been cases of parents wanting to kill their children. If it wasn't my fatherland that wanted to kill me, if it was only a few of its inhabitants, then what makes my fatherland different from the fatherland of those who ordained the killings and carried them out? They too spoke of their fatherland—all the time. If I am a part of my fatherland, then so is what happened to me since last year's exams. None of this could I discuss in my composition.

I was particularly attached to one image of my fatherland—our fatherland—and the place that gave me birth: the *good place*, the place where you felt safe and from which you could not be uprooted. But once you have been driven from your home and observed your fellow countrymen accepting it (indeed, rejoicing in it) then you will never again feel at home as you once had. Something has been destroyed, and your relationship to the place will never be as naively intimate as it was. My sister and I had wanted to feel at home again in the town after our weeklong return trip, but the house was empty, our parents gone, and there I stood, on the national holiday, 15 March, in the same square where I had once marched in formation to the national flag with my class.

There was a stone podium where the speakers stood and behind it a flagpole where the red, white, and green tricolor had flown at half mast before the war to indicate, as I have said, the painful fact that the country was incomplete, three-quarters of it having been truncated after the First World War. The flag would never fly at full mast until the lost territories had been reannexed. We wore dark blue trousers and white shirts. I can even remember some bright spring mornings when shorts and short-sleeved shirts were warm enough. The Catholic, Protestant, and Jewish schools stood side by side.

In my boyhood I was as unhappy as anyone that the flag was at half mast. I considered it unacceptable that the train should stop so long at the border, after Biharkeresztes, whenever we went to Nagyvárad to visit my grandfather and the tangled network of our relatives there, that one uniform should replace another, that we should have to go through passport control and customs. Once we crossed the border, we saw cement fortifications, as if war were imminent. From Berettyóújfalu to Nagyvárad is only thirty kilometers; from Berettyóújfalu to Bucharest is seven hundred. So Nagyvárad was more mine than the Romanian king's.

The family's oral tradition embraced a number of cities. In addition to Berettyóújfalu, there was Brassó, Kolozsvár, Debrecen, Miskolc, Budapest, Pressburg, Vienna, Karlsbad, Fiume, Heidelberg, Trier, Manchester, and New York. Rabbi relations may have lived in those great distant cities, but Nagyvárad was the true center of things, Nagyvárad with its cafés and theater, with its riverbank where, from the balcony of one of my great aunts, I would watch events unfold on the surface of the Körös through an opera glass.

If Nagyvárad was the sun, then the moon was unquestionably Berettyóújfalu, seat of Csonka-Bihar County. We had our county hall, our county prison, and our county satrap; we had balls and literary evenings at the Military Youth Center, sponsored by either the gentlemen's club or the Jewish women's organization. In elementary school we studied the geography of Berettyóújfalu and then of Bihar County, reciting in wonder how everything was to be found there: plains and snowy mountains, rivers, forests, mines, and—in the very center of it all—the modern city of Nagyvárad with eight hundred years of history behind it. I was a patriot of my region as well as of my fatherland and would jealously defend Berettyóújfalu against Derecske, its neighbor in the district.

Noticeable changes cropped up in the speeches given on the national holiday in 1945. Recalling 15 March 1848, a speaker called it more than a war of independence; he called it a "revolution." My position at school was that of polite outsider, and it continued to be so. The community that sang "Be unshakably faithful to your fatherland, O Magyar, for it is your cradle and some day your grave, nourishing you and covering you," a community that loved pathos, could not expect my Jewish classmates, present only as ghosts, to join them, because the fatherland in question had no interest in their graves: they had been turned to ashes in a small town in Poland, those two hundred children whose lives I was living, if I was to accept the mourning father's words.

The townspeople had generally made no comment about the Jews' being carted off. Some had even laughed at the sight of the old people struggling with their bags, and indeed they were laughable, thinking they would have need of their things, their familiar pillows and blankets, when what was awaiting them was the crematorium. The fact that they were loaded onto trains was met with the same indifference as news from the front or draft notices or the appearance of bombers over the town on a sunny morning: they were all so many historical events over which one had no control. It was the indifference that comes of an acceptance of fate mingled with fear and perhaps relief. "The town has become Jew-free," the local newspaper proclaimed. Hungarian had found its equivalent for the German adjective *judenfrei*. Most people probably felt that with husbands and sons at the front they had enough trouble as it was: news of the fallen kept coming, the harvest had to be brought in, the shops they had always frequented were closed. Then there were those who thought that it was their turn to own the shops, that their little girl should play this piano, their little boy sleep in that brass bed, that they could make good use of the linen cabinet and its contents. There was a place and a new owner for every head of cattle.

I was cold a lot in the early spring of 1945 in Berettyóújfalu. It still got dark early, and I would read by candlelight in the unheated living room, while the fat housekeeper, the wife of a delivery man, peeled potatoes and sorted peas by the light of an oil lamp near the kitchen stove. When her three-year-old son told his mother he was hungry, she unbuttoned an enormous, sagging breast and the child sucked. Either he climbed on the stool or she bent over. Nothing was real. There we were in Berettyóújfalu, though not yet home.

Every day I walked past the lowered blinds of my father's hardware store. Anyone could have gone up to the apartment through the side door and traipsed around in the debris, but it wasn't worth the trouble. Sometimes I went into the courtyard and up the steps to the second floor, where I walked through the empty rooms and looked down at the carts making their way along the main street. A couple sitting straight-backed on a coachbox, each in a lambskin hat.

I walked through my room wearing a heavy overcoat. The cold, dry smell of excrement emanated from the bath. The floor was still strewn with the assignments that had earned me the praise of my teachers and pages from photo albums: summers in the Transylvanian Carpathians, the peaks of Máramaros, my great aunts and cousins now gassed to death. I had not picked anything up off the floor or if I did I put it back. My previous year's coat was not yet tight or short: I hadn't grown an inch in a year; I may have shrunk. Standing in that pile of shame, that mockery of homesickness, I gazed at my astonished face in the surviving mirror and nodded at the little fellow who had found his way home after all.

A woman captured my gaze: a naked woman's body, a display-window mannequin. She was obviously a woman: she had breasts and inked-in pubic hair. Her eyes had been stabbed out with a dagger, her body riddled with bullet holes. Why did they shoot at her seeing she was a woman? I heard a rustle behind my back: Gypsy children were looking to see what I was after or had found, because there might be something in it for them too.

Walking along the main street on those late-winter mornings. I would be invited into one shop or another. It was a nasty March: muddy, gray, inflexible. We were apprehensive, between destinations, yet found it natural enough to be there and have someone provide for us. This was the place we had longed to be. We had looked forward to taking over as adults, but we were just children after all. The wind blew through the family letters in my old room and the prayer-book pages in the synagogue.

Our weakness was palpable: we could no more begin a new life than remove all the rubble; it was cold in our rooms and noisy in the kitchen, and the town had no library. I dawdled in the thinly stocked shops of the men back from forced labor as I once had in my father's. Two or three of them would team up, one buying, the other selling. Friends from the camp. Having lost their families, they had nothing else to do. For a while money could buy processed sugar or flannel or hoes, but soon the only valid currency was eggs or flour. Still, the door would open and customers come in. The young widowed men began looking at women again, the Jewish women trickling back from the deportation camps and the Christian women of the area, former typists, nannies, and housekeepers. If a wife had been killed, her younger sister might still be alive. A woman would enter house and bed, and children be born by the year's end. The loss of the original family was no longer a nightmare, rather a painful reality. If things worked out, you could mourn the dead in the company of a new wife and new children, though more in silence than in words.

But in 1950, just as returnees were getting on their feet again—gathering goods to sell, furnishing houses, filling them with families—the People's Government took over all businesses, all workshops, all houses, everything. You could see it coming. This was the second blow, the final blow to the Jewish community in Berettyóújfalu. The first had occurred in 1949, when a number of the men hung "Back Soon" signs on their doors, went out to the edge of town, and climbed into a truck, destination Israel. Jankó Kertész the shoemaker continued telling his juicy stories on a three-legged stool in Naharia in Hungarian: he had no lack of Hungarian-speaking clients. Jankó had lost his wife and two children.

In November 1944, after the Soviet troops had passed through Berettyóújfalu and set up their headquarters in the district courthouse, Balogh the blacksmith, the strongest man in the village, was elected president of the National Committee. During the few weeks of the Hungarian Soviet Republic in 1919, he had been the president of the Directorate. He was a man people trusted in extreme situations, though there was nothing particularly pleasant about him: he was a terrible grumbler, a malcontent. Nor with the black scarred pits in his face where sparks had landed could he have been called handsome. Loose oilcloth trousers, black boots, and shovel-like paws tipped with dark nails completed the picture. He would lug things here and there in anarchic bundles, meting out justice by giving a poor farmer a rich farmer's porker, though not doing himself any damage in the process.

Anyway, one day this Balogh went to headquarters (the former county courthouse) to lodge a complaint with the potbellied colonel against a Soviet soldier who had gone to the woman next door with a goose he wanted cooked, and taken her eiderdown cover to trade for bad moonshine. The commander stood the guilty party in front of the smithy's coal-cellar door. Then taking a running start, he gave the soldier such a kick in the rear that he tumbled down the stairs. There were no witnesses to what followed, but I heard that the soldier got nothing but water for three days, and when he was good and hungry, the colonel sent for him.

"Do you regret your offense?"

And *how!*

He would get something to eat then.

The colonel got on fine with the blacksmith, but the powers that be did not. Back in 1919 the gendarmes who took over after the fall of the Hungarian Soviet Republic had beaten Balogh the blacksmith black and blue, but he was still the strongest man in the village. In 1945 he again proved stubborn, and because he could not get along with the authorities he returned to his smithy. It was he in 1956 who led the demonstrations, carrying the national flag and becoming the president of the local Revolutionary Committee. When the old guard Communists came back to power, they, depraved weapon-happy drunkards that they were, dragged him out to the edge of the village and took care of him. He died soon thereafter.

My sister and I remained in Berettyóújfalu for another month. I don't remember how we got word that we would be going to Nagyvárad in a Russian truck, but László Kún, a cousin of mine who lived in Bucharest (the son of Aunt Sarolta, my father's favorite sister) went there to pick us up. No one asked us if we wanted to go, but my father's friends took it for granted that we needed to go where people would take us in for the long term. My cousin, a textile manufacturer and businessman, arranged for our lodgings in advance. The gray-green truck had a tarpaulin roof and benches in the back for passengers and was carrying so many packages of black-market goods that we had no place to put our legs. Behind the driver sat a sergeant who had learned the language of every country that the Soviets had moved through, and instantly found his place in each of their local economies. He sold me a Cossack hat and traded me a dagger for an alarm clock. (Today I still think warmly of that grinning sergeant. More of him later.) That autumn Nagyvárad and Berettyóújfalu had been in the same country, even the same county; by then, early April, they were in different countries. But by then it wasn't Bucharest or Budapest giving the orders; it was the Russians, along with the local authorities that always seem to pop up.

My sister Éva and I were taken to an address in Nagyvárad where some plump women were engaged in looking after a baby. My sister was happy to join them, while I gave myself up to pleasant solitude. I lived in an apartment one floor up, home to a forced-labor returnee who had lost his family. He was a prosecutor who traveled a lot on business and did not sleep at home, so the spacious apartment was virtually all mine. I would sit on the balcony sampling the liquors I found in the cabinet. It was perfect springtime weather, and I watched the fast-flowing Körös sweep everything away like paper boats. Lounging on the balcony with a book in my hand, I wanted things to stand still; I wanted to hold them as they were and protect them.

There are times during childhood, times of inspiration, when we know what we do not know even though we do not particularly need to know it, because merely existing, walking along the river or a row of shop windows or a peristyle is joy enough.

I make my way by smell in my grandfather's house, seeking a cupboard, an oak tree, a dining cabinet covered by a lace cloth, the porcelain figurines in a glass case easily penetrated by a bayonet. The inner turns of the garden remind me of dinners under the arbor. To live well you need more than means; you need a certain lightness, but most important, you need to stay alive. You need to give the beef broth and the coffee and the cigar each its proper due. There used to be a life in which everything had its time and place, with tasks to be done that stacked up neatly like ironed shirts in the wardrobe: a time to read and write letters, a time for the *Neue Zürcher Zeitung* and the *Pester Lloyd* and the government and opposition papers of the capital and provincial cities, a time to nap, a time for the café, for a walk, for the theater. There used to be a life in which there was no reason for grandfathers to hang their jackets on any but the same coat rack before changing into a tobacco-colored camel-hair housecoat.

In those earlier days of the late thirties there was plenty to talk about at table—once I was old enough to weigh the adults' words, that is. The rebellious sons of the bourgeoisie traveled to Paris and London, not Vienna or Abbazia. They did not go to Moscow. They were leaving Berlin. They would make impatient declarations at supper, eating with silver cutlery whatever the housemaid (or, in more modest households, the cook) served them when the kitchen buzzer rang, its button built into the table (or, in more modest households, hanging above it) to send the message that she could clear and bring the next course.

A serene permanence seemed to abide in the weekly menu and starched caps worn by the house staff. Even if faces changed from Juliska to Piroska, from Erzsi to Irma, from Regina to Vilma, there was little change in the preparation and serving of food. The younger members of the family were at a loss to explain what intolerable problem lay behind a change in staff, as they were satisfied with all of them, from Juliska to Vilma. They all married properly, with a proper dowry. Nor could the younger generation understand the odd new relationships being forced not only on themselves, but on everyone around them. More than one of the well-provided for heirs made the case for cohabitation.

Now those days were gone too. I stood on the balcony in an overcoat, watching the spits of foam jostling on the rocks: the Körös was a sweeping mass of water even when low. I went to see *Six Hours After the War* with its images of camp prisoners and the unforgettable inside-left soccer star: every day an armed policeman in one uniform or another would take them to clear rubble. Once I had spent the requisite amount of time with the baby and the plump women in the warmth of the second floor, I would go up to my room and read or close my eyes and concentrate on the river's thrum, gripping the armrests of my chair and waving my head back and forth until I was dizzy and could no longer think.

My month there passed quickly, even though I visited the bureau for returned deportees every morning. Camps began to be liberated at the end of April and the beginning of May. The men and women would arrive in their striped uniforms or various combinations of striped and civilian garments. They were gaunt, and their voices seemed to emerge from the bottom of a well. Their eyes were on constant alert, anticipating the next blow. The clients—the deportees—gathered in a large hall. Behind the windows at the counter, clerks would refer to a list that might shed light on who was alive and who dead. They also distributed civilian clothes. Many departed carrying the striped garments; others left the camp uniform there, better forgotten.

I asked the none-too-friendly woman behind the window whether she could tell me anything about my parents, which she could not. Leaving her our present address, I sat down on a chair in the hall and waited for them to come, because here they would receive not only civilian clothing but also a bit of money and information about where we were. And where would they go if not here? My mother, who was from Nagyvárad, would naturally come here: everyone went to the city of their birth. And it was from Nagyvárad that her older sisters and their children and grandchildren had left for the gas chambers. Someone might come back, though not the children. They would most certainly not be coming.

I tried to imagine my parents entering the hall, stepping up to the window, and asking after us, imagine myself dashing over to them and touching them. I wondered whether they had changed much, whether we would spot one another easily. Returnees showed us photographs of faces looking out at the camera with candor. The intervening year had carved the knowledge of death and mourning on one and all, even the most ordinary. One told me my parents' chances of survival would be better if they happened to have ended up in Austria rather than Auschwitz, though nothing was yet certain. So I found myself hoping that my parents were in what was still German-controlled territory—in other words, in constant mortal danger—because it would have been worse to imagine them in liberated Auschwitz.

I had heard about what had happened there. Since no other Jewish children from Nagyvárad and the surrounding region had survived, I was the only child waiting for parents at the bureau. The women sitting on the bench next to me explained that the Polish–Jewish inmates would take the children from their hands and pass them to a grandmother or other old woman: they wanted to save the younger women from having to accompany their children to the gas chambers if so directed by Dr. Mengele. The doctor must have particularly hated children if he sent young women and others still capable of working to be gassed just for holding the hand of a child: the children had to die, immediately, unconditionally. Children and those in physical contact with them were motioned by the doctor to the right the way you snap your hand over a mosquito buzzing around you in summer on the terrace. He saw my coevals as pests, not children. He saw the children's faces, yet did not see them, his eyes cataracted over with words, an officer, intelligent and imperious, carrying out his command to the letter. And since the command was to exterminate every last trace of them, there was no place for individual consideration: each Jewish child was a mere speck in the mass. It did not matter what sort of children they were; all that mattered was that they were Jewish. People said the doctor was no more than a vain young man with a handsome face, more interested in twins—that is, his scientific career—than in his anthropomorphic guinea pigs. What a nice gift for the Führer if medicine could help Germanic—or preferably just German—mothers to give birth to twins and limit the propagation of others. In a short time Europe would be teeming with fertile Germans.

At any rate, I was a real curiosity at the bureau. Some parents would not look at me; others looked at me and cried. One wanted to give me something I didn't accept; another shook me, then cried like the others. It was too much in the end. They had my address; they could find me. I stopped going.

I recently had a visit from a Berettyóúfalu acquaintance, the writer Tibor Tardos, who is now seventy-eight. For me he will always be the legend, the big boy. His father, the lawyer Henrik Tardos, was a friend of my father's who died of diabetes at the age I am now. I remember his bald pate as if it were yesterday. A clear-sighted man, he sent Tibor to Paris, where he preferred chasing women and tennis balls to studying: he wanted to be a writer. Bored with politics, he would not have thought of leaving on his own, but in 1938, after Munich, his father realized that the Allies would not protect Eastern Europe from Hitler —in other words, that our fate was sealed. He was a tall, affable man. He dressed well and thought straight. Not one to fall for rhetoric, he sensed the interests behind the words. He presented the county health officer with a gold cigarette case, and Tibor was released from military service and allowed to return to Paris. There he wrote surrealist books that his father would proudly show me, though he understood not a word. When he sent his son a telegram, he would ask my mother to translate it, since she was the only one in his circle of acquaintances who more or less knew French. After the war I stood before their bookcase as his father took down Tibor's books like relics. And relics they were.

"It was a good village," said the aged Tibor to me. "People lived side by side in peace until those German insanities started happening." Life had an order to it. In the movie theater owned by the father of our friend Karcsi Makk, the boxes on the left were for Jews, the boxes on the right for Christians. They would tip their hats to one another and nod their ambiguous nods. They were separate, yet together. Young peasants sat in the cheaper seats in front of them, Gypsy children in the first row. On Sunday afternoons the Apollo Theater offered a cross-section of village society.

The generation of our fathers needed no incentive to work. Diligence was in their blood, though there were those who aped aristocratic ways: hunting, playing cards, and taking drink with the gentry. Jews had their own tennis court, right next to the Christians', and the Jewish bourgeoisie engaged German governesses for their children and had them taught French or English if they could afford it. Friendships were separate from professional interests. Henrik Tardos in his capacity as lawyer for the Berettyóújfalu Jewish community demanded that my father remove one meter from a newly built multistory house. The community held that the house infringed upon the three-meter-wide service road running from the back of our garden to the synagogue behind it, the road I looked down on from the balcony every Friday evening. That is when the men in black hats would walk three abreast, their tallises rolled up under their arms and their prayer books in their hands, deep in conversation and not the least cramped for space. But the community leaders, friends and former classmates of my father, proved unmovable. They may have been annoyed at the idea of a multistory house on the main road, the only one at the time besides the community center, because on the Great Plain towns tended to expand horizontally into the distance. Imagination moved horizontally, and my father's vertical vision needed curbing. The proceedings went all the way to the Supreme Court, and although my father won the suit his friendship with Tardos remained intact. Nor was the subject broached at their Sunday-afternoon gatherings over coffee, cake, and liqueur.

I was surprised that Tibor did not know what had happened to his father. He was aware that he had been deported to Austria, but not that the Gestapo had arrested him with my father and one of the Kepes brothers. The other Kepes brother was taken to Auschwitz but came back with a number on his arm. They were robust men, not particularly well-educated but quick to take the initiative, worthy of respect, and full of good will. One was a lumber merchant; the other dealt in wines. They saw to it that their children went to university, but like Tibor's father they never left Berettyóújfalu. Their wives died in Auschwitz with one of their daughters. They were beautiful, educated girls, like Dr. Spernáth's daughter. Dr. Spernáth's son was a strapping young man. He is alive to this day, having survived the war, thanks to false papers, as a Wehrmacht officer. His parents were killed in Auschwitz.

There was reason enough for the Jews of Berettyóújfalu to be politically active and save their children by sending them away, even if they themselves remained. They were fine where they were: they had built houses, made lives, and earned reputations in plain view of everyone. Be it honor or shame, they had brought it upon themselves. They were known for the quality of the firewood, the wine, the cart-axles they sold. My son Miklós used to make fun of me when I asked him about the shoes he bought. "Are they nice and comfortable?" He may have realized I was quoting my father, but I approved of my father's concern wholeheartedly.

My mother and father came back from their Austrian internment camp at the end of May 1945. They cleaned out the house and started up the business again. They did not give the issue a second thought, as it would never have occurred to my father not to pick up where he had left off. At first there were just four shelves of goods, then six, then twelve. The shelves filled fast, as there were five children to support.

As a survivor, I owe my greatest gratitude to Providence, yet much as I would like to regard it as something other than coincidence, I am uneasy with every case of providential mercy. For if the Lord of the Fates willed my survival, then why not the survival of the other children? They were no more guilty than I, after all. I cannot be so generous as to hand over Vera, Gyuri, Kati, Jutka, Baba, Jancsi, Gabi, or Ica, to say nothing of Aunt Sarolta, Uncle Dolfi, Aunt Giza, Uncle Náci, Aunt Ilonka, Uncle Pista, Aunt Margit, Uncle Béla, Uncle Gyula and the rest to complete oblivion.

In place of a childhood there is an absence, a story that has not been and perhaps cannot be fully told. Two generations after the fact, I feel prompted to preserve the memory of the Jews of Berettyóújfalu. The synagogue is now an iron-goods warehouse. There was some talk of turning it into a concert hall, but nothing came of it. The Jews who return to visit generally go to see Annus Lisztes, a sharp woman in her eighties, one of the original inhabitants, who lives in the house of the former rabbi. "Come more often. It's your home town, isn't it?" she said to me last summer.

In August 1945 we got a phone call from the border crossing at Biharkeresztes informing us that István and Pali, two orphans traveling from their aunt's in Kolozsvár (which had once again become part of Romania) to their uncle's in Berettyóújfalu, were waiting there to be picked up. My parents happened to be taking a summer break in Hajdúszoboszló, and my father had left the business in my hands. I went to a carter who said he was too tired to go anywhere, but his horse and cart would go if I drove them. This was a staggering offer on his part; it was tantamount to entrusting a boy of thirteen with an automobile. Until then I had been allowed to hold the reins only if the coachman sat next to me on the box. Anyway, the carter hitched up the horses, and I climbed onto the box and gave the reins a tug. I could have taken the old road, but chose the new one, so I could drive the length of the town.

The sun had abandoned the stubbled field, leaving the landscape to cool. It was dark by the time I reached Biharkeresztes. I would have liked to hug István, but he just held out his hand. I babbled something about the horses. He had come from a real city where the cream of the Transylvanian Hungarian intellectuals were regular visitors at his uncle's villa. Whatever I told him was a mere village anecdote.

"How is stabilization going?" asked István, to raise the level of conversation. He was referring to the monetary reform. I was proud to give him some kind of answer and disappointed he had no interest in my cart, whose progress he called slow and bumpy. This was undoubtedly so. He barely watched while I watered the horses at the sweep. When I mentioned that horses had been stabled at the Újfalu synagogue by the Germans, then the Hungarians, then the Soviets, all he said was "Hm." He was through with Jews now that they had been swept away by history. I mentioned Uncle Béla, but this too irritated him. I still had my parents, whereas he was orphaned and had no reason to love his parents' bourgeois reality. He said that he had become a communist and that his father, had he survived, would be his enemy.

István had read Stalin's *The Questions of Leninism* several times and had even taken a crack at *Das Kapital*; I had read nothing of the sort. István had put up communist posters; I had put up nothing of the sort. I had attended various election rallies, drawn by the fact that there were several parties: what I liked about the communists was that they were communists; I liked the smallholders because they were smallholders. István had joined the Hungarian Communist Party at the age of thirteen. By fifteen he was an official Party activist, earning a salary by teaching *Das Kapital* to adults. At twenty he was expelled from the Party and the university for something he had written, and at twenty-three he played a significant role in the Revolution in Győr, so significant that when the Soviet tanks rolled in, his boss and friend, the elderly Attila Szigethy, told him to leave the country. Szigethy himself waited calmly to be arrested, and a short time later was to fall from the fourth-floor window of political police headquarters onto the cement courtyard below. I never joined the Party and never thought I should leave the country, not even after 1956.

István was more theoretical than I and had a more sensitive and radical morality than my own. He was a revolutionary, while I am conservative by nature: I prefer to let things be. My worldview was eclectic, and I did not adhere to any doctrine. Flitting about and refraining from headlong commitment, I could always correct my excesses the next day. Everything István said had an intelligent beginning, middle, and end. If I took a stab at something and he liked it, he would make an approving click with his tongue. He formulated every problem as if speaking to himself.

"This Revolution," he said to me at the end of October 1956, as we stood holding machine guns on the student national guard truck, "is not only against Stalin; it has no use for Lenin either." I was not the least shaken by this statement. By that point István had run through every conceivable issue based on an analysis of data he had smuggled from the State Planning Office and on his experience in the countryside.

"The only benefit of emigration is that I've got hold of a copy of Kierkegaard," he wrote to me from Oxford. What came after the defeat of the Revolution, a slightly less-communistic, more bourgeois communism, was something István did not find particularly tasteful. No one could be homesick for *that*! Had he not emigrated, he might well have hanged. If that kind of thing was to my liking, I was welcome to it.

István pretty much knew all three volumes of *Das Kapital* by heart, but capital itself left him cold. He was found dead in his bed in March 1960, a doctoral student at Trinity College. Gas poisoning, signs of suicide, no note. The previous night he had returned to his rented flat from his brother Pali's birthday party. He had moved out of College lodgings, which he regarded as a rubber-walled sanatorium and where he had had a servant. The housemaid called the police. He was buried in Oxford. The Budapest *Esti Hírlap* printed a small obituary on the last page. Not long ago someone said he had it on reliable authority that István had had "suicide committed on him." He was the best mind of the young post-1956 Hungarian diaspora, which may have given rise to the statement. Pali looked into the matter, but the source had gone silent.

Some time in the seventies I traveled to Berettyóújfalu with my children and our American cousin Tony, Pali's son. We cut a path through the man-tall weeds to the family plot, where Tony cried out, "Jesus Christ! I'm standing on my grandmother!" It was Aunt Mariska's marble grave. My daughter Dorka, tired of the graves, wanted to swim, so we sent her down to the Berettyó. The water smelled like pig manure. One of the cooperative stables was emptying its wastewater into it.

We walked the length of the town. The single-story middle-class houses on the main street, the homes of vanished Jews, stood gray and peeling. I drank *pálinka* in the railway bar. Everything was as it had been forty years earlier except that the hansoms were gone and the restaurant had become a bar. On the train an elderly Gypsy had given his son a slap for suspecting his father of stealing his money. The boy put up no defense, only cried and vowed to kill him. "I cannot strike my father, but I can shove a knife into his throat." A policeman with a German shepherd and a truncheon appeared on the scene. "Jesus fucking Christ! Why don't you respect your father? Put down that knife, and don't you be stabbing anyone on me here in the train. You'll get it back in Budapest."

"It's so *real!*" enthused Tony.

"Father feels most at home on trains like this," my son Miklós noted somewhat acridly.

Until 1948, when I was fifteen, I would regularly visit my parents' house in Berettyóújfalu. After that my father's hardware business and house were taken over by the state and my parents moved to Budapest to be with my sister Éva and me. From then on only letters came. They came from the local Party secretary to my university, saying that my father was a bourgeois and not merely a petit-bourgeois, meaning he was a class enemy, meaning I was unworthy of a diploma granted by the authority of the people.

Later, in the seventies, I went to the village of my childhood on several occasions to visit my friend Tóni Baranyi in the psychiatric ward of the hospital, which was run by a superb doctor, István Samu. Many of us had had great respect for Tóni's sharp mind and sardonic sense for the heart of any matter. He had his own room in the hospital, where he could smoke and read as he wished, and he sometimes put on a white robe. He could leave the hospital at will, but still required Dr. Samu's fatherly support and the friendship of a doctor couple. He helped work up patients' case histories through thorough questioning, thus playing the role he had filled in other mental institutions, the inmate prince who in intellect and learning towered over patients and doctors alike. His talent as a writer was evident primarily in the musculature of his formulations: his words hit their mark the moment he opened his mouth. At home in Pesterzsébet he would mostly just sit in his armchair and stare out of the window into the street at the similar working-class house opposite or read the only book in the room. He gave away all books once he'd read them. Having no desire for possessions, he was finicky only about his trousers. Otherwise he was no dandy. He would go down to the garden gate several times an hour to see if anyone had rung. He was ready to deal with any intruders, by force if necessary.

Tóni Baranyi always felt better after seeing his doctor friends in Berettyóújfalu, where he would go to the beach and have a swim in the Berettyó. The time I visited him, we had an animated conversation in the former Lisztes Restaurant. I was the only guest in the upstairs hotel, where I found the Gypsy boy who played piano at the restaurant in the evening playing chess with himself. Tóni and I sat in high-backed chairs in the restaurant's large main room, digging into wild boar sausage and garlic cabbage, drinking a heavy red wine, and watching a row of identical, well-nourished, self-confident peasant faces engaged in singing. The heavy-set men wore dark jackets, white shirts unbuttoned at the top, and rubber boots for the mud, and gripped their glasses with dark-skinned, thick-fingered hands. At one time the corner table had been reserved for the town notables; now, in the seventies, it housed detective types, the city and county police department having moved next door. They were telling jokes, jokes that were good if the commanding officer at the head of the table laughed.

Facing me, a young lady with a touch of a mustache brought a forkful of kidney and brains to her lips. Truck drivers waiting for the main course popped pork-crackling buns into their mouths to go with their beer. Some pried them apart with curiosity; others skipped the fuss and bit them in half. Dollops of sour cream glimmered on the stuffed cabbage, which, as it crumbled under the knife, revealed that it contained more rice than meat. The man who looked after the local dam was served a small vat of bean soup in which cubed beef swam in abundance. Soon tiny roses of fat glittered on his droopy, graying mustache.

Then the rectangular bottle of marc brandy came out, and a glass or two slid down the gullet, leaving not a trace. The flypaper hanging from the lamp had done its job and was completely covered. A double bass leaned against the wall under a color photo of the Gypsy band's leader, who had been playing here for years, his muttonchops running down to his dewlap in a wave. Now he was grinning, the violist earnestly chewing his mustache, and the *cimbalom* player using the paprika shaker with scientific precision as he polished off his roast beef and fried onions.

A thin young couple at the next table ordered osso buco, which they knocked against their plates to dislodge every last nugget, concentrating fully on the process to the exclusion of each other and lifting the marrow on toast to their excited mouths.

The long-limbed, slightly tipsy waiter gave the waitress a kiss on the neck. She recoiled. The hostess behind the old-fashioned cash machine drummed her fingers while studying the varicose veins in her legs. A row of cars decked in flowers pulled up, and guests poured in, half-happy, half-drunk, taking their seats around the long tables. The waiter started bringing out the brandy; the music was not far behind. Men in thick furs, leather jackets, and boots breathed in the aroma of the hot stew and cautiously bit into the pickled peppers. The guests discussed the trend to smaller portions. "They're looking out for our figures," said one. An enormous young butcher in a bloody apron danced into the kitchen with half a pig over his shoulder and flirted with the cook, while her apprentice, in a carefully ironed and folded white cap, extricated herself from the strident din.

A squat gentleman on our left, his ring digging deep into the flesh of his finger, was courting one of his lady colleagues. They had left headquarters for a fact-finding investigation, and now that the meetings were over there was time for a little celebration. Young workers on sick leave arm-wrestled. A crumb quivered on the mustache of a thick-armed Gypsy fellow, his broad fist hanging motionless. The walls were adorned with woodcuts of distant wars of independence. The waiter said the best thing to drink with wild-boar sausage was genuine Bikavér, Bull's Blood, which he poured from a special bottle. A salesman pulled a little bag of bicarbonate out of his pocket, removed a pinch with the tip of his pocketknife, and mixed it into his soda water.

A bearded young man who had gone through his cutlet and buttered peas was looking disgruntled, though there was nothing for it. He was telling a blond schoolteacher with a narrow face that knowledge is not the basis of love, because the more you know someone the more relative that person becomes.

"You mean the better you know me the less you'll like me?" asked the teacher.

This is not what the bearded young fellow meant: he was thinking metaphysically.

"I see," said the teacher, relieved. "Only metaphysically." (Why couldn't the fellow relax and stop pulling her leg?)

"The road to familiarity leads to exalted regions, the realm of icy peaks. Only a greengrocer would suppose that we find warmth among great minds. Chill breezes blow about us, perchance the indifference of sanguinity."

"You mean from your icy peaks I look common to you?"

This is not at all what the bearded young fellow meant. "We do not love the one who deserves our love, but the one that we in fact love."

Now what was the teacher to make of that?

The young man raised the ante: "God must needs be a believer, but the God He believes in cannot be He himself. If God knows of God, then he cannot be one with himself, but must then be as divided as I myself. In short, God must have another God. And so on, ad infinitum. Better not to think of it."

Tóni took a pill that, he claimed, sliced off the cerebral cortex. He washed it down with beer. In a short time he felt a bombing raid approaching and asked to go down to the bomb shelter. He spotted an emergency exit along one wall, but as it was blocked by a table of four corpulent guests he went over to them and said, "Please follow me through the emergency exit to the bomb shelter!"

The four large guests looked at him quizzically. "Where is it?" Tóni pointed to the blank wall.

"Leave us in peace, will you, Comrade?"

Tóni gave up his evacuation plans. They can bomb us if they want. A few years later he blew up his heart with drugs and vodka.

The next day I continued my solitary walks. My legs knew automatically where to turn. A schoolboy waited in a window.

"Who are you waiting for?"

"My parents."

This is where the domestic would lean on her elbows, waiting for the lady of the house to ring, while over in the next window the daughter leaned on a pillow, taking refuge from her French lesson. As a child, I knew who lived in all these houses, but by now the names were unfamiliar. The only familiar names I found were in the cemetery. A row of children's hats and women's legs in boots filed by, and faces stared through the fence waiting for what was to come.

In 2000 I accepted an invitation to Berettyóújfalu from City Hall (it was a city now, not a town). I was to give a reading to an audience of local citizens in the building that had once housed Horthy's Military Youth Organization. The reading and the discussion that followed were a bit on the somber side, whereas my hosts would have preferred that I be more emotional in my nostalgia: nurture warm memories, express my love for the old Berettyóújfalu. They wanted my heart to beat faster whenever I saw it rise on the horizon, this town that all three of my wives unanimously dubbed a dusty hole, but that made my heart quicken, that I found beautiful, the town of towns with the most intelligent arrangement of space. Approaching the former community building and national flag on the former Erzsébet Street, with the Calvinist church and school on the right and our house, somewhat higher than the rest, on the left, I had the sense of being at home. How many times had I experienced this sight on sunny afternoons, heading home on my bicycle from the river. I was sad to see the artesian well gone and the cinema disfigured, but at least the post office was its old self. I had a framed picture of the past inside me that overlay what I was now seeing, but even with the best of intentions I was unable to portray it with anything like the sweet reverie my audience expected.

I could not veil the deportation of the Jews or the plunder of the survivors by state appropriation with sentimentality. The town had deported its Jewish citizens and viewed all their possessions as its own, moving strangers into their houses. At the time my father called it highway robbery, and I agreed. Today the town is coming to see that my father and the others did it honor and were model citizens in their way. The vanished Jewish citizens are becoming a venerable tradition.

I found my grandmother's and grandfather's tombstones in the abandoned Jewish cemetery. My great-grandfather's tombstone had probably had another inscription carved on it. The hospital director, an intelligent man, told me the cemetery serves more than a hundred villages in Bihar County. Sometimes elderly visitors come from Israel and walk out to it. These children of émigrés are sober, naive, and cordial and take a hand in preserving the monuments, as does the town itself. The black-haired women with prominent cheekbones look familiar. The woman who is deputy mayor, a local and very kind, told me how much the town had looked forward to my coming and mentioned that her parents had known mine and me as a child. I felt my Bihar County roots that day. When something during my visual inventory caught my fancy, I felt the pleasure of one who belongs. True, they have filled in Kálló Creek, and the garden where we played soccer among the cherry trees is gone, as is the walnut tree by my window; indeed, the window itself is gone, filled in. And the synagogue is still an iron-goods warehouse.

II

Up on the Hill During a Solar Eclipse

ON A DAZZLING SUMMER DAY IN the last year of the twentieth century I had the opportunity to watch the world change colors and sink into gray darkness from the porch stairs of a crumbling wine-press house on Saint George Hill.

The noontime bells are pealing. I arrived yesterday. The countryside was beautiful, my family even more so. My account of the trip elicited laughter from my most critical audience, and I was pleased by the quantity and variety of the gifts I received: Áron had painted me a rich landscape with a wonderstruck deer that bore a striking resemblance to his father; Józsi had carved me a walking stick with the inscription *To Papa*, a nice long stick that will soon take me up the hill.

I had spent the entire day in travel—first by plane, then by train—but by evening I had reached this place of repose. Now, my back propped against the uneven masonry, I sit on the acacia-wood bench in the garden between lilacs and the walnut tree listening to the rush of the wind and swallows' chirping. I can feel waves beating between my forehead and the hill, which in primeval times seethed with volcanic magma, though for thousands of years now it has exuded nothing but fruit, water, and fragrance.

Most of the houses are inhabited by widows now. They have a better rapport with life than their menfolk had: men tend to pace and fidget, get in the way, wondering what in the world to do with themselves and ending up messing with varieties of afterlife; women potter around in the one we have.

When I sit at my desk with the window open, I can see the village world of Hegymagas: my sons eddying up amidst a horde of friends, the elderly neighbor women, the tractor man, the bulldozer driver, the housepainter, the groom, the vintners, the Gypsy family that always marches in a group, the young mothers pushing their infants up and down in carriages or leading them by the hand, the old ladies bent over their little purses, out for a wholesome stroll, the old men stepping gingerly, leaning on canes.

The locals parading by my window exchange greetings with me. The poorest old man in the village sometimes topples into the flowerbed in front of our house on the way home from the pub or nods off on the bench there under the linden tree, propped on his cane. If he had more money, he would just drink more. The old fellows are on their own now. For a while they can go on without the people who made their lives, and then comes the day when they cannot.

The days grow shorter now that summer's back is broken, though the sun is still well up in the sky. The noontime bells are pealing. A veil of fog covers the ridge of Long Mountain. Wheel marks escort me across the meadow, my legs practically whisking me over the springy ground. Untroubled by ragweed, I take a good whiff of the undergrowth. I run into a shepherd who complains about his right leg; I'm having trouble with my left. The shepherd feels better if he lies on his left side, but since it's bad for you to lie on your heart he spends the night twisting and turning. Clean spring water gurgles from the mouth of a century-old lion carved of wood into a mossy basin where tamarisks are budding. The smartest thing to do is to keep going up the hill.

Zsuzsi kneels beside me on the bench. "I'm going to draw something beautiful, so beautiful you won't believe it, and I'm drawing it for *you*." She draws a kind of latticework in red pencil.

It is soon done, and she asks for another pencil. "It's so beautiful: droplets falling from branches," she whispers.

I will be eighty when she is twenty, if I live that long. The fun was short-lived, like a holiday. Over before you know it. Every afternoon we go down to the lakeshore, where Jutka rents a kayak for Józsi, who was paddling away at the age of seven, climbing walls, scampering up ropes, speeding along on his bike in every possible position. Jutka got a new bicycle for her birthday and rode through the neighboring villages in white slacks. She came back flushed and enthusiastic. The other day she said she was despondent at feeling stupid. I attempted with great conviction to argue the contrary, but to no avail.

"So what if you *are* stupid? You're smarter than I am."

Jutka laughed.

"How long is there a point in living, Son?" my mother once asked me.

"Until we die, Mother," said I. "Till then for sure."

The mood at the breakfast table is bright for the moment. Not even Jutka has a headache. True, Áron was attacked in his sleep by a venomous snake and upon waking noticed a red spot on his leg right where he had been bitten, but he complains of no pain. Józsi asks about the plan for the day. Has the Bureau of Parental Services arranged for the proper abundance of entertainments for the People, the Little Ones? A full day's worth?

I give my assurance that we will arrange a trip to the circus in the afternoon. I call to ask whether there will be a show. Yes, they tell me, elephants included. I sit beside my wife in the car, passing her crackers to munch and water to swig. She never takes her eyes off the road.

Meanwhile there is no break in the process of enchanting the children and hushing them and taming Zsuzsi and coming up with ideas and encouraging them to shut their eyes and try to catch a few winks. I just stare ahead lazily, passing her the water. If Jutka is dissatisfied or (*horribile dictu!*) starts grumbling, I put up no resistance, because this is the best of all possible worlds. Even the physical decline that awaits me, the series of defeats that is old age, is more interesting than the hereafter. As for resurrection, well, of course I believe in it. It happens every morning until the show gets canceled for technical reasons.

Jutka will be forty-five the day after tomorrow; I will be sixty-six tomorrow. Both of us are Aries. We have been getting to know each other for twenty-some odd years. I sense what she is thinking even when she says nothing. Three children and a husband on her back, and all the practical issues of their daily lives. It takes no small effort to stay on top of it all, to pass out praise, find refuge in a corner, come up with incredible stories, talk through the day that has passed, and preside over the evening's ceremonies from the English lesson to the brushing of teeth to the climbing into bed. Once she emerges from the children's room after nine o'clock (often closer to ten), she too will go to bed soon. She has done her most elemental job.

Everything is so perfect at this moment that I fear something will come along to upset our lives, in which bitter tears and hysterical cries and nightmares and self-enforced exiles and escapes cast their shadows only up to a point. Each member of the family will remember only the happy moments when they think back on the old days.

I feel I have simply turned up here where I am now. The world has fallen into my lap or I into its lap. And some day I will simply be turned out. In a cool room on a hot afternoon I begin a story. I do not yet know where it will go.

In the middle of April 1945 I got a message saying my cousin László Kun would be arriving at four-thirty. He was thirty-seven at the time; I was twelve. I knew his first stop would be to say hello to the women of various ages in the downstairs apartment, including my sister Éva and the little baby (I no longer remember whose). Then he would come upstairs to the floor that at the time was mine alone, with its balcony overlooking the Körös, its library and liquor cabinet. Nothing was forbidden me. I could spend the entire day reading and wandering with no one expecting an account of my time (though I would not have minded being questioned and chided if I proved ignorant). This older presence was a soothing influence, Laci Kun representing the next generation in the family tree, and it had been decided— perhaps by Laci himself —that he would be our guardian, our bread-giving surrogate father until our parents, carried off in May of 1944, came back from the camps once the war managed to end. *If* they came. So I expected some direction from him.

Seated at a large round table, I fixed my eyes on the front door of the Nagyvárad apartment belonging to György Pogány. Then city prosecutor, he had started out as a lawyer, but soon had to serve in the forced-labor service units for Jewish men. His entire family had disappeared. When my cousin László Kun from Bucharest made his entrance, it seemed as if my father had walked in, but a head taller, broader in the shoulders, larger in every dimension, and ten years younger. He was a self-assured and elegant man in a flawless suit. You could see he had made it his own.

The new arrival was more urbane than the locals and had been spared the humiliation of being sent to a camp. Former prisoners, happy to be alive, could not afford his generosity: all they had was what fit in their knapsacks. "The Swedish Lord" was what I called Laci to my sister, though fully aware no such thing existed. Laci sneered at lack of generosity in others and could sometimes be haughtily, curtly dismissive of people. His parents had been of modest means, and he had no wish to follow suit. It is hard to be small-time when you are over six foot three.

He asked few questions, wishing only to know whether I was satisfied with my circumstances, and he assured me that we would not be long in that apartment: he would return in under a month to take us to his family, a wife and two children, in Bucharest. Then we too would be his children whether our parents returned or not. That was the last time we discussed such intimate subjects. When I asked him what I should do until he came, he took a wad of paper money out of his back pocket and set it down before me, saying it was mine and my only task was to spend it. He assigned my sister Éva the same task.

After that I ate a lot of cream-filled pastries and went to see the Soviet film *Six Hours After the War* several times. I understood neither the Russian narration nor the Romanian subtitles, but after several viewings I could follow the action. A young woman once flashed me a kind smile from a window. I went back several times, but she was gone. I could deal with loss.

I was growing a little wild: I would unbutton my shirt, reach under my arm, and scratch. This did not escape the notice of Aunt Zsófi.

"Oh, Gyuri, what has become of you? How you've let yourself go! It's only six weeks since we separated, and you've taken up such crude ways!" True, she smiled and may have been joking, but her words could be taken seriously.

A pair of brothers in transit sat at the dinner table, spilling the black humor they had picked up in the labor camp, where violent death was as common as seeds in a watermelon. They vied to win a smile from Aunt Zsófi, a smile whose unmovable reserve filled me with bliss.

Aunt Zsófi went her way early the next morning, while I walked up and down the Körös watching labor servicemen marching off to clean up rubble under the escort of an armed but shabbily dressed policeman. It would have been easy for them to escape, but apparently no one did. I looked for the house where my grandfather had lived three years before, and found strangers living there. They were not interested in my grandfather. They said they too had been bombed out of house and home. They offered me some rolls and jam, but didn't mind when I declined the offer with thanks. There was a little girl drawing in a corner of the kitchen. During the few minutes I was there she raised her head no more than twice, but even so we had a good look at each other. After that I walked past the house a couple of times hoping to run into her on her way back from school, but those meanderings did not bring the hoped-for encounter, which I had even fleshed out with a bit of dialogue. In my head we had some very serious conversations.

Later I stopped walking down that street or even in that general direction, because I happened to run into my Aunt Gizu there. She gave me a kiss, but I extricated myself from her arms, unable to forgive her for having abandoned us in Budapest without notice at the beginning of the Arrow Cross regime. I made no promises to visit her. She had found her way here to Nagyvárad to take over the house and possessions of her relatives. I left her with a remonstrative smile, without telling her our address.

Our upcoming trip to Bucharest filled me with a powerful curiosity, heightened by a yearning to travel and the excitement of anticipation. I had heard there were more Hungarians living there than in the outlying cities of Hungary itself. We had a long road ahead of us in the big, black Chrysler Imperial that Laci had purchased from the Queen of Romania, chauffeur included. Now that he was allowed to work again, he was doing business everywhere between Bucharest and Transylvania, including Kolozsvár and Brassó, and we had family to stay with all along the route.

Looking back, I see that I climbed a few rungs on the cultural ladder that year, moving from rural petit-bourgeois to urban intellectual circles, the latter calling for an ironical style as opposed to the naive nostalgia of my family background in Berettyóújfalu. People smiled at me when I expressed a desire to return there. I said I belonged in the village and considered everything else a mere way station.

Both our guardians—Aunt Zsófi, a fashion designer and historian of fashion, and Laci, a textile engineer and wholesaler as well as Romania's breaststroke champion and the assistant concertmaster of a distinguished amateur orchestra—would gladly have left their parents' origins in obscurity. This I could not accept, since I loved Laci's mother, the tall and robust Aunt

Sarolta, who knew just how to make me happy. Whenever we visited them in Nagyvárad, she would sit me out on the terrace overlooking the Körös and, if a wind was blowing off the river, wrap me in a silky blanket. Then she would set down a chocolate pastry with strawberry jelly and an opera glass so I could watch the water gurgling over the rocks and the fish jumping clear out of it. I could spend hours on end there. Now and then Aunt Sarolta would replenish my supplies from the adults' table and at my request give a brief summary of their conversation, which dealt mostly with the family and Laci's marriage to the tall, blonde, elegant, and noble-spirited Iboly, who always knew best and may have exceeded even Laci's ideal of perfection.

Iboly was from a good family in Kolozsvár, had attended university, played tennis, did gymnastics, spoke German, French, and a little English, and came with quite a nice dowry. She was unsurpassed in the theory and practice of manners. A movement at the corner of her mouth would register the faults in others' upbringing. She never said a word, and she was forgiving, but she noticed all the same.

Her father-in-law, Uncle Dolfi, had like my father been in the hardware business, but both his shop and his stature were smaller than my father's. I did not understand why Laci avoided mention of his parents killed at Auschwitz. Out of shame perhaps? Did he not want to look the horror in the face? Or perhaps he saw it all too well and found it unseemly to mention. Should all talk of humiliation and murder be taboo? My father had only the greatest love and respect for his older sister Sarolta, who had treated him with the utmost tenderness from earliest childhood: she always had something to give him—an apple, a spool of thread—and if there was uneasiness at home, if my grandmother got worked up over something (what with five children and a house full of people there could always be reason for pique), Sarolta would go into action and make so amusing a remark that my grandmother would turn red from cackling and her annoyance vanish—together with its perfectly valid basis. What is more, Sarolta had a perfect sense of judgment and proportionality. Witness her choice of the diminutive Uncle Dolfi out of all her suitors: he was the most human of the bunch. Uncle Dolfi looked upon his monumental wife in wonder. It probably never entered his mind to betray her, and Aunt Sarolta was the very embodiment of tranquil satisfaction, her only concern being for the children.

Sarolta's daughter, Laci's sister Magda, was the most beautiful girl I knew as a child. Once she summered with us in Hajdúszoboszló, where my passions included nuzzling up to her in the early morning to trade purrs and inhale her scent. For the most part I was the one to wake her, though she was not always in the mood, sometimes whimpering for me to wait and stop squirming under the blanket. But once her eyes were open, she had strange things to say.

She would say, for example, that only bad people amused her and that she would like to meet a pirate some day or at least an adventurer. She wanted to have a look at an honest-to-God decadent seducer, because the only people she encountered at the Nagyvárad theater or the pastry shop or the women's club ball or in the synagogue garden on Jewish high holidays were well-intentioned young men. The ones who looked interesting to Magda all left town for the big cities. Her own brother Laci had outgrown Nagyvárad and felt at home only in Vienna or Bucharest. He had so many girlfriends he couldn't count them on his fingers and toes combined.

Laci's visits were red-letter days for Magda. Together they would go down to the public bathing area on the Körös and show off their backstroke, breaststroke, and crawl, sinking their arms deep into the water and gliding gracefully forward. In Nagyvárad Laci generally appeared in the company of Magda, who was not beyond the occasional acerbic remark should any of her friends show conspicuous interest in her brother. Though I did not lay eyes on him until I was twelve, I had heard a lot about Magda's fabulous brother and seen him looking dashing—decked out in a riding jacket or tennis shorts—in photographs. I had also heard that Laci once gave such a slap to a young man for an undignified remark directed at Magda that the fellow tumbled backwards over a bench in a park square.

Magda let me in on her suspicion that her brother was not truly in love with his wife but she would at least give the children an excellent upbringing. I found it odd that Laci would use the familiar pronoun *te* with Iboly while she would address him with the impersonal *maga*, but they made a fine couple at evening events. In 1942 Magda made the acquaintance of a man twenty years her senior, broad in the shoulders and tanned to a copper hue. He was balding somewhat and working on a paunch. Now here was someone whose state of decay had a certain mystery about it. The interesting thing about bad people, she said, was that they were good anyway, in spite of themselves.

His surname was Flóra, and he ran rackets, or at least that is what my governess Livia informed my mother. This Mr. Flóra came for Magda at the Gambrinus Hotel in a Steyr Puch sports coupe and took her for long drives. This made both my mother and my governess uneasy. After lunch Magda would disappear, not to return until after dinner. He fancied unusual dishes like breaded chicken shaped into sticks; I was less drawn to such innovations. Once I saved one of the chicken sticks for Magda, but she didn't seem interested. She said she had eaten marrow custard at the Golden Bull Hotel in Debrecen. That turned my stomach.

Once an incandescent Magda and I were sitting on the terrace at the Gambrinus Hotel when Mr. Flóra took a seat with us. "How old are you, sir?" I asked.

I saw that he did not appreciate the question. Magda tried to skewer me with her gaze, but gave up. We sat in silence, letting Ákos Holéczy's Jazz Band and his singer Stefi Ákos move us, probably with a song of farewell. I despised that old coot with the woman's name—Flóra—and tried to trip him up.

How did he like the Alföld region? If he was less than enchanted, his goose was cooked. And so it was. He came up with the dullest of criticisms: it was flat and empty, there was too much distance between the one-horse towns, the cobblestone roads connecting them were hard on his roadster. I grew more pleased with his every word. If this fellow is so stupid, Magda won't be long in turning him out. But this was not to be. To my silent horror Magda happily concurred, even raising the ante: she understood him completely, this Flóra, this ape who lived on Budapest's fashionable Gellért Hill and skied in the Tyrol. She was of mountain stock herself—in spirit anyway—living, as she did, close to the Bihar Range. So it was the two of them against me, the Alföld yahoo. (Can you really be conspiring with *him*—you and he a *we*, and I just a *you* to you now?) This little roly-poly of a Flóra will come to regret his little fling, and you'll see what a slug he is! He'll make you retch! That very year proved me right: Magda, pregnant and abandoned, failed to cough up the sleeping pills she swallowed, and closed her eyes forever. Lying on the bedside table next to her, tied with a silk ribbon, were the letters she had written to Flóra. He had returned them.

Laci's arrival was a real event. He would rise up tall out of the back seat to greet everyone scurrying to meet him, then get a full report from each member of the family and its employees, dispensing praise and a few witticisms to point up our intellectual debility. You could never be sure on what grounds he would disapprove of what he heard. I sensed there was a sensitive instrument, quivering to every stimulus, working inside him, consigning everything clumsy, excessive, or petty to the black zone. I suspected he used his pipe to keep him from answering too quickly, and although the remark would have had more bite had he come right out with it, the contemplative pause carved veritable epigrams out of the smoke. There was no reason to take his words to heart, but if he trained all the power that was in his eyes on you, you were done for.

Laci was nothing if not talented, particularly when it came to starting good-sized businesses. When Austria aligned with Hitler in 1938, he had to make a quick exit from Vienna, where as successful executive and exquisite equestrian he had gained entrée into high circles. His quips and sparkling, intelligent smile, his flawless decorum would have sufficed to keep him there, but he also had a dignity, a power that drew others to flock to him: he was the kind of man upon whom people danced attendance, for whom they put their best foot forward. It was not easy to win the boss's approval, but they kept trying.

By the time Laci returned to Nagyvárad just under a month later, we had set our hearts on his becoming our guardian. Perhaps the reason I trusted him was that he so strongly resembled my father.

He was a good man even if Mimi, one of his girlfriends, was more often unhappy without him than happy with him.

One day a well-dressed young woman called to me on the street, asking my name with a lilt, suspecting who I was, based on Laci's description and our physical resemblance. I nodded. "Yes, I'm the one." I was amazed at having such a sweetly scented beauty in furs recognize me or even find it worth her while to do so. She removed her hat in the Japort Pastry Shop, let her dark golden hair tumble down her back, and ordered a tea. She placed her elbows on the marble table, rested her chin on her fists, and had a close look at me. Then she smiled as if to say, Let's get to it then!

I had been there several times and religiously ordered the cream pastries (scented vanilla, which had been my favorite at Petrik's in Berettyóújfalu as well), but this time, to make my new acquaintance happy, I responded enthusiastically when she pointed to the pastry case and said, "It's all yours!" This led me to conclude that the lady was inclined to excess. Mimi inquired about Laci and the family, wanting to know everything because, according to her, he was so taciturn and irritated by anyone's curiosity. "I will listen to what anyone tells me, but I won't ask anyone a thing," he once told me after I had barraged him with questions.

Mimi had a quick mind and a quick tongue and claimed to have read *Les Thibault*, a thick, two-volume *roman fleuve*, in two days. I had had a rather uncomfortable relationship with the book during the Budapest siege in the domineering presence of Aunt Zsófi: she made me hold a volume under each arm to keep my elbows at my sides and prevent me from leaning on the table "like a cow." Though properly trained thanks to the efforts of my mother and governesses, I was nonetheless inclined to recidivism when it came to elbows on the table. "You're not in a bar, you know!" was something I heard a lot. ("More's the pity," I would say to myself.)

In any case, my relationship with this ample novel, so filling and always ready to provide further nourishment, continued in Bucharest, because Iboly too had noted my pernicious propensity to rely on my elbows, to say nothing of fingering tumblers, as I had seen men do in the bars in Újfalu whenever I peeked inside. No sooner did I tell her about my grotesque connection to the Thibault family than she reached for the bookshelf and pulled down the very same edition. It had lost none of its heft in Bucharest. She tried to civilize me further by requiring me to lift buttered steamed peas to my mouth on the convex bottom of the fork rather than the top. (A decade or so later I wrote a long paper on Roger Martin du Gard out of chivalry perhaps or as a tip of the hat to that reliable master as I sampled proper bourgeois virtues after the intervening turbulence.)

The day I mentioned Aunt Zsófi's pedagogical procedure to Mimi, provocatively placing my elbows on the table, she said, "Your family is a bunch of scoundrels!" and tousled my hair. Her nails were long and, of course, painted red, which one month before the end of the Second World War was, I would venture to say, an uncommon spectacle even in the Japort Pastry Shop. She asked after our family. Her own was largely gone and had not been all that extensive to begin with. Mimi was the product of a less than regular marriage and had decided as a girl to grow up rich and famous. She later amended this with another wish: to stay alive. She thought she looked like Magda, or vice versa. The two of them had been the prettiest girls at school and were often compared. They got over this by praising each other's beauty. They never became close.

With her too, Laci refrained from speaking of his parents, victims of Auschwitz, but neither did he bring up the beautiful Magda, who never got there. "Thank God for that," Mimi would

have added. Even so, she had not had an easy time of it: she had
fled to Southern Transylvania in Romania, where Jews were not
being deported to Poland, only shot by the tens of thousands in
their own land. Like many others Mimi was taken to an island
from which there was no escape: all those who tried were shot,
and by spring only their remains were left.

Still, you could slip through the cracks by means of a paper
marriage or bribery or indifference on the part of the authorities: Mimi arrived in Nagyvárad not long after the Russians and
watched over her mother's apartment there, filling it with furniture of her well-to-do deported aunt, lighting the candles in silver
candlesticks. She came to know Laci's tastes and cooked his favorite meals, taking the edge off some and improving on others,
getting hold of the ingredients through mysterious, semi-obscure
supply chains. "That finicky cousin of yours is quite a gourmand.
It's begun to show on him. Have you noticed?" Mimi divulged
that she had let Laci's trousers out herself. A seamstress by training, she hoped to open a fashion salon in the center of Pest,
Szervita Square, perhaps—yes, she had picked out a spot next to
the Rózsavölgyi Music Shop. Laci would find her there after the
war, assuming neither of them got shot. Mimi had reckoned with
the possibility that Bucharest would not be enough for Laci, that
he needed Budapest, Budapest and Vienna, where he had spent
some good years. He had even divulged to Mimi what the name
of his company would be: Technicomp.

"Like the sound of it?"

"Hmm."

Laci would not have a partner because he liked making all the
decisions himself. Maybe he would use her in the clothing factory as a fashion designer, Mimi said, though nowadays it was
work clothes that were in demand. Well, they could be attrac-

tive too. Laci was supposedly stunned by her productivity: each time she came to Nagyvárad she showed up in a different outfit, designed and executed by her at astonishing speed.

"Your despot of a cousin does love novelty," said Mimi, "but don't worry, he won't trade you in! He's just a bit difficult and won't let himself be loved. He doesn't spoil me either, but you'll be fine," she added with a touch of envy, "because you'll be able to have lunch and dinner with him every day, while he's my eternal fiancé." She talked with a dreamy sadness and fretted about having let her hair down, but she had divined that Laci enjoyed talking to me.

And so he did. Laci and I even talked politics. He asked me to pick him up a copy of *Scînteia*, the Romanian Communist Party newspaper. When I asked why he wanted that paper in particular, he told me the same thing I had heard in Budapest from my beautiful dancer friend Magda, a few years before she was shot in the back while trying to escape over the border. She had reasoned then that the Communists were the most determined enemies of the Nazis, the Arrow Cross, and the Iron Guard, so they were the ones she trusted most. I replied that this was only partly true, since I had heard stories in Újfalu about Arrow Cross people turning Communist —once a bigmouth, always a bigmouth. But Laci chose to believe that industry was about to pick up and finally usher in the age of enterprise. I told him stories about the Russians and their drunken shooting sprees, about how I'd pulled one of them back to save him from falling into the well in Uncle Imre's courtyard while he was emptying his bladder.

Oh, of course, he said, he had stories of his own like that, but I should keep in mind that they were the liberators and I owed them my life. I acknowledged this, though I was a debtor on so many fronts simply for making it to twelve that I was growing lazy in matters of gratitude and felt that Laci's optimistic generosity towards the Communists was overly hasty.

As did Bibi, his assistant manager in Bucharest, who said, "*Les idées sont belles, mais le pratique, bon dieu, c'est tristement douteux.*" He would phone early in the morning and announce in his piercing, somewhat impatient voice, "Bibi here!" He was amazed I could not pass on his messages in French to Laci. When I offered to do it in German, he thanked me and said he'd rather not, German being a language he was steering clear of for the time being. Bibi was not at all impressed that the Russians had commandeered ten thousand automobiles in Bucharest in a single day, and made his feelings known at the table where he often took dinner with Laci and his family and they conversed over cigars and cognac like proper capitalists.

But to return to the despondent Mimi: it became clear during our conversation in the pastry shop that she was not only waiting in vain for her eternal fiancé but would go on waiting even if she married another. "And if some day that cousin of yours leaves his clever stick of a wife, and says, 'Come to me, Mimi,' then crazy little Mimi will run as fast as her feet will carry her. She'll dump her husband and family just to feel your precious cousin's heavy hand on her head."

A few lovely teardrops trickled down her nose, and she wiped them away with her scented handkerchief. I never met Mimi again despite her promise to visit me. I did see her once, however, though she did not notice me, or pretended not to. She had just come out of a building when a large, black Morris driven by a man in a crew cut, black glasses, and leather gloves pulled up. Mimi climbed in next to him and ran her hand through his hair. In light of what I had seen I considered Laci's passion for Mimi a reckless investment of his energy, yet despite my moral ruminations I concluded that Laci's putative infidelities did not make him unreliable as far as we were concerned.

Thus my sister and I decided to let Laci in on our secret: the buried gold. There were two kilos of it in a stainless steel box, about half in bracelets and other jewelry, the rest in different forms. The day after we arrived in Berettyóújfalu we made an energetic inspection of our house's grounds, which were nothing but rubble. We also peered into the warehouse that opened onto the courtyard and determined that the crumbly ground in one corner indicated some digging, but that there were no traces of it on the hard-tamped earth floor starting a meter from the doorpost.

We gave each other a nod: any nitwit would have thought to dig in a corner, but a meter out from the doorpost and the wall was an unlikely hiding place. While one box was gone, the other might still be in place, underground. But if we dug it up, it would not be safe with us. So we told Laci our secret and left it to him to work out where the goods could be stored. On the evening of the third day Laci said we would start digging at nine the next morning.

We took three cars and were escorted by five or six young Jewish men with holsters under their short coats, former labor servicemen who had lost their families and thought they were helping the sole surviving pair of Jewish children in the county. They had brought shovels and guarded the gate as they dug. It was a good while before the tip of a shovel struck metal. They lifted the box and placed it in a sack. We headed back immediately so as to meet the same border guards and Russian soldiers who had let us into Hungary that morning at the new crossing, approving our passports with a compassionate glance. They said something I could not understand, and off we went.

If our parents ever returned, they could not accuse us of being careless. We had no intention of letting Uncle Andor in on the secret, though he was very curious about our parents' hidden valuables. We said we had no idea about anything of the sort. We were very good at playing dumb.

We soon left Nagyvárad. I still remember the long goodbyes to the older women who had managed to stay alive. I had been accustomed to such staircase sentimentalities from earliest childhood. I recall the loud, almost paroxysmal greetings of my mother's sisters (Margit and Ilonka, destined for the gas chamber and crematorium) when I would recoil so as to be spared all but the final slightly mustachioed kisses that accompanied those yelps of joy. My mother, now ninety-five, still mentions her long-dead sisters and talks of having visited them recently or of their imminent visit to her. She asks whether I have seen one or the other recently. My attempt to awaken her to the truth feels fatuous and uncalled for even as I say it: "She's been gone for sixty years, Mother. You know that. They killed her at Auschwitz."

"Did they now?" asks my mother in amazement. "Killed her?" She might have been hearing it for the first time. She knows the truth; she just doesn't want to acknowledge it in her mental slumber. She would rather think of the childhood games they shared. She no longer recalls my father. What brings her the greatest happiness is a visit from her grandchildren and great-grandchildren or a certain gray tomcat when it springs into her lap on the balcony. Zsuzsa, the sensitive economist from Munkács who works as my mother's nurse, calls the cat Bandi; she feeds him and elaborates humorously on his character. My mother will sometimes do a little drawing or reading or walk through the garden on my arm. She eats what is served her, then falls silent, then asks a question, then falls silent again, then starts laughing.

When I visit, she holds her cane in her right hand and takes my arm with her left, and we take a few turns around the garden. Her forgetfulness may help her along the one-way course of years: she is letting go of her burdens, and the tapestries of memory slip from her consciousness layer by layer, leaving a smooth, unfurrowed optimism that asks only to be caressed. I stroke the soft gray hair on the back of her head and praise her, tell her how beautiful I find her latest drawing though a two-year-old might do better, and often feel the same dizzy optimism in myself, a tolerance and aloofness from the world, a mask that says, Any way at all is just fine. I feel my mother's face against my own and my father's smile coming to my mouth. Sometimes I come out with one of the silly things he used to say, the few that I recall. When I do, my sons give an ambiguous smile, not knowing what to make of me and my verbal oddities.

But let me return to my original story. There was silver in one of the boxes we dug up: trays, cutlery, sugar bowls, and candlesticks. My parents meant to sell it if we lost everything else. In fact, some of the rest ended up with relatives, and what little remained was still there a few years ago, at the end of the twentieth century (of glorious memory), in my mother's glass cabinet. Then one day, when she happened to be alone in her ground-floor flat, two stout old hags rang the bell. "You remember us, don't you, dearie? We shared a room at the hospital." They told her all kinds of stories about herself and their close friendship there, none of which my mother denied, though she had never actually been in a hospital. Why hurt their feelings if they were nice enough to pay her a visit? While one of them talked a blue streak, the other removed my mother's savings book from the drawer and her silver trays from the cabinet. They packed the goods into a bundle and took their leave, expressing their sadness at the prospect of not being able to return for a while. In response to their kind words my mother saw them off with a kind farewell of her own.

Before we approach the eight-hundred kilometer trip from Nagyvárad to Bucharest during the last month of the Second World War, this time under the patronage of my cousin Laci and in his elegant, once-royal, still chauffeured car, stopping on the way to visit my second cousin Ferenc Dobó at his house and garden near the Greek Orthodox Church in Kolozsvár and my uncle Ernő Klein, director of the Hotel Korona in Brassó, a bit of perspective is in order.

In the fifties, after the communist takeover, Laci became a department head at the Romanian Ministry of Industry (then the Ministry of Foreign Trade). Although he had been chief engineer at several factories, a respected expert who oversaw international negotiations, he remained under suspicion because of his bourgeois background: technically speaking, he was a class enemy. To determine whether he was a class enemy in spirit as well—or to use the parlance of the time, whether was also *subjectively* so inclined, the appropriate entities were mobilized.

One night, lying in bed next to his wife, he awoke to the glare of artificial light: four shapes in trench coats stood over him, each with a flashlight, grilling him about the whereabouts of a missing document. They took him to the Ministry, where he found the document in question, which was in the wrong folder. The whole thing turned out to be a farce, and they let him go, though from then on he no longer slept soundly. Thus the next visit by flashlight did not wake him from a deep slumber; indeed, he had been all but expecting it. He left the Ministry and sought a simple job: all he wanted was to keep his family in modest circumstances and be left alone. But this was not to be. Laci could not shrink into a small enough package to escape their harassment and interrogations. Iboly bought a knitting machine and started making sweaters for a cooperative.

In 1956 they filed a request to emigrate to Israel: it was the only way to leave. The entire family was released in 1958. We met briefly in Budapest, whence he was off to Vienna. There a friend asked Laci whether he had officially informed the municipal authorities that he was moving away for good when he left in 1938. Laci did not recall having done so. He looked into the matter and found that this was in fact the case. So after twenty years he was still a registered resident of Vienna and could apply for Austrian citizenship. Which he did, successfully. Thereafter he opened an elegant office in the center of town under the name of Technicomp. He particularly enjoyed traveling to Budapest as the representative of German, Dutch, English, and Swedish companies, arranging the purchase of chemical, oil, and food industry equipment for Hungarian enterprises. He sent his daughter Kati and son Stefan to the best schools in Vienna, but Stefan, the light of his life, died suddenly of meningitis.

Once Laci had more or less emerged from mourning, he and Iboly went to the Konzerthalle every week. He read all the major German-language newspapers and lunched in Mr. Kardos' restaurant not far from Technicomp. Every morning he crossed the City Park on the way to the office until one day he collapsed on a bench, having lost all desire to reach the leather armchair behind his enormous desk. Frau Reisner, his aged secretary, did not understand what had put Herr Kun into such a catatonic state, though according to Frau Kun it had happened once before: he had been interned in one of the better mental institutions in Bucharest, where he would stare at the puddles in the courtyard and give the tersest of answers to her questions. Here in Vienna it was the brick wall of a stolid public building from the previous century that he saw across the street, though he was not inclined to look out of the window.

In time he managed to pull himself together and make another go of it. The work intoxicated him again. He took up with a woman named Edit, a good match: elegant, intelligent, svelte, tanned at the pool by early spring, now a citizen of South America, originally a Nagyvárad Jewess. He enjoyed her witty, malicious pinpricks like a good massage. With ever-increasing momentum he traveled the world—America, Japan—putting together complicated deals for his clients. He often came to see his cousin Gyuri Gera and me in Budapest, paying amicable court to our young wives, until the secret service called him in and tried to get him to report on his domestic and foreign business associates and his burgeoning circle of friends. If he refused, there was not much chance of his doing business, as they could revoke his multiple-entry visa. "What can these people be thinking?" he asked us, as if his own experiences back in Bucharest had not made it perfectly clear to him what these people were thinking. They were thinking that if he did what his character dictated (and what I respected so much) we would not be seeing him in Budapest in the foreseeable future.

We were sad to see the end of our cousin, though thereafter it would have been more disturbing had he been allowed to visit. He wasn't, and our meetings were suspended for a long time. Laci lost his taste for Vienna as well. After seeing to his wife's funeral, he remarried in America and lived near his daughter Kati. Later he moved to Florida and from there to the world of shades.

I have presented these developments to give the reader a sense of the future trajectory of the man who sat to my right in the front seat of the car. In the back sat my sister and two women we knew, whom Laci had taken along as a favor. Behind their heads was the sack containing the heavy strongbox. Coming into Ploieşti, the driver swerved off the road and hit a milestone. The box flew into the air and hit the head of the woman who talked the most and loudest. The Chrysler ended up in the ditch below with the milestone on its roof. A Soviet military truck had veered towards us out of the opposite lane—its young driver may have fallen asleep—and the queen's chauffeur had skillfully yanked the wheel to the left. As a result there were no serious injuries— except for a bump on the head of the talkative lady.

We were picked up by a truck in the pouring rain. Laci sat in the open back, wrapped in a waterproof tarpaulin; we sat in the cab, where it was dry, with our lady guests. The entry into Bucharest was less triumphant than the departure from Nagyvárad.

Crossing rainy boulevards, we arrived at a fin-de-siècle boyar villa. Deep in the garden stood a three-story Bauhaus building completely overrun with woodbine. The garden also boasted a sandbox, a swing, and a small pool. Standing perfectly straight in the doorway of the third-floor apartment, wearing a soft camel-hair robe and exuding a faint scent of lemon, was the broad-shouldered Iboly. We found in her a good surrogate mother, mindful of her obligations, from meals to bathing to clean pajamas. Everything fell into place more or less as at home, before 1944: I had a bed and a desk, we had lunch at lunchtime and dinner at dinnertime, we were to be civilized at table, and we were to toss our underwear daily into the hamper, because a clean change was waiting in the wardrobe. After the morning bath I was allowed to go to the garden or shops with my two-and-a-half-year-old cousin Kati, who served as my interpreter: What I said in Hungarian, she repeated in Romanian. Invigorated by our team spirit and well-matched roles, we dutifully accomplished our appointed tasks, garnering praise from Iboly and Viorica the cook, a loud, amusing, passionate woman who called me a Dacian savage when she was dissatisfied with me. Laci's baby son Stefan, tossing and turning in his little bed, was the only other male in the apartment, because Laci left home early and returned late and was often away on long business trips.

While the Queen's Chrysler was being repaired, Laci drove around in a red Škoda sports coupe that was requisitioned out from under him somewhere between Torda and Kolozsvár by the Soviet soldiers who were always standing around in groups by the side of the road. Laci expressed his outrage, insisting on speaking to the commander and having the case officially recorded. The sound of the word *protokol* got the soldiers' dander up. They gave Laci a shove in the chest and jumped in the car. Laci, always one to do things by the book, found this an unorthodox procedure, but was still capable of laughing at finding himself once more in the back of a truck in the pouring rain.

Born under the sign of Aries like myself, he saw adversity as adventure and was unable to stay angry for long. He merely moved on to the next item on his to-do list, earning the money for a new car and accepting from the outset that it would turn out a losing proposition like the last. In those days luck was an ephemeral guest if it came at all, glittering in one spot for a spell, then evaporating just as quickly. He had two good years after the war, then four more after emigrating, but the last time I saw him—we were walking along Fifth Avenue looking for a certain tobacconist's where he had seen a cherrywood pipe in the window that had caught his fancy—I realized he had resigned himself to the pensioner's view of the world: he spoke highly of walks by the sea and had stopped making plans.

My father was unsuited to prosecutorial statements. Instead he would reflect, "What is this fellow trying to pull out of himself?" as if everyone had a few extra characters lurking inside, like suits in a closet. I imagined him saying to me, "And you, my boy, what do you want to pull out of yourself?" "Nothing, Father. I'm just waiting for the bell to ring in the front hall. Maybe I'll go down to the garden with Kati, but I'll always be where I can see you in case you come home."

One day Laci phoned from Nagyvárad to say that our parents were alive. They were at home in Berettyóújfalu, and we would be seeing them soon. How soon? *Soon.* He refused to go beyond the essentials. Our parents were probably as thin and sickly as other returnees. I didn't relish imagining what their fate had been given what I had heard of concentration camps.

In the meantime I hunkered down in that apartment so little like home. Everything exuded normalcy, yet things could have worked out much less favorably. In the last year of the war two English pilots had hidden out in the room where I was staying. Their plane had been shot down, and the resistance network brought them here. One evening during dinner the concierge rang the bell and asked who was living there besides the immediate family. "No one," said Laci. The concierge wanted proof, but Laci would not let him in. When the concierge tried to push his way in, Laci gave him a punch in the face that sent him tumbling down the stairs. "You won't regret keeping quiet about this," said Laci, helping him to his feet.

Even as we spooned our soup from Rosenthal porcelain bowls, the image of our parents taken from Nagyvárad and Kolozsvár to the gas chambers had floated in the air above the chrome-plated silverware and the covered soup tureen. Whenever they were mentioned, a silence would fall over the room and Iboly and Laci's faces strained to hold back the spasms tightening their throats.

With a nod from Hitler and Mussolini Hungarian troops re-occupied Northern Transylvania—and hence Nagyvárad and Kolozsvár—from Romania in 1940. In 1944 the Jews in Northern Transylvania were deported to Auschwitz, while the Jews in Southern Transylvania remained under Romanian rule. Thus my uncle from Brassó and cousin from Bucharest survived that critical year, while my relatives from Nagyvárad, Kolozsvár, and Berettyóújfalu, except those few young men drafted into forced-labor service units alongside the army, perished. Some of the men in the labor units were eventually shot into mass graves anyway, but others were left to live—the decision being determined at their commander's whim—and made their way back home. In other words, the fate of the Jews sent to forced labor depended on whether their company commander happened to feel like killing or rescuing them at the time. If he was a hardened fascist who stuck to his guns or if such a one replaced the softer and more feeling reservist, the Jewish men's days were numbered. Although I avoided imagining where my parents might have ended up, I had heard enough at the Office of Deportee Aid in Nagyvárad about what happened to those who managed to pull themselves off the train on the platform at Birkenau, where prisoners were divided into groups depending on their usefulness. If they had gone to work in the fields, they would occasionally find something edible.

We had no idea when Laci would arrive with our parents. Each day could be the day. The excitement of anticipation was great.

Suddenly I was no longer able to give my full attention to little Kati's meanderings in the garden. Yes, even Kati, to whom I owed a new fairy tale, could wait. The tailor in the ground-floor shop—he was supposed to measure me for a new suit, though I was perfectly content with the old one—could wait too. Indeed, I was glad I wouldn't have to hear him ask on which side, right or left, I put my "tool." I needed time for the most important thing of all: retiring to an elevated spot in the garden that let me keep track of all who arrived.

Finally the rumble of the familiar car, the slam of its doors, and the voices of several people, most prominently Laci's. Then a woman's voice: my mother's. I ran out to take my mother's bag from her hand. Éva too appeared, eager to take my father's rucksack. Bickering about who would take what was a restraining influence on the excitement of falling into one another's embrace. It would give the kisses time to dry. Walking into the garden, my father squinted in the bright June sunshine and dropped behind; my mother held out her arms. I had to gulp back my tears. Yes, these were my parents.

They were smaller, thinner, and older than the image I had been carrying in my mind. The eyes of both held the same probing question: Who are you, you who have been in my thoughts for so long? Laci left us to ourselves. There was a long silence during which we held one another's hands. I looked at them and nodded, then said the words *Mother, Father.* Then we did all sorts of things: we walked to a park my sister and I now knew inside out; we treated my parents at the Italian ice-cream vendor's. Gazing at a girl with black curls drinking from her palm at the fountain, then sprinkling the water over her hair, I felt a bittersweet peacefulness settle over me: how nice that the people around us had no desire to stake us out, turn us in, have us dragged off and exterminated. You can relax when no one around you wants you dead.

After dinner, in our pajamas, we squatted on our parents' bed and listened to one another's adventure novels. My mother told their story, my father commenting with an occasional grimace. On the forced march from Vienna to Mauthausen a dozen of them had dashed into the woods at a bend in the road at my mother's instigation. They were so quick that the guards failed to notice. It was early spring and survival in the woods was difficult. They encountered an SS unit and passed themselves off as Hungarian refugees. The soldiers were glad the group spoke German and was willing to cook the hares and deer they had found in the forest, so they all sat around the roast in a friendly mood. A pretty young girl among the escapees rather caught the fancy of the young and handsome unit commander, who engaged in some coy flirtatiousness in the interest of good relations.

This sylvan idyll, which lasted two weeks, turned out to have saved their lives, since none of those who reached Mauthausen— those who had not dared to escape at the time—remained alive.

My father's role in the adventure was to keep his mouth shut, as his acting would not have got him far: he was incapable of cheating or lying and had always kept his books assiduously, always paid his taxes, and never bought on credit (though he also enjoyed the minute discount he received from paying in cash). He would repeat ad nauseam the German saying *Ein Mann, ein Wort*—a man is as good as his word—but such simple-minded piety was dangerous. He would never have survived the war had he not yielded to Mother, who in the face of authority and laws was stronger-willed, more tenacious, impulsive. The commander, ever more frustrated by the forcefulness with which the young woman rebuffed him, eventually reported a band of escaped Jews hiding in the forest.

So in April 1945 they were packed into a wagon by Austrian gendarmes and traveled for days to reach a multipurpose camp located amidst cherry trees in bloom and housing people of every origin, a great many prisoners of war included. It was not an extermination camp, though, and it was there, in Krems, that my parents were liberated.

Mother's quiet yet determined resistance predated their ordeal. Take, for example, the case of the broiled sausage. The market square in Berettyóújfalu had an open kitchen stand from which the aroma of pork sausage wafted far and wide, enticing not so much mother as son, who had fallen into temptation. From whatever angle I sniffed, the sausage would win out.

Not that it had no competition: I was particularly partial to the smell of sunflower rolls—leftover sunflower seeds pressed into a disc and used as fodder—that filtered through that olfactory cavalcade. I was also drawn by the gentle whiteness of the tables where old ladies sold sour cream, butter, farmer's cheese, and ewe-cheeses big as a child's head. Ultimately my mother ceded to the pressure and bought a twist of sausage. Daringly we sneaked bites before lunch, sitting on the pinewood chairs in the kitchen and using my pocketknife. We ate quickly, like conspirators, hoping to conceal our assault on Jewish dietary proscriptions from my father, ever the good son, who though resigned to the fact that my mother bought rump of beef along with the shoulder, would have found the appearance of pork in the house unconscionable. In any case, our attempts at concealment failed: my father happened to come upstairs in search of my mother and got an eyeful of the sausage champers. And yet he pretended to have seen nothing.

My mother was willing to lie, to break the law if necessary. She had led the eager Gestapo officers and Hungarian gendarmes around the house and denied what needed to be denied. Women are better at that sort of thing. When my mother was arrested with my father in May 1944, they were first held for two days at the fire station in Berettyóújfalu. I thank my stars that my mother had the nerve to get herself locked up, leaving us children on our own. One of the gendarmes accepted a bribe to let my father into the room where my mother was being held and she told him in no uncertain terms to demand an audience with Chief Constable György Fényes at the local police headquarters, which was well disposed towards them. She thereby saved both Father and herself, since the train they were packed into went by mistake to Austria instead of Auschwitz, and in Austria chances of survival were sixty percent. She also saved us, because had she been at our side the gas chamber would have been our lot—mine for certain, and most likely Éva's as well. I never held her leaving us against her: a woman's place is at her husband's side.

At noon on the third day we took them lunch. Even food was now a political statement, an expression of solidarity and protest.

But there was no longer anyone to deliver the food to. At first we were glad to see that the doors to the holding area were open, but it turned out to be empty. One of the gendarmes told us they had been taken to a place near Debrecen, and next day we learned from the Chief Constable that they were on a farm that had been converted into an internment camp. He advised us not to go there, however, as we would not be allowed in. We took the roast home and nibbled at it, then put the rest away for dinner and played ping-pong all afternoon. At the camp the gendarmes questioned my father about the location of our valuables. He said that he had none, that all his capital was in the business. I don't know what they did to him, but by sticking to his story he saved our chances for starting over, at least in part. That gold, which he would trade for nails, wire, and pots when peace came, was for him what a last manuscript is to a novelist. They did manage to get information out of Uncle Béla, however, so they came to the garden and pulled the steel box out of the well. I remember hearing the water they pumped out gurgling into the street.

They were packed eighty at a time into cattle cars. My mother got hold of some Ultraseptil for my father, who was weakened by a fever, and whenever the train stopped she would help him off. They did the work they were required to do on the property of the Dreher brewing family in Schwechat under guards who were strict but not particularly cruel. They were lodged in a long barn. Nearly all the local day-laborers had been conscripted, so the group hoed the fields for potatoes, sugar beets, onions, and beans, occasionally slipping some under their shirts or into their pockets. They worked until winter, huddling together in the cold and keeping each other's spirits up.

In December they were taken to Vienna to clear rubble. They lived in a school building in Floridsdorf on the left bank of the

Danube, but worked in the center of the city, climbing over mounds of bombed-out houses to set the rubble into piles. Most of the Viennese pretended not to notice them, though a music publisher gave them buttered bread wrapped in paper and invited them in the evening for hot tea amidst carved mahogany music stands.

Laci encouraged my parents to stay in Bucharest for a while and rest. My father could eventually join his firm, Laci said, but first they had to shore themselves up physically and mentally. He probably made a few disparaging remarks about Berettyóújfalu: Why would my father want to go back after all that had happened? What was left for him there? As long as he was starting over, why not go into a more serious line of business? My father nodded, though to himself he must have been saying something along the lines of "Just keep talking, cabbage head." To his mind Laci was a megalomaniac.

So my father would return to his hardware business, for this was his trade and there was no one better at it in all Bihar. All he wanted was to be the person he had always been and greet the first customer who came into the store that summer. Things would have to be put in order. He would start with a few goods on a shelf or two over in the right-hand corner. Then he would expand gradually until ultimately the entire store, basement included, was stocked. The authorities would leave him alone. He still had a few friends in the village.

As for Mother, she had her heart set on Budapest, where the children had managed to stay alive. She rejected the notion that Berettyóújfalu was the place to start over. Everything had been split into separate nationalities. What had been was no more, nor would ever be again. Better to forget what cannot be restored.

But her Józsika was too stubborn to be dissuaded. He went on about his father and his grandfather and the fact that he knew virtually everyone in town by name. The madness had passed, and it was time to get to work. He took possession of his house, had it cleaned out, had new locks put on the doors. All he wanted was to be at home in his own house, to live where he had made his reputation. The fact that everything had been taken from him, that he himself had been taken off, was a passing insanity and could not happen again. No question about it. He would be stocking the finest English merchandise.

My mother kissed him on the forehead. "Oh, Józsika!"

I put my hand on his. He squeezed it and said, "That's how it will be, won't it, son?"

"Of course, Father, if that's what you've decided." Újfalu, naturally, yes.

But Újfalu proved a less than feasible option. First of all because only four years later my father ended up having everything taken from him again, this time in the name of the proletarian dictatorship, but also because retreating into the familiar little nest and longing for days of peace in the village—days that had never existed or existed only in Father's imagination—was little more than an obstinate, sentimental dream. Yet I have no trouble understanding my father's naive attachment to the village where he was born, the home of his parents and grandparents.

Laci was a bit annoyed at us for not accepting his offer. He had come to like us and regard us as his own; he had prepared for the day when we would become his children, and knew that to give us back to our parents was to lose us. Why shouldn't we all stay in the same city? In those days it was still possible to imagine Romania turning into a good country, and it was no fault of his that it did not. Neither did Hungary for that matter.

As a department head in the Ministry of Foreign Trade he negotiated with German and English clients who came to Bucharest, but since his colleagues did not understand the conversations they were in no position to write the requisite reports to their superiors. They suspected Laci of making secret deals with his visitors. The moment he received the slightest gift or sign of attention from them, they had him hauled before the political police for interrogation. He was trailed on the street; his house was searched. When he took sick leave, they moved a woman into the apartment as a cotenant, a woman who irritated Iboly no end with her transparently insincere coquettishness. Later, when Laci escaped from it all into a sanatorium, they moved an informer into the room's other bed. Posing as a patient, he would go through Laci's pockets as soon as he left for the toilet. Once Laci scribbled something on a slip of paper, then tore it up and tossed the shreds into the wastepaper basket. He came in from the corridor to find his roommate bent over the trash, retrieving the bits of paper to fit them together. They *wanted* him to know that he was surrounded, that the authorities needed more than a loyal expert who remained a political outsider. They needed all of him.

He became a truck driver instead: he had the physical strength to carry huge baskets of bread on his back. One day while he was making a delivery, a shopkeeper happened to hear him whistling "Yankee Doodle." Before the scandal got out of hand, Laci moved back to the sanatorium, grew a beard, and spent his days standing around the garden in pajamas or dishabille watching the leaves falling, silent for long stretches of time. Thanks to the intervention of a kind doctor he had access to recordings of classical music. Once they allowed him and his family to emigrate, he left everything behind. He would have done anything to remove his loved ones from that insane country.

Everyone could see that my father with his humble smile was the mainstay of the family. Though the fifth of the six siblings, he was the only son. The financial situation of his sisters was more precarious, and the younger generation disparaged his bourgeois decency, sense of proportion, and self-knowledge. I could sense my cousins' arrogance, the arrogance the intelligentsia feels in the face of middle-class stability.

My father was not at all receptive to communist slogans, always returning to the principle of free elections and rejecting the revolutions taking place all over the globe. "In an election you have many choices, son. That is all I know." He listened to the BBC during the war and after. He would also spend hours with Radio Free Europe, delicately turning the knob to minimize the jamming.

The trip back from Bucharest was a long one and mostly in trucks. Anyone with any kind of vehicle set up benches on it and became a chauffeur. There were about twenty of us seated in a very old contraption. Speed was out of the question, but limping along in a group made the trip easy to bear. I was interested to know who was sitting next to me and across from me. Who were these people with whom I got off occasionally to stretch? Opposite me was a Romanian girl about my age who ran down from the embankment at the edge of a wood and gave a shout of joy: *Vai, ce frumos!* (Oh, how beautiful!), though there was still plenty to worry about and many dead to mourn.

In Brassó we again visited Uncle Ernő, the hotel manager, stocky, polite, relaxed, though sometimes reticent. Before the war I had spent long summers with him in the woods belonging to my grandfather's family. He lived then in a large, wooden house in the snowcapped mountains of Máramaros, where he had been delegated by his family to plant trees and produce lumber. The company had a sawmill and a train of its own chuffing merrily up and down the mountainside. I felt on top of the world at five or six riding that little train hauling stripped tree trunks over the wide mountain tracks. My grandfather traveled all the way to and from the mill in his own upholstered passenger car.

I can see them now—sturdily built men, broad-shouldered, tight-bellied, and mustachioed: Uncle Ernő, my mother's older brother, and one of her brothers-in-law Pista, a misanthrope who, once the passion for cursing Jews had seized him, could be calmed only by the application of leeches to his back. Whenever I was a guest at their house, he heckled me after lunch, mocked me by saying I attended a *cheder*, a Talmudic school, which I did not—we simply lived near it—but old Pista was not one for fine distinctions. He was angry because his attempt at settling in Palestine had failed, and he was tired of constantly being a Jew. He loved the woods and fishing for trout in icy creeks. He loved feeding the pigs growing fat in their sties, and giving them a friendly kick in the rump, sprinkling groats for the chickens and decapitating them with a swing of the axe. Once he took me up to a part of the mountain where they burned wood for charcoal. He bought wild strawberries in glazed pots from the Gypsies. That rascally girl was there, the one who would frighten me by laughing and rolling her eyeballs so only the whites showed. I wanted to touch her, but lacked the courage. No one could top Pista at lighting campfires or roasting meat, and no one knew the crevasses and waterfalls better than he. It was a joy to help him skewer the bacon, chicken legs, onions, and peppers. And we had a good laugh wolfing down all traces of bacon as soon as we heard the chuff-chuff of the locomotive, which at this hour of the evening could only be carrying grandfather in his personal car.

The old gentleman liked to sit out on the porch of the wooden forest house, where his papers would be delivered to him, always a bit late. He would leave it only to accompany us to a small town in the Carpathians, where next to a lovely square stood the local prison. On Sunday afternoons the inmates would reach through the bars to sell their handiwork: wooden whistles and pipes, clacking roosters, birdcages. Their cells were their workshops. We would stroll along the tree-lined gravel path, watching them whittle. One of them had killed a man, we were told. He made slippers.

Grandfather, a cousin of the head rabbis of Trier and Manchester, read the masters of modern Jewish scholarship. He had been president of the Nagyvárad congregation at one time. He did not much bother himself with the details of the lumber industry.

When imaginary bats fluttered too thickly around Uncle Pista in the dining room, his head would grow so red that my great aunt Ilona had no choice but to bring out the pickle jars holding the thin, balled-up, wriggling leeches. Aunt Ilona would have her husband straddle the chair backwards and take off his shirt. Then she would set the leeches on the vast expanse of Uncle Pista's back—it was almost as wide as the dining table—one by one, in rows. They would set to work—pumping assiduously, growing thick and fat—and suck the red right out of Uncle Pista's head. Within a quarter of an hour Uncle Pista would reach the point where he lost all interest in the Jewish question: it was nonsense either way.

If I was in the mood, the two of us would cross the creek on a narrow plank, then proceed stone by stone across its other branch and arrive at a clearing where we could watch the deer walking along the path. When they caught sight of Uncle Pista, they would flinch and give a start, but he would just blink his eyes innocently and they would go back to their grazing or have a drink from the stream and move on along the path in a group. I very much enjoyed having Uncle Pista take me along on these excursions. He even forgave me for wetting the bed after a big lunch. Since I was already five, my mother would have punished me for such slovenly behavior by canceling all afternoon entertainments, but Pista would sneak me out of the house to the ice-cold creek, where, standing still as a statue he would reach into the water and in a flash grab a silver trout. Then we would settle down on a mossy outcrop, where Pista checked the brandy flask to see whether there was still some marc left, for what else can one do at dusk if one's feet are cold but have another pull from the flask.

In May 1944 Pista tied three trunks to his landau, took his seat on the driver's box in front of his wife and son, and like the other patriotic Jews in the region drove to the Nagyvárad ghetto. A freight train took them northward. Uncle Pista and Aunt Ilonka, my mother's favorite sister, were soon turned to ashes. Their son Gyuri Frank, my most kind cousin, died of typhus a year later in Mauthausen. He had taught me how to make world-champion soccer players out of overcoat buttons using a file and some pitch.

My uncles did not do a good job of analyzing future prospects when they conferred in the Golden Eagle Café in Nagyvárad. My mother's oldest brother Imre had held various jobs: he had been a croupier and a maître d', going from table to table with a friendly word to everyone. He always kept a table for his current girlfriend, a strawberry blonde, like all the previous ones. Imre had broad shoulders, a dark-brown tan, and a pin-stripe mustache, but he was bald and short. Sometimes he mounted the orchestra platform and took the leader's violin from him. Grandfather was less than enthusiastic about all this and steered clear of the café where his son Imre wasted his time with such madness.

Uncle Pista and my two Uncle Ernős would go there to see Uncle Imre, and the four of them would put their heads together and take counsel about how to survive the war. The most successful solution was the one Uncle Ernő Schwartz came up with: a coronary. No more did he hop into his smooth-riding Citroën and have his chauffeur take him on one of those sometimes mysterious trips of his. Whenever he was ferried to the kind of woman who made demands on him—the kind that gossiped to her girlfriends about who gave her the new ring or fur—Uncle Ernő had no choice but to stand in the doorway of Aunt Margit's room, rest his brow against the doorjamb, and complain to her about how low the human race had sunk: "Just imagine, my dear, they're going on about me again! This time about X and me!"

"Poor dear. Don't they have anything better to do? Maybe it's because you're such a big, handsome, strapping man and they're jealous of me and the children."

The children—Uncle Ernő took good care of them. He gave Éva's hand in marriage to a highly reputed pharmacist and arranged for Bandi to study in England and become an architectural engineer. His son Pál, though, whose triumphs at Exeter were more on the tennis courts than in the medical labs, he brought home and installed in his company: he, at least, would not organize a strike against his father as son Bandi had done after marrying a robust, red-haired woman active in the left wing of the Workers' Party, an lifelong advocate for the poor in Parliament.

Uncle Imre was killed in Budapest by the leader of an Arrow Cross patrol who refused to recognize his exceptional status. Detecting an inappropriate tone of voice in the officer, Uncle Imre informed him that he was speaking with a reserve lieutenant, whereupon the officer unceremoniously shot Uncle Imre in the head. My cousin, the architect Bandi Schwartz (later Andy Short) survived the war as an English doughboy. The beautiful wife and daughter of his easygoing younger brother Pál were sent together to the gas chamber because the mother would not let go of the girl's hand. Pali escaped from his forced-labor unit and organized a group of partisans of various nationalities and religions in the mountains of Máramaros. They lacked the weapons to conduct major operations but did manage to disperse the smaller units sent to pursue them.

Éva, the youngest of the three siblings, ended up at Birkenau, but a Polish prisoner pulled her daughter Kati's hand from Éva's and put it in the hand of Aunt Margit, the girl's grandmother, and although the two of them went to the gas chamber Éva remained alive. She worked in a factory, growing weaker and weaker and moving from camp to camp, until finally she received word in a hospital barracks that her husband Pál Farkas, a pharmacist and perfumer, was alive. Word of her got back to him as well, and taking heart at the prospect of meeting again they recovered and returned home.

In our family the older generations were generally bourgeois liberals and, if forced to choose a party affiliation, identified with the Social Democrats. As for the younger generations, they were radicals, Communists for the most part. Perhaps that is why I felt uncomfortable when my father, returning from the deportation camps, thought of nothing but reopening the hardware business in Berettyóújfalu and taking up the life he had once had. They might have known that nothing could be as before. But even though the young felt that radical change would affect everything in life and I might well have taken my place at my cousin István's side in that sneering communist chorus, I identified with my parents. When I asked István who could better manage our fathers' businesses in Berettyóújfalu (Ferenc Dobó's books, Béla Zádor's textiles, József Konrád's hardware) than they themselves, who had done it over a lifetime, he dismissed the question as insubstantial. "One of the assistants will take over," he said.

My father still believed in the return to what he thought of as normalcy: he would reopen his business in the ransacked house with a fraction of what he had once had and the customers would come and greet him and hold profound discussions on questions both timely and eternal, sitting in upholstered armchairs and eating food they had brought from home in their wagons—garlic sausage or paprika bacon or plain old salted bacon with bread and red onions—and drinking the fresh artesian water he provided. The staff, my father, and his regular customers, all on familiar terms, had so much to talk about in winter as they warmed themselves around the enormous iron stove or in summer as they enjoyed the cool, spacious room.

The younger family members, who had professional or humanities degrees and whose parents had been killed, wanted a radical break with the old order. "Why do you want things to be as they were?" they asked, seeing us move home—or at least to what we imagined to be home—with all our chattels. We should be happy to be alive, the sole surviving Jewish family in Berettyóújfalu, parents and children reunited. When our friends and relatives brought up their gassed wives and children, my parents maintained a somber silence.

People did not stop telling me I was living for the others as well as for myself. That frightened me. If it had been a mere bombastic phrase, I would not have minded the rebuke implicit in it, but I knew there was more involved: now I had to act as they would have acted had they still been alive or at least act in a way calculated to win the approval of my murdered childhood friends. Even with relatives I felt a mixture of tribute and antipathy in their response to my having survived and being able to return to the nest and live happily ever after.

Another issue soon insinuated its way into our talk: Were we bourgeois or communist? "Had my father lived, he might well be my enemy," István had told me. I was no enemy of my father, nor did he harbor ill will against us. It was only natural for him to take István and Pál Zádor, the sons of his late sister Mariska and cousin Béla, into his house. He did the same for my cousin Zsófi Klein. István and Pali spent a year in school in Kolozsvár, skiing down to the main square in winter, but by the summer of 1946 it was clear that Transylvania would revert to Romania and they came home to Berettyóújfalu.

The new age began for me in the summer of 1945. The family was together and out of mortal danger. Our old life had resumed its course, after a fashion, in the house at Berettyóújfalu, the hardware business having reopened on the ground floor. My sister was soon attending the *gimnázium* in Debrecen, taking room and board with the family of a retired officer. As for me, it was the dawn of freedom: I was now being privately tutored—meaning that every once in a while I went to see a teacher—and working in my father's shop, where three shelves were now filled with goods brought in from Budapest, Salgótarján, and Bonyhád. (They came in Studebaker trucks, now in Russian hands, which were used in civilian commerce and sometimes escorted by the Soviet military on roads not yet free of danger. Everything of course had its price.)

In December a second cousin of mine arrived on the scene. His name was Ernő Steiner, and he was a good-looking, active young man who refused to acknowledge the border separating Berettyóújfalu from Nagyvárad. He and his friends would race their jalopy of a truck across it through frozen fields carrying goods. "I always take two or three shots in the air to get the border guards to look back." Ernő had been liberated by the French in May. He could converse with them and had developed a taste for Calvados and Gauloises. Arriving home in the summer, he learned that his parents and younger sister had not survived, and although other families were living in their former house Ernő reoccupied his old room, telling the new residents to behave themselves and showing them the pistol he carried under his jacket. Ernő did not want to stay long and soon began carrying people, not just goods, westward. Many young Jews of his ilk had been sailing from Marseille to Haifa after returning from labor service to learn they were without families.

"I'm ready," said Ernő one day.

I gave him a questioning look.

"Ready for anything," he said dryly. His knapsack held everything he owned.

"Why not take over your father's business?" I asked.

Ernő gave my arm a stroke. "That chapter is over." But to acknowledge that I too had a point, he added, "Your father's still alive. You're helping him."

From the wheel of the truck he reached down to shake my hand one last time. I stood in front of our house and waved as he pulled away, en route to the Holy Land. Holy, he said, because they had given their blood for it. The next year in Haifa he would be active in disabling or sinking English patrol boats so the passengers on immigrant ships could maneuver their rowboats to the shoreline.

I wanted my own space and took over my old room so as to escape the wheezing and snoring of others and have the freedom to turn on the light whenever I pleased. I needed a room where guests could sit and talk, but where no one could just come traipsing in. My craving for privacy came from a desire to know the terrain: if the dogs reacted to late-night passersby, I wanted to know what courtyard they were barking from.

Although the churchyard adjacent to the garden had once provided many playmates, I currently had only my cousins István and Pali and Zsófi Klein. Zsófi had returned from Bergen-Belsen thin but tenacious and with no other place to go. There were now five children in the house. It was never quiet. We cooked in enormous pots. Leftovers were unknown.

My father took it for granted that he should support us all. He enjoyed being back in the saddle, watching the stock gradually spread from one wall to the next and rehiring his shop assistants. Some of the old customers hugged him and squeezed his hand seeing him there again by the door. "My Józsika," they called him, a form of address dating back to his childhood. He well recalled that there had been no hugs the previous year, but never mentioned it.

By the tile stove, which was still beechwood-burning in the winter of 1945–46, I listened to the conversations of the people who came to visit. A girl named Kati and I would cut holes in apples to remove the core and fill them cinnamon and molasses, sugar not yet having returned to the market. I was particularly interested in the opinions of Laci Nyúl, Kati's broad-shouldered and obstinate cousin. He had returned from labor service a tough customer and later barely escaped imprisonment by the Soviets. He wore a short leather jacket and high laced boots. His family had owned the local slaughterhouse, and he helped out at the butcher shop, where kosher and non-kosher products now co-existed. Immersed in blood to the elbows, he sliced pork legs and chops all day long. On the way to our house he would rub cologne into his chin. He had dreams of sties housing hundreds of pigs and a thoroughly modern meat-packing plant, a dream he would punctuate with endless views of the great figures of Hungarian literature. He held Mihály Babits in the highest esteem, knew the poems of Attila József, and brought a number of living authors—Milán Füst, Lajos Nagy, Lajos Kassák, Tibor Déry—to my attention. My sister would see him to the door; I humbly retired. Their parting words seemed to take longer than absolutely necessary.

On other evenings I would listen to the admonitions of the blacksmith's son, who provided me with sexological advice—for example, which notorious women in the village were best avoided. He had plans of becoming a mechanical engineer in Budapest. Laci Nyúl wanted to stay in the village and made us swear to vote for the Smallholders' Party, because if the Communists won he'd have to, as he put it, kiss his meat-packing plant goodbye, and my father his house and business. The Russians, not the Americans, would be giving the orders then. On dark winter afternoons he brought along a book of poetry. We had managed to trade up from a petroleum lamp to a gasoline one with a pump of its own, the white mantle growing taut and burning with a crackle when the flame caught it.

I would cut tobacco and stuff it into cigarette papers (I no longer remember who paid for it, though I'm afraid it was my father); I had fashioned a spinning wheel out of a bicycle wheel and would spin the long, white fur of angora rabbits for my mother to knit sweaters with; or I would move off somewhere to read. My time was my own. I spent summers on my bike, riding with my cousins to the swimming area or down to the Berettyó, where we would climb the pylon of the railroad bridge.

One day I found myself next to Marika on its sun-drenched concrete surface. Because she was four years older than I, it was an honor for me to lie next to her. Soon thereafter the activity repeated itself on the sofa of a cool room whose blinds had been lowered. Leaning on my elbows as she lay there on her back, I tried to reach under her skirt and stroke her thigh. Her resistance was mild, and as I touched her skin I had the impression she was not entirely lacking in interest. We both held our breath. Marika's aunt would leave us alone together for long stretches.

On days like these I should have been reeling off Latin declensions and conjugations for my blonde yet dull private tutor. When she phoned my father, he took me aside and asked whether I was going to my Latin lessons. "Of course I am," I said. "Most of the time." My father's gaze darkened, and he walked away. I wanted to spare my tutor, but I can't deny that I always took pleasure in skipping classes.

Inflation brought chaos. My father was not good at riding such waves or, rather, he could not do it at all. After the billions came the unfathomable trillions and then the period of barter, when customers brought wheat and bacon in exchange for his merchandise. My father having no use for wheat and bacon, they went moldy in the cellar. It was beginning to look as if commerce were utter nonsense, but my father kept at it, and once reliable money was minted in 1946 it began to accumulate. Whether he could keep his business, however, was unclear. The reassuring announcements being made could be interpreted in many ways. But then the Communist Party in its passion for state appropriation was moving from large companies to small businesses, with the result that after five years of a second flowering my father's hardware business was taken over by the state, which then turned him out of house and home with no reparations. Such was the law. The Smallholders' victory meant nothing: the Communists took over anyway. But he had reckoned with losing everything again. At least now they did not want to kill him.

Laci Nyúl's dreams remained just that. He enrolled at the Technical University in Budapest and went to work at a slaughterhouse to earn his keep. One day he fell asleep in the bathtub and the gas flame in the water heater went out. The gas poured noiselessly over him, and the exhausted Laci Nyúl slept on, forever.

In August 1947, when the last parliamentary elections were being held, I would ride my bicycle to the town hall in Berettyóújfalu, where they posted the results on a large board the moment they were phoned in. During the preceding weeks I had attended the campaign assemblies of every party and found something stimulating about each. I was fourteen and had completed a year at the Debrecen Calvinist Gimnázium with highest honors.

The previous September my parents had taken my cousin Pál and me to the four-hundred-year-old institution in a cart, together with our fees in the form of a chest full of food—because over and above the fees for room and board payment was required in staple goods: flour, sugar, bacon, smoked meat, beans, eggs, and preserves.

Debrecen was a big city in my eyes, unfamiliar and inscrutable. After lurching along the wide Market Street, the cart arrived at the entrance to the student dormitory, where bronze heads commanding respect stared out at us. An inscription on the interior facade admonished all that this was a place for prayer and study.

On the third floor a bleak, pave-stoned hallway led to sleeping quarters packed with iron beds. This room also served as the study area. The daily schedule specified that *silentium* was to be observed from three until five in the afternoon, during which time we were all to sit studying at the common table. The wake-up bell rang at six in the morning, when we ran laps around the courtyard. At the filthy sinks we could wash only down to the waist. A cowbell would summon us down to the cellar dining room, where a roux–thickened soup with cumin awaited us every morning.

We stood behind our chairs in silence while the others mumbled grace: "Dear Jesus, be our guest today, and bless what Thou hast granted us . . . He who food and drink hath given, let His name be blessed in heaven." I could have said the Jewish blessing "Blessed art Thou, Eternal God, King of the Universe, who bringeth forth bread from the earth," but I was not the praying type in those days.

The serving spoon would make the rounds from room monitor (whom we were bound to obey) down, according to age. The prayer did little to dampen the abuse of rank. The serving order went by class, the oldest class going first, the youngest last. If there was a big steaming bowl of goulash in a big porcelain tureen, it was only natural that the highest class should spoon out the most meat for themselves and all that was left for the "little buggers," those of us under fourteen, were the potatoes at the bottom. As a member of the fourth class I was in the lower school and therefore subject to commands like, "Bugger, bring me a glass of water!" A raw sense of fun made the vulgarity of it all seem natural. Endless jokes about farts filled the dormitory.

Pali was in the first class, at the bottom of the pecking order, while I, in the fourth, belonged at the top of the lower school and was thus ripe for rebellion. I put up with the hazing as long as I could. I even put up with the prank they called the star-kick, which consisted of sneaking up to a new boy at night and sticking strips of twisted paper between his toes, then lighting them. When the flame reached the skin, the victim would make huge kicks in the air and bolt up in alarm to see the flaming paper wafting through the room. Something to snicker at. (Even the little buggers had their established order, whereby one might end up sniggering at one's best buddies' misfortunes—or one's own.) I put up with the fact that packages coming to me from home were opened with the room monitor's approval and devoured without consulting me. (I was familiar with his type—a "cackler"— and as I will relate I eventually put my foot down.) Otherwise we got on well enough. I was good at my studies and let them play with my four-grooved Cossack dagger, which they would throw at the doorpost. My classmates, sons of village schoolteachers, priests, choirmasters, artisans, and farmers, wavered between intimations of justice, lording it over newcomers, and submitting to the authority of older boys. After lights out a Psalm was read. It was followed by witticisms about jacking off. I didn't know what that was.

One classmate shared the homesickness that came over me each evening, and we counted the days together. He told me that to get to his village from the station he had to cross a forest. There were wolves in the forest, he said, so occasionally he needed to sling a huge cudgel over his head. During the previous Christmas break he had set a whole pack running. I would have liked to believe my new friend.

Our house was thirty kilometers from the dormitory, which was doable by bicycle, though occasionally a friendly Russian sergeant, the polyglot who had accompanied us to Nagyvárad, would come and ask if I felt like going home: my mother was willing to certify a made-up illness for a few days. He was an interpreter at the headquarters in Berettyóújfalu and knew his way around the markets and the world of exchange in general. I traded him our kitchen alarm clock for a Cossack hat and that four-grooved dagger. We rode in his jeep, with me in back, my legs hanging over the side. He worried that I would bounce out: his driver drove at a hundred kilometers an hour. I was thrilled by the speed.

But it was also a pleasure to climb onto an ox-drawn cart with my mother, the driver perched listlessly on his plank and the two oxen taking their time, letting me have a good close look at every house and tree along the road. The familiar, thirty-kilometer trip between Debrecen and Újfalu would take a good six hours.

In my simplicity I was happy with any pace: all that mattered was that I was going home. And it was with a heart of stone that I watched the truck that served as the bus to Újfalu pull away from the Golden Bull Hotel in Debrecen with my mother aboard after three days in Debrecen, time mostly wasted in a group shopping tour to buy shoes for my sister Éva and cousin Zsófi. They would try on pair after pair, first in shops that seemed to hold promise, then in ever-more disappointing establishments. My mother was patiently respectful of the process, but I was bored and did not pass up the opportunity to express my scorn when the girls ended up with the shoes they had tried on in the first shop. My remarks were received with cool disparagement and labeled barbarian. My original inclination, to go into the first shop and buy the first thing that more or less appealed to me, remained unshaken.

This philosophy of random choice guided me in other areas as well: "God is good, and what he gives is good." My life has been shaped by chance meetings and telephone calls: the best dinner is always at the nearest restaurant; my first woman—I was fifteen at the time—was the nearest one in the raft of women lining up before me in the salon of the old-fashioned house of assignation. The approach probably had something to do with hunger: I barely grew at all that year. You had to take what there was.

Like Debrecen, for example. It was the closest of cities (with good schools) to my parents' house. The dormitory destroyed a few illusions perhaps, but I had excellent teachers.

My favorite place was the library. Whenever school got me down, I would go straight there. No one would ask me whether I had permission to be there or was just skipping class. Good as the classes were, I enjoyed reading more, so I often found myself at its entrance, a flight of wide, sloping wooden stairs worn down by many thousands of feet. I had to stretch to reach the handle on the door and was immediately captivated by the smell of floor wax and old books.

One day, while reading a light novel whose spine I had seen earlier on my mother's bedside table, I felt a tactful hand land on my shoulder. I turned to see our class advisor, Dr. József Salánky, who taught Latin and History and inspired both respect and fear.

"If my suspicions are correct, you, young man, should be in class right now. Is that not so?"

"Yes, it is."

We were face to face. I could deny nothing.

"I hope you are reading something worthy at least."

He had a look at the book by lamplight in the November darkness.

"This one is hardly worth missing class for," he said disparagingly.

I felt reduced to near nothingness but had to respond somehow.

"And what *would* be worth missing class for, sir?"

It was a cheeky question, but by saying "this one" he had given me a lead-in. He looked at me and said, "Wait!" He had access to the library's inner sanctum, forbidden territory to students. While he was on his mission there, I found it hard to return to my novel. He reappeared with a stack of books, set them down on the librarian's desk, and said to him, "If this boy comes back, give him these to read in the building." He winked at me and left. The librarian called me over with a glance and set the top book before me. It was *Crime and Punishment*. Later, in the school corridor, Dr. Salánky remarked to me that it didn't matter if I understood only a little of what was in those books. Whatever I did understand would be worth more than all of a bad book that was easy for me.

Eventually I had to leave the dormitory. What led to my expulsion was the practice of our being allowed out into the city after lunch (though we had to be back by three, which was the beginning of *silentium*, when we were expected to do our lessons, not play with jigsaw puzzles or tops or that wooden figure whose little red peanut would pop out when you pulled on a string). On one sunny November day I was on duty, which meant I was responsible for taking the key to the common room when we left for lunch and being there to open it for those who preferred the dormitory to town, perhaps because they felt insecure and needed to stick to their nests or because they wanted to study or simply because they were lazy. After a less than glorious lunch I forayed into town. I may have bought a jam roll from one of the glassed-in stands or a cluster of the grapes sold on corners. At any rate, I completely forgot about the damned key. In thrall to the pleasures of sights and tastes I got to the door of our common room to find ten pairs of eyes glowering at me. I arrived in a lighthearted mood, giving the boys a warm hello and making a casual apology. No one said a word, but I got a good slap in the face from the room monitor. Taking a step back, I charged into his belly with my head, which landed him on his behind. When they pulled us apart, he said I would regret what I had done.

The regulated life was no longer for me. I asked my cousin Zsófi whether Pali and I could move into her rented room, and she said yes. The next day the three of us were living in Zsófi's room in the Bishop's Palace. It had a fine view of the Great Church together with Market Street and the Golden Bull Hotel, where the Municipal Philharmonic Orchestra played Mozart and Liszt in the Blue Salon under the inspired direction of Dr. Béla Pukánsky, director of the Academy of Music.

In the fall of 1947 I moved from the ponderous Debrecen Calvinist Gimnázium to the lively Madách Gimnázium in Budapest. I rented a room in the flat of an elderly couple. I was a village boy, unsophisticated and starry-eyed, but Budapest was much to my liking. And this time I could wander the city as I chose, with no yellow star on my coat and no worries about danger lurking everywhere.

The school was nearly as interesting as the city. It had its own parliament and government, two newspapers, and a court with a judge and jury, prosecutors and defense counsels, and all sorts of cases, serious and otherwise, awaiting adjudication. There was a student representative at all grading sessions, and if he disagreed with the mark the faculty wanted to give to one or another of his classmates he had the right to veto it.

Politics was in the air, and there were Communists among the student body, although the boys generally preferred to play historical roles: Danton would observe that Robespierre, sitting at one of the desks in the back of the classroom, had a glowering countenance. Chénier was a kind, light-haired Jewish boy. We used to walk together on Margaret Island, reading Dante in the Babits translation. He would soon escape over the border, which in 1949 was no longer easy, and emigrate to the newly founded state of Israel to become general of a tank division. There was a good deal of role-playing in our class and a tremendous number of debates. I defended Mallarmé against the great Romantic Victor Hugo and the aforementioned Danton, who later became director of the Opera. (His fondness for spectacular effects was already in evidence.) We read a lot in those days: the second or third time I admitted to my friends that I hadn't read this or I hadn't ever heard that name, one of my friends called me an ignorant country bumpkin.

Yes, this was an age of politics, even at school. When was it permissible to kill? That was a burning question. Or should boys like us, fifteen or sixteen years old, go to a brothel (and if so, which one?) or *go out* with a girl? A girl? From a girls' school? What would you talk about? Your homework? One opinion was that you were better off talking to your Latin master. Ours was a wise man, though anarchy held sway in his classroom. (A translator of Plato does not get bogged down in discipline.) Mr. Kövendy would sit in the last row, and whoever gathered round him could drink in what he had to say while the rest went on with their racket.

The couple I boarded with was Arnold Konta—a former wine wholesaler and rowing and walking champion, then past eighty—and his wife. They could not afford to heat their large apartment, which was crammed with carved mahogany furniture, Shakespeare in English, Goethe and Schiller in German, Flaubert in French, plaques in black glass cases, ponderous paintings all over the walls, and bronze statuettes in every spot not taken up by something else. I found it all very depressing. At fifteen I detested the fin-de-siècle style and its eclecticism, and even the Jugendstil (or Secession, as we called it); I loved the cubism of modern architecture.

Mr. Konta was a short man; his wife Elza was quite tall. Every Sunday morning the natty old gentleman reached up and took his wife's arm (her shoulders were higher than his head), and they walked to the Museum of Fine Arts in Heroes' Square. He used to say you could look at a good painting a hundred times. He read some *Faust* every evening. Before sitting down to his desk, he murmured a short Hebrew prayer. His face was pink and jowly and fragrant from shaving. He took his meals in a housecoat redolent of tobacco and tied with a rope.

I would be walking along the Ring, and who would step out of one of the noble old buildings, each forming a quarter-circle, but Zoltán Kodály, white beard and all. (Whenever he appeared on the balcony in the hall at the Academy of Music, the house would give him a standing ovation.) I would bow my head as we passed, and the old man would nod. The garden and red sign of the Stück Pastry Shop filled me with melancholy. This is where I had sat with my father before accompanying him to the Nyugati Station whenever he visited me at the end of one of his buying trips. Much as I enjoyed sitting with him, I smiled to myself more than once at his naive but well-intentioned notions.

Every morning I would feel compelled to step off the sidewalk as I walked along Andrássy Boulevard two blocks down from the Ring: the building at number sixty, with its *gravitas*—and the heavy chains that bound its concrete pillars—would order me down into the roadway. In the last year of the war it had been called the House of Loyalty, the headquarters and torture chamber of the Arrow Cross. Anyone taken there had little chance of coming out alive. There had been concrete-walled torture rooms in place in the cellar by then, but the setup was not modern enough: the new regime dug deeper. Buildings outlive regimes, and this formerly upper-middle-class apartment building was home to the political police of the new system. The reconstruction was the idea of Gábor Péter, once a tailor, then a librarian for a fashion magazine, then head—general—of that police force. A major sat on either side of the padded door to his office, effective advisors no doubt. After 1956 they became official humorists, writing hilarious Christmas radio and TV programs.

With Gábor Péter at the helm of the State Security Agency, the Andrássy Boulevard facilities embarked on a visually dazzling expansion, gobbling up the large and lordly buildings around it one by one. No sooner were the inhabitants expelled than industrious stonemasons set about making it fit for the uses of the Agency. Red geraniums bloomed in a flowerbox outside every window, but guards carrying machine guns stood in every doorway and on every corner, and no one would have dreamed of playing games with them.

Soviet Pobedas, light brown and gray, and large, black American cars with curtains in the windows rolled out of the driveways. The next block was also part of the picture. The windows of the Lukács Pastry Shop on the corner—once a showcase of cakes and liqueurs, of glass chandeliers, velvet draperies, and marble tables—had been replaced by glass bricks impenetrable to the eye: it had become a club for State Security officers.

I later learned that prisoners who had signed confessions were assembled there among the Art Deco decorations to learn their show-trial roles. Since the baker and his masterpieces had been kept on, the prisoners got pastries for reciting their canned self-accusations by heart. By then they had gone through the preliminary phases of confession and torture. Most people proved capable of slandering themselves, even condemning themselves to death. All bets were off once the prisoner found himself alone in the cellar, crawling into his cell on all fours like an injured animal. As soon as you signed the papers and redeemed yourself, you got a hot bath. Now all you had to do was play your part. And this was theater at its most imaginative. You were spirited up from the cellar to the vanilla-scented paradise of golden angels and chandeliers and garlands and whipped cream, where a clean change of clothes and a dignified stroll along the slightly sloping marble floor could put you in the mood for any role. Down below, all relationship between the ego's visible and invisible aspects had been severed, the visible (and thrashable) part doing what it must, the invisible part looking on, astonished.

In 1949 I did not know much about what was going on in the cellar, but from the BBC I learned that the accused in show trials would say all sorts of things to incriminate themselves, that they were mere puppets, their will having been broken with beatings and chemicals. This seemed plausible, as they spoke like automatons, reciting more than repenting, as if meaning no longer mattered.

The cameraman father of a boy I knew told his son that the proceedings were filmed without the knowledge of the accused. Moreover, the trial was staged more than once, and the accused never knew which the "real" one was. The final film version was spliced together from several takes. Could the whole procedure have been just for the sake of the film? The director supposedly had friends among the accused.

A bit further up Andrássy (soon to be Stalin) Boulevard there was a private lending library that was taken over by the state in 1949. It was intoxicating for me, at fifteen, to take out novels by Steinbeck, Hemingway, Martin du Gard, and Malraux. The same neighborhood also boasted a respectable private house of assignation run by Madame Clarisse on the second floor of a neoclassical apartment building. By the end of the year it was all over: the private library, the private *maison de rendezvous*, and everything else private, including the private individual. Nor were we left in peace at school: we had to sing hymns of praise to the working class after each ten-minute break. Sometimes we slipped in a dirty rhyme or two.

When in the early sixties the State Security Agency moved out and the space reopened as Specialty Pastries, I would drop in after long afternoons spent investigating the living conditions of people on file at the Public Welfare Authority. I would sit with friends in velvet-upholstered chairs beneath the chandeliers' gold curlicues and Venetian glass and surrounded by blue-silk walls and gold-leaf friezes as trolley buses, the pride of Soviet technology, rumbled by. I was always on good terms with the old ladies in the cloakroom. I had many dates there, dates with beautiful women and odd women, with clever women and madwomen: I had just divorced my first wife. Those women are dead by now, or elderly.

Late in November 1983, when I was on a fellowship at the New York Institute for the Humanities, my wife Jutka and I rented an apartment on the corner of Fourth Street and Avenue A, four blocks from St. Mark's Place. One morning while walking along the latter we came upon a street fair. There were bands playing and a woman prancing around on stilts, enticing children to dance. We bought a table lamp for two dollars, and the seller wanted to prove to us it worked. We walked into a precinct house to look for an outlet. "Your honor is at stake," the policemen told him, smiling as they pointed to an outlet. The lamp did not light. They had a good laugh, black and white, men and women alike— then took pity on the salesman and pointed him to a working outlet. The lamp was fine. Filled with a sense of dignity, the salesman then told us that his mother was Hungarian and that he was happy to have us here in this part of town, properly called the East Village, not the Lower East Side.

I am standing at a Tarot reader's shop front surrounded by iron pipes, iron plates, and iron gratings. The mustachioed old fortune-teller likes to snooze in a rickety armchair in the window. The next two shops are bookshops. My novel *The Loser* is available in both. Back home it had to be published in the utmost secrecy, which bestowed an aura of heroic transgression on the publisher, Gábor Demszky. Here in America I ran into a samizdat plain-white-cover edition. It is so tightly spaced that the whole novel fits into two hundred pages instead of four.

Iván Szelényi and I also single-spaced our typescript of *The Intellectuals on the Road to Class Power*. The fewer the pages, the easier it was to smuggle it outside the country. That accomplished, I could turn back to my novel. But one day Biki (Tibor Hajas—poet, essayist, photographer, body-artist, film director, watchman, and warehouse worker) told us there had been a house search at Tamás's (Tamás Szentjóby—poet, painter, film actor, and Fluxus artist). They had been looking for pornography, but discovered our manuscript instead. They suddenly lost all interest in pornography. No, they had a 132-page typescript dealing with ideological issues and containing all sorts of seditious ideas. "Looks like 127/b is your genre: incitement against the state," said the good-humored, portly lieutenant colonel entrusted with my arrest and interrogation.

Now here we were, nearly ten years later, our consternation having shriveled to a series of comical anecdotes, standing in St. Mark's Place, looking over the offerings on the sidewalk. People put out anything with the slightest chance of selling, trusting to the market gods to make the proper match. Nor did the market gods let them down. For among the pulp novels and one or two good books were two familiar-looking soft-cover volumes—red on top, yellow underneath—with a Hungarian title: *Társadalmi*

Szemle (Review of Society), the theoretical journal of the Hungarian Communist Party, November and December, 1949. Stalin, then celebrating his seventieth birthday, was on the cover.

I picked up one of the yellowed volumes. Now the young black man proffering it was certain you could find a paying customer for anything under the sun. Supine on a New York sidewalk the *generalissimus* was none too imposing, but in the autumn of 1949 the whole world was sending him gifts, including a trainload assembled by the grateful Hungarian People with enough material—a sea of miniature locomotives, machine tools, and children's drawings—for an exhibition. What is more, there was a statue of him in every shopwindow. In butcher shops, for example, the wisest leader in the history of mankind was rendered in frozen lard, the artist's honorarium being paid in kind: fatback.

Suddenly there was a vacant flat on the first floor of the Andrássy Boulevard building. Its former inhabitant was the son-in-law of the President of the Republic, a self-assured squat little man with an equally self-assured and squat spouse. In the autumn of 1949 the shutters were rolled down. The son-in-law of the President of the Republic had been appointed ambassador to Cairo and moved there with his family. Then he was ordered home, denounced as a spy, condemned to death, and executed. It didn't take long. The large American car stopped coming for his wife. The movers came and took all their possessions heaven only knows where.

The year 1949 was the year of the Great Change, the great new rigor, as peace-loving, progressive mankind prepared for the seventieth birthday of the Lighthouse of the Peoples. The brass band of the Hungarian State Security Agency, as part of peace-loving and progressive mankind, had recently moved into the spacious apartment of the freshly executed Hungarian ambassador to Cairo, and there they rehearsed the *Stalin Cantata*. I was forced to listen: I lived on the opposite side of the courtyard. They rehearsed it bar by bar, playing each one hundreds of times, boring it into my head. "Stalin is our battle, Stalin is our peace, and the name of *Sta-a-a-lin* will make the world a better place." (The last line had slight meter and rhyme problems, but was ideologically pure.) Sometimes a booming chorus would sing along. It was all very festive.

In 1949 Stalin thought there would be a war with the West, so the eastern half of Europe needed to be unified according to the Soviet model. The Soviet model meant trials. They started by sentencing Archbishop József Mindszenty to life. Then came the tall, handsome, and popular Foreign Minister (previously Minister of the Interior) László Rajk, who was selected for the role of arch criminal and duly tortured until he testified against himself. The BBC called him a victim of the very methods he had introduced.

People were no longer as they had been. A kind of rigid intoxication seemed to have infused their faces. The fear radiating from the walls of 60 Andrássy Boulevard seemed to grow stronger as the geraniums in the windows grew redder. Every afternoon a million sparrows perched on the lindens and plane trees, turning the street into one great vibrating river of chirping. Might there be some ruse lurking deep in the innocence of sparrows? Like the newly refashioned puppet theaters waiting to receive jackbooted kindergartners with machine guns?

The brief period of normal civil life that followed the Germans' collapse was over now, I realized. Gone were the days of burning class records, of back-talk, of speechifying about Hugo and Apollinaire, Ady and Babits. My *gimnázium* days enabled me to experience the whole city, its swimming pools as well as its libraries, or visit my sister, or sit in a café with a boy who could really play the saxophone, or admire the classmate sitting behind me, who could belch the whole of *Rhapsody in Blue*, or hire his neighbor to drive off every teacher from my vicinity with his farts and thereby let me read in peace (though of course I had to smell as well as pay).

My Hungarian literature teacher encouraged my readings, inviting me to his apartment and lending me books. When he opened his glassed-in bookcase to me, it was as if a beautiful woman had undone her robe. Those were the days when I discovered manifold meaning in every line and found profound wisdom in clichés.

I was sixteen and entering my next-to-the-last year at the *gimnázium*. I walked into the room on the first day to find two students standing by the window. The others were sitting at their desks, looking stern and singing songs of the workers' movement with great enthusiasm. They scrutinized the latecomer with lowering anticipation to see what he would do. Would he take a seat and sing with us? One class, one community, one heart, one soul. If not, he could go and stand by the window with the other two and pretend not to know that standing there made him conspicuously suspicious, dead to the ideological and political unity that flexed its muscle in common song! There they stood—Pali Holländer and Laci Endrényi, the most sensitive boys in the class. Tall and thin, learned, dripping with irony, inveterate concertgoers, readers of Hemingway's *Fiesta* and Huxley's *Antic Hay*, and, as Junior Tacituses, fully equipped to enjoy the historical transformation in all its vulgarity.

But the brightest student in the group was sitting in the back row near the window, bragging that he had traveled to the border in a State Security car as a volunteer to denounce his Zionist schoolmates' escape. He had always been malicious, but his sarcasm was grounded in power now: he was a high official in the student association. Though he still had to attend class, he would seek out other student officials in the corridor, where they would discuss important, confidential issues of the Movement under their breath. No outsider could come near. And he was the one who gave the speech on the occasion of Stalin's birthday in 1949. He spoke of a Golden Eagle, of an unshakable will that pursued its goal ruthlessly, without mercy. On the first day of classes he read aloud a passage from *The Road to Volokolamsk* about how cancerous meat had to be hacked out of a body or the body would rot. He then spun a pretty little speech on the topic, repeating the word "rotten" several times while glancing my way.

When József Révai, a member of the Politburo, condemned the harmful delusions of the philosopher György Lukács in a page-long analysis, I was the only one in the class who stood up for Lukács. It was intolerable that a *gimnázium* student should disagree with the Party leadership. I was summoned to a disciplinary committee chaired by a student my age. His name was Ferenc Fehér and we later became friends. He despised Lukács at the time, but later saw the light. In a required paper on the Three-Year Plan I wrote that for me it meant the state takeover of my father's business and house, for the tired worker I used to see on the stairs it means long hours of work for low wages. My literature teacher could not bring himself to grade the paper ("There is nothing I can do for you, son; I have no jurisdiction in such matters") and passed it on to the headmaster. It wasn't long before I was expelled from the student association.

What I really wanted was to be expelled from the school. "You have outgrown this place," the literature teacher told me. "You are intellectually over-age." Which was flattering enough, though I couldn't tell whether he just wanted to avoid the unpleasantness that came from having me around.

My friend Pali and I once invited him to come rowing with us on the Danube. Sitting in a bathing suit on the coxswain's thwart, he displayed a fairly large belly, but also the broad shoulders to match. Now that we were à *trois* and on the water, he confided that he could not make his peace with Marxism and expected difficult years to come. "Terror," I said ambiguously, "is history's sacrificial festival." My teacher did not completely understand. Perhaps I did not either.

That summer, the summer of 1949, Budapest played host to the World Youth Assembly, and young Communists flooded in from the Soviet Union, China, and the countries of Eastern Europe. After the trial that condemned László Rajk and his associates and led to their execution the city was brimming with a vibrant energy. It might have been said that the only people not yet arrested were the ones whose trials the authorities had lacked the time to arrange. They were scheduled for the following year.

"This ice cream represents the penitence of the alienated mind," I said one day on the way home at an Italian gelato stand that had not yet been appropriated by the state. Pali gave a good laugh. His violin teacher had called Kant the only respectable thinker, so he was primed to appreciate my Hegelian quips.

Soon the *Weltgeist* gravitated to the brothel. We set our elbows on a piano covered with a large embroidered cloth and peered down from the balcony at the Ring sinking into shadow. We set out on a hunting expedition. We stepped through the door of that neoclassical apartment house with its spacious courtyard, its pale pink marble staircase, its slightly dirty red carpet. The bell gave out a restrained buzz behind the heavy brown second-floor door. First a servant girl, then Madame: "Do you want Éva again?" Yes. Éva was thin with small, pointed breasts and an indecipherable, lovely scent. Her hair was red—everywhere—and she had an identification number from Auschwitz tattooed on her left arm. She was nineteen, I sixteen. "Explain the Rajk affair to me," she ordered, because I had always been able to make things clear. Her breasts got goose pimples. "I don't want to be tortured!" She had a fur, and on occasion there was a car waiting for her. Sometimes she took my money, sometimes she didn't. When she did, I paid with the proceeds from books I had sold from my library.

Pleasant as it was to sit in the brothel kitchen, all those thighs together tended to dispel illusions. Later, when they closed the public houses and socialism retrained the girls as taxi drivers, the only one left leaning on her elbows in the second-story window was Madame. She underwent a second flowering, because the drunk and disenchanted men whose feet mechanically took them her way were happy with her for want of anything better. Her neck was wrinkled, but the skin lower down on her body was smooth. She would bend over the lace bedspread dramatically and spread her legs passionately. The lips of her sex were large and swollen. She kept it shaven and screamed in the soprano register.

Be it by cart, bike, or train I would go home to Berettyóújfalu for holidays whenever I could, but once I began my studies in Budapest I became a city boy. The story of my village boyhood was over—if a story can ever be truly over.

This was my last summer in Berettyóújfalu. On the hot week-day mornings the daughters of the town's proper families would lie out by the railroad bridge. When I was fifteen, I had sat with Marika by one of the hot pylons, a veritable box seat for viewing the daughters of the pharmacist and chief physician, district court judge, and Calvinist priest rubbing oil into their thighs down on the sandy riverbank. Whenever the train rumbled past, I would put a protective arm around my girlfriend.

Once a group of sweaty, dusty Cossack soldiers galloped down to the water from the embankment. They rubbed their horses down stark naked and, once the hides were shiny, splashed and tumbled and pushed one another under the water until, suddenly cold, they emerged, their bodies stark white atop the dark brown, wet beasts. The young ladies averted their eyes. Then the soldiers slapped on their red felt hats and rode in ever tighter circles around the tanned young ladies, whose hair peeked out from under swimsuits barely reaching their thighs. The sun shone fiercely. Then from nowhere came a whistle followed by a command. The soldiers snatched up their uniforms and boots and galloped off as quickly as they had come.

In the summer of forty-nine I often lay on a sofa under a crimson Persian rug in the Berettyóújfalu dining room reading *Remembrance of Things Past* and *Doctor Faustus*. I would lift Marika onto my bicycle and take her to the Berettyó for a swim. Those were the days of first love. Marika was a couple of years older than I was and sat in front of me in neatly ironed white clothes. I was honored. I rode down from the dam to the riverbank and came to a stop with a nice tight turn, which I always executed just so, with a hard brake and a tail skid. Once, though, under the weight of the two of us, we rolled into the water, still on the bike. This little accident did not do our love any good. Soon thereafter a guest of ours, a saxophone player, asked me whether I had serious intentions about Marika. When I pointed out I was a bit young to be thinking about marriage, he told me that *his* intentions were serious indeed. With an eye to Marika's domestic happiness I generously let her go. The saxophonist had tricked me: his intentions had nothing to do with marriage.

When I was fifteen and entering the sixth year at the *gimnázium*, I moved with my sister and cousin into a narrow street in the middle of the city, Vármegye. I lived in the servants quarters in flat number five on the sixth floor. Entrance to the booth of a room—it was barely big enough to house a table, a bed, a wardrobe, an armchair, and a bookstand—was from the vestibule. I was free from adult supervision, but received a monthly allowance from my parents, which I husbanded as I could. Once in a while my friend Pali Holländer and I took lunch at the Astoria Hotel. We would discuss the offerings on the menu in detail and even order a Napoleon brandy after dessert. The waiter did not ask young gentlemen their age. Certain practices had remained alive.

By the end of the month, however, I would be eating at the Astoria's stand-up restaurant on the corner of Lajos Kossuth Street and the Museum Ring. If I had enough cash, I would get layered cabbage for 3.50, if not, then bean soup with beans for 1.10; and if even that was too expensive, then the 70-fillér bean soup without beans, which, cheap as it was, came with bread. But then there were the terrifying moochers who came and stood in front of me, mumbling, hacking, whining, showing their toothless gums, fixing their eyes first on my plate, then on me. Sometimes I could make a deal with them: "I'll leave you half. Just don't stand right in front of me, please. Move over there!" But they never went far; they just watched, anxiously, to see whether I would keep my part of the bargain.

I knew the Astoria inside and out and had even stayed there in earlier days on one of my father's trips to Budapest. It had the smell of that special cleanser I had enjoyed sniffing at the Hungária. My father's lifeline had been cut, while mine was just beginning. With everything still before me it seemed natural to be starting from zero. That I lived in a cubicle of six square meters and needed electric light to read even in the afternoon, that all I had—and needed—were a bed, table, wardrobe, and bookcase, none of this was humiliating; it was uplifting. I liked having my own room, a bell jar where I could hide away, where another world was constantly in the making inside my head. I could easily step from one world to another, for a book was as much another world too as the strip of sky I could see from my window.

On the other side of narrow Vármegye Street stretched the yellow county hall, a large, ancient structure with an irregular roof that made me nervous, because workers nonchalantly clambered up and down it gnawing on snacks of bacon. "Parisian style," said people who had never been to Paris. No one lived directly opposite, so I could gaze out over the roof to the antennas, towers, cupolas, siren horns, and clouds.

Below us lived the wife of Baron Villy Kohner, and on the next floor down Baron Tivadar Natorp. I took a liking to the baroness, a lithe, tanned woman who went around in sporting clothes, and to the baron, stooped over, examining the ground before him with a cane. Both were forcibly relocated in 1951, as was a beautiful woman with a deep voice, a smoker who wore plaid skirts and let her thick and (naturally, I believe) red hair tumble carelessly down. She worked at the Turkish Embassy, where she was arrested. Yet another neighbor, a banker, was resettled outside of Budapest. A

Council chairman, a former *gimnázium* teacher, moved in below us. The young son of a military officer on the fourth floor came upon his father's pistol one day and shot the daughter of the postman on the seventh floor while playing with it.

I can still picture the friends who turned up in my apartment, sitting in the unupholstered armchair across from the bed or stretching out on the bed. István would speak of his comrades in the Movement and those dull, official rooms where they discussed how to make everyone just like them, the "new men." Actually István himself was somewhat "new" for me in this phase of his, different from what he had been (and would later be, when curiosity would drive him to chase the elusive tail of a truth that was just beginning to take shape). Now his words were more judgmental and at times directed against friends in the name of Party justice. The Party's logic was enough for him. For a year or two.

But he could also speak respectfully of a girl's hair or artistic talents or mock his colleagues for their human weaknesses, to remark of a great thinker that "It wouldn't hurt for him to bathe more often." He said the most intelligent things about the crisis of the planned economy, making his points with hard statistics. As part of his professional training, he was permitted to work in the State Planning Bureau and would smuggle out data on scraps of cardboard, holding them in his hand like Aladdin's lamp or a kind of theoretical miracle weapon to condemn the system in revolutionary language as retrograde. At twenty he realized that the market exists and can be done away with only at the cost of lunacy. My eyes grew wide as I meditated on how Uncle Béla's business acumen had resettled into his son, though István was interested in the market merely as a theoretical construct and had no intention of taking part in it.

I was a boy from the provinces in one of Budapest's best schools, the Madách Gimnázium. I was a cautious young man whose accent and dress betrayed his country origins. Mr. Tóth, the tailor from Berettyóújfalu, made my suits with golf trousers, which none of my classmates would be caught dead in. But what I yearned most for was a pair of what were then called "ski boots," shoes with a double leather sole, a strap on the side, and a buckle. I believed they would give me a more forbidding, masculine air. Ski boots were for making an exit, giving the slip, taking a powder, the kind of footwear that wouldn't tear up your feet or fall apart on you if you were being pursued.

I loved films with chases and never identified with the pursuers. I used to flesh out stories of friends' escapes over the border in my imagination, taking them through creeks and mined bogs. Pali and I had plans to row down to the southern border and suss out the possibilities for crossing, but the motorboat border guards never let us get close. We still fanaticized about swimming out underwater using a reed as a breathing straw or strapping a motor-powered propeller onto our bellies, even to the point of wondering whether the propeller would harm our private parts.

Yet when emigration became a realistic topic of conversation, when Hungarian Jews, too, could move to the newly founded state of Israel, even take all their possessions with them in large chests, when our parents asked us whether we would be willing to emigrate, my sister and I said no. Everyone we had feelings for, everything we enjoyed was here. I had by then a good few years invested in Budapest and had learned to take the bad with the good. I held fast to the places where both had befallen me.

"We'll stay," I said.

"What for?" said my father, and with reason, since he had been forcibly removed from everything he had created for himself. Although he never could understand the point of it, he acknowledged its reality and went on to earn a pittance by managing a hardware store in one of Budapest's side streets. As ashamed as he was to tell his customers day after day that he was out of this or that, he rejected with disgust the under-the-table deals made by his subordinates. He took a dim view of state-directed commerce. "Tell me, son. What's the point of all this?"

Since he was nothing if not insecure in the conceptual universe of scientific socialism, there was no use in my telling him what he should say the next day if it was his turn to discuss the Party organ's daily, *Szabad Nép* (Free People), at the half-hour ritual morning meeting, when basing their comments on the previous day's issue, the store's employees would condemn the web of deceit spun by the imperialists to destroy the cause of the working class. Neither my father nor the imperialists were up to the task.

"I'm no good at speaking," he would say, though in fact he had the gift of gab. Once retired, he would go shopping at the Great Hall and spend the entire morning chatting up both sellers and buyers, then stop on the way home to hear out his concierge.

I never spoke to my family about wanting to be a writer. All anyone saw was that I read a lot, pounded the typewriter, and published a few book reviews during my university years. My diploma qualified me to be a teacher of Hungarian literature.

Mother would have been happier to see me in medical school, but I would never have been accepted, given my bourgeois background. I had an "X" by my name, which meant, in communist terms, that I was more than a class outsider: I was a class enemy. I had applied for a concentration in French and Hungarian, but was rejected. I could count myself lucky to gain entry into the Russian Department, which was soon renamed the Lenin Institute, its purpose being the education of reliable cadres with a strong Marxist-Leninist background. But we "X's" never lasted long anywhere, and during my second year, two weeks after Stalin's death, I was barred from the university during the general mourning period. Once Imre Nagy came to power, the Ministry of Education allowed me to continue my studies in the Department of Hungarian Literature, but I was expelled again after Nagy's fall in March 1955. It was only through the intervention of my professors that I was permitted to re-enroll and complete my studies.

After receiving a degree in Hungarian Literature in the summer of 1956, I did indeed become a teacher, but also a member of the editorial board of a newly founded (though not yet circulating) journal *Életképek* (Pictures from Life). I did not have much time to enjoy those positions: my fellow students were fomenting a revolution. We got hold of some machine guns and formed a university national guard regiment that tried to defend the university against what proved an overpowering force. In the end, we surrendered.

I have mixed feelings looking back on those five years of study. I feel the same ambiguity I feel whenever I visit a university anywhere in the world to lecture on literature, give a sociology seminar, or simply talk to faculty members and their enthusiastic students. Gaining an overview of an entire field of study, having the chance to study all day (a chance that may never return later in life), agonizing in preparation for examinations, recognizing personal capacities and limits, worshiping some professors and disparaging others, thinking through the strategies for turning knowledge to use, living the excitement of first love, conversing with friends deep into the night, entering ignorant and exiting relatively well educated—no, we didn't waste our time. But even these memories are tinged with irony: I see the faces trying on various masks; I see an army of fresh self-images marching along a road of careers. Looked at one way, it is an arrogant new elite, but from another angle it is a nest of newly hatched eggs. Yes, it is a diploma factory, but then there is the master–student relationship, dramatic and elegiac for both.

Clearly politics deeply permeated my years at university, permeated them so deeply that it was a permanent backdrop for both professors and students. Being locked in and locked out, dealing with weapons inside and out (machines guns within, tanks without) is anything but normal. Any normal student role soon went by the boards. But even at the height of the Revolution I had no desire to shoot anyone: in the face of the armored units' overwhelming advantage I deemed speech to be the opposing force that would prove decisive in the long run, a conclusion I arrived at through concerted contemplation with all those who did not stream across the temporarily opened border to the West.

Half my classmates left, most of them becoming professors, mainly at American universities. We, the more recalcitrant ones, went underground, thinking that if we couldn't have it our way now we would provide the spirit of freedom with a mantle of disguise while we consolidated and reinvigorated the culture. As long as we were locked in, we might as well get to know our city, our country. Compulsion breeds intensity. The plan was to learn from people of experience, to spend part of our days in the library and part in tenements and back courtyards trying to save the lives of neglected children.

As for our evenings, we spent them in the literary cafés. Our post-university lives were thus a continuation of our university lives: the same circles of friends and lovers, a few professors, and the literary crowd. Word got out who was who. Everybody knew everybody else. It was a world with the intimacy of confinement about it, with the air of a guild. The university was merely a relatively brief interval in a lifelong course of study, though arguably it was the most stimulating, because everything was new: first exams, first serious writing, first apartment (or room at least), first lovers' cohabitation, first public role. These win out ultimately in the contest of memories, as their smells and colors are stronger than those that follow, perhaps because of the great hunger that precedes them. Who can possibly digest all that food, those books, those bodies, those experiences. Once the student years have passed, the marvelous hunger dissipates. My university career, deformed as it was by political vicissitudes, nourished my hunger for reality. I envy today's students their freedom, because politics does not stand between them and knowledge and they are spared the many senseless obstacles that affected our lives so harshly. At the same time, given that we can learn from the provocations and shocks of fate, no matter how unwelcome, I have no regrets that such was my lot.

Many years ago my mother tried to give me my deceased father's wedding ring; it did not fit onto my finger. Even during my first marriage, the moment I walked out of the door I slipped the new ring into my pocket. One day I forgot, and an entire class at the girls' *gimnázium* gave out quite a buzz. From that day on they thought Daisy and I were married. During her last year at the university she demonstrated her outstanding pedagogical gifts in the same school where I was a teacher in training. I used to observe her from the back row and unsettle her with mocking glances. They could have seen us in the golden spring of 1956 after the earthquake and flood or before the Revolution, strolling arm in arm through the neighboring streets.

Later, they could see me with Vera, my wife, as we walked the length of the Parliamentary Library (an afternoon home for many) along the thickly bound issues of parliamentary minutes of earlier days, then turned off into the last of the so-called research rooms, which were glass-walled and lined with colorful panels. From there, a heavy door opened into a corner room: the *sanctum sanctorum*, a room reserved for us, the chosen ones permitted to keep a typewriter, György Szekeres and me. He was forty, I twenty-three. Through the thick, heavy window behind my enormous desk I had a stunning view of the Danube, the chestnut trees lining the promenade on the Buda side, and behind them the six-story palazzi in various states of disrepair, towering with lordly dignity, with the placidity of the beautiful who know they are beautiful, even if the man in the street kicks up a fuss, even if bombs start falling, even if people are lined up along the embankment and get shot into the breaking ice floes, even if excursion boats thrum about on the green-gray water. But there is nothing thrumming about now, only the sound of a piano and drums from the boat by the Hotel Dunapart, whose nightclub stays open until four in the morning. Couples coming together in the bar can rent little furnished cabins.

I usually took the number two tram to get to the Library of Parliament, whose entrance, tall and fitted with brass door-knobs, faced the Danube. You had to pass by the guards. I would nod to them with respect. After all, they were guarding the gate that led to the very summit of our country. Going up and down the steps, students would report to one another on the subjects discussed in the colloquia that went on there. Girls from humanities departments would be sitting side by side beneath bronze-stemmed lamps, future scholars with double fields (French and Hungarian, History and English, Psychology and Folklore) gazing at the current scholars, the higher caste, the chosen ones permitted to do their work in the four-man "research rooms," which were separated from the large reading room by wooden-scrolled doors with panes of colored glass, their large windows looking out over the Danube and the Castle.

Girls in the humanities were generally in love, or wanted to be, and could be quite dramatic in their breakups. They would tell their girlfriends they had just poisoned themselves in their grief, that cruel animal having told them it was all over. In a quiet little Buda bar, while everyone was dancing, that . . . that *cad* had said it would be better to put an end to it now rather than later. But the truth is, it's no good putting an end to it ever, sooner or later. So now, when her head fell to the table, he would quake at the humiliation of it all. But her true-blue girlfriend would abandon her own private students and drag her off to the hospital as her mother had done before, and later that scoundrel would sit on the blonde angel's hospital bed, and she would open her eyes and fix her gaze on him, and they would rejoice in each other, shedding tears of gratitude, both of them forgetting all that stupidity: the boy that their love was over, the girl that her life was over as a result. Now nothing was over, and the library would be open again the next day from nine to nine.

Libraries were places of refuge, asylums furnished with things of lasting value. In the library of the Institut Français I found books that spoke openly and open-mindedly of things taboo here at home. I had access to journals in sociology and psychology. There were art books as well, and novels by the latest authors. At the Parliamentary Library I was granted a pass to the research rooms—white instead of pink—which gave me access to even the classified publications of the Telegraph Office. I shared space with some odd birds involved in mysterious research and horribly boring types who used their white passes to take notes on textbooks of Marxist literature, that is, to extract meaninglessness out of meaninglessness. They looked at me suspiciously, since everything I read inspired alienation in them. Still, I was tolerated and felt at home there; in fact, we were a large caste, the merely tolerated yet still comfortable.

I glance out of the window at the Danube: Vera is coming to pick me up. We loaf a bit, our arms around one another's waists under the arcade, or sit on the embankment steps if the weather is nice. This is an appropriately humble spot: compared with the contents of the library, my knowledge was zeropoint-zerozerozero and remained so for a long time to come. I stare longingly at the tugboats on the Danube. They had a cabin at the stern where the captain lived with his family, and in the morning his wife would hang his freshly washed shirts out to dry. Watching the lazy tugboat pull those white patches along with six barges attached to its stern, I would fantasize about learning the captain's craft and, after seeing to my daily tasks, sitting in a reclining chair and reading or indulging in free-flowing ruminations.

I had a typewriter at home and one in the library, old, black portables. Gyuri Szekeres at the next desk and I would out-clack each other by turns. I wrote without restraint on my Triumph, whose handle had come off, though I rigged up another from an old belt. My machine clattered like a cannon, though no more loudly than my colleague's, who had been sitting at the next table since his release from prison. In front of me, on a table covered with crimson felt and standing on lion-legs, lay books by Albert Camus, Raymond Aron, Emil Cioran, István Bibó, László Németh, and Miklós Szentkuthy that I was entitled to borrow for in-house use with my white researcher's card, obtained through recommendations from the Writers' Association and the monthly *Új Hang* (New Voice). Without the card the librarians would have spent a long time debating whether to lend me a book of suspicious orientation; with it they gave me most of what I asked for. The rare refusal, with the explanation that a special permit was required for the work in question (for which I would have to pound the pavement and work out some clever tactics), came not from some repressed, balding employee with a puffy mustache in a white smock but from a stunning (though white-smocked) blonde wonder, her every movement—like her voice and gaze—wispy and smooth. She had a large, vulturelike nose, and the corners of her mouth were sensuous and arch though she never smiled. She seemed enveloped by a silvery bell jar, and much as I toyed with the idea I made no particular effort to break through it: by gaining her, I would lose the library, because I would eventually leave her. This made librarians holy and untouchable.

Szekeres would tell us stories about university life in Paris, stories of right- and left-wing radicals alike. He told us about the time when during the German occupation he had been caught in a raid and patted down. He happened to have had a revolver on him, a revolver wrapped in a newspaper, so he held the newspaper over his head while they searched his pockets and found nothing. Hearing about this brilliant stroke of heroism, all we twenty-three-year-olds could do was blink. We had a good laugh when he told us about the time in prison when the inmates suddenly took heart because despite the horrendous political situation the food situation had improved substantially, then lost heart when the political situation started looking up but the old slops returned. It turned out that a highly reputed cook had been arrested when times were bad and released when they got better. So the bad food didn't mean the regime was cracking down; it meant the old cooks had come back. He didn't go into detail about the interrogations. All he said was that realism lacked the means to depict them. He told us to read Kafka, because only his overarching metaphors could approach our reality and he did not consider himself up to the task. We used to compete to be the first to read the latest issue of the *Nouvelle Revue Française*. I knew that the French secret police had delivered Gyuri to the Russian secret police on Glynecke Bridge, the Bridge of Melancholy, near Potsdam, because he had refused to return home or tell the French Secret Service about his role as a Hungarian operative in Rome, their price for a residency permit. As a result, he had to choose between becoming a traitor and spy or being handed over to the Communists, who had ordered him home from the embassy in Rome (he had protested against the Rajk trial in a letter) and eventually sent him to prison.

He was a learned man and handsome, with snow-white hair, a slight limp, and a deep, powerful voice—a true gentleman, *un homme de qualité*. He was a major in the French Army, a hero of the Resistance, a master of conversation, an editor of Proust translations, and a fine translator in his own right. Later he worked as a proofreader at the prestigious Európa publishing house, where he was eventually promoted to head of the literature division.

Sometimes my wife Vera Varsa dropped in, and the three of us would sit in the heavy armchairs under a portrait of Kossuth and talk. I noticed that Gyuri's warm and civilized way of addressing his words to her, looking into her face while deep in thought, was not a matter of indifference to her. She was also taken with his masculine modesty, his self-isolation, his kindness. She had a deep voice and would give serious thought to our conversation, lifting her upturned nose, wrinkling her brow, playing in her excitement with her thick, unruly bronze locks, opening her mouth as she followed the train of thought, then making an occasional comment expressing anger or enthusiasm. And there, in the typewriter room of the Parliamentary Library, just next to the Prime Minister's office, our little band grew so close that Gyuri Szekeres, through the inscrutable will of fate (and of Vera), took over my role not long after.

Looking out of the Parliamentary Library window, I would spy the philosopher Miklós Krassó, true to form, still blond, not gray as he would be in 1985 just before his death in a London flat, where he was fatally burned by a gas explosion. In the spring of 1956 he was bubbling over with ideas, bounding about, waving his arms, having a grand old time. I would be riveted for hours by our conversations about politics and philosophy. We would go to the Dairy Restaurant, where the bread girl listened to him, fascinated, whenever he stopped her to take packets of sugar for his rice pudding from her wooden tray. He would lunge into copious detail about the madness inspired by Fichte and so transfix her with classical German philosophy that jealous cries of "Bread!" "Sugar!" rose up from all corners of the room.

Flitting past Vera and me on the Kossuth Bridge one day, he apologized for his rush by saying he had to drop Hegel and go back to Kant, because nothing existed outside of Kantian morality, though that wasn't entirely possible, because you can't ignore history and you can't understand history without Hegel. Having spent years with Spinoza's *Ethics* and Hegel's *Phenomenology of Mind*, he was at home with the dilemma. As for myself, I was going on at the time about forked paths of consciousness and the simultaneity of events as an apology for my eclecticism (which I called pluralism). Why choose between Hegel and Kant anyway? There's room on the shelf for both. Vera could not approve of my thinking in such matters, because for her it mirrored an inability to choose in love. This one is beautiful, you say, but so is that one. She noticed that when out walking I couldn't help eyeing a woman if she was the least bit attractive.

How to gain, if not freedom, then at least free time, which is occasionally the same thing? One day István brought me the news that the Debrecen crematorium was looking for professional cremators. The crematorium was in operation only two days a week, but it offered terrific pay in exchange for the repulsion you had to overcome. Should we become professional oven-feeders, corpse-burners? We, of all people? At least in this case the bodies were going to the ovens voluntarily. We talked ourselves into it, fantasizing that we would fly to Debrecen and live in the Golden Bull Hotel, doing the work in white gloves and spending the rest of the week in the Parliamentary Library looking out over the Danube at the Castle in ruins. We wrote a dignified letter of application about how deeply interested we were in the job. We had heard the remuneration was excellent. Was this true? The director gave a polite response. They were indeed looking for employees and were delighted with the sincerity evident in our expression of interest. However, they felt it necessary to clarify one misconception, namely, the salary was one-tenth of the figure we had cited. The thought flashed through my then twenty-year-old mind that we might sell the corpses to the Institute of Anatomy. No need there. "You are a very cynical young man," said Professor Kis, head of the Anatomy Department and coincidentally President of the Council of Free Churches. "Earn your bread by the sweat of your brow!" I could have unloaded freight cars, but instead decided to proofread and translate.

Those were the days of the Twentieth Congress of the Soviet Communist Party and Khrushchev's Secret Speech. After my third expulsion from university I was reinstated thanks to the intervention of György Lukács. A group of friends would congregate at our place to ponder historical portents, certain as we were that we stood at the very center of history: Austria had recently been pronounced neutral, and changes were imminent. István was convinced, citing classified information he had found at the Planning Bureau, that the country was bankrupt. He said he had enough material to depose Rákosi should the opportunity arrive.

On the morning of 23 October 1956, the day the Revolution broke out, I was sitting alone in a sun-drenched corner room of an Andrássy Boulevard mansard that served as the editorial office

of the recently founded —and strongly oppositional—journal
Életképek before an ever-growing pile of awful poems submitted
by dilettantes, to whom I, as a neophyte literature teacher and
editorial apprentice, should long ago have sent polite rejection
letters. Instead I spent my time on the phone with friends and
lovers, keeping up with political developments. The student
demonstrations were banned at some points and allowed at others. It was all well and good that the students were marching,
but demonstrations in and of themselves did not particularly
attract me: I had done my share of compulsory marching on May
Day with my schoolmates. When we assembled, I always tried
to avoid having a flag pressed into my hand and to arrange things
so I could slink away inconspicuously and go rowing on the
Danube with friends. Foisting the flag off on someone else was
a pardonable, if low trick. Things were different on that particular
day in 1956, I concede, but even then I grabbed not a flag but the
wriggling shoulders of a bright girl I knew from the university.
I noticed her in the march, to which I had calmly taken the tram.
We crossed the Margaret Bridge together.

Carrying flags along the street had been allowed only on official holidays, while saluting the Party leadership, but what had
been forbidden yesterday was now suddenly permitted—simply
because we were doing it. I was not so ardent as to cut the insig-
nia of the People's Republic out of the middle of the flag; there
were plenty of volunteers for that. There are always plenty for
everything. During an uprising they turn up on the perimeter of
the march route on motorcycles or elbowing their way along or
shouting a slogan or two at the crowd from a car outfitted with
a loudspeaker and enthusiastically breaking into song. I knew
a few at the *gimnázium*, ready to stir up crowds with forced
enthusiasm.

That night, after leading my curious companion past the head-quarters of the Hungarian Radio, where we heard shots and shouts ("Jewish murderers!" yelled a man who had carefully with-drawn into a doorway), I returned home and told my wife, as I listened from the balcony to bullets crackling in the distance, that I would not take part in the shooting. But as the government had as yet no halfway measures like rubber clubs and water can-nons and the only choice was live ammunition or forbearance, escalation was unusually rapid. So in the end when a young poet ran through the university halls shouting, "Hey! Who wants a machine gun?" I told him I did, and soon I was propped on my elbows on the cabin roof of an open truck as a member of the student-organized national guard.

Together with my fellow writers, all in their twenties, we could have taken over the editorship of our monthly literary-political journal from the old guard, who were in their thirties. My editor-in-chief had traded his post for the mayoralty, and a multiparty system was in place. We had withdrawn from the Warsaw Pact, and the Soviet troops were beginning to withdraw from Budapest.

Then, suddenly, they reentered, four thousand tanks strong, first aiming their cannons at spots where they had spied machine-gun fire, then at spots where no one was shooting at all, just to be on the safe side or because the soldiers felt like it. There was a general strike, a nonstop holiday. The city was one big theater with audience participation. When you found yourself holding a machine gun or a stretcher, you didn't think about the future; you lived a concentrated version of the present with no thought of praise or prison. Bravest among the fighters were the miners, freshly released from jail and sometimes still in their striped uniforms, and wards of the state, boys and girls alike, back in the city from their institutions.

Fifty-six was the most memory-rich year of my youth, the year when unforeseen bravery replaced fear. Furs or jackets with astrakhan collars or gallooned overcoats or old Hussar uniforms— you could see all kinds of outfits in the mayor's antechamber. Loden coats too, of course, which were all the rage at the time. Everyone wanted to meet my editor-in-chief and obtain signed and sealed documents enabling them to found new parties and appropriate state-owned assets for their headquarters. The now armed young editorial colleague stowed his machine gun under his chair and waited patiently to see the official inside to discuss his literary journal. While the men set off with their official stamps, the student noted the brand of rhetoric that went with each style of coat. But without the daring of those young toughs out in the square the gentlemen in the antechamber would have had no hope. The family men setting out for the factories had gone through a lot to join the ranks of street fighters. It was a time when half-naked, brutally bruised or bulleted and spat-upon bodies were hanged by their feet in front of Party Headquarters. The victims of these lynchings came chiefly from the State Security Agency. Such was the price they paid for their terror. But when I looked into the dead men's faces, considerations of that sort seemed senseless. Walking home sporting a National Guard armband and toting a machine gun, I was asked by more than one woman if I would be kind enough to rub out one or another neighbor—you know, the one in the fourth-floor corner flat. I did nothing to appease the popular demand for murder.

It would be a wild exaggeration to say that I was an obsessed freedom fighter. What was I doing with a machine gun? It was an adolescent whim, a remnant of the war. Once in a while I imagined an armed group stomping up the stairs to eliminate us. (What would be the best corner of the front vestibule for me to shoot from?) I was a pretty good shot: I had earned the title of sharpshooter during my brief training as a soldier. I was also a political commissar, because when our commander once asked who knew when *Das Kapital* was published, the student soldiers in our regiment guessed either wrongly or not at all until I chimed in: 1867. At last! He praised me and appointed me commissar for one of the company sections.

At the time we had no live ammo, the First World War–issue bayoneted rifles we carried coming only with five rounds of blanks. The reason, perhaps, was to keep us from using our weapons otherwise than intended. Which is just what happened two years later, late in October 1956, when students in my cohort disarmed the Baja garrison officers and moved on Budapest in army trucks. (I was unable to take part in the operation, having been forcibly removed from the community of officers-in-training.) This was in keeping with the spirit of the times, when the word "revolution" felt good. Every revolution got the highest marks: the French, the Russian, the Hungarian. Our 1848 War of Freedom was the very epitome of all that was beautiful and good: the poet falls in battle for his homeland; only the rootless scoundrel lacks the courage to die when his time comes.

A young painter said she would be ashamed all her life if she did not go out to the garrison at Újpest and get herself shot. We had to go, said the excited envoy who came for us, because people were being shot. Were they shooting back? I asked. No, he said. They were being shot with mortar fire, all the way from Gellért Hill; they couldn't shoot back. "So why go?" "Just to be together." It was all I could do to hold the young painter back, thereby laying her open to a lifetime of shame.

The reason I missed out on my classmates' military operation was that during our theoretical training at the university I had smiled impertinently when a captain was at pains to describe how horrible the enemy was. "You there!" he bellowed." Yes, you, with the long hair! On your feet! You see, comrades? That's what the enemy looks like! Look at him, grinning at our worldwide struggle for peace. I order you to leave the room!"

I promptly stood and headed out of the classroom, a remnant of the grin still on my lips. Few of my classmates expressed their solidarity. They tended to be "serious" and were therefore inclined to have me expelled from the youth organization of the Communist Party. The majority thus raised their hands in favor of expulsion. A few abstained. Only two protested, but they were on the outs as well.

The most ardent supporter of my expulsion—the gifted recipient of a Soviet scholarship, a member of the board of the Students' Youth Association, and a past master at shaping the general mood ex cathedra (he is today a professor of social science)— established with painful gravity that I was fundamentally alien to the people. As I later learned, his diary exhibited a bloodthirsty animosity to Communists and Jews, though he never took part in the battles when the time came and in fact never left the small room Miklós Krassó provided him as a reward for his inquisitive mind. I am familiar with the contents of his journal because the room's primary tenant—Miklós's grandmother, who was then over ninety but still enjoyed the life-extending properties bestowed by curiosity—had dipped into the notebooks lying there on the table. She was curious about what that odd boy could be writing: not only did he fail to set foot outside the flat during those stirring times; he put his jacket on over his bare skin, because he never washed his shirt.

Miklós's grandmother immediately noticed the frequent appearance of the word "Jew." Though born a Presbyterian, she was perhaps particularly attuned to that sequence of letters since her parents had converted in the nineteenth century, the better to move freely among the other landowners and doctors. Seeing all the filth her lodger appended to that word, she took the first opportunity to turn him out. "Be gone, you miserable Tartuffe! How can you despise me so and live under my roof!"

She still called Russians by their pejorative Hungarian name, *muszkák*, and when she heard Trotsky mentioned in connection with her grandson—Miklós had given a successful lecture on him in London—she kept calling him Tolstoy: Tolstoy meant something to her, Trotsky did not.

Her grandson Miklós, though getting on in years, was constantly on the move, and I could only marvel at the whirlwind of energy that secured him a truck and the papers to carry out his plan. He managed it by making a scene in the chambers of the Revolutionary Council of Intellectuals, which had responded to revolutionary demands rather docilely by collecting information, assembling credible-looking reports, and weighing strategies. The inner sanctum was kept under guard, but Miklós broke through. What moronic impotence, he screamed. The intellectuals' place was in the street, in the armed insurrection! And he explained in detail what needed to be done. After putting up with him for a while, the Revolutionary Council of Intellectuals asked him what he would take in return for leaving them in peace. A truck and driver, replied Miklós, and a document stating they supported his recommendation for consolidating workers' councils.

Was that all? They were happy to get rid of him so cheaply. So Miklós drove from factory to factory, gathering up emissaries of the workers' councils, and that very day saw the formation of the Greater Budapest Workers' Council in Újpest. At the founding assembly Miklós made liberal references to Marx, Heine, Shelley, and Ady, but before he had finished they thanked him for his efforts and begged him to let them pursue their own ideas. Miklós was not in the least offended.

When, eight years later in Paris, I asked him about those events, he reminisced with amiable humor. After leaving the workers, he tried to bring György Lukács, the philosopher, together with Imre Nagy, the democratic Communist prime minister, hoping the symbolic collocation of their names would be a message in itself. I believe Lukács was named Minister of Culture, and I reminded Miklós about Lukács's previous stint as Minister of Culture during the short-lived Hungarian Soviet Republic. When Lukács held the post in 1919, he ordered the pubs closed, a move that did nothing to increase the popularity of the regime. Another reason the move bewildered me was that the philosopher enjoyed a good tipple.

Rum played the primary role in my consumption of alcohol. I would take it with a double espresso at the Saint Stephen Ring Casino Café, where a full-breasted baroness made the coffee, a former Social Democrat MP recently released from an internment camp let you grab his unusually long earlobes for a forint, and an occasional click of heels came from one of the corner tables (a monarchist message immediately following a Polish émigré's references to Dr. Otto Habsburg, rightful heir to the Hungarian throne).

For a day or two I served as bodyguard to the psychologist Ferenc Mérei, then patrolled the public squares of Budapest with my machine gun at the ready and visited a few editorial offices. I would hang up the long, heavy, dark-blue coat I had bought for a pittance at a consignment shop and use the next hook for the machine gun, as if it were an umbrella. Freed from this double burden, I enthusiastically presented plans for the revitalization of our journal.

Stopping at a café for something strong—the woman at the piano had an absolutely perfect, towering, platinum-dyed hairdo, as if these were the most halcyon of days—I watched a group of people rush past, a man out in front, the others in pursuit. They gunned the man down on some cellar stairs.

Walking through the halls of the university, I ran into Miklós Bélády, a beloved teacher of mine. We stopped for a moment face to face.

"Humanists with machine guns?" he said.

"These are changing times," I responded. "Better to be on the safe side." It was unclear to either of us what I meant. I had read Marx's thoughts on "realistic humanism." One protects one's family and oneself if one must.

I headed home to listen to the radio and read Erasmus and Tolstoy. In front of the Horizont Bookshop I had found a copy of Tolstoy's *Childhood, Boyhood, Youth* in the trash and removed it from the other books, most of which had been burnt to ashes.

It had not taken long for piles of refuse to accumulate in the streets. The streets were also full of posters demanding the immediate withdrawal of Soviet troops in the strongest terms. Nor was it enough for them simply to leave the country: they were to ask the pardon of the heroic Hungarian people, which they had ruthlessly dishonored with their recent invasion and unjustifiably extended stay, recalling in our memory the havoc wreaked by Russians in 1849.

On my way home I stopped off at the Writers' Association, where things were buzzing. You could feel a sense of importance emanating from the directorship as they prepared a public statement. It had to be at once brassy and silky, sonorous and deathly—a masterpiece, in other words.

Trucks coming in from the countryside had brought a bit of nourishment for the intellectual leaders, the conscience of the nation, behatted men who were good at pressing against wall or fence the moment they heard a burst of fire. In any case, a nice little package slid into my bag. Down in the restaurant writers were debating how far back to go: 1949? 1948? 1947? 1945? Even further? The day the Germans marched in? Was there an acceptable starting point? Or perhaps this day of revolution marked the dawn of a new era. This very day, with its giddiness, its swagger, its display of the dead. Liberation goes hand in hand with murder.

A stocky fellow made a triumphant entrance, his face flushed with glory: he had managed to shoot two Soviet soldiers and write two stories. His boyish pride suggested he now considered himself a man: he had gone from student to killer.

A reporter had heard that the Soviet tanks were pulling out. Another had heard precisely the contrary: railway workers had sent word that they were rolling in on wheels. He said the Old Man—meaning Imre Nagy—had just waved his hand at the news.

In the café on the corner of my building I heard a man in a Persian-collared overcoat assuring all and sundry that Konrad Adenauer was on his way, though the bearer of glad tidings had added "on a white horse," which turned them into a moronic fairy tale. The neighborhood's high-class whore, a former language teacher and genuine polyglot, was outraged that the swimming pool she visited daily had been closed. She also asked in stentorian tones whether anyone at the café had read Virginia Woolf's *Orlando*, because she had not yet decided whether she cared for it or not.

Before I could open my door, two other doors popped open, and that era's masters of information retrieval, the concert violinist and the filling station attendant, stormed me with their questions. Theirs was a resplendent new friendship. One moment they would feel the flush of victory, the next they would predict a house-to-house roundup, the men beaten and the women raped. And what would they collect now? Wristwatches again, as during the war?

Late on the evening of 4 November the art student—her name was Éva Barna—and I were standing guard with machine guns at the University's Humanities Division. Once in a while a tank came rumbling down Váci Street. That was the banal part. The important part was Éva's beauty, her striking, deep voice, and, most of all, what she said. She had read Camus' *Mythe de Sisyphe* in the original; I had not. A mean-spirited jealousy moved me to make some ironic remarks about Camus. Éva emigrated that December and eventually met Camus and corresponded with him. Between Éva and Camus stood only travel expenses; between Éva and me the Iron Curtain.

Vera made some phone calls. What she heard was enough for her. She had no desire to see the fallen, burned, or hanged sons of whatever nation; she longed only to leave and live among more reliable peoples: she would go to Paris to teach English and Russian, giving us something to live on; she would rent an apartment, set everything up, and I would follow. She said I should stop being so difficult.

On 11 November, after the defeat, Miklós Krassó and my cousin Pál Zádor told me they were leaving the next day and asked me to go with them. They had assured my passage. They showed me my name on the document. Their story was that we were going to persuade others to return home.

I refused. I said it couldn't be as bad as before. I would hold out. I would outlast the leaders. I had no wish to be swept into the great outflow; I wanted to know what was going on here, in these streets. It was an unfinished story, and I refused to tear myself away from it.

Among Biblical heroes I found Jeremiah particularly appealing: he knew in advance what would be—he prophesied the fall of the Hebrew commonwealth—and all he asked of the victor was that he be allowed to mourn his city and his people on its ruins.

I had no desire to look for clever ways out. I wanted a normal, simple life: the same stairways, the same cafés, things as they had been. Even if hundreds of thousands were leaving, millions stayed, and if I had friends and lovers among those leaving, others would come along. My books were here and the sky and the balcony overlooking the Danube and the hills of Buda across the water.

And if I did go, where would I go to? People were wandering off in different directions, but this was still the place where I'd find the most speakers of Hungarian; I'd have the easiest time finding my way around, around the streets, the words, the customs.

Yet I sanctioned their going because I suspected they would be in greater danger here than I. They would be less able to get on here because they were more active, more inclined to speak out, more lively, more passionate, more important than I. I who was just a kibitzer, an armed onlooker. Besides, my parents were here, and if no uniformed compulsion separated us now should I be the one to separate us just to make the life that was best for me? I did not feel any danger looming here. So what if they locked me up. I had heard plenty of prison stories from former inmates: you can have a life in there too. Behind bars I would still be myself. Or so I thought.

What about taking my parents with me? And be dependent on charities? Start my student career anew, on scholarships? No need for me to waste away in the classroom. Every morning I could sit down to my notebook at any number of tables, since I would still have the money for an espresso at Budapest's myriad coffeehouses. I would always be able to find work to cover the absolute necessities: I could translate, I could edit. I had no desire to be rich. I had been rich once. It was no great shakes.

Looking around me, I saw nothing but strategists. How did they deal with the issues, the obstacles? The patterns they assumed, born of compulsion, appealed to me, comical though they were. Every social type, after all, is a complex of clichés. Caricature needs recurrent elements. Life here abounded in provocations and hardships directly traceable to schematic thought. Psychic sprains were never far from our door.

What interested me was how thinking becomes reality not from habit or sober practicality or tradition but from the exertions of the willful mind, from bold dreams, from seeking the truth and then announcing it—how the noble turn base, ideals become a hell, and how, in the end, we will survive it all anyway because we are stronger, we everyday, pedestrian people capable of work, wonder, and contemplation.

If István had stayed, he might have been sentenced to death. Besides, who was I to judge my friends? Everyone who left was right, as was everyone who stayed. Everyone tried to heed the prompting of fate. My advice to myself was: As long as you are not in mortal danger, sit tight. Keep going, but don't rush. All your problems come from impulsive decisions. Just keep working quietly, steadfastly, inconspicuously, ceaselessly.

They searched Gyuri Krassó's apartment and took in Gyuri, Tamás Lipták, and Ambrus Oltványi. But not me, because, true to form, I was late. We were to meet at ten; I arrived at twelve. Gyuri's mother told me what had happened. They didn't find the mimeograph machine, which had been well tucked away. They let Ambrus and Tamás go, but later took Tamás away again.

That they didn't arrest me was a lucky break, suggesting that they had not found the list containing the signatures of the people who had received machine guns. Besides, I had never been particularly active, never stayed in one place too long. I observed things, but made no speeches, didn't belong to the elite of the youth organization calling for reform (I had long since been expelled), didn't even use its language or style. To my good fortune I was insignificant.

So my concierge did not report me after all, though he had seen me come and go with my machine gun and never displayed signs of sympathy. I buried it in the corner of a then still vacant Pannónia Street lot with Vera, my coconspirator (or rather lookout). Two or three years later a large apartment building went up on that site, and who knows what happened to my well-packed and well-oiled weapon.

One day I ran into my philosophy professor, pacing the Ring in the company of a classical philologist. He had joined the new Sovietophile patrol force and was carrying a machine gun and wearing the requisite gray overcoat. He was extremely well-read and capable of reconciling his professional interest in Kierkegaard with his duties as a Party soldier, which included efforts to re-educate me. He wanted me to eliminate all traces of the bourgeoisie from my person, toss them off like old clothes, to steer clear of my old friends and to marry a woman of working-class extraction, a Party member. He himself had done as much: his stern, solidly built wife was unsparing in her theoretical criticism. When all was going well, she called him comrade, but whenever any ideological tension arose between them she addressed him as sir. (There was an analogous practice in the public sphere: at the workplace we could be comrades, but under police investigation we were inevitably sir.) I merely nodded, seeing from his uniform how far he had gone in his intellectual odyssey, and he merely returned my reserved nod: he had no wish to make friends or trouble, which was fine with me. A weapon makes an eloquent sartorial accessory.

After the second coming of the Soviet tanks—this time in greater numbers and ferocity than on the eve of the uprising— that is, after 4 November, two hundred thousand out of ten million Hungarians left the country, young people for the most part, including half of my classmates, most of my friends and lovers, and my cousins and sister.

Fifty-sixers? After a brief stint of valor they had a choice: to go or to stay. Those who could go did, fleeing either the previous state of things or the future revenge. They trudged through snow and ice over the spottily guarded border. Just before Christmas Vera set off too with my sister Éva. They made it to the border and crossed in a midnight snowstorm, trudging on in the dark along roads marked with Austrian signs. Then they saw Hungarian signs again: they had probably walked around the same hill twice. My sister tried once more the next morning and made it across.

Vera came back on the evening of Christmas day and was a little impatient with me for not having bought a Christmas tree. We went down and managed to find a small one and some decorations. There were gifts and an improvised supper, candlelight and family happiness.

I did not leave in 1956. Every time the opportunity presented itself, I sat down at my desk and wrote. Whenever the time came to make a particularly important decision, I desisted, letting things happen as they would. The more dynamic ones left; the rest of us stuck it out, hardening into shape. When I think of them from a distance, I like them; when I meet up with them, I do my best to slip away.

Though I stayed, I well knew that the dark bell jar of reality and nightmares, the space where anxiety looked itself in the face, would close around me again soon enough. It was time to learn to cohabit with angst, yet ensure that it did not become master of the house. After 1956 people no longer tacked their thoughts up on trees. The spirit of fifty-six turned to the wall and pulled the blanket up over its ears. Most memories died out, there being no profit in keeping them alive.

The furniture in my sister's room had once been my parents' bedroom set. A carpenter at the beginning of the century had replicated Maria Terézia's bedroom, and I had angel faces gazing down on me from the head of the bed and from the wardrobe. Two naked angels held up a mirror that had once stood atop a dressing and makeup table with its many drawers, some locked, others not, depending on their contents. When I was a child, sweets, condoms, and a pistol were locked up, while more boring things like photographs, locks of hair, and milk-teeth were not.

This bedroom set survived the most extreme vicissitudes. In 1944, when both the German and Soviet command posts had abandoned the house, the poor of the village came and took away everything they could carry. The large three-doored wardrobe was the one thing they could not manage; they did not even smash the mirror, though they did their best to destroy all manner of other things. So the wardrobe was the only piece that stood there in one piece, a monument of sorts in the refuse-strewn house, a harbinger of a restorable order.

By 1960 the wardrobe had moved to the inner room of our sixth-floor Vármegye Street apartment with my bicycle on top. The makeup table served as my desk, though the angels holding the mirror had been disposed of by history, which at this point tended to resemble a collective disaster. When you get hit in the head, you stay down for a while before initiating the long struggle for restoration. We should be players in the match, not victims (or so I would tell my friends at our regular coffeehouse table).

In the early morning hours sometime in 1960 a drunk hacks below my window. I am sympathetic: we are the only ones up. We are surrounded by the kind of silence that amplifies snores, angry whispered words, the screeches of distant trains, the moans of trams rolling out of their yards. There is a flood of stimuli in

Budapest, but I can only take in small bits of it. In the hours before dawn we need not contend with the assault of distracting sounds, calls, and obligations that demand attention and dull us into indifference. Perhaps I am not a city person after all. When I go out to do field evaluations as a children's welfare supervisor, my job requires me to enter the living quarters of complete strangers as if I were in my own home. Within a couple of minutes I discover I am in fact at home.

"It's the man from the Council!"

A kitchen chair is shoved under my behind.

"Well, sir, you see, what happened was . . ."

The words gurgle up like water. I hope I can keep from nodding off.

Rezső Rajnai sleeps in the cellar wrapped in his coat. He sleeps only till dawn, when his drunkenness wears off. The cold wakes him up.

A police officer tries to throw his weight around. I might be able to take him down a peg or two. This I do with a secret passion.

A Jehovah's Witness spends his life being jealous of his wife. She could have him institutionalized permanently, but keeps having him released at her own risk to protect him from the stress. She brings him home; he tortures her some more.

The wife of an obstetrician's best friend gives birth while the friend, a cripple, waits outside in the hallway for the good news. The doctor reaches into the infant's eyes instead of his rectum, blinding it. A surgical error. He goes home and poisons himself.

I have a bad chill. My bones ache. I may have a fever. I had a fish soup at the Golden Pheasant for lunch, which helped me put the "House of Lords"—a rundown vagrant shelter where all my dealings are with toughs—out of my mind. Still, one stern word from me and the beating of sensitive hearts is immediately discernible under the threatening shell.

A woman's husband dies: he was standing on the sidewalk when a bus hit him and killed him on the spot. The woman gets a hefty pension to replace her well-situated husband. A year and a half later, the late husband's best friend leaves his wife and moves in with the widow. They marry. As a result, the widow loses her pension, which was larger than her salary. She has a kindergarten-aged son from her first husband, but finds little time for him. I ask her why they got married. They were already living together, weren't they? The woman smiles and blushes. I blush too, then take my leave.

An old woman who sold newspapers walked into the main distribution center and asked for her quota. In those days people were reading *Népakarat* (The People's Will), but they foisted *Népszabadság* (The People's Freedom) off on her. She went out and sold almost all of them. Three young men, armed, were walking quietly along Rákóczi Street when they spied her with a *Népszabadság*, tore it from her hands, fell upon her, and kicked her as she lay on the ground. As the woman was dragging herself away, one of them said, "Finish her off, why don't you."

"What for?" one of the others said. "She won't dare hawk that trash anymore."

The old woman's skull was fractured. She was blinded in one eye and has had neuritis ever since.

Now on to six more addresses, six new kinds of despair. But first I sit and pray on a bench in Bethlen Square. There is a synagogue nearby.

Now off to the darkest heart of the district. Mrs. Alabárdos and her daughter. She wants the girl to respect her. The girl will not. So she is cruel to her.

Then I grant absolution to a widower who has committed incest. His daughter forgives him as well. If I had him locked up, what would they live on?

I look in on little Lajoska Musztafa. His father, now dead, was Turkish. His mother has remarried. Her husband is a locksmith named Bogyi. The handsome young boy was proud of his Turkish roots and mourned his father. When they studied the Turks in school, however, Lajoska heard bad things about them. His fellow pupils started eying him, so he asked to take Bogyi's name. After which Lajoska Musztafa (or, rather, Bogyi) stopped mourning his father.

A young typist goes out to Óbuda for rowing practice. It is winter. The training grounds are empty, nothing but fields and gardens. Four kids attack her. Screams. All four rape her.

"I know what you look like! I'm going to report you!"

So the boys poke out both her eyes.

An old man sits down next to me on the bench. His face is soft but stubbly; he has few teeth; he wears his winter overcoat even in the sun; he smells. An old woman with a pointy nose sits down with us. Her speech and movements are sprightly, her legs wrapped in bandages under her stockings.

Woman: "What's for lunch?"

Man: "Tea, and bread with lard."

Woman: "Don't you cook?"

Man: "No, I don't."

Woman: "Kids?"

Man: "I had a son. He was executed."

Woman: "So you live all alone?"

Man: "With my bedbugs."

Woman: "But you must have a nice little pension."

Man: "Six hundred forints. I drink it up pretty fast. Then I don't eat, just the leftovers they give me."

Woman: "Where do you live?"

Man: "I've got a nice apartment, two rooms plus kitchen."

Woman: "Why don't you rent out one of your rooms?"

Man: "I did, but my tenant went crazy. He stopped paying."

Woman: "You should get married."

Man: "Yes, but I can't find a woman I like. If she's young, she might not take care of me, and if she's old I'll have to take care of her. So I'm picky."

I stop for a glass of milk. A wheezing old man underpays by twenty fillers. He walks with two canes. When the woman at the counter calls after him, he pretends not to hear. Every day he underpays by twenty fillers.

A woman is called into a police station and asked about a man they have arrested. He abandoned her not long before. She is either afraid or cannot bring herself to lie, and testifies against him. She is the main incriminating witness.

An electrician has recently lost his wife. Every evening he lays out a table setting for her, then eats alone. He can't stand television. He goes over to the wardrobe and takes out his wife's clothes one by one. "She wore this one on such and such a day and that one on another." That is how he spends his evenings.

The welfare officer has grown thick-skinned from his work. The office madness and his wife's nerves box him in. Unable to sleep, overworked, he learns to put a stern face on things.

The heavy iron chairs on the playground are screwed into the ground. In January 1945 I looked into the corner coffeehouse through the broken glass. It was crammed to the ceiling with the bodies of Jews shot dead in the ghetto. That was the day we went looking for Aunt Zsófi's mother in the ghetto hospital and found her alive but with a bullet in her face. Now the new wallpaper has a sunflower pattern. An energetic woman greets all comers, apologetically bemoaning the lack of one or another item on the menu as if conveying the news of a dear one's death.

Little shops are opening in the courtyards of the old apartment buildings, and people are withdrawing into them. Here in Elizabeth Town everything is cavelike. There is no pretense about the place; it is full of life and people-friendly. I am no stranger here; I understand everything muttered in its most distant corners. I know the crocheted cloths under the clay pots with dried flowers, the bursts of cackling women, the heavy clank of the iron doors. That tall, attractive girl reading a magazine has probably knitted her midthigh-length white sweater herself. Comfortable oldies emerge from the depths, the espresso machine clatters, and spoons and saucers clink. The man making the coffee never takes a break. The guests know him and make small talk. "Ate the flowers, dammit!" *Who* ate them?

During my *gimnázium* years Budapest's Elizabeth Town represented the heart of things, a magic place, the place where I could find anything I might wish for. The population density is highest there, and as they used to leave the main gates open I would catch whiffs of the human smells wafting out of open kitchen windows into courtyards. I would walk along the hallway-like balconies lining the courts as if looking for someone.

I used to trade books by weight with the blind antiquarian

bookshop owner on Hársfa Street. All that mattered to him was that what I brought in weigh more than what I took away.

"How is it you never go broke?" I asked him.

"You're still a pipsqueak, young man," he said. "You lack all understanding of the profundities of human stupidity and stochastic processes. You suppose that everyone brings in junk and takes away the good stuff, but the opposite holds just as often. Besides, what constitutes junk is a highly relative issue."

On the way to and from school I did some urban sociological field research, if we accept my friend Iván Szelényi's definition. Years later, when during a trip to Pécs for a study of urban society we spent the first three days simply walking around and I guiltily suggested we were wasting time, he responded no, we were doing genuine fieldwork. This put my concerns to rest. But the only time I did fieldwork in the strict sense of the word was from 1959 to 1965, when I visited Elizabeth Town families as a youth welfare supervisor for the Public Guardianship Council and wrote reports on their living conditions.

All I could do was set down my impressions, but the great consistency of those impressions gave them the weight of objectivity, and the recommendations I made led to measures affecting the lives of children. My beat was the area between the Ring and György Dózsa Street, and I saw six to eight families a day. There was hardly a building I did not pay at least several visits to. Most of the time I spent in apartments facing the inner courtyard rather than the street, so it was the less fortunate aspect of the area I came to know. Sometimes it seemed hard to sink any lower.

What has changed over the past forty years? Poverty is lasting; only the faces change. But poverty is more than a condition;

it is a blow, a disaster, a pit you fall into. How can you expect a person in dire straits to have the patience of a saint? When the well-to-do go off the rails, they may or may not pay a price; the poor have no choice: they kick, they scratch, they torture one another. Reviewers found the world of my first novel, *The Case Worker*, hellish. I found it quite normal: one's imperfections make one mortal, hence real. Moral philosophy must be built on human frailty, and our acceptance of it. Behave outlandishly and you scare people. They take you for a criminal or a lunatic who belongs in a prison or asylum, as if humans were cars and could be taken to the shop for repairs. Crazy people exist, but most of them get by on the outside; only a few give up and entrust themselves to institutions. Weakness and abandonment require assistance.

The more moneyed and better educated a country, the more it confronts issues of weakness, a condition that fosters a frightened, dependent, and childish relationship with body and mind, with sickness, fear, and sorrow, with intimations of mortality. People are frightened by portents of death, having had no training in dealing with their problems and pain. If something is not entirely as it should be, they are in a bad way. Yet the zone between a perfect state of affairs and a wretched one is where most of life plays itself out.

My workdays were full of decisions, and everyone I met was a challenge. Each of my clients required some kind of action. Some people need more than a cordial nod. But how far are you willing to go when an entirely helpless child enters your charge?

It was worthwhile to spend time in the kitchens of those one- and two-room apartments: each kitchen was interesting in its own way. It is only when you hear a hundred versions of the same story that you begin to understand and feel it. I had a daily wish to combat my overwhelming feeling of superficiality which, even as I flattered it by acknowledging its existence, I found stultifying. "They are all of them just like me," I said to myself every evening on the brightly lit tram after leaving my charges.

A yokel gawking at urban life, I was never blasé. I studied the metropolis, wanting to write about everything, taste everything through my words. Asking my questions and giving my curiosity free rein, I felt an infectious bliss. Budapest was an endlessly juicy tidbit. Even in twenty years a voyeur from the provinces could not get enough of it.

At the time I was also editing Tolstoy's diaries. Tolstoy would begin each morning with a vow and end each evening with a guilty conscience; he broke every vow: he drank, whored, brawled, played cards, and picked fights. I did not brawl or play cards.

One day I got up early, read some Tolstoy proofs, and went to the Magyar Helikon Publishing House where I edited Hungarian translations of Russian and French classics. The head of literature called me in. He wanted to appear in high spirits, but the stories he told were not happy ones.

F. had intended to marry a working-class girl designated by the Party when his "bourgeois" girlfriend informed him she was pregnant. Abortion was out of the question in those days. Socialist morality took the side of the girl; his fallibility took him to his girlfriend, a class enemy. The child would be born, but he could not simply leave his bride-to-be because of an ideologically and otherwise problematic woman. Like the poet Attila József, F. lay down on the train tracks in front of a locomotive. The train sliced off both his legs. The policeman who arrived on the scene established that his nice trousers were salvageable.

His fiancée visited him every day at the hospital. F.'s first question when he came to was: "Did you find my party membership card?" Two weeks later his bourgeois girlfriend came in and confessed that she wasn't pregnant; she had merely wanted him to marry her. In 1956 the miners got word that a Party bigwig lived on the fourth floor. F. was no Party bigwig, but he did happen to live next to the Party's district office. The miners stormed his apartment intending to take him off, then noticed his artificial legs. They knocked them together, enjoying the noise they made.

He was my boss at the publishing house. My fellow proofreader Tamás Katona and I would carry him in the elevator in our intertwined hands. Though somewhat embittered, he was unfailingly alert when it came to ideological matters. Yet by playing on his sentimentality, I managed to trick him: I published Isaac Babel and Bruno Schulz.

I would look at women with the alert hunger of a hunter. In those days I felt there was no simpler way to get to know people than by lying naked with them in the same bed. Conversation is better afterwards; it is permeated with reciprocal gratitude and openness. The girl who sold bread and the hairdresser, the girls studying at the university and the women colleagues teaching there, the soprano who lived across the way, the pediatric nurse— they all were frightfully interesting to me, every one different in her own way, miraculous in her uniqueness.

I would go to the station and pick out a train, then get off at a small-town station, take a room in a hotel, and look out onto the main square. The constricted undulations, the slow passings were all so many offerings of meat, in hiding until they burst into the public eye. I turned around as a woman with a nice body passed by, paused a moment, abandoning my original purpose, and set off after her. We entangled, then fell out of each other. A housewife babbling to her baby was a font as precious as old diaries discovered in the attic or the ferocious rancor of a divorce court.

I phoned a woman at the number she had slipped into my pocket among mutual friends. I canceled all my plans, went to the address she gave me, and tried to guess as I walked up the stairs what she would have on: underwear or armor? How did she arrange to be alone? What would her smell be like from up close? I go and sit down beside her, listen to her talk about all kinds of things. I have never yet heard a story that was entirely dull. And what will be the situation that gives rise to the quick embrace that encounters virtually no resistance? What is the touch that will make her shiver and whimper like a child? And what will happen afterwards? Will she phone me back or show up unexpectedly at impossible moments?

At sixteen we are awkward because our bodies are complete but our understanding still childlike. At twenty-seven we are ill at ease because our minds are adult but our blood still childlike.

I have a job, but a tiresome one. I should be a Confucian at the Guardianship Council and a Taoist at home. I laugh at the thought. Who could pull it off? I have a contract with the publisher for a book on Stendhal, but am not writing it. I have a love, but am nervously repelled by the idea of marrying again. I have friends, but know what they are going to say before they say it. In fact, I sometimes fear I know what I will be thinking the day after tomorrow. I have reached the point where each successive birthday only reminds me of what I have failed to accomplish during the stupid five years since the Revolution.

At our regular coffeehouse table I made some antideterministic remarks, unable to reconcile myself to the idea that I am the way I am as a result of the effect on me of others. I insisted there was someone inside me making complex decisions at every moment, though I didn't know exactly who it was. My decisions were not influenced by my father's wealth or my childhood sexual fantasies, I asserted in opposition to fashionable contemporary views, reverse determinisms I found tasteless and morally questionable. This is a land of sloughed-off responsibility, a land where people justify their acts, whatever they are.

In the library catalogue room a former professor of mine mentioned that he had been hearing identical antigovernment theories from various students of his and that when quizzed they all turned out to have talked to me recently. My teacher, who was in direct contact with the highest echelons, shook his head and said no good would come of this. I should think carefully about what I said. And to whom.

After the fall of the Revolution, in the "consolidated sixties," I encountered the touchiness of tyranny wherever I looked. The police captain and the concierge were the state's patron saints. They were granted practically nothing else but the right to high-minded rage and to vengeance on their fellow citizens in the name of the state. Do not imagine that people who appear intelligent, good-natured, and civilized will not go wild when presented with a chance to take umbrage in the name of the state. And there is no one they despise more than the person who exposes the vanity of their everyday treacheries, for that person denies their very raison d'être. Who is the traitor's most natural enemy if not the non-traitor?

I had a classmate whose mother happened to see her son standing on a chair in his room delivering an address. He was denouncing his friends, one by one, to the General Secretary of the Communist Party of the Soviet Union, Nikolai Sergeevich Khrushchev. On and on he went, his voice rising in intensity, until he fainted and fell off the chair.

It was always cause for celebration when we happened upon islands of terra firma in the ocean of verbiage. Reading substantive works during the years of censorship was a form of refuge, a suspension of the falsities that had elbowed their way into house and home. One good book in my bag was recompense for all the clichés that had to be endured. We can use literature to be hard on our fellow humans, but if we truly learn to read we can use it to forgive them and revel in their beauty. Since my *gimnázium* days I have believed that the constant discussion of substantive texts is what keeps humanity going.

From spring to autumn I sought out garden spots. There were still outdoor restaurants with tables decked in red-checked cloths, and I deemed it a mark of distinction to lunch in the garden of the Fészek Club with writers older than myself, the prize of the day being the chance to measure my mind against theirs and thereby establish I had a rightful place at the table. There would always be someone in the company who had just been abroad—to Paris, naturally—and would speak of it to the provincials, for whom Paris is as far off as the moon. But just as we had no desire to pop up to the moon, we could do without Paris. We had refined the art of determining who all and what all we could do just fine without. You could still play foot-tennis with a soccer ball in the street. Little girls still chalked hopscotch squares. You could still find mossy ruins and nooks for love trysts. It was still the fashion to carve arrow-pierced hearts and initials into tree trunks. There were still hideaways where a poet and his paramour could settle into a room on the basis of his verses.

The latent elegance of the city transcended all obstacles. You could still find white-haired watchmakers in nineteenth-century workshops and elderly, elegantly dressed Jewish salesmen in state-owned fabric shops. Waiters with prewar manners still served you in restaurants that still featured prewar pianists.

The only people in my neighborhood who could afford a car—a Škoda—were the saucy fashion designer and perhaps a writer or two or film director. The city still belonged to the pedestrians, a fact of which I took free advantage. To this day I have not learned how to drive.

We knew each other's habits in love: our lives were virtually open books. We were shut in together on the same stage, and love was our ethnography. We sought it out, then did what we could to escape its consequences so as to seek it out again. There were no girls in white boots leaning on their cars. Business pleasure and private pleasure were not yet distinct realms. If someone was in pain from, say, the infidelity (or, for that matter, the fidelity) of a partner, the chronicle of their heart's agony was met with sympathy rather than scorn. Everyone had a trusted friend to pour his heart out to; all secrets tended to become public knowledge.

Women in the center of town and at summer houses in the hills, women in every district, in little ground-floor rooms looking onto courtyards, women encountered in the night, women encountered in cafés staring back at you, letting their eyes rest on you, women looking down from the bend in the stairs above, entering a shop and pleasantly surprised to note the loyal perseverance of this still-unknown knight. Girls who hopped onto a tram, girls we hopped on after, and finally the embrace of unanticipated intensity, as if we had set off explosives inside each other.

They were looking for something more, or less, than I was. They were curious, and so was I. The bolder ones took the elevator; the more timid tiptoed up to the sixth floor and hesitated before ringing the bell. Thighs twisted and curled; nails clawed the bed; breasts swayed left and right; labia opened and closed, sopped and dried. You were good if you didn't toss her out, if you were willing to stick around, go for a drink, look at the falling snow, study the veining of a hand, hear out a family saga. They were psychologists and hairstylists, teachers and tapestry-makers, lawyers and medical assistants, opera singers and bookkeepers, ceramicists and bank tellers. What I like about many women is their two-sidedness: a woman without a hidden agenda is like a lily-of-the-valley without a scent. The lady comrade made it clear she disagreed with you in matters ideological, but demonstrated total agreement in matters sexual. Leaning against the banister, the doorjamb, the mirrored bureau, on the ground, in the bathtub, in the pantry, in the most unorthodox places. Sailing over hurdles, getting back at prohibitions, ending up in new beds beside new bodies observed with the exhilaration of a teenager.

The bed is warm, the radiator cold. I can reach the nose of the white Rococo angel with my left hand. I give it a pat. All's well with the world. I have developed a lifestyle not particularly suited to a married man, but permissible for one in the process of divorce. I go to bed early in the evening and get up at three a.m. Then I climb into the bathtub and lie back cross-legged, the cold water splashing over my chest. A goose-down comforter calls me back to its embrace in the unheated room. I deliberate whether to sanctify the day with a glass of tokay. (My sister Éva has had a case of tokay delivered to me from America.) My birthday is coming up, a number substantial if not round: twenty-seven. It is the year of our Lord Nineteen Hundred and Sixty.

I begin my day earlier than the schoolchild, earlier than the factory worker. I go out into the still-dark city, wending my way to the Pipacs Bar. They let me in; they are open until five. The guests are drifting homeward, and the only girls are the ones the taxis have brought back. There I sit by the jukebox, absorbed in the work of Samuel Beckett, engulfed by the smell of dusty curtains, polished shoes, coffee, cigarettes, beer, hairspray, and the body odors of a city where only every other apartment has a bathroom.

"Looking for decadence?" asks the pianist, his hands prancing around the keyboard. Am I looking for decadence? More a state of fallenness, the hour where makeup on wrinkles smudges, when the collar pops open behind the necktie, when the belt gets loosened a notch or two. The Finnish ambassador's son starts dropping glasses, but Gizi comes over and sweeps up the shards. "You just go ahead," she says. She gets a good tip for every sweep-up.

Out to the banks of the Danube, to the Pest abutment of the bombed-out Elizabeth Bridge! The little motorboat is not running yet, but I need to look at the water every morning from the steps that line the riverbank. It is not so long since we set out from here to a still backwater at the Tas locks, where the surface shone black and the waters lapped softly amid perfect silence. A factory owner whose plant had been appropriated by the state had survived the difficult Rákosi era by fishing there for sturgeon every morning and selling the catch to the better restaurants.

Leaving the Pipacs Bar one morning in early summer, I have a few words with the Petőfi statue: "Europe is quiet, Mr. Petőfi, quiet again. We're keeping our mouths shut as we did after 1848, after your revolution, and at least no one is getting shot into the Danube. But as you know, Mr. Petőfi, they hanged our Prime Minister, Imre Nagy, two years back. We were terribly broken up when the news was announced, and could think of nothing to say."

Ambrus Oltványi, our host that evening, made us excellent tea with a series of scything movements, a legacy of polio. Towering above us in bookshelves that reached to the ceiling was the intellectual history of the nineteenth century. We were overcome with the beauty of the view from his windows, but Ambrus tempered our enthusiasm. "Yes, it's beautiful all right, but beauty is a great thief of time."

Ambrus's father, Imre, was a great collector and patron of the arts, a former banker, a retired Minister of Finance, a great believer in civil society, and a translator of composers' biographies. He spent the worst years of communism in his bed in a silk robe, surrounded by teapots and ashtrays, the corner window darkened by a crimson velvet curtain. When his son speculated that the current regime might turn out a bit more liberal, Imre listened to him quietly as if he were a madman.

In 1961 I began a half-time job for Helikon preparing a ten-volume, onion-paper, leather-and-canvas-bound edition of Lev Tolstoy's collected works. My days passed under the sign of Tolstoy. I read *A Confession* sitting on the bank of the Danube by the remains of the Elizabeth Bridge.

It is a work unparalleled in its clarity of vision (particularly the first half), though lacking in personal humility in the face of the universe. It is an honest and passionate compendium of every pessimistic, existentialist, life-denying philosophy. Once the mind breaks away from the superficialities of a mechanical will to live and daily tasks and responsibilities and rejects its identity with its existence in time, in other words, once it begins to question life itself and has a good look at death (which it had previously lacked the imagination and freedom to know), it suddenly feels that mortal existence is distressingly pointless, repellent, and humiliating and that it is pointless to seek a goal or mission or anything higher into which one's individual existence may meld and find peace. Science is valid only when it deals with nature, which has no mind; it loses its validity the moment it tackles the human element. We have no goal, no future other than the pursuit of our own annihilation. The mind is incompatible with life. Consistent and logical thought leads to suicide.

The only way to keep suicide at bay, Tolstoy tells us, is to develop modes of behavior that skirt the issue. The common people, fettered by workaday struggles, are too dull to devote their lives to seeing things as they are. People surprised by death with a blow to the back of the head may be left out the equation. One pure type is the hedonist, who revels in intense pleasure, who does nothing but eat, drink, and make love; another is the scar-picker, who debases life instead of confronting death, who looks towards death half-crazed, with endless whining.

Then what sustains life? asks Tolstoy. What pulls a person through despair? What makes suffering worth the price? What pacifies the soul of the people? What structures our civilization? What in history transcends the personal?

Faith, answers Tolstoy. He first settles on religious faith, then searches for something personal. Faith and intelligence are unrelated. One cannot use the one to verify or support the other. After intelligence has done its work, faith demands its rights at the outer limit of our helplessness. (Faith and not God, Who is a consequence of faith, faith as one of the vital functions.) The concept of infinity does not arise from the circle of the finite. Faith carries us beyond the limits of the finite to a state of humility in the face of the infinite, a humility that releases us by undoing our very selves.

At this point his train of thought gives way to an apostolic brand of speech, which I did not follow in its stark moralizing tendencies, its idealization of the peasants and the poor, its depiction of the landowners' guilt, and its romantic opposition to civilization.

My own experience with the poor—manual laborers, people who have received the short end of the stick—has not borne out Tolstoy's claims. As I see it, we must all pass through the thinking man's stages of development. I can testify that Budapest's Chicago, Elizabeth Town, has developed a kind of raw, barroom variety of existentialism, the lives of its inhabitants subject to the same insoluble questions and same loneliness and consternation affecting those of us who are relatively well educated.

I would like to think I will never curse life, not even if I develop a serious illness. This is something I wrote forty years ago in the Kisposta Café. I prize *what is* with all its fortune and misfortune. I have no desire to break with this world or merge with it. For the time being I hope the world and I will keep staring each other down.

All I can assume about the future is that human life on earth will eventually disappear. This likelihood offers me no moral choice. I have always been amazed at how simpleminded religious concepts of the afterlife and communist-inspired (or other invented) utopias tend to be.

Both earthly and heavenly utopias presuppose a rejection of the world, of the here and the now. Any exaltation of the future entails a vilification of the present. Whatever my present existence may be like, I cannot wish for something radically and elementally different, because I do not believe in the possibility of such a thing. In fact, I find promises of theoretically good alternative states as repulsive as common lies.

Are we capable of living here in our bounded present, rejoicing when we can manage it, suffering when we are in pain, keeping the prospect of death before us, yet rejecting fear of the next time round, the other side?

Human beings are travelers, on their way somewhere. Once there, they are travelers no longer. Amidst all the suffering en route they naturally think of how nice it will be to get there, the way an exhausted person thinks of falling asleep to blank out everything. But it feels good to wake up the next morning too.

We live with three problems: the vexations of our daily existence, the uncertainty of our knowledge of the world, and the certain knowledge of our deaths. The believer says that God, the only truth, compensates for all this. Even the nonbeliever can hope for a friendly obituary or, in rare cases, a memorial tablet on the house where he lived. But some people require no compensation: they accept the problems and are unshaken by the ultimate uncertainty of their knowledge of the universe. How can one have certain knowledge of the universe when one can say nothing certain about one's nearest and dearest?

In this part of the world, people eat and drink a lot, buy ugly clothes off the rack, and watch television nonstop. They don't execute the opposition, because there is no more opposition. There are no happy and unhappy people; there is really nothing and no one at all. Our society is sometimes tedious, sometimes delirious. Having had it with uniformity, it is receptive to disorder of every kind. It is a glutinous heap, incapable of taking things seriously or knowing where to draw the line.

If you are looking for an elaborate, sublime apparition here, you are in for a disappointment. But if you feel you absolutely must have a genuinely local article, then try this: shapeless battles abandoned before they begin. All you can find here are the jumbled by-products of existence. Everyone is a snail, a caterpillar, a worm. We are strong on flesh, weak on spirit. People die of fatty degeneration of the heart. There is no slaughterhouse; it is all do it yourself. Premature debility carries you off.

I have tried to wring the self-pity out of my prose.

When I first met Júlia Lángh, who would be my wife from the autumn of 1960 to the autumn of 1976, she had floated into the Kisposta Café trailing blond hair and a rustling black raincoat and wearing a white blouse with a turned-down collar. She had just come from the university—where she had been accepted thanks to her perfect *gimnázium* record and a captivating articulateness—and entered the café, a first-year student in French and Hungarian, suppressing her timidity and wondering, "My God, what happens now? Who is that old man, that twenty-seven-year old?" She was not quite eighteen.

I would show up at six a.m. with notebook, pen, and ink, as if punching a time clock. It allowed me to watch the rendezvous, generally hurried, that took place before work.

Her overcoat unbuttoned, Juli sweeps in on the wind. It is better not to stand in her way, because she can bowl you over. (This gives a hint of things to come: while you gape at her in wonder, she has put breakfast on the table and talked Miklós into finishing his story some other time and Dorka to stop covering Miklós's mouth with her hand. But that is all a few years down the road. First she had to go through the university.) Her entrance does not go unnoticed. The waitress gives an approving glance to her inky-fingered regular: "Others have been pretty, true, but this one has the energy to match." Juli even has a manuscript in tow. The elderly gentleman emits a satisfied "Hmm." (She wrote well then, as she did forty years later, carrying our youngest grandchild in her arms on her way to the car, where our daughter-in-law sat at the wheel and our son Miklós sat calming his son Jankó, the three-year-old swooping eagle, as he spread a shielding wing over his three-month-old brother, who, he tells all and sundry, "is going bald.")

From that morning on, Juli and I saw each other practically every day for sixteen years. I could always be assured of stories: she is the kind of person whom elaborate things happen to, or who can make them happen. For her part she did not appear to find the stories of the aging welfare officer and part-time proofreader tedious and had no qualms about putting the necktied knight in his place when the stories turned into analyses. She was obviously free of all dishonorable intentions.

It was days before the first kiss, when her head leaned back just a bit. Then lips fused and bodies coupled to the point of exhaustion, leaving not a fingernail-sized patch on the other uncultivated—a mutual cultivation that continued until I checked two fabulous personalities in swaddling clothes out of the hospital across the street and put them in a cab.

Who are you? As we looked at each other, I tried to sail through her eyes to the harbor of the enigma. And who are those two figures in the slatted bed carrying on a mysterious conversation, sister supplying little brother with imaginative stories and he turning to her, the nearest authority, with his questions. Everything a family needed—except that I was not really there. The marriage classifieds of the day used to end: No adventurers need apply! They made me shudder.

During our courtship Juli would tactfully remind me to remove my arm from her shoulder when we neared her home, because the eyes in the windows had known her from earliest childhood and expected of her the sort of behavior befitting a young lady. Juli's grandmother asked her permission to leave the family's title of nobility hanging on the wall when her youngest granddaughter's suitor came to call, though she ultimately resigned herself to the fact that, though a polished gentleman to all appearances, he was (no use mincing words) a Jew. Jews can be decent, can they not?

There followed roughly sixteen years of cohabitation and submission to a common judgment—the children's gaze—confident as we were of the strict but fair verdict of Anna Dóra (1965) and Miklós István (1967) and hopeful as we were of their mercy.

The Case Worker appeared in 1969, the darkest book to come out during those years. I could not believe it was permitted to appear, so strongly did it call the regime's official self-portrait into question. No matter from what angle I read my words, I could find no hint of uplift, the hero and narrator of the novel merely handling his cases as best he can, trudging on, ever downward.

After 1956 many of us were in that situation. Our lives would straighten out only if the regime changed. But that did not seem possible. At best, change would be slow in coming. In the meantime we pulled our hats over our eyes.

In the morning I would report to my new job but soon abandoned it for the café on the corner, the Alkotás (Creation). Even so, I managed to get more done than those poor old fogies who run panting from tram stop to office. Signs of work flourished on my desk—charts, texts, slide rule (it was a planning bureau with liberal pretensions)—but the morning still belonged to me as it had in my earlier days as a welfare officer. I had begun to grow into the city. My person and my name were now recognized here and there.

It was in this context that Iván Szelényi and I did our first extensive urban sociological study in Pécs and Szeged. We used approaches current at the time. Walking into my first computer room I felt I was entering a temple: How does a system of settlement relate to the structure of society as a whole? How do people move in social space? How do they get where they are? I traveled the country using a flexible system of optics: at times a microscope, at times a telescope. I combined close-ups and long-distance shots within a single sentence. I had put politics on the back burner, my concern now being how we might put up with one another in a time that passes slowly.

I roamed about in search of useful conversation partners, walking the streets as if they were the stacks of a library filled with books I had never heard of. I sniffed around doorways and courtyards, copied out stairway and toilet graffiti (both offers and requests), and knocked about as if snuggling up to a woman with a boundless body.

The large hopes had gone up in smoke, but small hopes remained. At the time any celebration of life would have seemed a self-compromising form of kitsch, but love still served to counteract the constrictions of life. Amid so many prohibitions it felt good to eat forbidden fruit, break rules. The one-night stand had its honor.

And there was literature. Literature had remained an adventure. Who can tell what events will filter into our storytelling? The number of tellable tales far exceeds the number that can be put down on paper, and what we choose to put down on paper is arbitrary. You pull something out of the spectrum; you reject the rest. That is the karate of saying no.

The aim of a story is to be hard to forget. We writers take over selves we have never before inhabited. We look into the heads, and beds, of others. Can you be other than what you are? Once the child who needs no stories comes into this world, we must all start to worry.

As a child I would lie on my stomach in the darkness as it rolled in from the window in treacherous waves, pressing my fists into my eyelids to call up unforeseen images, images over which I had no control, withdrawing my will to let them flow where they pleased. Once they begin to flow, I told myself, let them happen, let them follow their own secret logic.

Later I would put off decisions, letting myself be swept into marriages (and jobs) and entrusting the progress of my life to happenstance. I felt that by doing something, I learned more about it than by not doing it. I felt a constant devilish temptation to escape the passage of time.

In 1973 I finished my second novel, *The City Builder*. Although the head of the Magvető Publishing House liked it, he felt he had to reject it because of its dark view of the world. (It was ultimately published in Hungary in 1977, minus certain passages, after it had come out in German and French, without official permission, in violation of the law.) Also in 1973—during a trial for incitement mounted against my friend Miklós Haraszti, the accusation centering on his superb essay "Piece Work"—the political police declared me a suspect and carried out several searches of my apartment, confiscating my diaries, firing me from my job, and depriving me of the right to travel abroad for three years.

In the spring of 1974, Iván Szelényi and I rented a peasant house in Csobánka, a mountain village not far from Budapest. The "sexton's house" was part of the parish priest's residence and led to a friendship with Father Zsigmond, a Benedictine monk. It was in this house that Iván and I wrote *The Intellectuals on the Road to Class Power* in secret. We planned to publish it abroad.

On New Year's Eve in 1974, a large group gathered in the one-and-a-half room studio apartment of the painter Ilona Keserű. We were surrounded by her colored arcs depicting female bodies, birds, and gravestones along with her engraving equipment and other tools. There was a mood of excitement in the air. It was reminiscent of sixty-eight. Our cultural region was preparing for something new. A subculture, in the broadest sense, had formed. There were alliances of friends in every possible field: everybody knew everybody else, and we met regularly. There were rival schools as well, and the tribal chiefs cast jealous glances at one another in the Young Artists' Club. The secret police cast their own glances, so as to prepare a precise description of the age in all its color. The Counterreformation was in full swing.

Having lost my position as urban sociologist the previous year, I was working as an assistant nurse at a work-therapy mental institution in the countryside. I directed story readings and excursions and chatted with the patients. My experience in the mental institution was indispensable for the novel I had just begun, *The Loser*. I learned a lot from both staff and patients. Rationality was part and parcel of our state culture, or had at least come to be absorbed into it, while critical attitudes—dissident attitudes, if you will—depend on *transrational* decisions. They may be matters of faith, they may result from a quick blow, but they are inevitable. You follow the path open to you, risk or no risk. But why? Is it intellectual gratification? A command issued by the hedonism of thought? It was sheer pleasure to think through the possibilities.

Friends of mine, superb minds and personalities, would poke a finger to their foreheads if we met on the street and ask me if I had lost my mind. "Have you no idea where you are living?" they would ask Iván and me. The simplest explanation for our (to them) incomprehensible acts was that we had understood something and written it down just because we felt like it.

Early one summer morning thirty years ago the doorbell rang and five men burst into my apartment brandishing a search warrant.

The Major looked over my papers, sat down at my desk, and said, "I'll crush you like a leaf." He was a nervous, pedantic man who bragged he would clean up the mess I had made in my filing cabinet. He told me that if I kept my keys in a leather pouch as he did they would not pull my jacket pocket out of shape. He instructed my children not to tangle up the tassels on the rugs. (At his house they had a special brush for keeping them straight.) He then informed his wife he would soon have done with the suspect and would hurry home so they would not miss the movie. That was how I found out that I was a suspect.

I asked him how I could have incited anyone to hate the basic institutions of the Hungarian People's Republic with my diary entries, when I kept them locked up in a filing cabinet. Nothing could be simpler, he said. If I had a visitor and went into the kitchen to make coffee, he could hop over to the filing cabinet, take out the diary, and read it. That was all it took, and there you had your criminal act, with me as criminal, my seditious diary as corpus delicti, and as victim—my curious but ideologically innocent guest who, during the time it took me to brew him coffee, had made his move. I always invite my guests to the kitchen when I make coffee, I told him. "The kitchen?" he asked, concerned, as if this would constitute an affront to my guest. Yes, I told him mildly. That's where coffee gets made. I also told him my friends didn't do things like poke through my manuscripts. The only people I knew who engaged in such warped practices were your people. Professionals, in other words, who were not susceptible to being incited to hate the fundamental institutions of the Hungarian People's Republic.

"Your daughter is eight years old. *She* can read her father's notes. The moment she lays eyes on them the conditions for regulation 127/b have been satisfied. In fact, I don't even need to establish the fact of her having seen them, only the possibility that she has. If the key is in the lock, the crime can take place— a *criminal act*, mind you. Because what you think is your own business, but once an enemy thought acquires objective written status, that is no longer a private matter."

I imagine he had just recently learned the phrase "acquires objective status." The Major liked sounding scholarly. "Besides, the key to the file cabinet is not on your key ring." This was hard evidence—of which he was duly proud.

The next day he sent a police car for our son Miklós's nanny. Erzsi had instinctively asserted that the Engineer's filing cabinet was always locked and she had never seen the key. The Major barked at her to stop lying. Erzsi blushed, then rose. A retired textile worker, she was a model proletarian and a member of the Workers' Guard. The young man had no right to call her a liar. She had worked her entire life in the same factory, lived in the same house. He could ask her coworkers or her neighbors whether she was a liar or not. (When she retold the story recently, she gave a little laugh and said, "The fact of the matter is I fibbed a little.")

In any case, the Major was unimpressed. When the Department of the Interior rescinded my right to travel abroad for three years and the Major personally saw to it that I was dismissed from my job (if I insisted on writing something that was bad for me, I must be suffering from a maladaptive disorder), their logic found support with certain friends of mine, all bright, decent people in their own right, who wished me well but took it for granted that challenging authority would elicit a stern response. Some thought me crazy, others devilishly clever—but I was really quite guileless. In any case, I was now a freelancer after eleven years in the employ of the state.

Not that I had ever wished for a public role, a podium under my feet. The Major had saved me from an institutional career. If anything, my goal was internal emigration: a garden I would leave only to satisfy obligations I felt obliged to comply with. I had no desire to win or to lose, just to hold out a while longer. God forbid I should be the carrier of some first person plural. I shun the high ground that inspires envy. Even while under the employ of the state I managed to avoid having a single subordinate. I am at home only in groups where all are equal and speak in their own name—and feel free to tease one another. When required to speak or read on a stage, I slip back down as soon as possible.

After 1973 Iván and I could be sure that every document ultimately reached *them*, that *they* read every sociological interview we made. We wrote; they read. Research became evidence: every fact became part of the case against us; every wiretapped word made it stronger. Words could sweep you away, force you into roles, set traps for you to fall into, turn against you; they could make you do things you never dreamed of.

I first encountered Iván Szelényi at some meeting or other and found him standoffish, but then most of my friends are standoffish. He asked me from behind his pipe, "So you people are doing a survey too?" My answer came out a dilettantish jumble that only reinforced the wearily magnanimous superiority of the fellow, whom I judged to be five years my junior (about twenty-eight to my thirty-three). His jacket and tie were perfect. Everything about him bespoke the civilized young scholar, a rare bird in our context.

I was taken aback by the *you people* as well. So my office and I were a *we*? And he was with the Academy's Sociological Institute. But we soon realized our institutions could pool forces and create a new wave in Hungarian urban sociology. Our incipient friendship provided an added stimulus, but neither mentioned it explicitly: we were too bashful. Suddenly I was a young Turk reformer in a planning and research institute of the ministry. Iván and I—published professionals from Budapest, presenters at conferences where the most the local eminences could do was make a comment or two—mocked or disparaged things they still found interesting and respectable.

As I have said, Iván taught me that walks are the sociologist's primary modus operandi: If you want to know what a city is like, walk its streets. Observe the rocking chairs along the narrow, sloping sewage gutters that go by the name of thoroughfares in Pécs's poverty-stricken Zidina neighborhood. Watch the grandmother telling stories to her grandchild. Note the mirror up by the window enabling the old woman to follow who is walking along the street, ensuring her a constant flow of fresh information from the outside world.

Iván had an eye for such details along with a propensity for good dinners with our mostly local colleagues, who became our sources for gossip and local folklore. The morning after, they would take us to the Gypsy settlement or to the new row of elegant apartments they dubbed "Cadre Ridge." We also paid visits to any number of locals: council presidents, party secretaries, ancient barons, priests, schoolteachers, blacksmiths, gardeners, merchants, miners.

I would step out of my front door in Budapest at eight a.m., and by ten the propeller plane had me in Széchenyi Square in Pécs, where I began the day at a marble table at the Café Nádor, watching the locals coming and going southern style, in waves. Then Iván and I would set off, exchanging greetings with the people we met—men leaning on shovels in their gardens, women with net shopping bags, short-skirted, ponytailed girls whom we asked for directions.

We were the saccharine-smiled, arrogant sophisticates who had seen so much of the world. I had spent a total of maybe two months in the West; I had written in a café on the Île de la Cité, observed the blue-aproned peasants in a nearby village, and lain at the nearby seashore in Normandy alongside the great *transatlantique*, the *France*. Iván was a hopeless cosmopolitan who had spent a year in America on a Ford Foundation grant. When I asked him to describe New York, he said, "You're in New York and you're tossing and turning with insomnia because you have no lion. So you grab your wallet and out you go and before you know it you've got a lion on a leash."

"Hmm," I said to myself. "Why didn't this man go into literature?"

One night a good ten years later I had trouble sleeping in New York and went into the first grocery store I found to ask where I could get my hands on a lion. "Wouldn't you rather have a nice tongue sandwich?" asked the owner, a strapping fellow with a smile to match.

Which all goes to show that research and a sense of humor are not mutually exclusive and that you could do good work under the old system as well. The orange Volkswagen that was the vehicle for our merry pop-sociology, with our younger colleague Róbert Manchin at the wheel, took us to one after another of the hundred-odd villages we had chosen at random. In a parsonage we devoutly touched the four-hundred-year-old desk on which the Calvinist preacher Gáspár Károlyi had translated the entire Bible from Hebrew and Greek. We would take large bags of children's clothes out to the Gypsy settlements, where kids ran out of their shanties naked through the snow, bombarding us with their "Money, Mister! Give us money!"

Sometimes we thought we would simply observe them and describe their social structures; sometimes we imagined that if we managed to define the situation reforms might come of it. But the system, the ultimate subject of our observations, searched our apartments one day, initiating what would become a long series of unpleasantries, probably under the impression that if they put us on strict notice and isolated us, others would learn from our example and we would either come to our senses or leave the country as our Russian, Czech, and East German dissident colleagues had. We were naive perhaps, but so were the authorities. We persevered.

We persevered with Iván's peripatetic method, lugging the tape recorder up hill and down dale, discussing our subjects while perching on Serbian gravestones in Csobánka or a bench at the base of Oszoly Cliff. Then came the precise formulation beneath old brown rafters and bugging devices. We grew accustomed to passing the narration back and forth, giving signals to one another, rewording sentences that, though perfectly fine to begin with, assumed added luster from an unexpected twist or transition.

Our primary theme was how the regime was being ground down through conflicts among parties of opposing interests. The table of contents was as clear as a Christmas tree; only the ornaments were wanting. But Iván's main concern was the relationship of trunk to branch, while I was more interested in content and improvisation. Every time our exhaustive conversations helped us to make a point more clearly, we earned a refreshing hike up the Oszoly Cliff. We fleshed out my old idea that history was the locus of the intellectual, the knight of totality, the poet of thoughts, explanations, principles, and nightmare scenarios, the elevating force and the force of outrage. Look to the words, for in the beginning was the word. Look to the modelers of sentiment, the confectioners of feeling. Look to their own rhetorical gumbo. Before long it dawned on me that our exchange of ideas was beginning to intrigue me more than socialism's miseries and even socialism's prospects.

One day we heard there had been a search in the Ágnes Heller–Ferenc Fehér household. Their agenda being dissident like ours, we grew more cautious. A few times we wrapped the typescript in a plastic bag, placed it in a box, and buried it, though in less careful moments we simply hid it in the coal bin under the coal. That every room in the bell tower had a bugging device in a saucer-sized porcelain holder recording our every snore or key stroke or love groan—of this we had no inkling. We did not consider ourselves important enough. True, we had heard of Solzhenitsyn's deportation to the West, of exiles domestic and foreign; we had heard that Andropov, the former ambassador to Budapest, was now at the head of the Soviet Secret Police and shaking things down, purging the resistance counterculture, but it never occurred to us that our Hungarian counterpart would resort to similarly coarse measures. Before long we had to accept the fact that they were doing so: I had told my wife that there was a key in the silver sugar-cube container in my mother's glass cabinet, and the next time they raided the house, that was the first place they went.

From then on, whenever we needed to discuss anything to do with writing and manuscripts or politically sensitive encounters, we wrote it out on slips of paper we then flushed down the toilet. It also became second nature to look for nooks and crannies the size of the typescript. What we wanted to conceal most was how far along we were. I was afraid the manuscript would be seized as soon as it was completed, so I always denied any progress. When asked on the phone, "Are you working?" I would answer I was just pottering around.

"You are an intellectual resister," said one of my interrogators. Until then I had not thought of myself as such, but I liked the way the police officer put it. I grew more sensitive to the police lexicon. I spotted the eye watching me from a little hole scratched in the paint of the window of a shop in our building, a shop that was never open. I sensed that two faces were following me from two windows in the building across the street. I started recognizing the men in cars that rolled slowly past me and the old man leaning on his elbows in the courtyard and the people behind me whose footsteps never let up and the car parked by the front gate. I had the clear feeling that the policeman who came to the bell tower to check my papers and ask what I was doing in the town was an integral part of the machinery whose charge was to ensure the survival of the Great Lie.

Since we paid little attention to either communist or anticommunist ideologies, we befouled the self-images of the unofficial and official intelligentsias alike. Feeling insulted in the name of the intelligentsia, even our opposition friends took issue with *Intellectuals on the Road to Class Power*. What had happened, we concluded in the book, was that the intelligentsia was ensuring that the system functioned effectively by refraining from calling the power hierarchy into question, while perceiving itself as an abused victim and thereby absolving itself of responsibility.

One hot Sunday afternoon my friend the film critic Yvette Bíró brought a sad and skeptical Czech film director to the garden at Csobánka. Iván and I felt an immediate intellectual affinity with him and graced him with our most precious thoughts, but all he did was shake his head. "You'll be behind bars before you finish. And such bright people!"

One sunny morning my friends Gabriella Hajós (Zsabó) and György Jovánovics came out to Csobánka with me. While Zsabó stood watch down below, the sculptor took before-and-after photographs: first of what those ugly, old-fashioned bugging devices looked like in situ in the loose clay, then of what the loose clay looked like without them. I had ripped them out like carrots. Not knowing what to do with them, I tossed them into the kitchen cupboard along with the other trash. That evening, as usual, I took the bus and commuter train back to Budapest. The next day, when I reentered the Csobánka house, I noticed that my treasure was no longer in the kitchen cabinet. I was not such a free spirit as Václav Havel, who hawked his bugging devices at the flea market.

We did not intend to publish our book in Hungary; we wanted it to come out in normal countries, that is, in the West. I imagined it my duty as a citizen to see to the publication of the book, after which whatever happened did not much matter. My wife helped us to type it up, and we asked a friend of mine, Tamás Szentjóby, to photograph it page by page, the few photocopy machines in the country being under the supervision of the political police.

Walking along Péterpál Street in Budafok, where a row of houses once belonging to vintners ran up the hill, I was reminded of my hometown. We are so fatefully shaped by the place we lived before the age of ten that only in a similar setting can we feel at one with our perceptions. I kept returning to the second chapter in my novel, the one on childhood and the family. Life, for me, was beautiful, and to the question "How are you?" I generally answered—strange as it might seem to an outsider—"Great." This feeling dates from my days at the *gimnázium*, when all it took to make me happy as I left the house in the morning was the knowledge that I had no obligations for the day and could go off by myself.

One day, out of the blue, another friend, Tibor Hajas, came to say that Tamás had been arrested: searching his apartment for pornographic literature, the authorities had come upon our manuscript. The couple necking constantly by my front gate turned out to be police officers. Ambulances and taxis would follow our steps, as did all sorts of conspicuously average-looking men and women—or odd-looking men and women, if they wanted to be noticed. Since things like this could happen solely with the permission of or on the orders of Party Headquarters, we could only deduce that our own arrests were not far off.

We told each other that come what may our efforts had been worth it, and agreed on a story: we had no idea whose manuscript it was or what it was. Disowning one's work was a remnant of an earlier time, when you could get years for partial authorship of a leaflet.

Iván's wife Kati and I saw him off to the Belgrade train. He still had a valid exit visa for Yugoslavia. Naturally he was taken off the train and sent back. We were green at the game of resistance.

One day two men followed Iván into the sauna at the Csillaghegy pool with orders to arrest him. They sweated it out there on either side of him for three-quarters of an hour, taking his arm only when the three of them stepped out of the pool's main entrance together.

I had a desire, undoubtedly childish, to give them the slip, throw off their calculations, spoil their game. At least I could gain time. Once word got out, the decision-makers might come under pressure from writers or even their children. I asked my first wife Vera to put me up for a while.

I doubt I had been in Vera's seventh-floor apartment for more than two days—reading, watching the birds in the gutter and the slow-working roofers on the building across the street (who were watching me as well, since they were not real roofers) when the officers of state security knocked on the door. It was 23 October 1974. They had first gone for Vera at her school, bringing her with them as a witness, but all they wanted was me. They did not even bother to ransack the place. I thanked Vera, shoved a toothbrush into my pocket, and followed the plainclothesmen out of the house.

Lieutenant Colonel Gyula Fehér, who politely asked me to forgive him for taking up so much room in the back seat, was my interrogator. He told me he had suffered a great deal reading our work, unaccustomed as he was to such vocabulary and train of thought. Despite doses of strong coffee he had fallen asleep more than once over it.

"So the study did not particularly provoke you," I said.

"Not at all," he acknowledged.

"Then why am I here?"

The Lieutenant Colonel lifted his arms skyward.

The handwriting sample established the corrections to the typescript to be in my hand.

"Is this your work?" I said it was, thus breaking the agreement I'd had with Iván, who stuck to the story that we'd had nothing to do with the manuscript. I thought they would be unable to bring formal charges against us, because no one had seen the text besides its authors; in other words, they had jumped the gun. I decided they wanted to annihilate the book by confiscating every copy.

I found confinement tolerable: getting up early, swabbing the floor in the cell, eating bean soup and potatoes with noodles. The prison library supplied readable books, and the authorities allowed me to sign an authorization enabling my wife to pick up the royalties I had received from the American publication of *The Case Worker*. The Lieutenant Colonel regularly recited his favorite scenes from Hašek's *Good Soldier Švejk*. We did not speak about the book itself, only about the other copy. The expert had determined its existence, based on the confiscated copy, whose cover showed the traces of carbon paper.

One morning I woke up sensing I had gained a perspective on the matter. I would suggest they put it out as an in-house publication alongside Trotsky and Djilas. They might think me an idiot, but there was no harm in that. The point was to nip this in the bud or at least before it entangled others. Friends were bound to have their apartments searched and be summoned and questioned as witnesses. We needed to gain time. We would publish the book once things calmed down. (Iván had hidden the "real" second copy and the working manuscript.) I would work on my next novel, *The Loser*, and find a safe place for it.

In the meantime, we would give the authorities the feeling their work was not in vain. I would let them have the third copy, which could not possibly have carbon marks on the cover. They would have obtained a manuscript with some police value and could hope, for the moment at least, that the book existed nowhere else. I decided to let them have it on two conditions: that they release us both immediately and that the person in possession of the manuscript suffer no ill consequences.

Such was the line I gave them the following day. A few hours later the Lieutenant Colonel, acting on the authority of his superiors, accepted my terms. I took a seat with him in the police car, and off we drove to the flat of my sister-in-law, Zsuzsa Lángh, and her husband Ernő Sándor, who had done some fancy driving to ditch the car trailing them, get the manuscript to their place, and hide it in their tile oven. Both were at home. Pale and stunned, they acceded to my request that they turn the manuscript over.

That very afternoon, all three of us—Szelényi, Szentjóby, and I—were released on probation. An official decree forbade us from publishing the hostile document (the book) or even communicating its contents verbally. Any violation would result in criminal prosecution. Should we feel unable to adapt our activities to the laws of the Hungarian People's Republic, the authorities would countenance our emigration. We could even take our families with us. Iván said he would give it some thought, but I told them, "No, I am a Hungarian writer."

Then our case received a bit of attention in the Western press—Kissinger had supposedly asked about us—and we both decided to emigrate together with our families and proceed with our work at a university in the West. We would need job offers and visas and an exit passport, all of which we pursued through official channels.

Although life in the academy abroad seemed feasible, I had trouble picturing myself as a grateful émigré and (if all went well) university professor: I would tire of it; it would seem a waste of time. On days when something kept me from writing, I would be nervous and grumpy and get the urge to escape to a spot where

I could go out into a garden for some air, where no one would bother me.

I was an enthusiast, yet infantile. On my first day in a new city—east or west, large or small—I could imagine spending the rest of my life there. This would be *my* window and so on. Yet walking through town the next day, I had the urge to move on, generally homeward. To Csobánka, perhaps, where, surprisingly, no one searching the house had ever lifted the tabletop in my bell-tower room, where the notes for my novel lay untouched.

I settled back into my routine, writing in small lined notebooks in Budapest cafés. A button-eyed observer often watched me ply my trade. When there is danger, when the crowds stampede, stand still. I would abandon plans to emigrate, I wrote to György Aczél, the Party official in charge of cultural affairs, if they published my novel *The City Builder*, called off the police harassment, and let Szelényi leave. The way I put it, my decision to remain in Hungary was a sacrifice, a gift, though in fact it was the desire to continue the life I had led hitherto, a life I considered neither fruitless nor disagreeable. Aczél replied that no one could prescribe conditions to him but that he did not find my requirements outlandish.

It was painful to both Iván and me when I informed him we would not be a team writing in the West. You could stay too; we'd get by somehow, I thought. And he: You promised to come, and now you're going back on your word. Do you really think you'll be able to write your books, publish them in the West, and continue to take your constitutional through the streets of Budapest? Yes, that's exactly what I thought. And that's what happened. Thus began the decade and a half of my life as a banned, underground writer.

Children are smart. When I was arrested and Juli found her hands full, she took our seven-year-old Miklós to stay overnight with Feri Fehér and Ágnes Heller, who had a son about the same age. Miklós played with him all afternoon, but when evening came he took Feri aside and asked him with a touch of an aristocratic intonation, "Are you a good person?"

Sensing what he meant, Feri answered, "Yes Miklós, I believe I am."

"Good," said Miklós. "Then I'll sleep at your place."

Influenced by tendencies I observed in myself and those around me at the mental institution where I began to work at the time, I tried to view mental illness as a behavioral strategy, an individual concept of the world. The patient may act strange, but he sees himself as an innovator. Such might be well be a description of my type of dissident, I thought. The hero of my novel was committed to an asylum. Confiscated copies of the novel were condemned to destruction by court order as "hostile material." Not me, just a few years of my work.

Ultimately the mental institution is a reflection of state power. The illnesses there are fed by that world, which provides its causes and its symbols. Rationality was part and parcel of our state culture (or at least claimed to be), while critical attitudes—dissident attitudes, if you will—depend on transrational decisions. You follow the path you believe in, risk or no risk. But why? Intellectual gratification? The hedonism of thought? It was sheer pleasure to think through the possibilities.

After being dismissed from everywhere at the age of forty-three, I no long needed to put up with nerve-racking types (though I had always handled them fairly well), so I exiled myself to a garden, where, relaxed, I had plenty of time to sort things out. Enough money had come in from my writings to keep us going for a few more months. But our lives were not without risks—the aforementioned house searches, bugging, surveillance, and the three-year travel restriction—and my wife Juli was banned from the radio, where she had been giving insightful and refreshing book reviews every morning just before eight.

Writing counts as action only in unusual circumstances. Throughout most of the twentieth century writing had a chance to become action here in Hungary. All it had to do was go beyond the norm. Almost any statement was an opportunity for anti-state agitation.

Just after I lost my job a thick-browed colleague stuck his head into my office and whispered, "You sealed your own fate." But I despised the idea of begging my way back into the fold. Officially sanctioned normality contains all the symptoms of neurosis. Only the free are healthy, and the healthy are their own masters. The sick are directed by others: they are dependent, they cannot take care of themselves, stand on their own two feet, make decisions, see things as they are. They see what they want to see— or what they fear.

Excluded from regular employment, I recognized my condition as consistent with the logic of the centralized party state. Hence it did not enter my mind to make the rounds of the editorial offices. I knew they had no choice but to reject my work out of hand. And yet I occasionally experimented with submitting an article. The weak-willed did not even respond, while the stronger wrote something to the effect that they did not dare publish me. Ultimately I let up: I was ashamed to have put them in such a position.

I was now convinced I was not cut out for steady jobs in the East or West. Much as I respected all those who sawed and sanded, taught, or examined patients, I was thrilled to be released from it all, and viewed my life as an endless holiday. Only the typewriter's thump lent a touch of respectability to my activity—after all, typists were considered workers—but in fact, thanks to the generosity of the system, I was a pipe-smoking rocking-chair adventurer.

Too lazy and inept to handle the organization that went with oppositional activities, I did not get much involved, especially since political activism started early in the morning—my best time of day—which I never would have considered giving up. I stuck to formulating and distributing antipolitical texts.

It was hard for insiders in the old system to imagine that anyone would leave their ranks in the state power apparatus for civilian life. But representation, respect, and remuneration I needed like a hole in the head. Some make time to do what they like; others do not. The Gypsy nailsmiths from the outskirts of Csobánka had time to go into the woods and gather mushrooms whenever it rained. If a CEO headed for the woods on a workday morning, people would think him insane. I admired artisans supporting their families from their homes and gardens, oblivious of professions requiring them to report to the boss at a fixed time every day.

But even as I sat in the small Gypsy pub in Csobánka looking deep into my golden-yellow marc, I had to admit it was better to walk in the sun in a foreign city than pace the same five steps up and down in a cell here at home. Why then did I cling to the homeland?

The white walls in the Csobánka sexton's house and the dark wooden cross-beamed ceiling had not changed in over a hundred years. Beyond the grassy area at the kitchen door stinging nettles grew among the fruit trees. To the left of the door stood a marble table, once a tombstone. That is where I worked. The garden produced an abundance of fruit: sour cherries, walnuts, apricots, pears, and endless plums. In fat years a couple of the more tired branches would break under the weight of their yield.

A small lane arched upward past the house. It was called Red Army Boulevard and was sprinkled with white, gravelly sand and an occasional tuft of grass. On Sunday mornings the elderly, black-clad, kerchiefed and bonneted women of the village wended their quiet way up the lane clutching prayer books. Few people used the lane during the week, so I was assured of privacy. Only the parish priest might drop in of an afternoon, but he soon went his way. "Our humble respects for the fever of creativity!" he would say, leaving the memory of many smiles.

If I made a noise stepping out of the house, the deer at the end of the garden would prick up its ears, slink behind my back, and butt me gently with its peach-fuzzed antlers. The dog would bark, then fling himself prostrate while the deer rubbed its belly. But the deer's best friend was a feisty Japanese cock that slept with it, burrowing under its belly to keep warm. The cock's alliance with the deer reinforced its cockiness, and it would bluster like a rowdy and give horrific crows with a voice as thin as its body.

I had set a few stumps in the grass for seating, but they had been taken over by ant colonies. If I gave one of them a kick, it shook their world like an earthquake, sending them pouring to the surface in a frenzy, saving eggs and crumbs and bumping into one another in zigzag paths of panic. Desperate, tens of thousands streamed up from the depths, blackening the stump in a mad society that, seen from above, behaves not a whit more reasonably than our own. Once the danger (during which they occasionally bite off one another's heads in terror) has passed, they will boast of their heroism and the trials they have suffered. I give the trunk one more kick and the ants swirl out in even greater torrents. May they enjoy the shocks of history. After chaos comes peace, when they will have to reorganize and depose the incompetent leaders. In the company of the deer, the dog, and the cock I observe the ants coming to their senses, crawling back into the fissures of their shaken universe. The fickle god's wrath has faded.

Cloaked in my jaded and enigmatic cruelty, I, the Lord, head back to the house. Why should I, incorrigible scoundrel that I am, refrain from exerting my power as long as I have it?

The way I spent my time was my reward and my punishment. I concocted wiles to trick my congenital stupidity. If I was unpleasant, I had to put up with an unpleasant character. *L'enfer, c'est les autres*? What if it's me? Locked in a dark room, the only light from a screen: myself in an endless loop.

I enjoyed going back from Csobánka to the wild chestnuts along the bank of the Danube in Buda. I found something to my liking in almost every café and pub and did not mind the slowness of life. What comes of its own accord is enough.

From age forty to fifty-five I was a nonperson in my country, a person whose very presence violated the regulations. My response to the prohibition against working and publishing? An unchecked, internal, authorial freedom. I distributed my work in samizdat, usually Gábor Demszky's underground press. Not only did I receive no fee, I regularly contributed to the printing expenses, considering the dissemination of my works in Hungary a public service.

I could spend the day at my desk and the evening with people I wanted to see. There were a few I would rather not have seen, the ones who stood around on the corner or sat in a car by the door. They accompanied me everywhere, but kept a respectable distance, not really disrupting my solitude. Blacklisting and internal emigration were not so much blows dealt by fate as the result of a decision on my part, so it was my duty to cope with the vexations that went with them.

It was impossible to be normal here at home, and putting a good face on it was an unpardonable offense. The critical intelligentsia saw itself as a separate camp: us, with the police on our trail, versus them, bearers of the prevailing mindset and therefore police-free. People published all sorts of attacks on me, but I neither responded nor penned any of my own. I could never understand where their hostility came from. It took the utmost self-discipline and sense of humor to keep from going mad.

At eleven I was compelled to accept the reality that the spirit of the age was doing its best to have me shot and tossed into the Danube. Bad experiences made me suspicious earlier than most. Big words? Big words can turn people into child murderers.

As a banned author I had the luxury of being free from the expectations of others: I didn't need to embrace local public prejudices; I didn't need to be confident or outraged or despairing; I didn't need to worry about the authorities taking umbrage at what

I wrote. I required no future different from the present I was living in if for no other reason than that I did not believe in the possibility of a different future.

I am watching the Moscow May Day celebrations on television: a giant soldier extending his arms across the entire facade of a building, tight phalanxes lined up in Red Square. The flag-bearing gymnasts along the edge of each formation are dressed in white. Only the most distinguished—winners of workers' competitions—are allowed to appear in the square. Under the pictures of Marx, Engels, and Lenin there are pictures of the current Party leaders, and beneath those the men themselves. Every participant at the great assembly holds a little red flag in his hand. Filmed from above, the network of roads stretching through those human colonnades looks geometrically regular. Between the carpet of citizens (the first-string squad, as it were) and the complex of platforms (with Lenin's mausoleum as its center) stands a wall of white-gloved policemen at attention; above them—the marshals, their medal collections clinking and flashing on their chests, along the parapet of the mausoleum—the leaders of the Party and the government, dressed in the state's version of men's fashion: a dark gray overcoat and a dark gray hat pulled down to eyebrow level. Dour old men waving at the crowds there to hail them.

Bugle fanfares. Brezhnev doffs his cap and steps up to the microphone. He struggles with a text written by others and full of long words. A face covered with the wrinkles and bags of arrogance. Behind him, gruff and motionless, the other leaders, their hands behind their backs now, jaded faces sunken inward, obviously heedless to his words. "Warm greetings, the struggle for the workers' happiness." The leaders turn their heads sternly, left, right. When the boss has finished, the two leaders standing next to him initiate the applause. The crowd takes it up. Once in a while the men on the parapet remove their hands from their pockets as if out of a sense of obligation and strike them together a few times. They have absent faces with no curiosity. Athletes on large platforms carry those faces past the parapet.

This is the seventies. I go out onto the highway, where a sign indicates that taking pictures is prohibited. Of what? A missile silo? A radar station? The forest entrance of an underground weapons factory, accessible by a high-quality cement road? The small hill sloping up to it could house a tomb. The miniature bugging devices manufactured there suffice for all Eastern Europe.

The surrounding fields are uncultivated; grazing is prohibited. Through the strips of forest that line the road I catch glimpses of gray concrete buildings, guard towers, targets, bunkers, all ringed by a concrete fence covered with furls of barbed wire. Officers' housing is hidden behind a painted brick wall at the edge of the village. Children play ball behind barbed wire; husbands walk with their wives among the prefabricated apartment buildings; shaven-headed soldiers run back and forth along a beam three meters off the ground wearing full marching gear and carrying machine guns; little flags of indeterminate symbolism flutter atop the dusty hills; a jeep carrying two drums of milk pops out of nowhere.

Soviet troops—temporary guests in the country for thirty years now, athletic, pimpled kids smelling of sweat and foot cloths, staring through the fences of the garrisons where they were confined for months on end—wore the sad looks of sons separated from their mothers combined with a touch of arrogance. Guarding their armored vehicles and rocket launchers, they would gape with wild envy at the natives in colorful clothes walking and driving by. The only time they would be seen individually was on their way to the station for the Moscow express after their one-or two-year stint. Odd occupiers they were. Everything they had was beat up. Even the vehicles looked jerry-built.

A somber procession of trucks has been flowing past in an endless iron stream, each truck towing one out of commission, every second vehicle unusable. Only after two hours does it come to an end and we can go and buy our milk and bread.

I was always a bourgeois by nature and a dissident by compulsion. We inhabited a mad world in which the written word seemed to carry unfathomable weight, when in fact it did not. The most important structural component in the defunct political system was its thought, its texts, its curricula. That being the case, I sat down every morning to produce sentences that could pass for incitement against the state, and a good many people who deserved better dashed around spying to make sure a few warmed-over clichés did not see the light of day. My bag held neither bomb nor revolver; it held only a notebook. Just when I thought I was getting used to the situation, I ran into a young man who was being followed by three cars for having made copies of one of my studies. The cowboy-and-Indian games involved in publishing a few hundred copies of a dissident text unofficially kept both sides busy. No country house containing printer's ink and thinner escaped police surveillance.

Here at home I led a muffled existence. Living in Eastern Europe meant being constantly prepared for defeat and backwardness but also to question what it is to be human. There was no real dictator, only a long line of downtrodden individuals, each imagining that everyone in front of them was an informer and everyone behind them a reckless anarchist. But once informing has become common currency—and the informer the model citizen—what is left to inform about? Where is the truth whereby we can recognize the liar?

"Waiter! The bill, please! And would you be kind enough to tell me where I might find God?"

"I recommend the golden noodles with vanilla sauce, sir."

"In that case, could you tell me when things will improve?"

"Never."

In 1976 I received a fellowship from the DAAD, the German Academic Exchange Service, for a yearlong stay in West Berlin. My three-year travel ban having expired, I wrote a letter to Premier János Kádár requesting permission for a one-year stay abroad. Unusual as it was in those days, not only I but my wife and two children received a passport with the necessary stamp.

Given that Juli was a teacher of French and did not speak German, she decided to take the children to Paris. Nor had she any intention of returning: she had no wish to go on living in a police state. My feeling was that since I had started out as a Hungarian writer I might as well finish as one. This led to a divorce, my wife remaining in Paris with our children, who were entering their teens, and I returning home in 1979 after an extended, two-year stay in the West.

After walking Budapest for five days, I stopped being amazed that people were speaking Hungarian. My nose was no longer struck by the stench of unrefined gasoline. The dark gray buildings, the dusty shopwindows, the electrical wires sticking out near the staircases, the half-finished repairs in the courtyards, the pocks of bullets from the war and 1956—everything looked familiar again. I took down the things my mother had put up on the walls except for a photograph of my children. I bought the books that looked interesting, sat in each of my armchairs in turn, and spent time in apartments whose familiar decay did not surprise me. I took pleasure in the spreading boredom.

I tried to make out what had happened in my absence. A little more was permitted. The long-haired, self-styled avant-garde artists had had haircuts; the young women had learned to cook and were having babies. People who had longed to go abroad had come to grips with the idea of trying to be happy here at home. Young historians were proud to question the Party line about 1956 and surprised that it caused no great stir in the world. Political dissidents were becoming chief architects, theater directors, and editors-in-chief, buying better cars, taking trips abroad. There were jokes they could no longer laugh at.

I made a raw kind of peace with it all and with the somnolent passing of time and things. I shrugged my shoulders. "Everything's fine with me. You're all fine just as you are." The apartment was full of silence and nights that were not always easy.

If I switched on the light and looked around, I was amazed to see where I was. Persian rugs on the floor, a matching (if improvised) set of furniture that had seen better days, an Empire table with copper inlay that bore a tea saucer's marks, and the library, in disarray, with shelves reaching up to the ceiling. The cracks in the once white, now gray walls sketched the face of a camel, which I used to scan to establish where I was. I never had the room replastered. My wish was to leave behind as few traces of myself as I could and intervene as little as possible in the lives of those around me. In spite of everything, this was the only place where I could speak without making grammatical errors, where I did not need to be embarrassed every time I opened my mouth. I ran into my former boss. Until the authorities ordered him to fire me, he had been kind and called me into his office for chats, but once the political police said the word he had dismissed me on the spot. He had trouble extending his right hand after transferring the dog's leash to the left one. He too had had a stroke. All he remembered was what good friends we had been.

Looking around on the boulevard, I would think that everyone was a Communist, everyone I saw there—not just the Party members or the flag-wavers, everybody. Even people who hated the system, because they could not stop thinking about it. Not just the coachman, the horse too. Everyone who lived here. Including myself.

From my childhood until 1989 I lived with the consciousness that anyone who followed his own path had to reckon with the possibility of ending up between guard towers. By shaping his own life, the iconoclast made it more likely that others—and less likely that his own self-neglect—would kill him. The anxious desire to make life last as long as possible is a form of suicide.

Sitting at the marble gravestone table in Csobánka, I even remembered things that had not happened to me. But whatever you remember did in fact happen to you. Since the life of a mortal lasts no longer than the fall of a raindrop, I cling fast to anything inhabited by time.

Back from my Csobánka hermit's lair to my Buda apartment I receive a telephone call from a friend in telephone code: Had I heard the news? We meet at the Angelika Pastry Shop with its view of the eclectic neo-Gothic Parliament, where representatives approved every single motion submitted. (We recognized the lady and two gentlemen who came in the wake of the phone call for the pleasure of seeing and listening to us.) Had I heard, he asked, that Gábor Demszky had been openly followed for days on end, and when they stopped him for not using his directional signals they found the manuscript of my novel *The Loser*. They'd hauled him into the district police station, confiscated the documents, and taken minutes of the interrogation. Nine miniature bound copies of my novel were confiscated at the publisher's. *That* again?

In idyllic Csobánka one tended to forget where one was living.

In 1982 I entitled an essay I wrote there "Antipolitics," given that everything was political. A few years later a panting Demszky dashed up to my place with a heavy bag over his shoulder—fresh copies of *Antipolitics*. Written and published in secret, it argued that the time had come for a peaceful end to the Iron Curtain and the missile dialogue. The matter should be handed over to the Europeans. After the attempts at freedom in Budapest, Prague, and Warsaw had been quashed and avenged, Moscow and Berlin were next. Send home the Russian troops! Bring on the Russian tourists!

Europe, and particularly Central Europe, has Berlin to thank for so much. Think of the millions of lives lost, think of the decades wasted because of Berlin's arrogance. Had Berlin not instigated a war, there would be no Soviet troops in Budapest shoring up a system in which the publication of an uncensored book turned into a midnight secret, a conspiracy, a criminal act ("the preparation and circulation of materials containing incitement to action against the state") that could get you as much as eight years.

From the armchair I had a view of the top of the cliff, and by standing I could catch a glimpse of Jutka's dark head and long thighs. She was inspecting the fruit trees one by one, while studying a useful little book called *A Small Garden Is a Thing of Great Joy*. She was planning to plant dill, asparagus, bok choy, and eggplant. There would be flowerbeds, a lawn, and perhaps a child as well.

We are both Aries. Once I tossed out an offhand remark, and she answered with something brusque. I left in a huff, and she hurled mugs and spoons and unseemly curses at me from the balcony. She told me to wait, then ran down and tore my shirt to pieces. I went home in tatters. The phone rang. It was the voice of a frightened girl telling me to come back. I changed shirts and returned.

I see you twenty years ago, in a colorless woolen sweater, cotton stockings wearing thin at the heel, and the dark blue, baggy Chinese linen trousers fashionable in the subculture of the time. You are lying in the grass reading Goethe's memoirs when your head drops. A few minutes later, you lift it with a jerk. It is etched with the pattern of grass. You say you've had a good sleep because the book was so nice and boring.

Our daily lives melded, as did our memories. Silently we watched the shadows move. Most of our choices are in fact discoveries. Someone rings our doorbell and slips into our life, leaving the silk nightshirt bought at the flea market on our hook. If I wanted independence, why choose the dependency of family? Such was the question I asked myself before marrying for the third time. The following were my arguments against the move, which I put forth with ever weakening conviction: The man with a family is a prisoner: he can no longer assert he has nothing to lose. The married man is condemned to domesticity, the paterfamilias to simplemindedness. A wife is like the state: she is curious about everything you do and observes you in secret. Isn't it enough to have the state listening in? (True, I do not generally kiss the bugging device.)

The women I stayed with longest were the ones I most feared to upset. The less fear I felt, the sooner I beat a retreat, the sooner I chose another to step into my room without knocking. Mere whim drew me to some, but it was no whim that I was attracted to Jutka's voice, Jutka's touch, smell, movement, speech, and way of thinking, all from the very first night, or that the feeling has stayed with me for some twenty years.

Delicate, restrained, cautious, gently laughing, humming, and proffering considered judgments, Jutka came to West Berlin with me in 1982 for my next stay there, having been my partner in Budapest for three years by then. She proudly announced that she could understand the radio in German and had no trouble with French; English was a foregone conclusion. She loved golden leaves, rye bread with gorgonzola, and a Macon burgundy.

After our return everything was as before. Once, in 1987, the border guard checking my documents at the computer screen disappeared and brought out another guard, who found and confiscated the manuscripts of some talks I was planning to give. The Department of Education would return them to me should it see fit.

"But how can I lecture without them?"

"That's your problem."

"Well, that's the end of my talks," I said.

He liked that.

But it was all just an experiment, a ruse: the text had been smuggled out and the German translation was waiting for me in the West.

Looking out of a car window in Berlin, I see a peaceful, clean, and ordered city. Everything works. Not *almost* everything, *everything*. What you see in the shopwindows is what you see people wearing, which suggests that people change their possessions frequently and hence have no need to grow too fond of them. If I lived here, my wish would be to acquire means with a clean conscience. I would worry about spiritual frigidity, surround myself with prudent formalities, and carefully plan my time.

Back home there is a purple fog in the streets: the exhaust of east-bloc cars. That summer Jutka finished a book on death and funerals in Budapest at the beginning of the twentieth century. Her mood was far from funereal, however: she was more concerned with diapers.

I refuse to cling to situations and refuse to run from them. I have pure chance to thank for every turn in my life, including my three wives. One day I happened to catch a glimpse of Vera's hair in a classroom, though I had seen her a hundred times before. Juli plopped down on the arm of my chair at a happy gathering and stayed for sixteen years and two children. Jutka rang my doorbell one day in Paris—we were compatriots and lived on the same floor—and asked if I would like some coffee. The coffee never materialized, though a marriage and three children did. In the most traditional manner I have discovered the simplest purpose for life in my children and grandchildren, for whom I mean to stick around as long as possible.

Notes to myself: there is no point calling the attention of others to what I do not want or do not know. I have been shameless enough. No one wants to look at my bare chest anymore, so I'll wrap a scarf around my neck instead.

Nothing I come out with is of any use for anyone. It might have been once, but those days are gone. The day is approaching when I shall no longer set my glasses on the nightstand or say good night to my wife before withdrawing to my room. It won't be long now before my eyes are like two glazed chestnuts.

Every life is better than no life; every life, including the pain that goes with it, is good. True, getting through the daily grind is like wading through seaweed, but I can get through all sorts of things, therefore I am. And given the fact that I am alive, the question of why is as inane as fly droppings on a grape.

At twelve I survived National Socialism; at fifteen I saw Communism take over. Communism and I grew old together. Decades passed in active, disciplined resignation. Since I was fifty-six by the time the regime collapsed, I spent the best years of my life in the shadow of its stupidity. Still, I never watched my country from afar. I groped my way around in it.

Life was slow, which I did not regret, because there was so much of it. Humans are made mortal, hence real, by their imperfection; frailty and mortality are synonyms in the moral sense. Moral philosophy can rest only on frailty and our acceptance of it.

If every written description of human reality constitutes literature, then perhaps so does man himself. The novel's main character may be a welfare lawyer or city builder or retired revolutionary, but these are just naive masks, for there are no welfare lawyers or city builders or retired revolutionaries who ponder their lives with such profundity when lying in bed or sitting on the bench of a mental institution. Interior monologue does not occur in complete sentences.

All my life's more important choices have sprung from my decision as an adolescent to become a writer: I refrained from crossing the temporarily open border in 1956, chose jobs that required observation, became interested in people at the lower end of the social ladder (not that I was so high up myself, with my small salary, small apartment, and two or three changes of clothes), accompanying my former fellow student Tamás Csillag to the housing project at the Old Buda Brick Factory and spending the next seven years in Elizabeth Town as a supervisor of children's welfare. Then I grew curious about Hungary as a whole, the outlying cities and villages, and took a position with an institute of urban studies.

It is summer. How little the people of Budapest try to cover up their bodies, whether beautiful or ugly! I put it down to the city's sensuality and the survival of a pre-Christian, pagan lust for life. Budapest always goes whole hog: Stalinism, the Revolution, the compromises of the Kádár regime, you name it. It experiments with strategies of survival, grinding up the system to soften it, reviving old traditions—anything to curb the damage. Remember that Budapest was the first city in Eastern Europe to proclaim its freedom. The city is more enduring than the government; it has never let that pagan lust for life be taken over by ascetic delirium. There are plenty of upstanding cynics around here who do not think suffering is more moral than good cheer.

Even my internal emigration was basically a chance happening: one morning at dawn my doorbell rang, and in they came, picking apart my filing cabinet and dismissing me from all institutions. Then came the changes in 1989, and soon thereafter I had a phone call inviting me to be the president of International PEN. It was a serious offer, and it behooved me to accept it and do a good job.

Some authors love to play it tough; they are not satisfied until they have brushed with mortal danger and can recount it to their readers. I am not that type. I am of a more placid nature. But once in a while I run smack into fate's outstretched palm.

The good things always come on their own, the gifts of fate (or Providence, if you will), but the bad too come randomly, unexpectedly: there it is, and that's that. The ravages of fate are not something we can sense approaching or prevent. We make our way along a stairway of the gifts and accidents that constitute chapter divisions.

I do not like to be engulfed by the situation I happen to be in at a given time; I would rather look at it from the side or from above: I enjoy backing off and moving on. What is this compulsion, this current sweeping me on, this whistling wind, this gentle breath? The wish to slip the traps? To keep from being surrounded?

I was born in 1933. I was six when the Second World War broke out, eleven when survival meant the collaboration between fate and vigilance, particularly for Jewish children from the Hungarian provinces. When my parents were taken away in May 1944, my sister and I received an invitation to move to Budapest. Staying in Berettyóújfalu, waiting it out, would have been the normal thing to do. Had we done it, we would not be alive today. I owe my life to Budapest. It provided refuge for my sister and cousins and me; it kept us out of Auschwitz. All that mattered to me then about Budapest was its size: it let us be needles in a haystack. By May 1944 it was clear that people in the provinces would do nothing to stop the deportations, that they were following the dictates of a government that wanted to make all cities and towns *judenfrei*. The official culture around me has always been deceitful and, except for a few exceptional years, hostile to me. Although I had committed no crimes against it, I would eventually realize the time had come to start.

Every word puts the writer in a new situation. He is carried onward by the throat-tightening intoxication of improvisation. If a person's choices and actions count for anything, then this day, from the rising up unto the going down of the sun, is his constant pilgrimage. There is no line between everyday and holy acts.

The tactful pilgrim recognizes the possibility that dialogue with a saint is forever one-sided. He may spend his whole life speaking to someone who does not exist. Yet even if he never gets an answer, if the saint never reveals himself, he has no trouble addressing him, the eternal *here and now*.

On such secret, private pilgrimages we retrace the steps of a route long since traveled, reliving a past event, leaving the land of servitude and trudging the road of suffering to the cross. Our man brings the lamb, the most valuable offering of all: the son. He gladly offers his neck to the heavy blade. He appears before the godhead-in-hiding to offer It his life. So it is with books: a constant struggle with the angel fate has delivered us to; an eternal plodding, pinning down traces, making stations visible. The writer's path as pilgrimage? The parallel is perhaps justified by the pursuit of the unattainable: writing the book after which no other books need be written, after which there is only the bell, the flash, and loss of consciousness. They put all they've got into that last book, thinking about it during every waking moment, living with it, a lover full of promises, yet ultimately elusive.

I would have liked to write the kind of book I could have been called away from at any moment, one that could never be finished, only stopped. One more glass, one more pipe, and nothing for me to be ashamed of.

Who is observing me? Who is the all-seeing guardian of my fate? Why not just say someone. If He has created me, He can watch me. Our dream is a universe that is made for us and looks after us. If we weave God into a story, He turns out like a person who is ever at our disposal, even if He does occasionally go into hiding. Our Father is a good deal like us. If He is equally Lord of Life and Lord of Death, then he is both good and evil, as we are, and He simply mimics the game being played on earth, uniting the mind and blind happenstance.

I used to hold sin to be fatuous and shallow: the sinful are impatient and scatterbrained, panic-stricken and hysterical. Could they have but imagined the consequences they might never have sinned in the first place. Lately I have been inclined to think that hatred and cruelty are independent passions and can fill a life, be it stupid or intelligent. Even the most determined relativist can distinguish between a decent person and a scoundrel, especially if he is affected by the behavior of the party in question. Our sense of whether a person is good or evil works instinctively, the way we blink when something gets into our eye. I smile a lot. My father also had the gift of smiling. It stems from our simple natures. The smarter you are, the angrier you are. When asked whether I am happy, I respond: often. When asked whether I am ever unhappy, my answer is: rarely. Which goes to show how simple I am.

While I was studying in Berlin on a German fellowship in 1977, my mother was my main tie to Budapest. She was my only blood relative in Hungary. A terrible correspondent, I phoned her every week. I tried to keep her happy with gifts and alleviate her financial condition, and in the spring I invited her to Berlin for a month: a pair of warm boots is no substitute for a smile and long leisurely talks peppered with *édesanyám*—literally "my sweet mother"—which in its slightly antiquated Hungarian sounds perfectly natural, yet cannot be translated naturally into any other language.

When we part, I kiss her hand. The joints in her fingers have grown a little thicker, and she remarks with humorous regret that light brown spots have appeared on her skin. "Old age is ugly, my boy. Nothing nice about it." By way of consolation I tell her that even an old face can be beautiful if it reveals a good soul. I have refrained from asking myself whether my mother was beautiful. That she never was. But her eyes have an oriental kind of mystery that has grown brighter and more meditative with age.

My mother was happy about my being a writer. She would read reviews of my works in German, French, and English with a dictionary at her side, looking up every word she did not know. She would say a few words of praise, then begin to worry whether the work in question would be published in Budapest and get me into trouble. No need to write about absolutely everything, she said. "You can write something that is good and still not provoke *them*, my boy."

She would have been terribly gratified to see me on Budapest television and have her friends phone her the next day, to be congratulated by her old hairdresser or the young woman caretaker in the building or perhaps the neighbor with the friendly face, whose husband had been a prison guard known for his restrained behavior.

My mother was hardly surprised at my trouble with the state, as she herself had had less than pleasant experiences with the authorities. She felt her modest pension to be insufficient, but would have been perfectly satisfied with half again as much. At midday she ate a little soup with potatoes and an egg or two on the side. Listening to old man Kádár would put her to sleep. "You've had your say," she would tell him, switching off the television.

At six in the morning she would drink a cup of coffee in the kitchen, then go back to bed and read or listen to the radio until eight, then spend an hour exercising and bathing. She never went to a private doctor, not wishing to spend the money; the free clinic doctors suited her just fine. She was overjoyed to get a two-week, union-sponsored pass to a medicinal spa every year. On those occasions she shared a room with her old friend Marika. Marika never married and was a touch crotchety, but Mother was used to her eccentricities. They would have espressos in the café and watch television in the common lounge. They might also indulge in a jigger of brandy of an afternoon (though a bottle of cognac could last half a year in my mother's cabinet despite the fact that she offered it to guests).

I did not stay on in San Francisco in 1978, though I might have chosen to work for any number of causes: the American Indians, or the Catholics of Northern Ireland, or the gays of the Castro district, or tanning-room devotees protesting nuclear energy, or Australian Aborigines. I might have chosen South Korean CEOs, communards from the Pyrenees, instructors of bioenergetic analysis, Sufi gurus, levitating meditators, faith healers, or Jews for Jesus. I might have joined an African resistance movement, offered to help the developing world, or I might simply have stayed on, playing with films, holograms, videos, computers, visiting prisoners in jail, converting to homosexuality, or moving into the pink house where Janis Joplin committed suicide. But I didn't. I could have landed a teaching job in some provincial city, where at this moment I would be walking onto the main quad, past the bank to the café, where I would be ordering apple juice in a paper cup and looking out over the young men and women made angry and headstrong by trying to work their way upward. But I didn't do that either.

The books on my shelf are alive, entreating me to look at them, take them out of the darkness, follow them. Boxes fill and pile up behind me, my abandoned writings pursuing me. I delay opening them and restoring lost time. So many faded pictures, names now just barely familiar. But when the heavens are kind, a chink opens up and something comes out of nothing.

My work goes better in the village than in Budapest or Berlin, where I spend most of my time. Since I live my life in both kinds of place, however, the extremes of pro- or antiurban cultural philosophy are alien to me. In fact, the tension between the two is my domain: I enjoy moving back and forth between density and sparseness, between the natural and the artificial; I have no desire to drop anchor at either end.

I dash out of the house into the meadow. You cannot see this spot from the village. I stop and turn around. The vast emptiness is refreshing—the surrounding hills, the ruins of a castle sacked three hundred years ago, the solitude. There is no one here in the bright noon light. It is no effort at all for me simply to be.

The years have come and gone, and I am still here at the Academy of the Arts in Berlin, stressing the first syllable of German words in my Hungarian way. I give the Germans what advice I have and make my umpteenth introductory speech. I've been reelected president. There were no other candidates.

I support my family as best I can and do my best to stay out of their way. I recognize (and accept) the fact that my wife is boss of the hearth, and I do everything in my power to obey her. I try to provide warmth and encouragement to the family, knowing they will have troubles enough—anxieties, failures, loneliness, sadness, losses—the extent of which a parent can never know. I am content to start each day with the patter of footsteps around me.

I might just as well be a conscientious farm animal, giving regular milk and getting by on modest fodder. For the family I am not Mr. President; I am a simple smile at all the goings-on around the kitchen table. Who can tell how true to life my descriptions are? Even my mother is a product of the imagination when I write of her, as I am myself when I am my subject. Whatever is made of words is narrative, not reality.

In tonight's joint panel discussion of the Berlin Academy of Art and Academy of Science we are to delve into the question of whether science and art are not mere luxuries. Of course they are. Almost everything human is a luxury: morality, religion, conversation, recreation, love, mourning—luxuries all. As it is a luxury whenever a person does not steal or cheat or kill the weak or denounce his competitor with a real or trumped-up accusation. Only in barracks, prisons, and concentration camps are there no luxuries.

I have been informed that I shall not escape the final agony, that I shall not be resurrected, and that on the other side there will be nothing at all. In response to this I shall call for a white horse and, taking a deep breath, a white widow as well, and make cynically merry in the dark of night when the rest of the family is sleeping. I do not acknowledge my sinfulness and expect practically nothing of others.

The narrator prepares: he has taken his medicines, lifted his weights, kept himself alive. If he obediently follows the path of his pen on the paper, he can invent and vicariously experience situations with the aid of his imagination. Today is the novel, the eternal today. The best hours are those in which nothing can happen unless he is the cause. The narrator's freedom means life imprisonment. He even writes when no one encourages him to so do. What is he after? More days, more sentences, and the well-being of his dependents.

He is ignorant, helpless, and perplexed, with no choice but to look his decline in the face. Meanwhile his past, his fortune, has appreciated in value. Old photographs assure us we are the same people we were as children. Tell me a nice, boring story, my friend. We'll fill in the gaps, go round and round, repeat ourselves.

I have been a spy for the writing profession in all my roles: welfare officer, urban researcher, dissident. (The things we get ourselves into!) With the political changes in 1989 I turned oracle for a while, a role that required some reflection. Does this mean I strayed onto the path of sin by selling myself to the devil of worldly vanities?

I get up. There is a cramp in my leg. I stumble, hopping from the table to the armchair and back. I lie down and groan: standing was better. Images from a sleepless night, a night too long. The only remedy is to sit at the desk and do what I usually do.

Every sentence is an independent entity, a freestanding unit, a closed circle, as if internal cohesion were drawing together a fistful of magnesium buckshot. Picture a pile of fish roe or a clump of bees stuck together on a tree branch after you shake it. More than once I have felt like vanishing unnoticed like a drop of water falling from the spout.

A brook is babbling under the wooden bridge. A neighbor's hen has gone mad. It has rained a lot lately after a long drought. The grapes have begun to shrivel: the stalks have sucked them dry. We are sitting out on the terrace. The clouds are shedding tears, and moisture hangs in the air. Birds are chirping lazily, and the elders are blackening. A poplar begins to shimmer in the bloody disc of the sun, as if suffused with glass.

At the end of the dock I am struck by the suspicion that I have reached the very end of the end, that there is nowhere to go from here. As an adolescent I imagined one would have to sit at the end of the dock for hours before profound thoughts would come. Given that no such thoughts come to me now, I trudge up Saint George Hill to the sunlit garden stairway of the crumbling winepress house. There is hang glider floating above, and the heavenly figure speeding in my direction brings a sudden shade and wind.

The woman who lives next door stumbled on her way back from shopping. We helped her home and looked in on her a few times, but after lying down for a while she was back at it: shaping her pretzels, adding a coat of egg white and a sprinkle of grated cheese. I look forward to munching on them and drinking her vintage. I smell ducks roasting behind her: her grandchildren are coming tomorrow.

In the afternoon I go out to where there are people and movement. I stare in wonder at the goods in market stands, holding up a wine goblet, buying a whistle and a string of beads for my daughter Zsuzsi, a jackknife with a carved handle for my son Józsi, and for Áron, the boy poet who disdains possessions, several portions of shish kebab. Jutka buys some red basil for her herb garden.

We visit the artists' festival in the nearby village of Kapolcs. We see a wooden pig with gleaming eyes and a little screen in its mouth showing the slaughter—but in reverse order, from sausage to living animal—in copious detail. We hear its yelps and observe the details of its disembowelment projected large, as the eyes are removed and sliced and the blood stirred. We have the feeling we are eating one another, draining one another's blood into a bowl to make sausages or serve it, steaming fresh, over browned onions.

Then comes a Punch whacking at ghosts, but once he has whacked them aplenty and they have whacked him back, once all those *palacsinta* sticks have been put to good use, the rain, till then only a drizzle, starts coming down hard and the show is stopped. Drums and cymbals fill the street. The bus can't move. A slender girl takes her bows, the grotesque head on a wooden, collar-like apparatus on her shoulders bobbing up and down. A booted actor clacks his booted hands, then splits into a four-legged creature or, rather, two figures that have it out with each other, shaking blood- or flour-speckled skulls over their backs. The eye pops out of one of them like a tomato.

I became part of the cavalcade, standing there with an enormous green-and-white Dutch umbrella in my hand next to my sons as they bolt down one *palacsinta* after the other. The churches, sheds, and pubs all around are full of things to see.

The only sad note is Summer Santa pulling his sleigh, his cotton mustache drooping, melting off his face. He has lost his way and ended up in summer, inconsolable as he drags his empty sled over the gravel in search of a better world. Last year he was the Bad Boy of the Village, slapping the bottoms of the prettier women, tossing a bottle far away when he found he'd been given mineral water for his thirst, and sneezing gargantuan sneezes which fascinated Áron and Józsi. But he's on his good behavior this year: after a few words he moves on, downhearted, never giving up hope of finding a nice world full of snow for himself.

In a pub we find a tableau vivant and *cimbalom* music, outside—trucks with actors jumping and sneering and screeching and stomping something fierce, little children searching for their mothers, balls rolling off, drivers yawning, beer, wine, and *pálinka* flowing. A robust fellow stops the cars asking people to taste his beer, which he has brought in a fire truck.

My sons liked the Summer Santa best of all and then the four-legged, two-headed wonder. Zsuzsi liked both of them best.

It will soon be 2000. I am sorry to trade in all those nines—svelte, swollen heads—for the potbellied zeroes. With its large, backward-looking head, the nine seems so intelligent, while the three zeroes signify self-satisfied achievement.

The millennium is over. It's time to pay the bill. Here comes the waiter.

"I had a twentieth century," I tell him. He pauses. I don't see why. I've made it clear I intend to pay.

"What about the second millennium?" he asks.

"Must I pay for that as well?"

"Who else?"

"Fine. Add it to the bill."

But the waiter shakes his head sadly. "What about the first millennium?"

I am seized with fear. "How far back do you mean to go? You can't hold me responsible for everything, can you?"

"Who else?" he says, shaking his head again sadly.

This time I'm angry. "I want to see the owner, the Lord Himself!"

And what does God do? He appears on the balcony. In person. He points a finger at me. I get up from the table, look Him in the eye, and point my finger at Him. We stand there for quite some time. Host and guest, father and son.

"I shall call for your mother," He finally says.

"And I for your daughter," I finally say.

The women come. The children have not yet had dinner. We are told to wash our hands, take our seats, and stop our bickering. "Stubborn old asses. Still pointing fingers." We sit, nonplussed, the Old Man and I, waiting to be served.

After dinner the Old Man will not give up. "That bill of yours still wants paying." We are about settle on a price. I hold out my hand. The Old Man's hand rises. I wait for it to reach mine. Where does it stop? I do not know.

Where is home? Where I stand, inside a solar system. Where I sit, holding my pen tight. Here in the bed where I awake, where I set off for the bathroom, where I step out of the door and greet whomever I happen to meet.

Home is those few square kilometers where my paths come together. Home is the Jewish cemetery at Berettyóújfalu, unused for fifty years, my grandmother's tall gravestone and my grandfather's, just as tall, in black granite. (My great-grandfather's, in white marble, is less than half their height.) Home is in the classroom I wanted so desperately to escape as I stared at the bakery sign across the way. (My schoolmates were murdered and the school torn down.)

Where is home? Where they don't strike me dead. Where I know my children are safe. Where the individual and the word are held in high regard. Where being who I am and thinking what I think are granted the benefit of respect. Where there is a quiet kitchen nook for postprandial conversations over wine. Where the children play hide-and-seek and build bunkers. Where Jutka sits reading, feet up, in an armchair. Where I can stop for a glass of wine here and there on my way up the hill and, after the friendly invitations, prance my way down again.

Home is in the middle of the Elizabeth Bridge, where, coming home from my travels, I murmur, "How beautiful!" It is a house overgrown with woodbine, where I search for my key, climb panting to the third floor, a bag on each shoulder, and hear sounds within. Lively sounds. I have arrived.

JOHN MacARTHUR

THE FREEDOM

FOR

AND POWER

GIVE

OF FORGIVENESS

NESS

CROSSWAY BOOKS
WHEATON, ILLINOIS

Cover design: Josh Dennis

First printing, trade paper, 2009

Printed in the United States of America

Unless otherwise indicated, Scripture quotations in this book are taken from the *New American Standard Bible®*, copyright © 1960, 1962, 1963, 1968, 1971, 1972, 1973, 1975, 1977 by The Lockman Foundation and are used by permission.

Scripture quotations marked NIV are taken from *The Holy Bible: New International Version®*, copyright © 1973, 1978, 1984 by International Bible Society. Used by permission of Zondervan Publishing House. All rights reserved.

The "NIV" and "New International Version" trademarks are registered in the United States Patent and Trademark Office by International Bible Society. Use of either trademark requires the permission of International Bible Society.

Scripture quotations marked KJV are taken from the *King James Version.*

Scripture quotations marked NKJV are from *The New King James Version,* copyright © 1984 by Thomas Nelson, Inc. All rights reserved. Used by permission.

ISBN: 978-1-4335-1130-1
PDF ISBN: 978-1-4335-0956-8
Mobipocket ISBN: 978-1-4335-0957-5

Library of Congress Cataloging-in-Publication Data

MacArthur, John 1939-
    The freedom and power of forgiveness / John F. MacArthur.
      p.   cm.
    ISBN 13: 978-0-89107-979-8
    ISBN 10: 0-89107-979-3 (alk. paper)
    1. Forgiveness—Religious aspects—Christianity.   I. Title.
    BV4647.F55M33   1998
    234'.5—dc21   98-11274

LB		19	18	17	16	15	14	13	12	11	10	09
14	13	12	11	10	9	8	7	6	5	4	3	2

Contents

Introduction

Vengeance is popular today; forgiveness is not. Retaliation is often portrayed as a virtue reflecting healthy self-esteem. It is heralded as an inalienable right of personal freedom. Vengeance is evidence of macho strength.

Dirty Harry takes aim at the perp and, challenging him to flee, intones, "Go ahead. Make my day." That is the existential moment in which his persona is defined. He will achieve personal fulfillment if he can kill the miscreant.

Our society is drunk on the grapes of human wrath. Road-rage, disgruntled employee rampages, drive-by shootings, and other crimes of vengeance are the hallmarks of this generation. No wonder so many people are wracked with guilt, anger, depression, and other destructive emotions.

Early in my pastoral ministry I noticed an interesting fact: nearly all the personal problems that drive people to seek pastoral counsel are related in some way to the issue of forgiveness. The typical counselee's most troublesome problems would be significantly diminished (and in some cases solved completely) by a right understanding of what Scripture says about forgiveness.

People who come for counseling generally fit into one or both of two categories. There are some who need to understand how God's forgiveness is extended to sinners; and there are others who need to learn to be forgiving. In other words, some people are struggling with their own guilt; others have a sinful propensity to blame others and withhold forgiveness for wrongs done. (And many people struggle with both guilt and blame.)

Both tendencies are spiritually and emotionally debilitating. Both are capable of making life wretched. Both can spawn a multitude of related problems. And both can be remedied only by a better understanding of and obedience to what Scripture teaches about forgiveness.

I have often defended the notion that doctrine is inherently practical. What we believe determines how we think, how we behave, and how we respond to life's trials. Abstract beliefs never remain abstract; they inevitably manifest themselves in behavior. A right belief system therefore lies at the foundation of all truly righteous conduct.

Yet I frequently hear people complain that biblical exposition and doctrinal instruction are too impractical. Here is a topic that utterly refutes that notion, for there is no way to deal with either guilt or blame unless we comprehend what Scripture teaches about forgiveness. In other words, the most important practical aspects of Christian living ultimately hinge on the soundness of our doctrine on issues such as guilt, forgiveness, reconciliation, and all related topics.

This book examines forgiveness from the perspective of what Scripture teaches about the subject. My concern, as always, is sound doctrine. But my ultimate aim is to show the practical ramifications of this vital doctrine and to help you, the reader, learn to respond biblically to your own guilt, as well as to forgive others who have wronged you.

In the process, we will address a number of important questions about forgiveness and how it affects our personal lives:

- Can we be sure of God's forgiveness?
- If Christians are forgiven already, why do they need to confess sin in their daily lives?
- How are we supposed to confess our sins? Do we confess to other people, or to God alone?

• Does God ever withdraw His forgiveness from someone who has received it?

• Should the forgiveness we extend to others be *unconditional*?

• How do we reconcile Jesus' teaching on forgiveness with His instructions for carrying out discipline against people who willfully live in sin?

• If we are to forgive seventy times seven, as Jesus taught Peter, do we ever have cause for questioning the legitimacy of a repeat offender's repentance?

• Isn't God concerned about justice too? If I simply forgive those who have wronged me, where's the justice in that?

Forgiveness is not an easy subject, especially in a complex age such as ours. It has become fashionable these days to speak of "forgiving" oneself (often a dodge for those who refuse to deal rightly with guilt), while laying blame for *our* shortcomings at the feet of parents, government, or society as a whole. Can these modern ways of handling guilt and blame be reconciled with Jesus' teaching on forgiveness? I believe they cannot, and in this book we will explore together what Scripture has to say about the subject and see why God's principles of forgiveness are infinitely superior to all human ways of reckoning with guilt, blame, mercy, and justice.

Almost no concept is more important to the Christian faith than forgiveness. The Gospel itself is a message about God's forgiveness, and Christ's teaching was full of exhortations to His people to be forgiving to one another. He set an incredibly high standard, teaching us to forgive even the most stubborn offenders.

In fact, let's be honest: the standard at times seems impossibly high. How can we overcome our natural human inclinations and learn to forgive the way God demands of us? That is part of what we will explore in this book.

But, first of all, though, we must come to grips with what Scripture teaches about sin, guilt, and *God's* forgiveness. And when we do, we will actually be thankful that the standard Jesus set is so high—because it's based on the forgiveness God Himself extends to us. Our need of divine forgiveness is infinitely greater than any forgiveness we might ever be called upon to extend to our fellow sinners. The person who keeps this truth in view will never have a serious problem forgiving others.

God is the consummate forgiver. And we depend every day on His ongoing forgiveness for our sins. The least we can do is emulate His forgiveness in our dealings with one another.

Yet there is a natural, sinful tendency for all of us to minimize our own sins and magnify our blame of others—to treat ourselves with mercy and demand retribution against others. If we would only learn to be more repulsed by our own sin than we are at the wrongs others commit against us, we would be well on the road to spiritual health. On the one hand, we urgently need forgiveness. On the other, we desperately need to forgive.

These things were constant themes in the teaching of Christ during His earthly ministry. His parables, His preaching, and even the Lord's Prayer all emphasized the truth that those who are forgiven must also be forgiving. Some of His harshest sayings were spoken to people who were unwilling to forgive.

Already you might detect that forgiveness is not an altogether comfortable study to pursue. In fact, I soon realized while preparing the material for this book that there are fewer topics *more* convicting.

Yet in the big picture the message is positive and hopeful. Without God's forgiveness we would have no hope whatsoever. And when we learn to forgive others, a host of life's difficulties suddenly are settled. Forgiveness, we discover, is the starting point for resolving life's most troubling problems.

So I offer this book with the hope that it will be a remedy for many caught in the grip of modern humanity's spiritual and emotional malaise. If you are struggling to forgive, or are searching for forgiveness, this book is for you. If you are grappling with guilt, or angrily blaming others, this book is for you too. As we study the freedom and power of God's ultimate gift, my prayer is that your heart will be drawn closer to our God, who is always eager to forgive—and that you too will learn to be an eager forgiver.

ONE

The Ground of All Forgiveness

He made Him who knew no sin to be sin on our behalf,
so that we might become the righteousness of God in Him.

2 CORINTHIANS 5:21

Forgiveness. Nothing is more foreign to sinful human nature. And nothing is more characteristic of divine grace.

Fallen humanity finds God's forgiveness terribly hard to understand. As individual sinners, we all know firsthand what a struggle it can be to forgive others who have wronged us. Some people therefore find it impossible to envision Almighty God as anything other than stern and unforgiving. Others, knowing that Scripture teaches us God is merciful, imagine that He is so completely indulgent that no sinner really has anything to fear. Both misconceptions are fatally wrong concerning divine forgiveness.

Compounding that problem, our attitude toward forgiveness tends to vary, depending on which side of the equation we look at. When we are on the receiving end of mercy, we naturally esteem forgiveness as one of the highest of all virtues. But when we are the aggrieved party, forgiveness often seems a gross violation of justice!

And yet, all would no doubt recognize *both* justice and mercy as great virtues. Who among us does not desire to be forgiven when we know we have done wrong? And who does not despise injustice, particularly when we are the ones against whom a wrong has been committed?

So how do we reconcile these two great virtues, justice and mercy? More important, how can *God* reconcile them? If He hates injustice, how can He countenance the forgiveness of a transgressor? How can a perfectly holy God pardon sinners?

That's easy for God, you may be thinking. *After all, He can simply choose to forgive us and declare all our offenses null and void. He can just excuse the sinner and let sin go unpunished.*

But that is a deficient view of God and an unbiblical way of looking at forgiveness. God cannot and will not simply acquit transgressors by ignoring the evil they have done. To do so would be unjust, and God is a God of perfect justice.

Here we must be extremely careful to keep our thinking biblical. Some people tend to take the grace and forgiveness of God for granted, while ignoring His absolute righteousness. Others thunder a lot about the justice of God, while saying little about His grace. Both truths must be kept in balance if we are to understand what Scripture teaches about forgiveness.

FIRST, THE BAD NEWS

God does not forgive by simply looking the other way when we sin. The Bible repeatedly stresses that God will punish every sin. Galatians 6:7, for example, gives us this solemn warning: "Do not be deceived, God is not mocked; for whatever a man sows, this he will also reap." In Exodus 23:7 God says, "I will not acquit the guilty." Nahum 1:3 is unequivocal: "The LORD will by no means leave the guilty unpunished." In the gospel message itself, "God's wrath is revealed . . . against all ungodliness and unrighteousness" (Rom. 1:18).

Scripture describes the relationship between God and the sinner as enmity (Rom. 5:10; 8:7). God hates sin, and therefore all who sin have made themselves God's enemies. "God is angry with the wicked every day" (Psalm 7:11, KJV). He hates those who do iniquity (Psalm 5:5).

All sinners are in the same boat. Those who violate some minor point of God's law are as guilty as if they had broken every commandment (Jas. 2:10). And the real truth is that no one's sins are trivial (Rom. 3:10-18). All people are born with an insatiable penchant for sin (Ps. 58:3). They are spiritually dead (Eph. 2:1), reveling in their own sin, objects of God's holy anger (v. 3), and utterly without hope (v. 12). From the human perspective, this is a truly desperate state of absolute futility.

God, on the other hand, is perfect, infinitely holy, absolutely flawless, and thoroughly righteous. His justice must be satisfied by the punishment of every violation of His law. And the due penalty of our iniquity is infinitely severe: eternal damnation. Nothing we can offer God could possibly atone for our sin, because the price of sin is too high.

Fallen humanity's predicament is as bleak as it can be. Every person is a sinner, caught under the looming sword of God's judgment. By nature we are "children of wrath" (Eph. 2:3), utterly enslaved to our own sin (John 8:34). We have no innate ability to love God, to obey God, or to please Him by any means (Rom. 8:7-8).

The situation seems irreversible: we are accountable to a holy God whose justice must be satisfied, and yet we are guilty sinners, incapable of doing anything whatsoever to satisfy God's justice. Left to ourselves, we would all be doomed.

Any hope of the sinner's ever being justified by any means would seem to be out of the question. God Himself says it is an abomination to justify a sinner, equal to the sin of declaring an innocent person guilty: "He who justifies the wicked and he who condemns the righteous, both of them alike are an abomination to the LORD" (Prov. 17:15). "He who says to the wicked, 'You are righteous,' peoples will curse him, nations will abhor him" (Prov. 24:24).

Again and again, God Himself expressly forbids anyone to declare a sinful person righteous.

NOW, THE GOOD NEWS

But Scripture tells us that God *does* justify the ungodly (Rom. 4:5). He covers their transgressions (v. 7). He refuses to take their misdeeds into account (v. 8). He declares them righteous, completely forgiving their sins. Do you see why the Gospel is such good news?

How can God grant such forgiveness without compromising His own standard of justice? How can He justify sinners without rendering Himself unjust? How can He forgive sinners without breaking His own Word, having already sworn that He will punish every transgression?

The answer is: *God Himself has made His Son, Jesus Christ, the atonement for our sins.*

Multitudes of Christians would nod their heads knowingly at the sound of that statement. But comparatively few are actually well-equipped to articulate the doctrine of the Atonement clearly, or to defend it against the many attacks that the enemies of truth constantly lob its way.

So while it may seem like we're about to cover ground that is familiar to many readers, I would urge you not to skim this section or assume you have heard it all before. I hope, in the remainder of this chapter, to unfold the truth about Christ's substitutionary work in such a way that you will gain a fresh, new appreciation of the depth and significance of this most vital of all Christian doctrines.

This truth lies at the very heart of the gospel message. It is the most glorious truth in all of Scripture. It explains how God can remain just while justifying sinners (Romans 3:25-26). And it is the only hope for any sinner seeking forgiveness.

THE MINISTRY OF RECONCILIATION

Perhaps the most important single passage in all of Scripture about Christ's substitution on sinners' behalf is found in 2 Corinthians 5. Notice how the idea of forgiveness permeates the context. In fact, *reconciliation* is Paul's whole theme in this passage:

*God . . . reconciled us to Himself through Christ, and gave us the
ministry of reconciliation, namely, that God was in Christ reconciling the world to Himself, not counting their trespasses against them,
and He has committed to us the word of reconciliation. Therefore,
we are ambassadors for Christ, as though God were entreating
through us; we beg you on behalf of Christ, be reconciled to God.*

—2 COR. 5:18-20

Variations on the word *reconcile* are used five times in those few
verses. Paul mentions, for example, "the ministry of reconciliation"
(v. 18). That is his description of the evangelistic task. "The word of
reconciliation" (v. 19) refers to the gospel message. This is how he
characterizes the Gospel: it is a message of reconciliation. The duty
of every minister of the Gospel is to tell sinners how they can be reconciled to God.

Reconciliation to God presupposes complete forgiveness. So
our theme of forgiveness is very much at the heart of this passage.

The truth is glorious: God has a plan by which He can accomplish the very thing that seemed so completely impossible. There *is*
a way to satisfy His justice without damning the sinner. He can both
fulfill His promise of vengeance against sin and reconcile sinners.
He can remain just while justifying the ungodly (Rom. 3:26).
"Lovingkindness and truth have met together; righteousness and
peace have kissed each other" (Ps. 85:10).

THE AUTHOR OF RECONCILIATION

Notice that the sinner's reconciliation is both initiated and obtained
on the sinner's behalf wholly by God. The redeemed person con-
tributes nothing of any merit whatsoever to the process. Paul says
this clearly: "Now all these things are from God, who reconciled us
to Himself through Christ" (2 Cor. 5:18).

The relationship between God and the sinner is *never* restored
because the sinner decides to change his ways and make amends
with God. In the first place, no sinner ever would or could take such

a step toward God. Remember that the sinner is in total bondage to sin, morally unable to love or obey God; he is willfully at enmity with Him (Rom. 8:7-8).

Furthermore, as we have seen, no sinner could possibly do enough to satisfy the demands of God's perfect righteousness. Sinners who think they deserve God's favor only compound their sin with self-righteousness. Their baseless hope of earning divine merit is actually a further insult to the infinite holiness of God, whose only standard is an absolute perfection unattainable by fallen humanity.

Sinners have no way to quench God's righteous anger, no capacity to satisfy His holy justice, and no ability to meet His standard of absolute perfection. In other words, no sinner could ever atone for sin. Sinners have broken the law of God and are therefore banished eternally from His presence.

Self-reformation is out of the question. Even if sinners *could* reform themselves, they could never pay the price to atone for wrongs already done. "Turning over a new leaf" cannot nullify sin already on the record.

To make matters worse, a sinner's best efforts at good works are always tainted with sin and therefore cannot merit God's holy favor. "But we are all as an unclean thing, and all our righteousnesses are as filthy rags" (Isa. 64:6, KJV). John Bunyan, who saw this truth clearly, once said that the best prayer he ever prayed had enough sin in it to damn the whole world.

So it is ridiculous to think that a sinner might simply decide to be reconciled to God and therefore effect a reconciliation.

Why does this truth deserve so much stress? Because many people have the misguided notion that reconciliation is something the sinner is supposed to accomplish by deciding to stop rejecting God. Often you'll hear some well-meaning Christian attempt to evangelize non-Christians by suggesting that by a sheer act of the will, any sinner can end his or her rebellion against God and in doing so, effect a reconciliation. That is a deficient understanding of the Gospel, based on a deficient understanding of the seriousness of human depravity. To suppose that any sinner could or would choose to restore a right relationship with God is to grossly underestimate the bondage of sin and its power over the sinner's will.

Besides, the greatest impediment to our salvation is not even our hostility against God. It is *His* wrath against us. The reconciliation Paul describes in 2 Corinthians 5 is not accomplished because we decide to accept God, but because He decides to accept us.

Therefore, if any reconciliation is going to be accomplished, God Himself must be the author and finisher of it. Reconciliation with God can never be accomplished by a sinner's self-efforts, because all such efforts are themselves inherently sinful. That leaves the sinner with only one hope: if reconciliation is to be achieved, God Himself must be the initiator and author of it.

God is not at all a reluctant Savior. It was He who came seeking Adam and Eve after they fell (Gen. 3:9). It was He who sought His wayward people and pleaded with them to repent and receive His salvation. It was God weeping through the tears of Jeremiah for His sinful people (Jer. 13:15-17). It was God who was depicted in the story of Hosea going into the slave prostitute market and bringing His unfaithful, sin-stained wife back and treating her with love as if she were a chaste, virgin bride (Hos. 3:1-3).

By contract, the gods of the pagans were either hostile and demanded appeasement to withhold their murderous intent—or they were indifferent and needed to be awakened to the cries of their worshipers. God is neither hostile nor indifferent. He is by nature a Savior.

This is the good news about forgiveness—"namely, that God was in Christ reconciling the world to Himself, not counting their trespasses against them" (2 Cor. 5:19). There *is* a way for sinners to be reconciled to God. Through the atoning work of Christ, God Himself has accomplished what seemed impossible. The enmity can be removed, the sin forgiven, and the fellowship restored—by God Himself, not by the sinner. That is what the gospel message proclaims.

Romans 5:10-11 says, "While we were enemies, we were reconciled to God. . . . [We] exult in God through our Lord Jesus Christ, through whom we have now received the reconciliation." God provides that reconciliation. He accomplishes it. And we dare not think we can contribute one ounce of merit to the process.

Paul echoes the same theme in Colossians 1:21-22: "Although you were formerly alienated and hostile in mind, engaged in evil deeds, yet He has now reconciled you."

Wherever the language of reconciliation is found in the New Testament, the stress lies on *God's* working to bring it about. Nowhere is the sinner ever portrayed as the one who can accomplish reconciliation. Nowhere are sinners ever led to think that they can work their way back into God's favor. The opposite is true.

On the other hand, however, nowhere in Scripture is God ever depicted as reluctant to reconcile sinners to Himself. On the contrary, it is God Himself who lovingly initiates and effects reconciliation on behalf of the sinner—and He offers reconciliation to all who will believe.

When the apostle Paul pleaded with sinners, "We beg you on behalf of Christ, be reconciled to God" (2 Cor. 5:20), he was not suggesting they should seek to make amends with God, but was simply urging them to receive what *God* was offering *them*.

This is the distinctive of Christian forgiveness. Every man-made religion ever concocted teaches that there is something the sinner must do in order to appease God. Biblical Christianity alone teaches that God has supplied on the sinner's behalf all the merit that is necessary to please Him.

THE MEANS OF RECONCILIATION

Here, then, are the basic truths underlying the Christian doctrine of forgiveness: God is the one who must accomplish forgiveness of sins; it is not possible for the sinner to earn his way back into God's favor. And if God is going to show mercy to sinners, He cannot do so in a way that violates His perfect justice. He has sworn to punish the guilty, and that oath must be fulfilled; otherwise, justice is not satisfied. So, until God's wrath against the guilty is fully meted out, forgiveness remains an impossible violation of divine righteousness, and no one can be reconciled to God.

The wrath of God against sin therefore poses the biggest obstacle of all to any sinner's forgiveness.

Do you find that truth shocking? Many modern readers will. Too many people think of divine grace as a sort of benign forbearance, by which God simply excuses sin and looks the other way— as if grace involved a lowering of the divine standard in order to accommodate what is unholy. Scripture teaches no such thing. Again, God Himself has sworn that every transgression and disobedience will receive a just penalty (cf. Heb. 2:2), and He cannot relinquish His perfection in order to indulge the wicked. To do so would compromise His own righteousness.

So how does God reconcile sinners to Himself? On what grounds can He extend forgiveness to sinners? Here we are brought face to face with the need for atonement. If God's wrath is to be satisfied, if God is going to be *propitiated* to the sinner, a suitable atonement is required. God must fulfill the demands of justice by pouring out His wrath on a substitute. Someone must bear the sinner's punishment vicariously.

And that is precisely what happened at the cross.

The apostle Paul distills the whole Gospel in one simple statement in 2 Corinthians 5:21: "He made Him who knew no sin to be sin on our behalf, so that we might become the righteousness of God in Him."

You may read that and think, *What does that have to do with forgiveness?*

The answer is, everything. While on the face of it this may seem a hard verse to understand, it sets forth the ground of all forgiveness. The truth the apostle Paul means to convey here is the whole basis for how God redeems sinners. I doubt there is a more important verse anywhere in Scripture for understanding the Gospel.

This profound truth is the key to understanding divine forgiveness: God made the sinless Christ to be sin on our behalf, so that we might become in Him the very righteousness of God. Let's carefully dissect this crucial verse of Scripture.

Substitution

First, it speaks of substitution. It means that Christ died *our* death. He bore the punishment for *our* sin. He Himself suffered the wrath of God that we deserved. God "made Him who knew no sin to be sin on our behalf, so that we might become the righteousness of God in Him."

In simple language, the apostle Paul's point is this: God treated Christ like a sinner and punished Him for all the sins of all who would believe, so that He could treat them as righteous and give them credit for Christ's perfect obedience.

Think about the profound implications of this truth: Christ's death was a payment for the sins of those who would believe. He substituted for them before the bar of judgment. He bore their guilt and suffered punishment in their place. And the true nature of the suffering He sustained was infinitely more than the humiliation and nails and flogging that accompanied His crucifixion. He received the full weight of God's wrath against sin.

In other words, as Christ hung on the cross bearing others' sins, God the Father poured out on His own sinless Son every ounce of divine fury against sin. That explains Christ's cry at the ninth hour, "'Eloi, Eloi, lama sabachthani?' which is translated, 'My God, My God, why hast Thou forsaken Me?'" (Mark 15:34). There's a very real sense in which God the Father *did* forsake the Son—judicially. As Christ hung there, God was discharging against His own Son the unrestrained fullness of His fierce wrath and displeasure against our sin!

When we think about this, it is a shocking doctrine. God the Father heaped punishment on His own Son for guilt that rightfully belonged to others! Yet, astonishing as it is, this is the clear teaching of Scripture. The apostle Peter wrote, "He Himself bore our sins in His body on the cross, that we might die to sin and live to righteousness" (1 Pet. 2:24). Isaiah 53, picturing the sufferings of Christ in prophetic language, says:

> *Surely our griefs He Himself bore, and our sorrows He carried; yet we ourselves esteemed Him stricken, smitten of God, and afflicted. But He was pierced through* for our transgressions, *He was crushed for* our *iniquities; the chastening for* our *well-being fell upon Him, and* by His scourging we are healed . . . the Lord has caused the iniquity of us all to fall on Him.*
> — ISA. 53:4-6, *emphasis added*

Isaiah goes on to add this staggering statement: "The Lord was pleased to crush Him, putting Him to grief. . . . He would render Himself as a guilt offering" (v. 10).

The death of Christ "*pleased*" God? That is exactly what Scripture teaches. Repeatedly the Bible says Christ died as a "propitiation" for our sins (Rom. 3:25; Heb. 2:17; 1 John 2:2; 4:10). The word *propitiation* speaks of an appeasement, a total satisfaction of the divine demands on behalf of the sinner. This is a marvelous truth. It means Christ paid the full price—the ransom—for sin on behalf of those He redeemed.

People often misunderstand what this ransom involved. "The Son of man came . . . to give His life a ransom for many" (Mark 10:45; cf. 1 Tim. 2:6). But contrary to what many think, the "ransom" spoken of in such passages is not a payoff to Satan. Satan is in no position to demand a payment for the redemption of souls. (See Appendix 1 for further discussion of this.)

Instead, the "ransom" paid is an atonement rendered to satisfy the justice of God. Christ ransomed His people by paying on their behalf the penalty for their sin that was demanded by divine righteousness. The price of redemption was the full wrath of God against an innocent, perfectly righteous victim! That, and that alone, could atone for the guilt of sinners.

Many find this doctrine distasteful. Liberal theologians often protest that this notion of atonement makes God seem harsh and unsophisticated. They deny that God demands any payment—particularly a blood sacrifice—in order to be propitiated toward sinners. God, they protest, has no need to "get even" with the sinner for sin or to demand a payment of any kind. They claim divine goodwill is a sufficient basis for the forgiveness of sinners. If God wants to forgive sin, they say, He can do so freely.

But to hold such a view is to relinquish God's justice for the sake of His benevolence. It makes God's forgiveness cheap, and perfect righteousness expendable. Far from exalting God, the liberal view demeans Him by compromising His righteousness.

Scripture plainly teaches that only a blood sacrifice can atone for sin and appease the wrath of God against the sinner. God told Old Testament Israel, "The life of the flesh is in the blood: and I have given it to you upon the altar to make an atonement for your souls: for it is the blood that maketh an atonement for the soul" (Lev. 17:11, KJV). Hebrews 9:22 states it succinctly: "Without shedding of blood there is no forgiveness."

So atonement by shedding of blood is absolutely essential to the forgiveness of sins. Forgiveness is impossible without a satisfactory, substitutionary sacrifice. Scripture teaches this plainly. The wrath and justice of God must not be downplayed in our understanding of His forgiveness.

Another grave misunderstanding about Christ's sacrifice on the cross is fast gaining new popularity these days. Known as the "governmental theory of the Atonement" (or sometimes "moral government theology"), this teaching suggests that Christ's death was proof of God's wrath against evil, a graphic demonstration of God's displeasure over sin—but not a literal payment for sins. Those who advocate this view deny that our guilt was actually transferred to Christ, and they also deny that His righteousness can be imputed to sinners.

Moral government theologians often sound evangelical. They speak and write a lot about "revival." (In fact, a site on the World Wide Web touting this kind of theology is called "Revival Theology Resources.") They quote writers whose names are familiar to evangelicals, such as Charles Finney and Albert Barnes. Occasionally they will insist that they believe in a *kind* of substitutionary atonement. But the distinctive of their theology is their insistence that neither guilt nor righteousness can be transferred from one person to another. So they have ruled out the only kind of substitution that ultimately matters for the biblical doctrine of justification.

That is why the "governmental" view of the Atonement is actually a serious compromise of the central truth of the Gospel. It amounts to a denial that Christ's death on the cross was payment for *anyone's* sins. In effect, it leaves sinners with no atonement at all and suggests that in order to gain justification they must amend their own lives, rid themselves of their own sin, and cleanse themselves from further defilement by sustaining a life of obedience. Since Scripture clearly teaches that such self-reformation is impossible (Jer. 13:23), this view of the Atonement in effect nullifies the biblical promise of salvation. (See Appendix 1: "How Are We to Understand the Atonement?")

But as noted earlier, all the self-reformation in the world cannot atone for past sins, nor can it provide the perfect righteousness necessary to please God. The whole error of apostate Israel consisted in thinking they could establish a righteousness of their own, apart from the righteousness God provides on believers' behalf: "Not knowing about God's righteousness, and seeking to establish their own, they did not subject themselves to the righteousness of God" (Rom. 10:3).

The clear teaching of the Bible, from beginning to end, is that sinners cannot atone for their own sins in any way. A perfect sacrifice was therefore needed to atone for sin on their behalf. This involved shedding the blood of an innocent substitute (this means death, not merely bloodletting). And the substitute must bear on the sinner's behalf the full punishment for guilt, not merely a token penalty (cf. Isa. 53:5). Only such a perfect sacrifice could satisfy the demands of God's justice and thus propitiate Him toward sinners. That is exactly what Scripture says Christ's sacrifice provided:

God set [Christ] forth as a propitiation by His blood, through faith,
to demonstrate His righteousness, because in His forbearance God
had passed over the sins that were previously committed, to demon-
strate at the present time His righteousness, that He might be just and
the justifier of the one who has faith in Jesus.

— ROM. 3:25-26, NKJV

We unequivocally reject the liberal notion that this doctrine of vicarious atonement places God in the same category as ancient heathen gods who supposedly demanded blood sacrifices in order to be mollified. The atoning work of Christ has nothing whatsoever in common with pagan notions about propitiation and offended deities. The God of Scripture is not at all like the gods of ancient Canaan, or even the more sophisticated gods of Greek mythology. He is not temperamental and irritable, requiring some sacrificial inducement in order to placate a fiery temper. We're not to think of God's wrath as equivalent to a bad mood. His righteous hatred of sin is a fixed and holy disposition, not a volatile temperament. His demand that sin be atoned for is an essential matter of divine righteousness, not a fatuous need for vengeance.

Nor should anyone imagine that Christ's sacrifice was necessary to overcome some reluctance on the Father's part to save sinners. God is inherently loving and eager to save, taking no pleasure in the death of any sinner (Ezek. 33:11).

Still, it is the clear teaching of Scripture that, as a simple matter of divine justice, the only acceptable atonement for sin was a blood sacrifice, a suffering substitute who would bear the full wrath of God on the sinner's behalf. Since it had to be one who "knew no sin," Christ is the *only* worthy substitute, and His dying on the cross rendered the atonement that was necessary to provide forgiveness for sinners.

This doctrine of substitutionary atonement is therefore the whole ground of God's forgiveness. Apart from Christ's atoning work, no sinner would ever have any hope of salvation.

The entire foundation of the sinner's reconciliation to God is the reality that Christ died bearing the guilt of our sin. He died in our place and as our substitute. He took our punishment and freed God to impute righteousness to us.

Imputation

The notion of imputation is important in explaining 2 Corinthians 5:21. *Imputation* speaks of a legal reckoning. To impute guilt to someone is to assign guilt to that person's account. Likewise, to impute righteousness is to reckon the person righteous. The guilt or righteousness thus imputed is a wholly objective reality; it exists totally apart from the person to whom it is imputed. In other words, a person to whom guilt is imputed is not thereby actually made guilty in the real sense. But he is accounted as guilty in a legal sense. It is a reckoning, not an actual remaking of the person's character.

The guilt of sinners was imputed to Christ. He was not in any sense actually tainted with guilt. He was merely reckoned as guilty before the court of heaven, and the penalty of all that guilt was executed against Him. Sin was imputed, not imparted, to Him.

This is a remarkable statement: "[God] made Him who knew no sin *to be sin* on our behalf." It cannot mean that Christ *became* a sinner. It cannot mean that He committed any sin, that His character was defiled, or that He bore our sin in any sense other than by legal imputation.

Christ had no capacity to sin. He was impeccable. This same verse even says, "[He] knew no sin." He was spotless. He had to be spotless in order to serve as the perfect substitute. He was holy, harmless, undefiled—separate from sinners (Heb. 7:26). He was without sin (Heb.4:15). If sin had besmirched His character in any sense—if He had become an actual sinner—He would have then been worthy of sin's penalty Himself and thus unqualified to render payment for the sins of others. The perfect Lamb of God could not be other than spotless. So the phrase "[God] made Him .. to be sin" *cannot* mean that Christ was tainted with actual sin.

What it means is simply that the guilt from *our* sins was imputed to Him, reckoned to His account. Many Scriptures teach this concept: "He was pierced through for our transgressions, He was crushed for our iniquities" (Isa. 53:5). "He Himself bore our sins in His body on the cross" (1 Pet. 2:24). He bore "the sins of many" (Heb. 9:28).

So in 2 Corinthians 5:21, Paul's simple meaning is that God treated Christ as if He were a sinner. He imputed our guilt to Him and exacted from Him the full penalty for sin—even though Christ Himself knew no sin.

The guilt He bore was not His guilt, but He bore it as if it were His own. God put *our* guilt to Christ's account and made Him pay the penalty for it. All the guilt of all the sins of all who would ever be saved was imputed to Jesus Christ—reckoned to His account as if He were guilty of all of it. Then God poured out the full fury of all His wrath against all of that sin, and Jesus experienced it all. That's what this verse means when it says God made Christ to be sin for us.

Justification

This verse also contains the answer to that troubling question of how sinners can be justified. In the same way that the guilt of sinners was imputed to Christ, His righteousness is imputed to all who believe.

Scripture repeatedly teaches that the righteousness by which sinners are redeemed—the whole ground on which they are made acceptable to God—is a righteousness that is *imputed* to them. As early as Genesis 15:6 we read that Abraham "believed in the LORD; and He reckoned it to him as righteousness." Romans 4 uses Abraham's justification as the model for how all believers are justified.

So the notion of imputation is crucial to understanding how sinners can be reconciled to God. Christ was "made . . . to be sin" because our guilt was imputed to Him. We become righteous by the imputation of His righteousness to us. It is that simple.

Note the important implications of this: Christ, dying on the cross, did not actually *become evil* in order to bear our guilt. By the same token, we do not actually have to *become perfect* in order to be credited with His perfect righteousness. How is the righteousness of justification obtained? Only by imputation. Just as God put our sin to Christ's credit, He puts Christ's righteousness to our credit.

That means our forgiveness is not dependent on some prior moral reform on our part. Every believer is forgiven immediately, just like the thief on the cross. No works of penance are necessary, no meritorious rituals. Forgiveness costs us nothing, because it already cost Christ everything.

The union with Christ that accompanies every sinner's true conversion will inevitably result in a changed life (2 Cor. 5:17). Every true Christian is being conformed to the image of Christ (Rom. 8:29-30). But that life-change in no sense merits divine forgiveness. Forgiveness is fully ours before the first evidences of Christlikeness are even visible, because Christ's atoning work has already paid the price of our sin in full, and at the same time provided us with a garment of perfect righteousness that is the birthright of every believer.

When God looks at the Christian—even the most godly, most consistent Christian you can imagine—He does not accept that person on the virtue of the Christian's own good life. He considers that person as righteous solely by virtue of the imputed righteousness of Christ. That is the whole point of 2 Corinthians 5:21. That is what Scripture means when it says God "justifies the ungodly" (Rom. 4:5). And that is the very heart of the gospel message.

Christ's perfect righteousness is infinitely superior to any righteousness that we might devise on our own. That's why the apostle Paul, discarding years of fastidious pharisaical obedience to the law, said it was now his great hope to "be found in Him, not having a righteousness of my own derived from the Law, but that which is through faith in Christ, the righteousness which comes from God on the basis of faith" (Phil. 3:9). Paul said that the highest kind of righteousness it is possible to obtain for oneself is like "dung" (v. 7) compared to the righteousness of Christ that is imputed to believers.

The believer is clothed with the righteousness of Jesus Christ. The perfection of that righteousness is what defines every believer's standing before God. It is why all Christians are given such a high position of privilege (seated with Christ in the heavenlies, according to Ephesians 2:6). It is why Scripture says that "there is therefore now no condemnation for those who are in Christ Jesus" (Rom. 8:1). Their sins are already eternally forgiven, and as believers they are covered with the perfect righteousness of Christ.

How does one obtain this forgiveness? By believing. In Romans 4 Paul's whole point is that sinners are justified only through an imputed righteousness, and that imputation occurs only through faith:

> *What then shall we say that Abraham, our forefather according to the flesh, has found? For if Abraham was justified by works, he has something to boast about, but not before God. For what does the Scripture say? "And Abraham believed God, and it was credited to him as righteousness." Now to the one who works, his wage is not credited as a favor but as what is due. But to the one who does not work, but believes in Him who justifies the ungodly, his faith is credited as righteousness.*
>
> — vv. 1-5

Faith is the *only* prerequisite to this justification. No work can earn it. No ritual can be the instrument by which it is obtained. In fact, Paul goes on to point out in verse 10 that Abraham was justified *before* he was circumcised (cf. Gen. 15:6 with Gen. 17:10). So circumcision, as important as it was in the covenant God made with Abraham, *cannot* be a requirement for justification or a means to it.

If God justifies the ungodly solely through faith (Rom. 4:5), of what does this faith consist?

It is a refusal to trust anything *but* Christ for salvation. It means the abandonment of self-righteousness and a single-minded reliance on Christ alone for salvation. It therefore involves a sincere love for Christ and hatred for all that displeases Him.

He offers forgiveness and eternal life freely to all who will come to Him. "The Spirit and the bride say, 'Come.' And let the one who hears say, 'Come.' And let the one who is thirsty come; let the one who wishes take the water of life without cost" (Rev. 22:17).

Dear reader, if you understand that you are a sinner and long for freedom and forgiveness from your sin, turn to Christ even now. He will not cast out any who come to Him (John 6:37). He is eager to forgive and reconcile sinners to Himself. All else that we have to say about forgiveness is moot if you do not know the forgiveness of God for your sins. You need read no further if this issue remains unsettled between you and God. "As though God were entreating through us; we beg you on behalf of Christ, be reconciled to God" (2 Cor. 5:20).

JUSTICE AND FORGIVENESS RECONCILED

In Christ, God's justice and His mercy are reconciled. "Lovingkindness and truth have met together; righteousness and peace have kissed each other" (Ps. 85:10). These two seemingly irreconcilable attributes of God have been reconciled.

God has reconciled sinners to Himself. I hope you can begin to appreciate the wonder of this reality. All Christians are forgiven an unpayable debt, not because we deserve it, not as a reward for doing penance by which we somehow pay for our own sins, but solely on the basis of what God Himself has done for us.

That inestimable gift of free forgiveness becomes the ground on which all other kinds of forgiveness are based, and also the pattern for how we are to forgive others. As we probe more deeply into this subject of forgiveness, please keep in mind all that God has done in order to provide forgiveness for us. If we keep in perspective how much God forgave, and how much it cost Him to forgive, we will soon realize that no transgression against us can ever justify an unforgiving spirit. Christians who hold grudges or refuse to forgive others have lost sight of what their own forgiveness involved.

God's forgiveness is the pattern by which we are to forgive, and the best model of that is Christ Himself. In the chapter that follows, we will examine what may be the most graphic example of divine forgiveness anywhere in Scripture.

TWO

Christ's
Dying Prayer

They crucified Him. . . . But Jesus was saying,
"Father, forgive them; for they do not know what they are doing."

LUKE 23:33-34

If anyone ever had good reason not to forgive, it was the Lord Jesus. He was the ultimate and only true victim—totally innocent of any wrongdoing. He never wronged another individual, never spoke a lie, never committed an unkind or unloving act, never broke the law of God, never had an impure thought. He never yielded to any evil temptation whatsoever.

Scripture says, "[He] committed no sin, nor was any deceit found in his mouth" (1 Pet. 2:22). He "has been tempted in all things as we are, yet without sin" (Heb. 4:15). He is "holy, innocent, undefiled, separated from sinners" (Heb. 7:26).

No one was *less* worthy of death than He. Even the evil Roman governor Pontius Pilate testified repeatedly, "I find no guilt in this man" (Luke 23:4; cf. Mark 15:14; John 19:4, 6).

And yet Pilate, conspiring with other evil men, using false and trumped-up charges, condemned Christ to death and killed Him in the most brutal manner imaginable. Throngs of people were whipped into a frenzy of hatred, demanding His death unjustly (Mark 15:11-14).

Through it all, Christ was led as a lamb to the slaughter (Isa. 53:7). Submitting to the indignity and injustice, He surrendered His life without resistance, without threat, and without retaliation. In fact, all that suffering and injustice was for the express purpose of making Him an atoning sacrifice for the sins of the very ones who put Him to death!

Forgiveness was what filled his heart, not condemnation or revenge. He had said, "The Son of Man did not come to destroy men's lives, but to save them" (Luke 9:56, margin). "For God sent not his Son into the world to condemn the world; but that the world through him might be saved" (John 3:17, KJV).

You might think, *It was one thing for Christ to be so forgiving. He knew it was in God's plan for Him to die. He had a mission to fulfill, and it involved His death. He understood all that from the beginning. Surely God does not expect me to suffer such wrongs so easily!*

But the manner of Christ's dying is explicitly set forth as an example for every Christian to follow:

> *Christ also suffered for you, leaving you an example for you to fol-low in His steps, who committed no sin, nor was any deceit found in His mouth; and while being reviled, He did not revile in return; while suffering, He uttered no threats, but kept entrusting Himself to Him who judges righteously.*
>
> — 1 PET. 2:21-23

TURN THE OTHER CHEEK

The principle of forgiveness was a feature of Christ's teaching from the beginning. The Sermon on the Mount includes a whole section instructing the disciples to suffer patiently when wronged: "You have heard that it was said, 'An eye for an eye, and a tooth for a tooth.' But I say to you, do not resist him who is evil; but whoever slaps you on your right cheek, turn to him the other also" (Matt. 5:38-39). Many people misunderstand the intent of that passage, so it is worth a closer look.

First, it is important to understand that Christ was not teaching universal pacifism. Some have suggested that this section of the Sermon on the Mount rules out the use of force or violence in every situation. However, that cannot be, because Romans 13:4 expressly assigns civil authorities the right and duty to "bear the sword"—meaning to use force, including deadly force when necessary—in the capacity of "an avenger who brings wrath upon the one who practices evil." So a policeman who kills a criminal in order to stop the commission of a crime, or an executioner who kills someone judged guilty of a capital offense, is acting with an explicit mandate from God.

Second, the passage does not rule out self-defense in wantonly criminal attacks. Jesus is teaching how we should respond to insults and affronts against our personal dignity (vv. 39-42), not criminal threats to life and limb. Furthermore, this passage certainly does not suggest that a husband should refuse to defend his wife, or that a father should decline to protect his children. Those who see in this passage that kind of radical pacifism have twisted Jesus' intent.

Third, Christ was not nullifying any principle of Old Testament law. He was correcting an *abuse* of the law found in rabbinical tradition. The eye-for-an-eye principle was given by divine inspiration to Moses, and therefore it could not have been an evil principle: "If a man injures his neighbor, just as he has done, so it shall be done to him: fracture for fracture, eye for eye, tooth for tooth; just as he has injured a man, so it shall be inflicted on him" (Lev. 24:19-20; cf. Exod. 21:24; Deut. 19:21).

We know that Christ was not declaring this law null and void, because He himself stated in Matthew 5:17-18, "Do not think that I came to abolish the Law or the Prophets; I did not come to abolish, but to fulfill. For truly I say to you, until heaven and earth pass away, not the smallest letter or stroke shall pass away from the Law, until all is accomplished." So there is no possibility that Christ meant to alter or amend the moral standard of the Old Testament law.

What did He mean then? If verse 39 doesn't actually rescind the eye-for-an-eye law and replace it with a kinder, gentler principle, what is the point of this passage?

Here's the issue: the eye-for-an-eye principle was given to govern matters of civil justice. It was a guideline for judges meting out punishment for civil infractions, to insure that the punishment fit the crime. It was a merciful principle, limiting the punishment according to the gravity of the offense. And in all cases where the eye-for-an-eye principle applied, *judges* were to find the offender guilty and assess the penalty, not the injured individual (Exod. 21:22-24; cf. Deut. 19:18-21). Nowhere did the Old Testament ever permit an individual to take the law into his own hands and apply it against those who had wronged him personally.

Unfortunately, rabbinical tradition obscured the necessary distinction between matters of civil justice and petty personal wrongs. The rabbis had misapplied the eye-for-an-eye principle, employing it to argue that individuals are justified in seeking personal revenge for all wrongs done against them.

Jesus was simply correcting that misconception. He was also making some necessary distinctions between public and personal offenses, between profound and petty ones. A slap on the cheek is no real injury. Let the one who wishes to follow Christ simply turn the other cheek. But if the victim deems the assault a criminal offense, let him go through the proper procedures of civil law and allow *others* to determine guilt and assess penalties. No one has a right of personal retaliation. To do so is to make oneself judge, jury, and executioner. That violates the spirit of everything the law teaches about civil and personal justice.

So Jesus' instructions about turning the other cheek establish two categories of offense: one petty and personal, the other profound or public. In the latter case, someone besides the victim must determine guilt and assess the penalty. In the former case, the injured party wishing to glorify God should simply suffer the wrong patiently.

DO NOT RESIST HIM WHO IS EVIL

Jesus' words in Matthew 5:39 sum up the principle that applies to petty personal offenses: "Do not resist him who is evil; but whoever slaps you on your right cheek, turn to him the other also."

That verse has been badly misapplied over the years. One cult in the 1970s was famous for applying the *King James* translation of that verse ("resist not evil") in the most extreme fashion, going so far as to worship Satan alongside Christ!

Obviously, Christ was not teaching that evil agents should simply be allowed to have their way in all circumstances. Jesus Himself opposed evildoers constantly, through both His teaching and His actions. On two occasions He even made a whip of cords and drove out those who were profaning His Father's house (Matt. 21:12; John 2:15).

Elsewhere, Scripture instructs us to resist the devil (Jas. 4:7; 1 Pet. 5:9). We are to oppose false teachers by refuting their lies (Titus 1:9). We are to resist evil in the church by excommunicating evildoers (1 Cor. 5:13; see chapter 7 for a fuller discussion of church discipline). Paul even taught that church leaders who continue in sin should be rebuked "in the presence of all, so that the rest also may be fearful of sinning" (1 Tim. 5:20).

It is equally clear, for reasons already mentioned, that the principle of nonresistance and the turn-the-other-cheek rule cannot be meant to keep civil government from punishing evildoers. To apply these principles in the civil arena would be to surrender society to chaos. Civil government is ordained by God precisely "for the punishment of evildoers and the praise of those who do right" (1 Pet. 2:13-14; cf. Rom. 13:4). Justice obligates us both to uphold the law and to insist that others do so as well. Reporting crime is both a civic responsibility and an act of compassion. To excuse or help cover up the wrongdoing of others is an act of wicked complicity with evil. To fail to protect the innocent is itself a serious evil (Jer. 5:28-29).

So there's absolutely no room in Scripture for the notion that our response to evil should always be passive nonresistance. That cannot be what Jesus is teaching in Matthew 5:39.

But what did Jesus mean when He said, "Do not resist him who is evil"?

Again, He was forbidding personal retaliation, revenge, spite, resentment, or a combative response in the face of a personal or petty injury. The word translated "resist" speaks of a militant reprisal. The idea involves personal vengeance. Christ is simply teaching exactly the same principle the apostle Paul set forth in Romans 12:17-19:

> *Never pay back evil for evil to anyone. Respect what is right in the sight of all men. If possible, so far as it depends on you, be at peace with all men. Never take your own revenge, beloved, but leave room for the wrath of God, for it is written, "Vengeance is Mine, I will repay," says the Lord.*

In this manner we can often overcome evil by doing good (v. 21).

A LAMB TO THE SLAUGHTER

Someone will point out that Christ's crucifixion was neither petty nor private. So it doesn't really fit in the category of those minor personal offenses we ought to overlook, does it?

No, but it *does* clearly fit in a third category of offenses Jesus also mentions in His Sermon on the Mount: persecution for righteousness' sake. Our Lord taught that we are to suffer gladly when our suffering is for the sake of righteousness:

> *"Blessed are those who have been persecuted for the sake of righteousness, for theirs is the kingdom of heaven. Blessed are you when men revile you, and persecute you, and say all kinds of evil against you falsely, on account of Me. Rejoice, and be glad, for your reward in heaven is great, for so they persecuted the prophets who were before you."*
>
> – MATT. 5:10-12

Notice the response Christ calls for when this type of wrong is suffered: "Rejoice, and be glad." That is not describing a giddy, capricious joy. It isn't talking about a masochistic delight over suffering. It is a calm, settled peace—exactly the kind of spirit shown by Christ Himself in the midst of His trials.

Scripture repeatedly portrays Christ as a lamb led to the slaughter: "He was oppressed and He was afflicted, yet He did not open His mouth; like a lamb that is led to slaughter, and like a sheep that is silent before its shearers, so He did not open His mouth" (Isa. 53:7). The emphasis is on His silence and His passivity. He was suffering for righteousness' sake, and it would have been wrong of Him to fight back. Why?

In the first place, He had no legal recourse. Both official Rome and the Jewish Sanhedrin conspired together to kill Him. In this case, although the offense against Him was both profound and public, He had no means to seek legal redress. There was no higher earthly court of appeal to which He could go. His only option was insurrection. He put a stop to that idea in the Garden of Gethsemane when He rebuked Peter and told Him to put His sword away (John 18:11). Violent resistance was not justified in such an instance, no matter how wrong His persecutors were, and regardless of how totally innocent He was.

Jesus reminded Peter that if He were inclined to resist, He could simply pray to the Father and immediately have heavenly armies dispatched to His aid: "He will at once put at My disposal more than twelve legions of angels" (Matt. 26:53). So Christ *could* have stopped His crucifixion if he had chosen to.

But had He done that, His earthly work would have been incomplete, and sin would have remained unatoned for. The Father had given Him this cup to drink, and He would submit to the Father's will, no matter what the cost. He would overcome evil with good.

One of the significant factors about the crucifixion narratives in all four Gospels is the silence of Christ before His accusers. When legitimate questions were put to Him, He answered honestly but briefly. For the most part, however, He remained silent. The high priest was frantic to find some reason to accuse Him, but Matthew 26:63 records, "Jesus kept silent" (cf. Mark 14:61). Brought to Pilate, he stood in utter silence while the chief priests and scribes listed false accusations against Him (Matt. 27:12). Mark 15:4-5 records the following: "And Pilate was questioning Him again, saying, 'Do You make no answer? See how many charges they bring against You!' But Jesus made no further answer; so that Pilate was astonished." When Pilate pressed Jesus about where He was from, John 19:9 records, "Jesus gave Him no answer." Luke says Herod also "questioned Him at some length; but He answered him nothing" (Luke 23:9).

That is why Peter, an eyewitness to much of the drama, wrote, "While being reviled, He did not revile in return; while suffering, He uttered no threats, but kept entrusting Himself to Him who judges righteously" (1 Pet. 2:23).

"FATHER, FORGIVE THEM"

When Christ *did* speak in those final hours before He gave up His life, it was clear that His mind was not on revenge—not even on self-defense. *Forgiveness* was the predominant theme of His thoughts throughout the whole ordeal of His crucifixion.

For example, at the height of His agony, at the very moment when most victims of crucifixion might scream out in fury with a curse, He prayed for forgiveness for His tormentors: "Father, forgive them; for they do not know what they are doing" (Luke 23:34).

Bishop J. C. Ryle wrote, "These words were probably spoken while our Lord was being nailed to the cross, or as soon as the cross was reared up on end. It is worthy of remark that as soon as the blood of the Great Sacrifice began to flow, the Great High Priest began to intercede."

Do you see the glory of that? Although Christ is the sovereign, eternal, omnipotent God, He did not threaten, He did not condemn, He did not pronounce doom on His crucifiers. Instead of lashing out against them, He prayed for them.

Jesus had earlier taught, "Love your enemies, and pray for those who persecute you" (Matthew 5:44). But who would have thought that teaching would be carried to such an extreme?

Like so many aspects of our Lord's death, this manifestation of divine mercy was a fulfillment of Old Testament prophecy. Isaiah

53:12 foretold it: "He poured out Himself to death, and was numbered with the transgressors; yet He Himself bore the sin of many,
and interceded for the transgressors."

This was the hour for which Jesus had come (John 13:1). Many
times His enemies had sought to kill Him before His time (cf. John
7:30; 8:20). "I lay down My life," He said. "No one has taken it away
from Me, but I lay it down on My own initiative. I have authority
to lay it down, and I have authority to take it up again. This commandment I received from My Father" (John 10:17-18). Everything
that was happening in those dreadful hours was according to "the
predetermined plan and foreknowledge of God" (Acts 2:23). It was
all coming to pass *"in order that the Scripture might be fulfilled"* (John
19:28; cf. vv. 24, 36; Mark 15:28).

This was the reason for which He had come (John 3:17). The
whole point of the Incarnation was forgiveness. It was the very thing
Jesus was dying for. It was what He was praying for. And it is what
He exemplified in His death. Again, He gave us an example we are
solemnly charged to follow. If you don't feel somewhat inadequate
to answer that calling, perhaps you have not understood the full significance of it.

The scene at the cross includes a remarkable contrast. Here is
Jesus, humbly submitting Himself to His Father's will, "obedient
to the point of death, even death on a cross" (Phil. 2:8). And there
is the mob, jeering, taunting, egging the murderers on, determined
at all costs to fulfill their evil deed. They came together in that awful,
sacred moment—the solitary, spotless Lamb and the murderous,
contemptible crowd: "And when they came to the place called The
Skull, there they crucified Him" (Luke 23:33). Again, it was all coming to pass according to "the predetermined plan and foreknowledge of God" (Acts 2:23), *"in order that the Scripture might be fulfilled"*
(John 19:28). But at that moment, surely only the Lamb Himself
understood that God's will was being done.

Inevitably someone will ask whom Christ was praying for. Was
it the Jews who had conspired to sentence Him to death? The

Roman soldiers who actually nailed Him to the cross, then gambled for His clothing? The mocking crowd who taunted Him?

The answer must be all of the above, and more. In one sense the scope of that prayer surely extends beyond the people who were there that day, to every person who has ever trusted Christ and so received His forgiveness. After all, our sins put Him there. We are every bit as culpable as the men who actually drove those nails through His sinless hands and feet.

Now, "Father, forgive them" was not a prayer for immediate, unconditional, indiscriminate forgiveness of everyone who participated in Christ's crucifixion. Rather, it was a plea on behalf of those who would repent and trust Him as their Lord and Savior. Jesus was praying that when they came to grips with the enormity of what they had done and sought God's forgiveness for it, He would not hold it against them. Forgiveness does not belong to those who stubbornly persist in unbroken unbelief and sin and rebellion. Those who carried their steely hatred of Him to the grave were not absolved from their crime by this prayer.

Forgiveness is offered to all, freely (Rev. 22:17). God is as eager to forgive as the prodigal's father was. He pleads for every sinner to turn to Him in humble repentance (Ezek. 18:3-32; Acts 17:30). Those who do, He promises to receive with open arms and unrestrained forgiveness. But those who remain in infidelity and defiance will never know God's forgiveness.

So Christ was praying for those who would repent of their evil deed. The sin they were guilty of was so unbelievably horrific that if these people had not actually heard Him pray for their forgiveness, they might have assumed their sin was unforgivable. (See Appendix 2, "What Is the Unforgivable Sin?")

Why did He pray, "*Father*, forgive them," when in the past He had simply forgiven sinners Himself (cf. Luke 7:48)? After all, hadn't He already shown that "the Son of Man has authority on earth to forgive sins" (Matt. 9:6)?

Yes, but now as our sin-bearer, He was taking our place, dying in our stead, having surrendered every divine prerogative, including His own life, on our behalf. He hung there before God as a representative of sinful humanity. And so He appealed to *the Father* to forgive the transgressors. He was at that moment identifying Himself with the very ones whose irrational hatred of Him had brought Him all these sorrows. Such is the wonder of divine mercy!

Jesus' words, "For they do not know what they are doing" (Luke 23:34) obviously do not mean that those who killed Him were wholly ignorant of the awful *reality* of their crime. The Jewish leaders knew that they had falsely accused Him (Matt. 26:59). Pilate knew that Jesus was an innocent man (Luke 23:4). Anyone even slightly aware of what was going on would have seen that a great injustice was being done (Mark 14:56).

Yet these were blind people led by blind rulers (Acts 3:17). They were all utterly ignorant of the magnitude of their atrocity. They were completely blind to the spiritual light of divine truth.

Their ignorance, however, did not excuse them. Ample evidence testified to the truth of who Jesus was. The people had heard Him teach, and they "were amazed at His teaching; for He was teaching them as one having authority, and not as their scribes" (Matt. 7:28-29). They had witnessed His mighty works (John 10:32-33). In all probability, some of those now clamoring for His death were the same people who earlier had followed Him just for His miracles' sake. Some of them may have even been among the multitudes He fed (John 6:26). Perhaps many of them had been part of the throng who just a week earlier had hailed Him as He entered the city (Matt. 21:8-11)! Surely these people could not have been ignorant of the many things Jesus had said and done in their presence. Two things are certain: their ignorance itself was not excusable, and ignorance certainly did not excuse their crime of murder.

Yet our Lord in His great mercy prayed for their forgiveness. Spiritually, they were blind, utterly insensitive to the awful reality of what they had done. It was not as if they consciously and deliberately were trying to snuff out the Light of the world. Their own minds were utterly blind to that true Light, and therefore they could not have understood the full enormity of their crime. "If they had understood it, they would not have crucified the Lord of glory" (1 Cor. 2:8).

Was Jesus' prayer for their forgiveness answered? It certainly was.

THE PARDONED THIEF

The first answer to that prayer came in a most dramatic way, even before Jesus died.

Both Matthew and Mark record that Christ was crucified between two thieves. These men were probably insurrectionists as well as robbers. Roman law rarely crucified men for mere thievery, so the two criminals were probably guilty of crimes against the government as well. They may have been in league with Barabbas, who was both a robber (John 18:40) and a murderer and was also guilty of sedition against Rome (Luke 23:18-19).

In any case, these were men who lived their lives outside the law. The crimes of which they were guilty had been deemed capital offenses, and one of the thieves ultimately confessed that unlike Christ, they were both indeed worthy to suffer death (Luke 23:41).

So these were grossly immoral men, and the hardness of their hearts is evident in the fact that even while they were being crucified, in the midst of their own excruciating agonies, they both poured scorn on Christ. When the chief priests and scribes taunted Him by saying, "He saved others; He cannot save Himself. He is the King of Israel; let Him now come down from the cross, and we shall believe in Him" (Matt. 27:42), "the robbers also who had been crucified with Him were casting the same insult at Him" (v. 44; cf. Mark 15:32).

Imagine how deeply ingrained someone's rancor would have to be to jeer at an innocent victim while the mocker himself was deservedly in the same predicament! These men were unspeakably evil malefactors. Surely they were the very worst of a bad lot surrounding Christ while He was dying. How amazing to think that Christ sought God's forgiveness for people as evil as this!

Luke, who recorded Jesus' prayer for His adversaries' forgiveness, also adds a remarkable postscript to the account of the two thieves. There came a point in the taunting where one of the two thieves experienced a dramatic change of heart. Watching Jesus suffer such abuse silently, without returning threat or insult to His taunters, that thief was smitten in conscience and repented. As both hung there dying, that man pleaded with the Savior, "Jesus, remember me when You come into Your kingdom!" (Luke 23:42).

His simple statement was actually a profound confession of faith. The man had clearly come to see the depth of his own guilt. He confessed that his own punishment was just and that Christ was guiltless (v. 41). His behavior immediately changed from wicked taunting to humble praise. He implicitly acknowledged Jesus' rightful claim to be Lord of the kingdom of heaven (v. 42). It is unlikely that the condemned criminal appreciated the full significance of Christ's death, but at that very moment, while that thief was receiving the due penalty for his crimes against Rome, Christ was atoning for the man's sins against God.

How did the man's scorn give way so quickly to worship? Flesh and blood had not revealed the truth to Him, but his eyes had been opened by a sovereign act of God. In the final moments of his earthly life, God graciously gave him a new heart. He had done nothing to merit divine grace. On the contrary, right up to the very end he was cursing, taunting, and mocking Christ, even though he himself faced certain death and after that, divine judgment.

But the sight of Christ's suffering in silence, the Lamb of God being led to the slaughter, awakened in that thief's heart a holy fear of God, and he finally rebuked his cohort: "Do you not even fear God, since you are under the same sentence of condemnation?" (Luke 23:40)—and with that statement rebuked himself as well. "We indeed [are suffering] justly," he confessed (v. 41), "but this man has done nothing wrong."

Knowing that he was utterly without hope on his own, the thief asked Christ for the smallest of favors: "Remember me." The request is reminiscent of the desperate plea of the publican who "was even unwilling to lift up his eyes to heaven, but was beating his breast, saying, 'God, be merciful to me, the sinner!'" (Luke 18:13). It was a cry of despair, a last-gasp appeal for the smallest token of mercy, admittedly undeserved.

Jesus, eager to forgive even the most hateful scorner, granted the man's request, and far more: "Truly I say to you, today you shall be with Me in Paradise" (v. 43).

Wrapped up in that promise was the full forgiveness of every evil deed the man had ever done. Nothing was required from the sinner himself to atone for his own evildoing. No works of penance were assigned him, no threat of Purgatory was made; he did not even receive a rebuke for having waited so long to come to Christ. He was immediately granted full entrance into the heavenly kingdom: "*Today* you shall be with Me in Paradise." Christ's atonement was sufficient to obtain full and free forgiveness for this most vile of sinners.

Scripture records no other words between Jesus and the dying thief. Both were suffering unspeakable agony. Soon both would enter Paradise, Christ having paid the price of the thief's sins, and the thief having been clothed in the perfect righteousness of the sinless Savior. A miracle of forgiveness had occurred!

SUPERNATURAL PHENOMENA

All of this occurred under a somber veil of darkness. Matthew says, "From the sixth hour darkness fell upon all the land until the ninth hour" (27:45). The darkness that fell upon the land was no mere eclipse. It could not have been. Passover always fell on the full moon, making a solar eclipse on this particular day out of the question. This was a supernatural darkness signifying divine judgment. God had judged humanity's sins, and as a result, the Light of the world was about to die. It was the most solemn moment in the history of the universe, and only darkness was appropriate for such a moment.

Matthew also records a remarkable series of incidents that happened at the moment of Jesus' death.

And Jesus cried out again with a loud voice, and yielded up His spirit. And, behold, the veil of the temple was torn in two from top to bottom, and the earth shook; and the rocks were split, and the tombs were opened; and many bodies of the saints who had fallen asleep were raised; and coming out of the tombs after His resurrection they entered the holy city and appeared to many.

– 27:50-53

Christ's death was no chance mishap, though it must have appeared to everyone present that chaos now ruled. The Shepherd was stricken and the sheep scattered. To the little band of observers who remained in the flock, all of this surely seemed a great victory for the forces of evil. Nature itself seemed in chaos. Darkness, an earthquake, and overwhelming gloom prevailed. It appeared to the human eye that the universe had been plunged into utter hopelessness.

Nothing could be further from the truth. Christ Himself remained in complete control. He had told the Pharisees, "I lay down My life so that I may take it again. No one has taken it away from Me, but I lay it down on My own initiative. I have authority to lay it down, and I have authority to take it up again" (John 10:17-18). Chaotic as the events may have seemed, at no time did God relinquish His sovereign control to the evildoers. On the contrary, numerous times in the crucifixion accounts we are told, "that the Scripture might be fulfilled" (John 19:24, 28, 36). All things were proceeding in accord with the divine plan.

When Christ died, He simply bowed His head and yielded up His Spirit. No one could have taken His life from Him against His will. At no time did He lose his deity or His sovereignty. All that occurred was part of His plan—a plan designed to make possible the forgiveness of sins.

What seemed like chaos in nature at the moment of Christ's death was actually a meaningful series of supernatural events, orchestrated by God, signifying that forgiveness was complete.

The Veil Rent

Notice that the veil of the Temple was torn "from top to bottom" (Matt. 27:51). That speaks of the veil that separated the Holy of Holies from the rest of the Temple. That veil marked a line no one was to cross, except for the high priest, who entered once a year with the blood of a sacrifice on the Day of Atonement.

Much of the book of Hebrews, especially chapters 9 and 10, discuss the significance of this veil, which signified "that the way into the holy place [had] not yet been disclosed" (Heb. 9:8). The annual sacrifices only symbolized a perfect sacrifice, yet to come, which, when offered, would put an end to all sacrifices forever (Heb. 10:11-12). The New Covenant, based on the shedding of Christ's blood, was then initiated.

Inherent in the New Covenant promises is the guarantee that sins are forgiven forever (vv. 16-17). "Now where there is forgiveness of these things, there is no longer any offering for sin" (v. 18). Therefore, according to the book of Hebrews, every believer can boldly approach the Most Holy Place—the true, heavenly mercy-seat—by the blood of Jesus (v. 19).

The tearing of the high-hanging veil from top to bottom signified that it was God Himself who tore the veil. Forgiveness was both complete and permanent. From that day on, the ceremonies and priestly functions in the Temple had no more significance. Within a generation, the Temple itself was destroyed, and with that, the Mosaic sacrificial system was sovereignly terminated.

The Earth Shaken

Matthew 27:51 continues, "The earth shook; and the rocks were split." Earthquakes in the Old Testament were always a graphic object lesson about divine wrath. When God delivered the law to Moses at Sinai, "the whole mountain quaked violently" (Exod. 19:18). Even in the Psalms, the shaking of the earth always signified the terror and wrath of the Lord (18:7; cf. 68:8; 77:18; 97:4). The final judgment will commence with a global earthquake like none ever seen before (Heb. 12:26-27; Rev. 6:14-15).

The earthquake of Matthew 27:51 accompanied the wrath of God against sin, poured out on His own Son. This moment marked the culmination of God's judgment against our sin, as the Son of God yielded up His spirit, and the earth shook in horror.

The Dead Raised

At that same moment, another miracle occurred: "The tombs were opened, and many bodies of the saints who had fallen asleep were raised" (Matt. 27:52). The other Gospels do not mention this incident. "Many," not all, of the saints in and around Jerusalem were raised. The term is relative and could refer to as few as a dozen or so. The low-key way in which Scripture describes this miracle seems to rule out a wide-scale resurrection. These people rose from the dead, no doubt in glorified bodies, and "after His resurrection they entered the holy city and appeared to many" (v. 53). There were enough of them to establish that this miracle had indeed occurred. No more is said about these people. Having borne witness of the Resurrection, they no doubt ascended to glory—forerunners of the event described in 1 Thessalonians 4:16.

All of these phenomena occurred instantaneously, and thus at the darkest hour earth has ever known these miracles of triumph signaled that something truly wonderful was occurring. Christ had purchased forgiveness. The Great Shepherd had given His life for the sheep.

And even at that moment God was redeeming sinners. Matthew 27:54 records: "Now the centurion, and those who were with him keeping guard over Jesus, when they saw the earthquake and the things that were happening, became very frightened and said, 'Truly this was the Son of God!'"

A CENTURION BELIEVES

A centurion was an army officer with command over a hundred men. This particular officer was undoubtedly the one supervising the crucifixion of Christ and the two thieves. He and some of his troops had probably kept guard over Jesus since the trial in the Praetorium, Pilate's Jerusalem residence. They may even have been among the soldiers who arrested Jesus in the Garden of Gethsemane the night before; so they may have witnessed the entire ordeal from the very beginning.

These same soldiers doubtless participated in Jesus' scourging. They would have been the very ones who dressed Him in a mock robe, placed a crown of thorns on His head, blindfolded Him, beat Him, spat on Him, and taunted Him (Matt. 27:27-30; Luke 22:63-64). They were the same men who had nailed His hands and feet to the cross, then cast lots for His garments and brazenly taunted Him in the midst of His agonies.

They had heard Pilate declare Jesus' innocence, so they knew He was no insurrectionist. Nothing about His actions or behavior made Him any real threat to Rome or the nation of Israel. To these soldiers He must have seemed a stark contrast to the many criminals they had helped crucify. Their taunting suggests they initially wrote Him off as a lunatic or a deranged religious fanatic.

But the supernatural darkness, the earthquake, and the way Christ endured His sufferings all began to have an effect on these soldiers. Mark says that the manner of Jesus' death finally opened their eyes to who He really was: "And when the centurion, which stood over against him, saw that he so cried out, and gave up the ghost, he said, Truly this man was the Son of God" (Mark 15:39, KJV). These soldiers had undoubtedly watched countless victims of crucifixion die, but none had ever died like Jesus. The strength required to cry out as Jesus did was unheard of at this stage of crucifixion.

Matthew says that not only the centurion but also the soldiers with him "became very frightened" (Matt. 27:54, KJV). The Greek expression refers to extreme fright—a kind of panic. This sort of fear often occurred when people realized who Jesus really was. In fact, the expression used here is the same one Matthew employed to describe the disciples' reaction when they saw Jesus walking on water (14:26) and the reaction of the three disciples on the Mount of Transfiguration when they saw Christ in His glory (17:6).

These soldiers at the foot of the cross suddenly realized whom they had crucified, and the result was sheer terror. As fearful as the darkness and earthquake must have been, they were nothing compared to the realization that the One whom they had killed was indeed the Son of God—the very One whom the Jewish rulers had wanted crucified for claiming to be the Son of God! And so in the centurion's statement of faith, he borrowed the very words used by the Jewish leaders who accused Jesus before Pilate ("He made Himself out to be the Son of God," John 19:7).

The testimony voiced by the centurion seems to be a genuine confession of faith on behalf of him and his men. "*Truly* this was the Son of God!" (Matt. 27:54). Luke records that the centurion's response was an act of genuine worship: "He began praising God" (23:47). Ancient tradition says the centurion's name was Longinus and that he was soundly converted and became one of the earliest members of the Christian Church.

That centurion and also any of the soldiers who shared his faith were an immediate answer to Jesus' prayer for His tormentors. God Himself saved those men in answer to His Son's dying plea for mercy on their behalf.

How do we know? Because salvation is *always* a work of divine grace. The faith of these men was proof of God's work in their hearts. "No one can say, 'Jesus is Lord,' except by the Holy Spirit" (1 Cor. 12:3). Jesus made it clear, even to Peter, that God is the source of all true faith (Matt. 16:16-17). Only God Himself could have changed the hardened hearts of that centurion and his men.

UNTOLD MULTITUDES

The centurion and his men were not the only ones struck with fear at the manner of Jesus' death. Luke records that Christ's crucifixion ended in sadness and terror for most of those who had clamored for His death: "And all the multitudes who came together for this spectacle, when they observed what had happened, began to return, beating their breasts" (Luke 23:48).

Hours before, this had been a bloodthirsty mob, shrieking with vicious delight for the death of Jesus. Now that they had what they wanted, it left them with nothing more than despair, grief, and horror. The triumph they had expected left them hollow and hopeless. The crowd dispersed, and everyone slunk back to their homes in fear. The beating of their breasts signified alarm and a measure of remorse. But unlike the centurion, who worshiped God, these people were lacking genuine repentance. Unlike the soldiers, they made no confession of sin and no confession of faith in Christ.

Still, that prayer from the cross was being answered by God. It seems apparent from the biblical accounts that many of these same people were among the 3,000 who were added to the Church in one day (Acts 2:41). Who knows how many of those people, and the thousands of others saved in Jerusalem in the weeks that followed, had been part of the bloodthirsty mob at the crucifixion.

Peter, addressing the multitudes at Pentecost, implied that many of them were the same ones who had actually participated in the crucifixion of Christ. Peter actually charged them with guilt for the deed: "Therefore let all the house of Israel know for certain that God has made Him both Lord and Christ—this Jesus *whom you crucified*" (Acts 2:36, emphasis added).

And they did not deny their guilt. It had evidently weighed heavily on them since they walked away from Calvary beating their breasts. When they heard Peter's words, "they were pierced to the heart, and said to Peter and the rest of the apostles, 'Brethren, what shall we do?'" (v. 37).

Peter then urged them to repent and trust Christ, and the result was dramatic: "Those who had received his word were baptized; and there were added that day about three thousand souls" (v. 41).

They, too, were God's answer to His Son's dying prayer. Jesus' prayer, in a sense, led to the miracle at Pentecost.

But the 3,000 converted at Pentecost were only the beginning. It could very well be that by the end of the apostolic era the majority of those who actually participated in putting Christ to death were brought into the Kingdom in answer to His prayer for forgiveness!

Furthermore, in a sense every pardoned sinner who ever lived is an answer to Christ's prayer. Since our guilt put Him on the cross in the first place, we bear responsibility for His death just as surely as those who actually drove the nails through His hands and feet. And the forgiveness He extended on the cross to those who put Him to death is the same forgiveness He extends to sinners today. We who have experienced such forgiveness have a solemn duty to extend a similar mercy to others as well (Eph. 4:32).

What a high standard He set for us! His refusal to retaliate, His silent acceptance of others' wrongs against Him, His prayer of forgiveness, His eagerness to forgive—all set an example we are expected to follow.

How quickly our flesh recoils from following that example! When we suffer wrongfully, it becomes very easy to rationalize a counterattack and painfully difficult to follow our Lord's steps. But like Him, we must keep entrusting ourselves to the One who "judges righteously" (1 Pet. 2:23).

Can we look at this scene on the cross and understand the depth of His passion, then justify our own unwillingness to forgive any offense our neighbor might have committed against us? The answer is obvious. Should we not have mercy even as we have received mercy (cf. Matt. 18:21-35)? As those who have been forgiven much, we owe much, both to our Lord and to our fellow servants (cf. Luke 7:47). May the Lord grant us grace to follow in His steps of mercy!

THREE

If We Confess
Our Sins . . .

If we confess our sins, He is faithful and just
to forgive us our sins and to cleanse us from all unrighteousness.

1 JOHN 1:9

One of the first verses many new Christians memorize is 1 John 1:9, because the promise of forgiveness and cleansing is such a rich comfort to those who have struggled all their lives with guilt.

But that verse is the focus of some controversy these days. A handful of popular teachers are claiming that since Christians are *already* forgiven, they should never ask God for forgiveness, and to do so is an expression of unbelief. They insist that 1 John 1:9 has nothing to do with Christians.

One of the best-known proponents of this view is Bob George, popular author and radio speaker. George characterizes Christians who pray for forgiveness as people "who live in daily insecurity . . . [Christians] who doubt whether all their sins are forgiven."[1]

George and several others who share his views claim the *only* way to enjoy one's liberty in Christ is to forget about guilt forever and embrace God's forgiveness as a wholly accomplished fact because of Christ's work.

There's enough truth in that viewpoint to make it extremely confusing to many sincere believers. As we saw in chapter 1, believers' sins *are* forgiven, atoned for by Christ. Christians are freed from the guilt of their sins and are clothed in the perfect righteousness of Christ. Their justification before God is an accomplished fact. Scripture says, " There is therefore now no condemnation for those who are in Christ Jesus" (Rom. 8:1). "Who will bring a charge against God's elect? God is the one who justifies; who is the one who condemns?" (Rom. 8:33-34). "Christ redeemed us from the curse of the Law" (Gal. 3:13).

So from the perspective of God's judgment-throne, the sins of believers are forgiven even before they are committed. God as Judge has thoroughly punished Christ for our sins, and He refuses to hold those sins against us in judgment. "Blessed are those whose lawless deeds have been forgiven, and whose sins have been covered. Blessed is the man whose sin the Lord will not take into account" (Rom. 4:7-8). All Christians are in this blessed state, and those truths are the whole basis of our liberty in Christ. That much is undeniably true.

But it is not the *full* truth. Don't get the notion that because of justification God pays no mind whatsoever to our sin. Don't think for a moment that believers can simply wallow in sin without provoking God's displeasure. Don't view personal remorse over sin as some sort of hindrance to spiritual health. Don't conclude that praying for God's forgiveness is something a Christian should never do. Such thinking is patently unbiblical; heresy is not too strong a word for it. Christians who think they can sin without causing offense to God and without seeking their heavenly Father's forgiveness are badly deceived.

Let's take a closer look at these issues.

ARE BELIEVERS SUPPOSED TO PRAY FOR FORGIVENESS?

I recently received a newsletter from one of these ministries known for teaching that Christians should never seek God's forgiveness. In a cover article, the founder of the ministry writes:

You've probably heard people pray like this: *And Lord, we ask you to forgive us for all our sins.* But hold it. Why do forgiven Christians ask God's forgiveness? Do they not believe they are forgiven? If they believe they're forgiven, then why do they ask for it repeatedly? Their prayers reveal unbelief.

A few paragraphs later, he proposes what he thinks is a better way to pray:

> How frequently do you hear someone pray, "And, Lord, I thank You that I stand before You a completely forgiven man. Thank You that I am as spotless as the driven snow"? Those words are rare, but they thrill the heart of God because they demonstrate faith that the man believes God who says we are forgiven in Christ (Eph. 4:32). There is no way you are going to cozy up to God if you feel He is increasingly upset with you. To feel secure, you must believe that He does not hold one single sin against you. Here is a bold statement: It is impossible for a Christian to ask God's forgiveness for a besetting sin the umpteenth time, then snuggle up to Him. He will feel like God's patience is being stretched to the limit.

There's one fatal problem with that whole approach to the subject of forgiveness: it's the very opposite of what the Scriptures teach.

Christ clearly taught His disciples to pray, "Forgive us our sins" (Luke 11:4). Those who argue against praying for forgiveness generally try to explain away that phrase in the Lord's Prayer by suggesting that it belongs to another dispensation—either the Old Covenant under Moses' law, or some yet—future legal dispensation. They believe Jesus was teaching law, not grace, when He gave the Lord's Prayer. Therefore, they insist, teaching people to petition God for forgiveness is tantamount to living under law, not grace. And to expect Christians to pray in the manner set forth in the Lord's Prayer, according to this view, is legalistic.

One man who advocates this view wrote me a letter in which he said:

> The Lord's Prayer belongs to the Old Covenant era, when law, not grace, was the governing rule. Does any believer today really imagine that God's forgiveness is contingent on how we forgive, so that we earn His forgiveness by forgiving others? Is it true that if I do not forgive others God will not forgive me? And are Christians supposed to fear that God will withdraw His forgiveness from believers who refuse to forgive those who have wronged them? We must conclude that the provisions of the Lord's Prayer are law, not grace. *Conditional forgiveness does not apply to Christians.*

That reveals a basic misunderstanding. Forgiveness is not offered on different terms in the Old Testament and New Testament eras. Even under the Old Covenant, salvation was always by grace, not by law. Believers were justified through faith alone, not by works. Paul's whole argument in Romans 4 is that the saved of all time are redeemed in exactly the same manner as Abraham: on the ground of a righteousness that is imputed through faith alone (vv. 1-5). That includes Old Testament saints living under Moses' Law, such as David (vv. 6-8). Their sins were forgiven in the same way ours are, and they too were clothed with a perfect righteousness imputed to them by faith.

In other words, limiting the Lord's Prayer to the Old Covenant era—or any other dispensation—does not alter the plain fact that Jesus was teaching already-justified people that they should pray for God's forgiveness.

WHY ARE WE SUPPOSED TO SEEK GOD'S FORGIVENESS IF HE HAS ALREADY JUSTIFIED US?

If justification takes care of sin past, present, and future, so that there is no condemnation for those who are in Christ (Rom. 8:1), why do believers need to pray for forgiveness? Aren't we praying for something that is already ours?

Let's back up and look at the subject biblically. First of all, it is a simple matter of fact that Scripture plainly teaches redeemed people to pray regularly for forgiveness. That is clear in many of the penitential psalms (Ps. 6; 32; 38; 51; 102; 130; 143); it is clear in the Lord's Prayer; and it is also what 1 John 1:9 describes.

As long as we live in a sinful world, with our own sinful tendencies, there is a sense in which Christians, though eternally cleansed by the washing of regeneration (Titus 3:5), still need daily cleansing from the effects of their sins.

The perfect illustration of these two kinds of cleansing is found in the apostle John's account of the Last Supper, when Jesus wanted to wash Peter's feet. At first Peter was reluctant to have Christ serve him in such a humiliating fashion. He told the Lord, "Never shall You wash my feet!" (John 13:8).

Jesus replied, "If I do not wash you, you have no part with Me."

Peter, always brash, decided that a foot-washing would therefore not be sufficient for him: "Lord, not my feet only, but also my hands and my head" (v. 9).

Jesus' reply draws a clear distinction between two kinds of cleansing: "He who has bathed needs only to wash his feet, but is completely clean; and you are clean, but not all of you" (v. 10).

Bathing illustrates the forgiveness of justification. Those who are justified are forgiven the penalty of sin forever. They do not need to be justified again. The day-to-day effects of their sin still need to be dealt with, however. Sin needs to be confessed and forsaken regularly, and the pardon of a loving but displeased Father must be sought.

The verb tenses in 1 John 1 also demonstrate this. A literal rendering of verse 7 reads, "The blood of Jesus His Son keeps cleansing us from all sin." And the verb tense in verse 9 also denotes continuous action: "If we are continually confessing our sins."

So neither the confession nor the cleansing spoken of in 1 John 1 is a one-time, finished event. These verses simply do not support the idea that God pays no heed to the believer's daily transgressions, as if our justification once and for all made sin an utterly moot point for the Christian.

Yet the question nonetheless seems to trouble many Christians. Why must we seek God's forgiveness if He has *already* granted forgiveness in justification?

The answer is that divine forgiveness has two aspects. One is the *judicial* forgiveness God grants as Judge. This is the forgiveness that was purchased by the atonement Christ rendered on our behalf. This kind of forgiveness frees us from any threat of eternal condemnation. It is the forgiveness of justification. Such pardon is immediately complete and never needs to be sought again.

The other is a *parental* forgiveness God grants as our Father. He is grieved when His children sin. The forgiveness of justification takes care of *judicial* guilt, but it does not nullify His fatherly displeasure over our sin. He chastens those whom He loves, for their temporal good (Heb. 12:5-10).

So the forgiveness Christians are supposed to seek in their daily walk is not pardon from an angry Judge, but mercy from a grieved Father. This is the forgiveness Christ taught us to pray for in the Lord's Prayer. The opening words of the prayer, "Our Father," demonstrate that a parental rather than a judicial relationship is in view. (This is also true in 1 John 1, where "fellowship . . . with the Father, and with His Son Jesus Christ" is the subject matter, again suggesting that the forgiveness in verse 9 is a parental rather than a judicial forgiveness.)

Judicial forgiveness deals with the *penalty* of our sins. Parental forgiveness deals with sin's *consequences*. Judicial forgiveness frees us from the condemnation of an aggrieved, omnipotent Judge. Parental forgiveness sets things right with a grieving and displeased but loving Father. Judicial forgiveness gives us an unshakable *standing* before the throne of divine judgment. Parental forgiveness deals with the *state* of our sanctification at any given moment and is dispensed from a throne of divine grace (Heb. 4:16). As Judge, God is eager to forgive sinners; but as a Father He is equally eager to keep on forgiving and cleansing His children from the defilement of their sin.

IS GOD EVER ANGRY WITH HIS OWN CHILDREN?

The mere suggestion that God can be displeased with His own children is enough to raise the defenses of many who believe that never, under any circumstances, can the sins of a child of God provoke divine displeasure. One Christian who was confused about these issues sent an e-mail to our ministry:

> Are you saying God will become angry with His own children? If we're clothed with Christ's righteousness, how could God even see our sin? And if He can't even see our sin, how could He ever be displeased by it? I thought God was never displeased with any Christian, because He accepts us in Christ, as if we were as righteous as Christ. And He is *well-pleased* with His beloved Son.
>
> Besides, if we believe God gets angry with His own children when they sin, can we honestly say we believe He has forgiven us in the first place?

Unfortunately, more and more Christians seem confused by such questions. Bad Bible teaching has pushed the concept of radical grace to the point where some seem to believe that God is obligated by the terms of justification to blithely accept the believer's sin and disobedience. Some who have imbibed these doctrines evidently imagine that because Christ has atoned for our sin, God is no longer entitled to object when we disobey.

But to hold such a view, one must ignore or explain away several important doctrines of Scripture.

For example, as we have seen already, Scripture clearly teaches that God disciplines His children who disobey:

> *You have forgotten the exhortation which is addressed to you as sons, "My son, do not regard lightly the discipline of the Lord, nor faint when you are reproved by Him; for those whom the Lord loves He disciplines, and He scourges every son whom He receives." It is for discipline that you endure; God deals with you as with sons; for what*

*son is there whom his father does not discipline? But if you are with-
out discipline, of which all have become partakers, then you are illegitimate children and not sons. Furthermore, we had earthly fathers
to discipline us, and we respected them; shall we not much rather be
subject to the Father of spirits, and live? For they disciplined us for a
short time as seemed best to them, but He disciplines us for our good,
so that we may share His holiness. All discipline for the moment seems
not to be joyful, but sorrowful; yet to those who have been trained by
it, afterwards it yields the peaceful fruit of righteousness.*

– HEB. 12:5-11

What is the nature of the parental discipline God administers to His
children? This is crucial to understanding the nature of the forgiveness Jesus taught His disciples to seek.

Bob George draws a stark contrast between *punishment* and *discipline*. He writes:

> Though ["discipline" and "punishment"] are often thought to
> mean the same thing, they are very different. The confusion
> of the two concepts probably comes from our experiences
> with well-meaning but fallible human parents, who often dis-
> ciplined us in love, but also sometimes punished us in frus-
> tration and anger. We then project those characteristics upon
> God, and assume that he acts the same way. However, noth-
> ing could be farther from the truth. This error is one of the
> final strongholds of legalism that must be corrected in order
> to enable a person to rest in God's grace. Let's begin by get-
> ting a proper definition of the terms.
>
> *Punishment* is a penalty imposed on an offender for a
> crime or wrongdoing. It has retribution in view (paying some-
> one back what he deserves) rather than correction. . . .
>
> *Discipline*, on the other hand, is totally different. Discipline
> is training that develops self-control, character, and ability.[2]

There is some truth in what George is saying. Sheer punishment
often has no goal other than the administration of justice. The death

penalty, for example, has no remedial design. Its aim is not to reha-
bilitate the offender, but to mete out the due penalty of a capital
crime.

And it is also true that discipline sometimes carries none of the
punitive connotations of chastisement. George's example of discipline is a basketball coach who puts his team through a hard work-
out in order to get them ready for competition. The goal is not to
punish the players, but to get them in shape. George writes:

> Punishment and discipline sometimes *feel* the same to one on
> the receiving end! But the sharp difference can be seen in both
> the *attitude* and the *goal* of the one doing it. The attitude behind
> punishment is *anger* and *indignation*, and its goal is justice; the
> attitude behind discipline is love, and its goal is the benefit and
> development of the person.[3]

Is it true, however, that discipline *never* involves punishment? Is
it also true that punishment never serves a corrective purpose?

No, it is not. For example, George himself illustrates "punishment" with an anecdote about a policeman who cited him for
speeding. He writes:

> You see, the law officer isn't interested in why you were
> speeding; he doesn't care whether or not you did it on pur-
> pose; nor is he interested in hearing about all the other days
> that you did abide by the law. All he knows is that you broke
> the law, and here is your penalty. You will also notice that he
> did nothing to compliment the 50 other drivers he saw that
> were within the speed limit. He just sat there, unresponsive,
> until there was a violation, then he got into action. That's
> punishment.[4]

But if George means to imply that a traffic citation serves no corrective purpose, he is quite wrong. Speeding tickets are designed
partly to punish and partly to deter future offenses. If the fine is
costly enough, it helps remind the offender not to commit repeat

violations. That is part of the lawmakers' intent when they establish the fines—and it is also quite often the officer's stated intent when he writes the citation. ("I'm going to cite you to help you remember not to speed next time.")

So a traffic ticket is partly punitive and partly corrective. *Many* punishments involve a measure of corrective discipline. And discipline—particularly the parental discipline described in Hebrews 12— often includes a punitive aspect as well.

George wants to separate the two in a way that suggests they are mutually exclusive. He is expressly denying that God's discipline of believers involves any punitive aspect. George writes, "*God, under the New Covenant, never deals with His children on the basis of punishment....* He is not dealing with us in anger, nor with a demand for justice."[5]

But does that square with what Scripture actually says? No, it does not. The basketball coach comparison is not the imagery Hebrews 12 employs. Rather, that passage pictures a displeased Father. Scripture pictures God administering discipline to believers with a rod. Yes, He disciplines His children in love, and for their good, and with a goal that is more corrective than it is punitive. But there is nonetheless a punitive element in the discipline described by the writer of Hebrews. This is firm yet loving parental chastisement—a spanking, not merely a practice drill prescribed by a benign coach-figure.

Furthermore, correction itself always contains the recognition that something is being done wrongly. Any good coach benches the undisciplined player, or makes him pay (as well as learn) by special workouts. That may include a punitive purpose, and it should produce a sense of shame.

This is crucial, because God's hatred of our sin is a manifestation of His love for us. His love is like that of a parent, not the detached benevolence of a coach who merely hopes his team will win. And the punitive element of the Lord's discipline is as much a manifestation of His love as is the corrective element.

The words used in Hebrews 12 to describe this discipline are important. They are rendered, in various translations, as "scourging," "chastening," "rebuke," and "chastisement." Those are fitting terms to convey what the writer of Hebrews is describing. They imply a parental punishment, colored by disapproval, mixed with sternness and a degree of severity. *Anger* is not too strong a term, with the caveat that we are describing a fatherly variety of indignation, and not the wrath of an offended judge.

Scripture itself repeatedly employs the language of holy anger to describe God's disapproval of His children's sins. For example, Moses recounted the Lord's response to the rebellion of the Israelites at Kadesh-barnea:

> *Then the LORD heard the sound of your words, and* He was angry *and took an oath, saying, "Not one of these men, this evil generation, shall see the good land which I swore to give your fathers, except Caleb the son of Jephunneh; he shall see it, and to him and to his sons I will give the land on which he has set foot, because he has followed the LORD fully." The LORD was* angry *with me also on your account, saying, "Not even you shall enter there."*
>
>   – DEUT. 1:34-37, *emphasis added;*
>   *cf. 3:26; 4:21*

He described a similar incident at the foot of Sinai, when the Israelites worshiped a golden calf:

> *I fell down before the LORD, as at the first, forty days and nights; I neither ate bread nor drank water, because of all your sin which you had committed in doing what was evil in the sight of the LORD to provoke Him to anger. For* I was afraid of the anger and hot displeasure with which the LORD was wrathful against you in order to destroy you, *but the LORD listened to me that time also.* The LORD *was* angry enough with Aaron to destroy him; *so I also prayed for Aaron at the same time.*
>
>   – DEUT. 9:18-20, *emphasis added*

When Solomon did what was evil in the sight of the Lord, 1

Kings 11:9 records, "Now the LORD was angry with Solomon because his heart was turned away from the LORD."

Moses, Aaron, and Solomon were all redeemed men, fully justified through faith. Their standing before God was in no sense dependent on their works. Their sins were fully forgiven in the judicial sense. Yet Scripture says they angered God because of their sin.

Similarly, Christ was "indignant" with the disciples for refusing to allow children to come to Him (Mark 10:14). He rebuked Peter on several occasions, at one point addressing him as "Satan" (Mark 8:33). He also harshly rebuked James and John (Luke 9:55-56, NASB margin).

So the notion that God is always benign, never displeased with His children, is quite foreign to Scripture. The idea that His discipline never includes any punitive component is also simply wrong. The promise of God to those whom He loves is that He will chasten them as a father chastens his children. That chastening, though done in love and always for our benefit, is nonetheless a true expression of divine anger over sin—even the sins of His own children.

Listen to this provision of the Davidic Covenant:

> *"So I will establish his descendants forever, and his throne as the days of heaven. If his sons forsake My law, and do not walk in My judgments, if they violate My statutes, and do not keep My commandments,* then I will punish their transgression with the rod, and their iniquity with stripes. *But I will not break off My lovingkindness from him, nor deal falsely in My faithfulness."*
> — PS. 89:29-33, *emphasis added*

Christians never need to fear facing God's wrath as their eternal Judge, but they will definitely face His fatherly disapproval and correction when they sin. According to Hebrews 12, such discipline is the strongest evidence of His love for us. So don't ever buy into the notion that God is never angry over His children's sin. The fact that He is vexed with our sin is the very proof of His fatherly love for us.

WHAT DOES CONFESSION ACCOMPLISH?

What happens when we, as already-justified believers, confess our sins and seek God's fatherly forgiveness? First of all, it is important to understand that we do not lose our salvation when we sin. Confessing sin is not a matter of regaining lost salvation or renewing our justification.[6] Scripture teaches that those whom God justifies, He also glorifies (Rom. 8:30). The elect don't fall out of the process before reaching the goal. "He who began a good work in you will perfect it until the day of Christ Jesus" (Phil. 1:6). Our sin might displease God, but it cannot separate us from His love (Rom. 8:38-39).

But what does Scripture say? "If we confess our sins, He is faithful and righteous to forgive us our sins and to cleanse us from all unrighteousness" (1 John 1:9). *Forgiveness* and *cleansing* are the two aspects of that promise. As we have seen, the forgiveness spoken of here refers to a parental forgiveness, not the forgiveness of justification. It speaks of a subjective, relational kind of forgiveness. It is simply a restoration to the place of blessing in the eyes of a displeased father.

Similarly, the cleansing spoken of in these verses is not the washing of regeneration. Regeneration imparts new life, often pictured in Scripture as the washing of the heart (Jer. 4:14; Titus 3:5); but the continual cleansing described in 1 John 1:7-9 is a spiritual washing to rid believers of the defilement caused by sin in their daily walk. This type of cleansing is the very thing Jesus was illustrating when He insisted on washing Peter's dusty feet.

Clearly it is believers who are being addressed in 2 Corinthians 7:1: "Therefore, having these promises, beloved, let us cleanse ourselves from all defilement of flesh and spirit, perfecting holiness in the fear of God." There Paul indicates that we, by means of obedience and true repentance, participate in an ongoing cleansing from sin.

So 1 John 1:9 likewise is speaking of an ongoing pardon and purification from sin, not the cleansing and forgiveness of salvation. We're not to think that the pardon of justification and the washing of regeneration eliminate any need for Christians to deal with the subjective reality of sin in their lives. In the words of Puritan commentator Matthew Henry:

> The Christian religion is the religion of sinners, of such as have sinned, and in whom sin in some measure still dwells. The Christian life is a life of continued repentance, humiliation for and mortification of sin, of continual faith in, thankfulness for, and love to the Redeemer, and hopeful, joyful expectation of a day of glorious redemption, in which the believer shall be fully and finally acquitted, and sin abolished for ever.[7]

That's why Scripture teaches us to be continually confessing our sins and seeking God's daily forgiveness and cleansing. He is both faithful and just to forgive—*faithful* because it is His promise to us in the covenant relationship, and *just* because He has already made atonement for our sins.

CAN WE AVERT GOD'S DISCIPLINE BY CONFESSING AND SEEKING HIS FORGIVENESS?

Does God's forgiveness utterly nullify the fact that we have sinned? When we confess our sin and seek God's forgiveness, will He immediately withdraw His discipline and free us from the consequences of our sin?

Some believe that forgiveness should nullify all sin's consequences. This issue inevitably arises, for example, when a Christian leader who has fallen into immorality professes repentance and then wants to return to a position of leadership in the church. Predictably, the fallen leader will plead his case by pointing out that God has forgiven him for his sin, so past sins should not be a factor in considering him for church leadership.

Yet, the basic biblical requirement for all elders and deacons in the church is that they must be "above *reproach*" (1 Tim. 3:2, 10; Titus

1:6-7). The expression speaks of the leader's public reputation. "Above reproach" means there is nothing of which he can be accused. It does not speak of sinlessness, or no one could qualify. But a man who is "above reproach" is someone whose life is not marred by any obvious sinful defect or scandal that hinders him from standing before the flock as an example of consistent godliness.

Some sins, particularly scandalous sexual sins, carry a reproach that cannot be blotted out even though the offense itself is forgiven (Prov. 6:32-33). Forgiveness restores the person to a right relationship with God, but the stigma and scandal of the sin sometimes remains. In such cases a man may be forgiven and yet disqualified from spiritual leadership, because his life has not been a model of godly virtue.

God promises to deal mercifully with those who confess and forsake their sins. Scripture says, "He who conceals his transgressions will not prosper, but he who confesses and forsakes them will find compassion" (Prov. 28:13).

However, there is no promise in Scripture that God's forgiveness will eradicate *all* the consequences of our sin. We have already observed that forgiveness does not necessarily erase the public reproach attached to scandalous sins. Forgiveness also does not necessarily avert divine discipline for sin.

When David sinned with Bathsheba, for example, many months passed before David was humbled enough to confess his sin and seek forgiveness. Scripture records that Bathsheba went through her entire pregnancy and delivered a son before Nathan came to confront David about his transgression.

During those months of disobedience, David was evidently suffering severe emotional and spiritual distress because of his sin. He wrote of that time, "When I kept silent about my sin, my body wasted away through my groaning all day long. For day and night Your hand was heavy upon me; my vitality was drained away as with the fever-heat of summer" (Ps. 32:3-4).

This was all part of God's discipline against David. His peace was taken away, and the weight of his guilt even affected him physically.

In spiritual terms, his unconfessed sin ruined the sweetness of his fellowship with God. The relationship was hindered on David's end. The problem was not that God refused fellowship with David; rather, David's own sin kept him from seeking God as he had when his conscience was clear. In Psalm 51, a psalm about this specific episode of sin, David wrote, "My sin is ever before me" (v. 3). Sin obscured David's view of God and thereby became an impassable barrier to the rich joy of the fellowship David had always enjoyed with the Lord. Compare David's comment in Psalm 51 with the confession he made when he was pure before God: "I have set the LORD always before me; therefore my heart is glad and my glory rejoices" (Ps. 16:9). But while David's sin remained unconfessed, it was the sin that was always before him, obscuring his view of God.

For God's part, He was "displeased" (2 Sam. 11:27, KJV). But it was God who sought David's restoration.

The story is well-known. Nathan the prophet confronted David with his sin. He did so subtly, by telling the wayward king a parable whose moral lesson described precisely the kind of wrong David had committed (2 Sam. 12:1-4). Failing to recognize himself in the parable, David decreed a death sentence against whoever was guilty of such a crime.

"You are the man!" was Nathan's chilling reply (v. 7). Then, continuing, Nathan prophesied about God's discipline against David:

> "Thus says the Lord God of Israel, 'It is I who anointed you king over Israel and it is I who delivered you from the hand of Saul. I also gave you your master's house and your master's wives into your care, and I gave you the house of Israel and Judah; and if that had been too little, I would have added to you many more things like these! Why have you despised the word of the LORD by doing evil in His sight? You have struck down Uriah the Hittite with the sword, have taken his wife to be your wife, and have killed him with the sword

of the sons of Ammon. Now therefore, the sword shall never depart from your house, because you have despised Me and have taken the wife of Uriah the Hittite to be your wife.' Thus says the LORD, 'Behold, I will raise up evil against you from your own household; I will even take your wives before your eyes, and give them to your companion, and he shall lie with your wives in broad daylight. Indeed you did it secretly, but I will do this thing before all Israel, and under the sun.'"

— vv. 7-12

David's immediate response was confession, followed by sincere repentance. The record of his repentance is Psalm 51.

Yet the Lord did not withdraw His discipline in return for David's confession. God stayed the death sentence David himself had unwittingly decreed, but He did not rescind His chastisement altogether:

Nathan said to David, "The LORD also has taken away your sin; you shall not die. However, because by this deed you have given occasion to the enemies of the LORD to blaspheme, the child also that is born to you shall surely die."

— vv. 13-14

Here is a perfect example of how justification erases sin's eternal condemnation, but not necessarily its temporal consequences. God forgave David's sins, but He did not erase the consequences— even though some of those consequences were divinely imposed as a means of punitive discipline.

In fact, David bore the consequences of that sin for the rest of his life. From this point on, his life became a chronicle of tragedy. As Nathan foretold, David's own wives were defiled in broad daylight by someone in his own household—his son Absalom (2 Sam. 16:22). Nathan's words to David make clear that God permitted this as a consequence of David's sin and as a way of chastening him. Could God have sovereignly stopped all the evil consequences of David's sin? Yes. Why did He not, especially after David repented?

Scripture does not provide a complete answer to that question, but we are given a hint in 2 Samuel 12:14, where God says to David that the discipline would occur "because by this deed you have given occasion to the enemies of the LORD to blaspheme." If God had allowed David to suffer no consequences for his act, the enemies of God would have had occasion to dishonor Him.

Furthermore, the chastening was part of God's covenant with David, and proof of God's love for him. In 2 Samuel 7:14 God promised, "I will be a father to him and he will be a son to Me; when he commits iniquity, I will correct him with the rod of men and the strokes of the sons of men, but My lovingkindness shall not depart from him, as I took it away from Saul, whom I removed from before you."

God had made an inviolable covenant with David and his house forever. And at the heart of that covenant was a vast promise of divine mercy for David. But along with the mercy came divine chastening when David sinned. The same principle applies to all the elect: "Whom the Lord loveth he chasteneth, and scourgeth every son whom he receiveth" (Heb. 12:6, KJV; cf. Prov. 3:12).

Far from being evidence that God has not *really* forgiven our sins, His loving discipline is proof that He has not cast us away. "For what son is there whom his father does not discipline? But if you are without discipline, of which all have become partakers, then you are illegitimate children and not sons" (Heb. 12:7-8).

WHAT DOES IT MEAN TO CONFESS OUR SINS?

The aim of genuine confession is not to avoid the earthly consequences of our sin. Read David's prayer of repentance in Psalm 51 and take note of this. David's confession focused entirely on sin's *guilt*, not its consequences. When he prayed the prayer recorded in that Psalm, David had already learned that he would suffer horrible consequences for his sin. His own children would dishonor him. His wives would be taken from him and made to commit adultery in broad daylight. The child he had conceived in his adultery with

Bathsheba would die, bringing him almost unbearable grief. God had already told him through the mouth of Nathan that all these things would certainly occur. David knew they were coming when he wrote Psalm 51.

Yet that great prayer of repentance includes no mention of sin's consequences. David made no complaint against the severity of God's discipline. His outrage in that Psalm was reserved for his own sin. That's because it was the *sin* that most disturbed David, not the *chastisement*. He wrote:

> *I know my transgressions, and my sin is ever before me. Against You,*
> *You only, I have sinned, and done what is evil in Your sight, so that*
> *You are justified when You speak and blameless when You judge.*
>
> – PS. 51:3-4

David was saying he regarded his discipline as totally just. Let no one question the righteousness of God for His treatment of David. David himself simply admitted that he was guilty as charged and deserved whatever consequences the Lord saw fit to bring against him.

That is precisely what it means to confess our sins. In 1 John 1:9, the word translated "confess" is the Greek verb *homologeo*, literally, "say the same." To confess our sins is to say the same thing as God says about them. Confessing our sins therefore means acknowledging that God's perspective of our transgressions is correct.

I once heard a Bible teacher claim that all God requires for forgiveness is that we simply name our sins—cite them—and He forgives. Another preacher I heard claimed all that is necessary is that we be aware of our sins. That is not what this verse teaches. Nor does confession merely mean *admitting* our sins. One can admit one's sin without truly agreeing with God's perspective. Acknowledging guilt is not the real sense conveyed by the word *homologeo*. Instead, to "confess" our sin in the truest sense involves despising the sin, being grieved by it, and judging it. That is what it means to say the same thing as God concerning our sin.

Must we keep a list of sins and confess every individual offense in order to get cleansing? That is not what this passage suggests. Agreeing with God concerning our sin is a constant attitude, not something done mechanically with a sin by sin checklist. Again, the verb tense in 1 John 1:9 speaks of continual confession. The apostle John is not calling for a one-to-one ratio of sins and confessions, but rather a constant, perpetual agreeing with God concerning our sin. And when we find ourselves, like David, enslaved to a particular sin, the only way to restore joy and harmony in our fellowship with God is repentance and confession.

TO WHOM DO WE CONFESS?

The confession spoken of in 1 John 1:9 is not confession to an earthly priest. Roman Catholicism is well-known for taking this verse, marrying it to James 5:16 ("Confess your sins to one another"), and employing those verses as justification for the priestly confessional booth.

Multitudes live in fear that if they do not regularly recite an inventory of their sins and seek the absolution of a priest, they might die with unconfessed sin and end up in hell. In effect, that makes confession of sin a meritorious work, as if the act of confession, combined with acts of penance, could somehow contribute to the atonement necessary to erase sins. All of that is foreign to Scripture, and certainly foreign to 1 John 1:9. This passage has nothing to do with confessional booths and rosary beads.

Here again, the verb tense is significant. Remember, "If we are confessing our sins" speaks of a continuous attitude, not a sacramental routine. This is in essence the apostle John's description of all true Christians—those who are continually saying the same thing as God about their sin. He is describing a characteristic of the true believer, not establishing a sacrament for doing penance.

In fact, there is nothing whatsoever in this context about confessing to other people. The confession the apostle has in mind is wholly Godward.

Is there ever a time when Christians ought to confess their sins to fellow Christians? We know that confession to God is *always* appropriate. Is person-to-person confession ever necessary? Yes. There are at least two situations that warrant this type of confession.

One is when we are seeking help from stronger, more mature Christians who can help us bear a burden, hold us accountable, pray for us, or otherwise be of help in overcoming bad habits and the difficult circumstances of sin (Gal. 6:2). That is the kind of confession in view in James 5:16: "Confess your sins to one another, and pray for one another so that you may be healed. The effective prayer of a righteous man can accomplish much."

The other time when person-to-person confession is appropriate is when we confess an offense to someone whom we have sinned against, in order to seek their forgiveness. This is part of the reconciliation necessary when we have directly wronged someone (Matt. 5:24). This is not to suggest that we are obligated to confess to someone every time we have an evil thought about them. But when our sins have caused another person real hurt, confession to the injured party is an appropriate, and even necessary, aspect of reconciliation.

However, what is in view in 1 John 1:9 is a Godward confession that ought to be characteristic of every Christian.

DO OUR SINS REMAIN UNFORGIVEN IF WE FAIL TO CONFESS?

One author whose works I read several years ago was an advocate of the checklist view. He believed that Christians should inventory their specific sins and confess them one by one. According to him, God forgives only the sins we specifically confess. All sins committed in ignorance, and sins forgotten or otherwise unconfessed, remain utterly unforgiven until the judgment-seat of Christ. At the *bema*, he said, Christ will deal with those unconfessed sins and punish us for them (though he believed Christ's work on the cross would guarantee that our punishment for those unconfessed sins would not include hell).

This man was a Protestant, but his view is very similar to the Catholic notion of Purgatory. It is at least as serious an error as the teaching of those who say Christians should never confess their sins, because if Christ's atonement does not provide judicial forgiveness for *all* our sins, then Christians will have to atone (at least partially) for some of their own sins. Such a doctrine is an implicit denial of the sufficiency of Christ's atonement.

Again, believers *already* have the fullest kind of judicial forgiveness. The apostle John wrote later in this same epistle, "I am writing to you, little children, because your sins *have been forgiven* you for His name's sake" (1 John 2:12). He used the past tense there to underscore the fact that the eternal question of our forgiveness is forever settled. The threat of condemnation for our sins is gone (Rom. 8:1).

Again, 1 John 1:9 is simply speaking about an attitude that is characteristic of *all* true Christians: they are the ones who as a pattern are saying the same thing as God about their sin. When they cover their sin, as David did, they do not prosper. They forfeit their joy. They reap divine displeasure. They experience divine chastening.

But when they confess and forsake their sin, there is the guarantee of divine compassion (Prov. 28:13). God, who disciplines sinning saints because of His love for them, also delights to shower the brokenhearted and repentant with His mercy and compassion.

FOUR

Put That on My Account

Accept him as you would me. But if he has wronged you in any way, or owes you anything, charge that to my account.

PHILEM. 17-18

Scripture everywhere teaches that those who have been forgiven much are obligated to forgive others (Matt. 18:23-35; Eph. 4:32; Col. 3:13). Christians are therefore to be characterized by a forgiving spirit.

God's forgiveness of sinners is sometimes referred to as *vertical* forgiveness. The sinner's forgiveness toward others is *horizontal* forgiveness. In the chapters that follow, we will look at several passages of Scripture that deal with horizontal forgiveness and probe the issue of how we are to forgive one another.

We begin with a look at one of the shortest books in all the New Testament. The epistle to Philemon is also the briefest and most personal of all of Paul's inspired works. Even though the word *forgiveness* never appears in the book, that is the whole subject of the epistle. It is a superb case study on how forgiveness should operate in the life of every believer. It also graphically illustrates how grace can reconcile a broken relationship and restore the offender.

THE CAST OF CHARACTERS

The drama behind this little epistle is touching: a remarkable providence brought the lives of three men together—a runaway slave, the offended slave owner, and a godly apostle. These men were vastly different from each other except in one regard: they all were believers in Jesus Christ and therefore members of the same body (1 Cor. 12:12-14).

Before becoming a Christian, however, Onesimus (the slave) had run away from his master and fled to Rome. Rome was a haven for runaway slaves because they could easily mingle with the large population there and avoid detection.

In Rome, Onesimus somehow encountered the apostle Paul, who was under house arrest while awaiting trial on false charges of sedition. The details of their meeting are not given in Scripture, but it is clear that Onesimus became a Christian as a result of the apostle's ministry (Philem. 10).

Philemon was the slave owner whom Onesimus had wronged. He too had come to faith in Christ through Paul's ministry, possibly years before, during Paul's time in Ephesus (Acts 18-20; cf. 19:26). Philemon owned the home where the Colossian church met (Philem. 2; cf. Col. 4:17). He seems to have been a wealthy and influential man, at the opposite end of the social spectrum from Onesimus. Yet he was a devoted Christian, regarded by the apostle Paul as a beloved "fellow-worker" (Philem. 1).

Onesimus also became a treasured friend and fellow laborer to the apostle Paul, ministering personally to Paul during the apostle's imprisonment in Rome, when many other Christians were fearful of associating with Paul because of the stigma and potential persecution (cf. 2 Tim. 1:8; 4:10-16).

THE PLOT

Both Paul and Onesimus must have been very reluctant for the slave to return to his master. Paul even stated that sending Onesimus back was like sending his "very heart" (Philem. 12). Yet Onesimus needed to seek his master's forgiveness for the wrong he'd done.

Onesimus was guilty under Roman law of some serious crimes. He had defrauded his master by running away, a crime tantamount to stealing. It may well be that he had actually stolen money too, because Paul offered to reimburse Philemon for anything the slave owed (v. 18). It was a serious matter in Rome to be a fugitive slave. If Onesimus had been captured by slave-catchers, he might have been imprisoned, sold for ransom, or even killed.

Possibly for that very reason, Paul waited to send Onesimus back to Philemon until someone could escort him. That opportunity came when it was time to send Tychicus to Ephesus and Colossae with the epistles Paul wrote to the churches there. Paul's epistle to the Colossians introduced Onesimus to that church, which would henceforth be his home church. Paul called Onesimus "our faithful and beloved brother, who is one of your number" (Col. 4:9).

Tychicus' presence ensured some degree of safety for Onesimus on the journey back to Colossae; but from a human perspective, the return to Philemon's house held a significant personal risk for Onesimus. Under Roman law, Philemon had full power to punish a runaway slave any way he saw fit. Multitudes of Roman slaves were tortured and put to death for far more petty offenses. As a standard practice, runaway slaves were branded with an F (for the Latin *fugitivus*) on the forehead, to make it impossible for them to hide if they should run away again. At the very least, a runaway slave would be given a severe beating. (In the century before Paul's time, a famous slave revolt led by Spartacus had been suppressed, and from then on Roman law was especially harsh with slaves who rebelled against their masters.) Yet Onesimus returned willingly and apparently without hesitation to his master. That speaks of the genuineness of his faith.

THE BACKDROP

Slavery was the universal practice at the height of the Roman Empire, and issues related to slavery are interwoven in the drama of this epistle. So perhaps a word is in order about the biblical perspective on slavery.

First, the slavery countenanced in Scripture is an indentured slavery, meaning that the slave entered into slavery by contract with the slave owner—usually for a set period of time (cf. Exod. 21:2-6). There was nothing inherently oppressive or unjust about such a relationship. In fact, the slave-master relationship was supposed to work much like modern employer-employee relationships in which contracts are involved. When Scripture instructs slaves to obey their masters, it is tantamount to telling employees to submit to their bosses.

Some aspects of Roman slavery *could* actually be beneficial for the slave. Many slaves dressed, ate, and lived at a higher standard than poor freemen. Slaves might be physicians, teachers, artisans, musicians, or accountants. Many slaves who learned such trades could ultimately buy their freedom. Some slaves even owned property. Wise slave owners used such incentives to motivate their servants. Some slaves and their owners developed close bonds, almost like a family relationship. Slave owners often granted beloved slaves freedom in their wills.

But *most* Roman slavery was not so benign. Slavery throughout the Empire was continually beset with abuses and harsh practices that were inherently immoral. Many Roman slaves were acquired and held by forcible means, rather than being properly indentured. Slavery in Rome digressed to the point where slaves were regarded as mere property. In the worst situations, Roman slaves were deprived of the right to marry and were bred like animals. It was also not unheard of for slaves to be killed on a mere whim by their masters. There is no moral defense for anyone to claim such absolute power of life and death over a fellow human.

Why does not the Bible expressly declare slavery immoral? Because, in the first place, it was the *abuse* of slavery, not servitude per se, that was evil. There is nothing inherently immoral or unjust about one man's serving another. Indentured slavery, practiced without the abuses that often accompanied Roman slavery, was no more immoral than the modern relationship between a business owner and a contract worker.

Furthermore, all abuses of slavery *are* condemned in Scripture, either directly or by clear principles. For example, the man-stealing on which the slave trade in early America (and much of Roman slavery) was based is expressly condemned in Scripture (Exod. 21:16). The inhumanity and injustice often perpetrated by evil slaveholders is likewise denounced throughout Scripture (cf. Lev. 19:15; Isa. 10:1-2; Amos 5:11-14).

It would have been wrong for the early church to turn aside from her calling in order to conduct a campaign for social reform, civil rights, or the abolition of slavery. It is equally inappropriate for the church today to flirt with such causes. When social reform becomes the sole focus, the gospel message is inevitably obscured by the human-rights agenda, and the work of the church is thus compromised.

Instead, the early church undermined the abusive system of Roman slavery by reaching both slaves and slave owners with the Gospel. What occurred between Onesimus and Philemon is simply one example of how the master-slave relationship was transformed throughout the Empire as the Gospel spread. By urging Philemon to receive Onesimus as a "brother" (Philem. 16), Paul defined the relationship between Christian master and slave in a way that made abuses unthinkable.

THE LETTER

Paul's epistle to Philemon was no doubt sealed and given to Tychicus to carry on his journey, along with the epistles to the Ephesians and Colossians. The letter is a gentle prompting to Philemon, reminding him of his duty to forgive, and an appeal for extreme mercy toward Onesimus. It shows as clearly as anything in the New Testament the magnanimity of Paul's heart, and his love of mercy.

Forgiveness was clearly on Paul's mind as he penned all three of the letters Tychicus was carrying. The epistle to the Ephesians includes this: "Be kind to one another, tender-hearted, forgiving each other, just as God in Christ also has forgiven you" (4:32). And the Colossian epistle expands on the same thought: "As those who have been chosen of God, holy and beloved, put on a heart of compassion, kindness, humility, gentleness and patience; bearing with one another, and forgiving each other, whoever has a complaint against any one; just as the Lord forgave you, so also should you" (3:12-13).

Those verses sum up precisely the message Paul wanted to give Philemon in particular. Having developed a warm affection for Onesimus, he longed to see him reconciled to Philemon, whose friendship and support Paul also cherished.

The epistle to Philemon is unique in the Pauline writings for several reasons. First, it is the only inspired letter written to an individual who was not a pastor, and it is the only one of Paul's inspired writings dealing with purely personal issues. That is, it was not expressly given as instruction for the Church at large, though in effect it *does* instruct all Christians on the importance of forgiveness. And the fact that it was ultimately included in the canon of Scripture means it was distributed to the churches for everyone's edification. But that may have been Philemon's choice. Paul addressed the epistle only to him and his household.

Second, and even more remarkable, this is the only one of Paul's epistles where he downplays, rather than asserts, his apostolic authority. He does this with very good reason. His aim was to appeal to Philemon to forgive freely, not to pressure him into forgiving by the force of his authority—"that [Philemon's] goodness should not be as it were by compulsion, but of [his] own free will" (v. 14).

The epistle was *deliberately* an appeal, rather than an order, as Paul told his friend: "Though I have enough confidence in Christ to order you to do that which is proper, yet for love's sake I rather appeal to you" (vv. 8-9). Paul, conciously declining to assert authority over Philemon, appealed instead to their love for one another (v. 9), Philemon's sense of spiritual partnership with Paul (v. 17), and Philemon's own great debt to Paul, who had brought him to Christ (v. 19).

The letter is addressed not only to Philemon, but also to Apphia (who must have been Philemon's wife) and Archippus (no doubt their son; cf. Col. 4:17). Paul thus appealed to the whole family to set the example of forgiveness for the church that met in their home (v. 2).

THE APPEAL

Paul apparently knew Philemon well. The apostle had been God's chosen instrument to bring Philemon to Christ. The two were longtime friends and had ministered alongside one another. They had other close friends in common. For example, Epaphras, Philemon's former pastor in the Colossian church, was presently Paul's companion in Rome (v. 23). Paul had great confidence in Philemon's character, and that is why he made such a tender appeal to his friend rather than simply issuing a command with the weight of apostolic authority.

Philemon's reputation as a godly and loving Christian was evidently widespread. It had reached as far as Rome because Paul writes, "I hear of your love, and of the faith which you have toward the Lord Jesus, and toward all the saints" (v. 5).

Such love for the saints is characteristic of all true Christians. The apostle John wrote, "We know that we have passed out of death into life, because we love the brethren" (1 John 3:14). Love for one another is the natural, and expected, by-product of a knowledge of God: "Beloved, let us love one another, for love is from God; and everyone who loves is born of God and knows God. The one who does not love does not know God, for God is love" (1 John 4:7-8). Clearly, some measure of love for the brethren is present in every believer.

But Philemon's love was extraordinary. He was renowned for his great love of the brethren. Even Paul drew comfort and encouragement from what he had heard about Philemon's affection for the saints. He wrote, "I have come to have much joy and comfort in your love, because the hearts of the saints have been refreshed through you, brother" (Philem. 7).

In other words, showing love to the saints was the ministry for which Philemon was well-known. His hospitality and love for the people of God was a predominant feature of his character, and everyone could see it. Not only had he opened his home to the church at Colossae, but he also was especially devoted to the task of refreshing the hearts of his fellow believers (v. 7).

The Greek word translated "refreshed" in verse 7 is *anapauo,* a military term used to describe an army resting after a long march. Philemon's ministry among the saints had a rejuvenating and invigorating effect among the struggling and often-persecuted early church.

Nothing in the biblical record suggests that Philemon was an elder or teacher in the church. He seems to have been a layman with a ministry of support, hospitality, and encouragement. But the overflow of love from his heart was legendary.

Those very virtues were the basis of Paul's appeal on behalf of Onesimus. Although Onesimus had left Philemon's household as a runaway slave, he was returning as a brother in Christ. The slave-master relationship would be superseded by a whole new relationship. Onesimus and Philemon had become spiritual brothers, and Paul knew that Philemon would recognize the duty this placed on him, for in Christ "there is neither slave nor free man . . . for you are all one in Christ Jesus" (Gal. 3:28).

Here is the heart of Paul's appeal to Philemon:

Therefore, though I have enough confidence in Christ to order you to do what is proper, yet for love's sake I rather appeal to you—since I am such a person as Paul, the aged, and now also a prisoner of Christ Jesus—I appeal to you for my child, whom I have begotten in my imprisonment, Onesimus, who formerly was useless to you, but now is useful both to you and to me. And I have sent him back to you in person, that is, sending my very heart, whom I wished to keep with me, so that on your behalf he might minister to me in my imprisonment for the gospel; but without your consent I did not want to do anything, that your goodness should not be as it were by com-

*pulsion, but of your own free will. For perhaps he was for this rea-
son parted from you for a while, that you should have him back forever, no longer as a slave, but more than a slave, a beloved brother,
especially to me, but how much more to you, both in the flesh and in
the Lord.*

— vv. 8-16

Paul's appeal to Philemon contrasts sharply with the approach he
takes in all his other epistles. Here he does not appeal to doctrinal
principles or divine law, but to Philemon's own love for the
brethren (v. 9). Since Onesimus was now a brother in Christ, Paul
knew Philemon would be naturally inclined to demonstrate love to
him.

Paul used a similar approach with the Corinthians when he
sought to encourage their giving. He appealed for each person to
give with a willing heart: "Let each one do just as he has purposed
in his heart, not grudgingly or under compulsion; for God loves a
cheerful giver" (2 Cor. 9:7). A forceful appeal to duty would no
doubt have been effective, but the reward for choosing obedience
gladly is so much more rich, and Paul did not want to rob them of
that reward. Likewise, with Philemon, Paul was so certain of his
friend's willingness to do right that he saw no need to employ
strong-arm tactics.

Was it Philemon's duty to forgive? Yes. To refuse forgiveness for
Onesimus would have been disobedient to the clear teaching of
Christ (cf. Luke 17:4; Matt. 6:15).

Withholding forgiveness is also a violation of the eternal moral
law of God. Jesus, expounding on the sixth commandment ("You
shall not murder," Exod. 20:13), taught that the Decalogue's prohibition against killing also rules out both anger and a vengeful heart:

*"I say to you that every one who is angry with his brother shall be
guilty before the court; and whoever shall say to his brother, 'You
good-for-nothing [see margin],' shall be guilty before the supreme
court; and whoever says, 'You fool,' shall be guilty enough to go into*

the hell of fire. If therefore you are presenting your offering at the altar,
and there remember that your brother has something against you,
leave your offering there before the altar, and go your way; first be rec-
onciled to your brother, and then come and present your offering."
                                                    − MATT. 5:22-24

Thus Christ not only condemned anger and spiteful words, but He
also placed on every believer the duty to seek reconciliation when
we know a brother is estranged by some offense we have committed. That entails a willingness to confess guilt when we have been
wrong, and a willingness to forgive when we have been wronged.
Whether we are the offender or the offended one, we should
actively seek reconciliation, and that always involves a willingness to
forgive.

Lest someone think this duty applies only to fellow believers,
remember the Second Great Commandment: "You shall love . . .
your *neighbor* as yourself" (Luke 10:27). In answer to the question
"Who is my neighbor?" Jesus gave the Parable of the Good
Samaritan, thus including even the most despised and outcast in the
circle of those whom we are to love as we love ourselves.

Loving others as we love ourselves clearly implies the duty of
forgiveness. This consists in a refusal to hold grudges, a refusal to
retaliate when the offense is personal against us, and a willingness
to extend full and complete forgiveness to all who seek it. It does not
mean we should look the other way when we see someone in sin
(see chapter 7). But in the case of a repentant brother, as Onesimus
was, there is no justification whatsoever for withholding forgiveness. Philemon would have been sinning had he done so.

Consider this: a sin against us always involves a greater sin
against God. David's adultery with Bathsheba, for example, was a
sin against her. It was a sin against her husband, Uriah (whom David
arranged to have killed). It was a sin against Uriah's family, now
deprived of a beloved relative. It was a sin against David's family,
who bore the consequences of his deed for generations. And it was

a sin against the entire nation of Israel, for David was their trusted king, example, and spiritual leader.

Yet in Psalm 51, David's great prayer of repentance, he says (v. 4), "Against You, You only, I have sinned and done what is evil in Your sight"—as if the sins against other people were not even worth mentioning. They paled in comparison to David's sin against God, and he wanted to make sure God knew he understood that. It was not that David was hard-hearted or impervious to his sins against others. Those sins were enormous, involving the killing of Uriah, the stealing of his wife, the compromise of Israel's national purity, lies told to just about everyone, and a host of other wrongs. But as great as his sins were against other people, the sin against God was infinitely greater. And God was therefore the *first* one to whom David appealed for forgiveness. God was the only one who mattered eternally. If God forgave David, then David could seek the forgiveness of others and could seek to make restitution where possible. But since the offense against God was the greatest, it was the first thing that had to be dealt with.

If every offense against us involves a greater offense against God, and if God forgives the offender, who are we to *withhold* forgiveness? Whatever Onesimus' offense against Philemon, he had sinned even more seriously against God. If God had already forgiven him, Philemon was in no position to withhold *his* forgiveness. If God forgives the greater offense, it is sinful to refuse to forgive the lesser one. Are we more just, holy, or deserving than God? Are we a higher court, with a more demanding law? Obviously not. Then whom God has forgiven, we dare not condemn. Those who refuse to forgive or who seek their own revenge have in effect usurped the authority of God.

Philemon also had a duty to the entire church at Colossae to forgive Onesimus. Had he refused to forgive the newest member of that fellowship, the entire congregation would have suffered. The unity of the group would have been broken, and their testimony to the unbelieving community would have been hurt.

So looked at from virtually every angle, Philemon had a clear responsibility to forgive Onesimus. Yet rather than pressing that duty on his friend with the weight of apostolic authority, Paul gently appealed to Philemon as a beloved brother, knowing that Philemon's maturity in Christ was such that he would gladly forgive one who had seriously wronged him.

THE CHALLENGE

There is no historical record of precisely what wrongs Onesimus had committed against Philemon. We know, of course, that he had run away, leaving his obligations unmet, defaulting on the stewardship that had been entrusted to him, perhaps even stealing from Philemon in order to finance his flight (cf. v. 18). His running away no doubt left Philemon in something of a bind.

So despite Philemon's personal commitment to Paul, his love for the saints, and his Christian maturity, there was no reason for Paul to assume that forgiving Onesimus would come easy to him. Onesimus' return very well might stir some intense emotions within Philemon. Philemon had every human reason to be angry with Onesimus and to resent what the slave had done. Paul nonetheless had enough confidence in his friend's character to frame his appeal as a request rather than a command.

Imagine Philemon reading this letter. Onesimus was probably standing in front of him. Philemon might have been surprised and at first was probably none too pleased to see the slave who had caused him so much trouble. But as he read Paul's letter his heart must have been moved by the manner in which the apostle wrote.

Notice that the apostle refers to himself as "Paul, the aged . . . now also a prisoner of Christ Jesus" (v. 9). Paul was probably about sixty at the time this letter was written. But he is probably referring to something more than his chronological age. This may have been a subtle reminder to Philemon of all the things that had taken their toll on Paul over the years—imprisonments, lashings, beatings, stonings, starvation, shipwrecks, thirst, cold and exposure and the resulting sickness (cf. 2 Cor. 11:23-30). His frail body had been severely aged by such things, and he constantly felt the pain of it. Furthermore, he remained a prisoner. He knew his dear brother would not want to add to his woes. And so on Onesimus' behalf, he subtly reminded Philemon of his own sufferings. Surely Philemon could not turn down a request from a friend who had endured so much suffering on Christ's behalf.

THE ACT OF FORGIVENESS

Paul lays out Onesimus' case in a way that would touch Philemon's heart:

> *I appeal to you for my child, whom I have begotten in my imprisonment, Onesimus, who formerly was useless to you, but now is useful both to you and to me. And I have sent him back to you in person, that is, sending my very heart, whom I wished to keep with me, that in your behalf he might minister to me in my imprisonment for the gospel. . . . For perhaps he was for this reason parted from you for a while, that you would have him back forever, no longer as a slave, but more than a slave, a beloved brother, especially to me, but how much more to you, both in the flesh and in the Lord. If then you regard me a partner, accept him as you would me. But if he has wronged you in any way, or owes you anything, charge that to my account.*
>
> − vv. 10-18

That request to Philemon outlines three crucial aspects of forgiveness.

Reception

"Accept him" (v. 17). Paul petitioned Philemon to open his life and household to Onesimus and to take him back. Philemon may well have been naturally disinclined to do that. After all, Onesimus had wronged him once. Why should the disobedient slave be given another opportunity? Most slave owners would have simply branded the runaway slave's forehead, and then sold him or demoted him to the lowest level of responsibility.

Therefore, Paul gave Philemon several reasons to view Onesimus in a new light.

First, he was *repentant*. When Paul wrote, "I have begotten [him] in my imprisonment" (v. 10), he was talking about Onesimus' spiritual rebirth. Paul was saying he had personally led Onesimus to Christ. Onesimus was Paul's own child in the faith, as was Philemon himself (v. 19). Paul wanted Philemon to know that he was sure the slave was soundly converted.

The very fact that Onesimus returned with Paul's letter to Philemon was evidence of the reality of his repentance. His presence before Philemon was tantamount to saying he was willing to accept whatever punishment Philemon deemed fit. It is significant that Onesimus did not stay in Rome to hide behind Paul's apostolic authority while Tychicus took the letter to Colossae on his behalf. Rather, Onesimus, no doubt at Paul's encouragement, went back to face the man he had wronged and to personally seek his forgiveness. He would accept the consequences of his wrongdoing, and that meant he would bear whatever punishment Philemon decided was fair. All this was certainly "fruit in keeping with . . . repentance" (cf. Matt. 3:8).

Second, Onesimus was *transformed*. "If any man is in Christ, he is a new creature; the old things passed away; behold, new things have come" (2 Cor. 5:17). Onesimus, formerly a useless rebel, was now "useful" (v. 11). This is a reference to the slave's name (a common one for slaves), which means "useful." Paul assured Philemon that Onesimus' transformation was genuine. His entire life had been turned around by Christ. The useless one was now a precious brother, certainly useful to Paul, and potentially useful to Philemon.

Third, Onesimus was *proven faithful*. He had spent enough time in Rome with Paul to demonstrate his faithfulness to Christ. Paul's confidence in and love for the converted slave were firmly grounded. Onesimus had served Paul well and thus proved himself willing to share the reproach of Christ. Other more seasoned associates of Paul would turn away when the rigors of persecution became too much for them (2 Tim. 4:10). But Onesimus, even as a new believer, devoted himself to serving Paul.

There was an irony in all this. Having sinfully fled from his bond-service to Philemon, Onesimus by divine grace had become a bond-servant of Jesus Christ. The very service he had refused to Philemon, he now willingly devoted to the apostle Paul. And it came at an important time—when the aged apostle was in a state of dire need. In fact, Onesimus had become so useful to the imprisoned apostle that Paul said sending him back to Philemon was like sending his own heart (v. 12). Had he been able, Paul would have kept Onesimus in Rome by his own side. But he knew Onesimus needed to go back and reconcile the broken relationship with his master.

Paul also knew that Philemon himself would have been in Rome if possible to minister to Paul. So Paul assured Philemon that he regarded Onesimus' service to have been offered "in your behalf" (v. 13). But not wanting to presume any further on his dear friend's graciousness, Paul concluded that it was now time to send Onesimus back. The relationship between these two brethren needed to be reconciled. And so Paul appealed to one friend on behalf of another: "accept him" (v. 17).

Restoration

Paul suggested that all these events were orchestrated for a good reason by Divine Providence: "For perhaps he was *for this reason* parted from you for a while, that you should have him back forever, no longer as a slave, but more than a slave, a beloved brother, especially to me, but how much more to you, both in the flesh and in the Lord" (vv. 15-16, emphasis added).

Indeed, it is hard not to see the hand of God in the story of Onesimus. Providence orchestrated his meeting Paul in a place so distant from Colossae. Divine grace drew him to Christ and transformed his whole life and attitude. And now under the Holy Spirit's guidance, Onesimus was going back to seek reconciliation with the master whom he had defrauded. In the midst of it all, the apostle Paul gained a friend and loving servant, not to mention the encouragement and help he drew from Onesimus. And now Philemon was getting his servant back, having unknowingly loaned him to the dear friend whom he longed to help but had no earthly way of ministering to. Only God could wring so much good from an act of human sin! (Compare Gen. 50:20; Rom. 8:28.)

Paul asked Philemon not only to accept Onesimus, but also to restore him. More than merely restoring him to his former position as a slave, Paul asked Philemon to receive him as "more than a slave, a beloved brother" (v. 16). Some have misunderstood this expression, inferring that Paul was asking for Onesimus' emancipation. But there is no reason to read such a conclusion into Paul's request. As noted earlier, the apostles did not regard our Lord's Great Commission as a campaign to free slaves. Elsewhere Paul wrote:

> *Let each man remain in that condition in which he was called. Were you called while a slave? Do not worry about it; but if you are able also to become free, rather do that. For he who was called in the Lord while a slave, is the Lord's freedman; likewise he who was called while free, is Christ's slave.*
>
> — 1 COR. 7:20-22

Nonetheless, Paul urged Philemon not to receive Onesimus as a *mere* slave, but also as a brother in Christ. Paul, familiar with Onesimus' commitment to Christ, knew the slave would be a rich source of joy, encouragement, and fellowship to Philemon.

Restitution

Paul now makes an astonishing proposal to Philemon: "If then you regard me a partner, accept him as you would me. But if he has wronged you in any way, or owes you anything, charge that to my account" (vv. 17-18). Paul was offering to make restitution on

Onesimus' behalf for whatever amount his wrongs had cost Philemon.

Restitution is fair and right; and when we seek another's forgiveness, an offer of restitution is always appropriate. The Old Testament civil laws demanded restitution in most cases where a wrong could be measured in terms of money or property. For intentional wrongs, the law demanded restitution with one-fifth interest (Num. 5:6-7).

Onesimus' running away had no doubt cost Philemon dearly. He certainly would have had to pay for someone to replace Onesimus. It is also possible that Onesimus' sin included embezzlement of money or property from Philemon. The slave was in no position to demand that Philemon forego restitution. He was also in no position to repay what he owed. So Paul graciously offered to pay on his behalf.

While restitution is always just and good, the kind of grace showed by Paul is even better. The most loving, magnanimous thing Philemon could do would be to forgive the slave's debt altogether. But Paul did not want to place Philemon under compulsion to forgive the offense. So he personally offered to make good on Onesimus' debt.

These verses are a wonderful illustration of how imputation works (see our earlier discussion). Paul asks Philemon to credit Onesimus with the apostle's own merit: "accept him as you would me" (v. 17). And he wants Onesimus' debt put to his account (v. 18). That is precisely how Christ justifies the believer. Having paid the debt of our sin, He imputes to us His own righteousness, and God receives us on that basis (Rom. 4:5).

Paul was modeling for Philemon the very sort of Christlike attitude he hoped to see his friend display toward the repentant slave. Nothing is more Christlike than assuming someone else's debt so reconciliation can take place. Paul was willing to suffer the temporal consequences of Onesimus' sin in the same way that Christ had willingly suffered the eternal consequences of all the sin of all the redeemed of all time.

Although Scripture does not record Philemon's response, it is likely that he saw the point of Paul's example and forgave Onesimus' debt entirely. In doing so, Philemon himself would have shouldered his offender's debt, which is precisely what Christ did in dying for our sins. That is why the act of forgiveness is the consummate expression of Christlikeness.

THE COST

Whether Philemon forgave the debt or not, Paul was so committed to seeing reconciliation take place that he reiterated his promise to repay the debt. In order to make it like an official contract, he signed the pledge in his own handwriting: "I, Paul, am writing this with my own hand, I will repay it" (v. 19). Paul normally dictated his letters, and then to insure their authenticity, he often wrote a brief closing greeting with his own hand (see Col. 4:18; 2 Thess. 3:17). In this case, early church tradition recorded that Onesimus was the one who acted as Paul's amanuensis. Then Paul dramatically closed the letter with this written I.O.U. Thus he underscored his great desire for the reconciliation of these two brothers and formally sealed his promise to Philemon with a binding, contractual guarantee.

Onesimus had no means to repay the debt himself. He was a mere slave, for one thing. Moreover, since his conversion in Rome, it seems he had devoted himself to the apostle Paul's service (cf. vv. 11-13; Col. 4:9), and that probably meant he had not acquired any kind of paying job. Paul, on the other hand, may well have had enough financial resources to pay the debt because the Philippian church had been so generous with him in his time of need (cf. Phil. 4:14-18).

However, as an aside, Paul reminded Philemon that he himself owed Paul an unpayable debt: "lest I should mention to you that you owe to me even your own self as well" (v. 19). By all rights, if Philemon put Onesimus' debt on Paul's account, the debt would *automatically* be canceled because Philemon owed Paul a far, far greater debt. Onesimus' debt to Philemon was measurable in numerical figures; Philemon's debt to Paul was an eternal, spiritual obligation. Paul, after all, was the one who had introduced Philemon to Christ. That was an incalculable debt that Philemon could *never* repay.

This is a perspective *every* Christian should have. We all owe our very existence to the immeasurable grace of God. That is a debt we cannot hope to repay. At no time are we justified in withholding grace from others. If our eternal offenses against God have been paid for by Christ, cannot we shoulder the burden of a temporal offense that someone else has committed against us? This principle is the very message of Jesus' parable about the unforgiving servant (see chapter 5).

There is no doubt that forgiveness is costly, and this episode illustrates that fact. But the most costly forgiveness of all was bought by the atoning sacrifice of Jesus Christ, and those who benefit from that great gift have every reason to forgive others, despite the cost. Whatever offense we bear from those who wrong us is comparatively paltry, no matter how great that offense may seem by human standards.

THE INCENTIVES

Paul, it seems, was confident of Philemon's willingness to forgive Onesimus' debt entirely. That may be what he referred to in verse 21 when he wrote, "I know that you will do even more than what I say." Nonetheless, Paul subtly suggested a few additional incentives for Philemon to forgive the prodigal slave.

Paul himself hoped to see the fruit of Philemon's forgiveness, and as an additional incentive for Philemon to be magnanimous, Paul informs him that he may shortly visit him in person: "At the same time also prepare me a lodging, for I hope that through your prayers I shall be given to you" (v. 22). It is possible, even likely, that when Paul penned this epistle, a trial date was set for him to appear before the imperial court, and it seems that Paul fully expected to be released. From Rome, he hoped to return to the churches he had founded in Asia Minor. This too would have an effect on Philemon's conscience. He could hardly be praying for Paul's return to Colossae unless he forgave Onesimus. He would not want his dear friend to show up and be disappointed in him. Such accountability to his spiritual father would move him to do the right thing for Onesimus.

The closing verses of Paul's epistle give a couple of other subtle incentives for Philemon to forgive. Paul writes, "Epaphras, my fellow prisoner in Christ Jesus, greets you, as do Mark, Aristarchus, Demas, Luke, my fellow-workers. The grace of the Lord Jesus Christ be with your spirit" (vv. 23-25).

First, by conveying greetings from five men known to Philemon, Paul reminded Philemon that all of them would be witnesses to his treatment of Onesimus.

Second, quietly included in that list of names is Mark. That refers to John Mark, author of the third Gospel. Mark was a cousin of Barnabas, and as a young man he had accompanied Paul and Barnabas on their first missionary journey. Along the way, he left the group and returned to Jerusalem (Acts 13:13). Mark's defection caused Paul to lose confidence in him. Later Barnabas wanted Paul to take John Mark on their second missionary journey, but Paul refused. Paul felt so strongly about the matter that he and Barnabas parted company over it (Acts 15:37-39). The apostle Peter evidently took Mark under his wing and helped bring him to maturity (1 Pet. 5:13). In time John Mark proved himself, even to the apostle Paul.

By now Paul had long since forgiven Mark. Mark ultimately became so much a part of Paul's ministry that shortly before Paul died, it was Mark whom he asked to be sent to him: "Pick up Mark and bring him with you, for he is useful to me for service" (2 Tim. 4:11).

The earlier tensions between Paul and Mark were widely known in the church. The episode even became a matter of record in the book of Acts. Luke, who wrote that account, was also known to Philemon; so he is included in the list of those whose greetings Paul conveyed in this epistle. So without Paul's even saying it, his own example of having forgiven Mark stood as yet another encouragement to Philemon that he should do the right thing with Onesimus.

THE OUTCOME

Did Philemon forgive Onesimus? Though Scripture does not expressly record how the incident turned out, there are several reasons to assume that Philemon's response was everything Paul hoped for. For one thing, Paul's epistle found its way into the New Testament canon. This was, after all, a private letter to Philemon, and it is highly unlikely that he would have allowed it to be circulated among the churches if he had chosen to reject Paul's advice.

Furthermore, if Philemon was the man of character Paul portrays him to be, it is unthinkable that he would have refused Paul's counsel. (If he was *not* the loving and godly man Paul described, then we would have a problem with the trustworthiness of Scripture.) Furthermore, if Philemon had refused to grant forgiveness to Onesimus, it is highly unlikely that the early church would have received the epistle into the canon without someone's protesting. So the very presence of this epistle in the canon is very strong evidence that Philemon did as Paul requested.

History records that Paul was released from prison just as he hoped (v. 22). We know that he traveled much in the remaining years of his life, and if he fulfilled his plans, he would have returned to Colossae to see for himself how well his two sons in the faith had reconciled with one another.

A few decades later, shortly after the turn of the first century, Ignatius, one of the early Church Fathers, wrote three epistles to the church at Ephesus. The first two of those epistles refer to the pastor at Ephesus as "Onesimus, a man of inexpressible love." Whether it was the same Onesimus is impossible to tell. If so, he would have been an old man, probably at least in his seventies by then. If this was a different and younger Onesimus, he may have been someone named for the old slave who had made himself useful to the apostle Paul.

Only heaven will reveal the full truth about the end of the story. And there we will learn, I'm certain, that the fruits of one act of forgiveness are unimaginably far-reaching. In this case, before Philemon ever forgave, the seeds were sown for a rich harvest of spiritual fruit because Paul's brief letter of appeal to Philemon found its way into the New Testament, where it continues to challenge us all to forgive others as Christ forgave us.

And for Paul and Philemon and Onesimus, the reconciliation of this broken relationship would have been one of those sublime moments when everyone came out triumphant—Paul because he shared in the joy of reconciling two dear friends, Onesimus because he was forgiven an unpayable debt, and Philemon because he received the eternal blessings that come to the one who forgives.

FIVE

Forgiving
One Another

*As those who have been chosen of God, holy and beloved,
put on a heart of compassion, kindness, humility, gentleness and patience;
bearing with one another, and forgiving each other, whoever has
a complaint against any one; just as the Lord
forgave you, so also should you.*

COL. 3:12-13

For a Christian to be willfully unforgiving is unthinkable. We who have been forgiven by God Himself have no right to withhold forgiveness from our fellow sinners. In fact, Scripture plainly commands us to forgive in the same manner as we have received forgiveness: "Be kind to one another, tender-hearted, forgiving each other, just as God in Christ also has forgiven you" (Eph. 4:32).

Since God *commands* us to forgive others, refusing to do so is an act of direct disobedience against Him. Let me say it plainly: refusing to forgive is a horrible sin.

Forgiveness reflects the character of God. Unforgivingness is therefore ungodly. That means unforgivingness is no less an offense to God than fornication or drunkenness, even though it is sometimes deemed more acceptable. Certainly it is more frequently found in the open among the people of God than the sins we typically regard as heinous. But Scripture is clear that God despises an unforgiving spirit.

As God's children, we are to mirror His character. At salvation we are given a new nature that bears God's spiritual likeness (Eph. 4:24). So forgiveness is an integral part of the Christian's new nature. An unforgiving Christian is a contradiction in terms. When you see a professing Christian who stubbornly refuses to relinquish a grudge, there's good reason to question the genuineness of that person's faith.

Yet to face the issue squarely, we must all admit that forgiveness does not come easily, even as Christians. Often we do not forgive as speedily or as graciously as we should. We're all too prone to nurse offenses and withhold forgiveness.

As we have seen, forgiveness is costly. Forgiveness requires us to set aside our selfishness, accept with grace the wrongs others have committed against us, and not demand what we think is our due. All of that runs counter to our natural, sinful inclinations. Even as new creatures, we retain a remainder of sin in our flesh. Sinful habits and desires continue to plague us. That is why Scripture commands us to put off the old man and clothe ourselves with the new (Eph. 4:22-24; Col. 3:9-10). And the new man is characterized by forgiveness. Notice that in both places where the apostle Paul employs such terminology, he highlights forgiveness as an essential garment for "the new self" (Eph. 4:32; Col. 3:13).

Forgiveness is so important to the Christian's walk that it was never far from the focus of what Christ taught. His sermons, His parables, His private discourses, and even His prayers were all filled with lessons about forgiveness. In fact, this was so much a running motif in Jesus' earthly sermons and sayings that one would have to be willfully blind to miss the point.

For example, as we have seen, at the heart of the Lord's Prayer is this petition: "Forgive us our debts, as we also have forgiven our debtors" (Matt. 6:12). Both the context and the cross-reference in Luke 11:4 indicate that the "debts" referred to here are *spiritual* debts; "debtors" are those who have committed transgressions against us.

It is significant that of all the phrases in the Lord's Prayer, it was *this* phrase that Christ saw fit to explain in the most detail. Immediately after the prayer's amen, He turned to the disciples and said, "For if you forgive men for their transgressions, your heavenly Father will also forgive you. But if you do not forgive men, then your Father will not forgive your transgressions" (vv. 14-15).

That has always been a difficult passage for expositors. At first glance it seems to make God's forgiveness revokable. Some have cited this verse to argue that if we refuse forgiveness to those who offend us, God will *withdraw* His forgiveness from us, implying that a Christian who does not forgive can lose his or her salvation.

But as we saw in chapter 3, the forgiveness spoken of here is not the *judicial* forgiveness of justification. It is the daily, *parental* forgiveness we are to seek when our sin has grieved our heavenly Father. One interpretive key is the prayer's address: "Our Father." This is a prayer for parental, not judicial, forgiveness. What Jesus is actually saying here is tantamount to: "If you refuse to forgive, your heavenly Father will discipline you severely for *your* sin of unforgivingness."

A well-known parable found elsewhere in Matthew's Gospel perfectly illustrates the point. Usually known as the Parable of the Unforgiving Servant, this often-misunderstood passage and its context contains some of Scripture's richest truth about forgiving one another.

PETER'S QUESTION

The parable was Jesus' response to a question raised by Peter. Having heard so much on the subject from Jesus, the disciples could not have missed the importance He placed on forgiveness. But they no doubt all had questions about how far He expected them to go in forgiving one another. As usual, Peter was the spokesman for them all.

Christ's teaching about forgiveness must have seemed radical to the disciples. What He taught contrasted markedly with what the rabbis of His time believed. We already mentioned in chapter 2 how the rabbis had twisted the eye-for-an-eye provision in the Old Testament and were using it as justification for personal vengeance.

Obviously, forgiveness was not necessarily regarded as a high virtue by most of the influential religious teachers of Jesus' day. In fact, the rabbis usually portrayed forgiveness as optional. The rabbis *did* acknowledge that the Old Testament permitted and even encouraged forgiveness in some cases. However, they strictly limited to three the number of times any person could be forgiven for the same offense.

They believed they had biblical authority for that view. They drew support for it from the book of Amos, where God pronounced doom on the enemies of Israel with these words: "For three transgressions of Damascus, and for four I will not revoke its punishment" (1:3). In that same chapter God pronounced similar judgments against Gaza, Tyre, Edom, and Ammon, always with the words, "For three transgressions . . . and for four" (cf. vv. 6, 9, 11, 13). In other words, each of those hostile nations was permitted three offenses that God overlooked, and He judged them for the fourth offense.

The rabbinical scholars reasoned that if God forgives men only three times, it would be presumptuous and even wrong for mere creatures to forgive their fellow creatures any more than that. So they set a limit on the number of times forgiveness could be extended.

No doubt because of the stress on grace and forgiveness throughout Christ's teachings, the apostles knew that He was calling them to a higher standard. Since Christ Himself had never quantified the number of times forgiveness is to be granted, Peter wanted to get some clarification. Matthew 18:21 says, "Then Peter came and said to Him, 'Lord, how often shall my brother sin against me and I forgive him? Up to seven times?'"

Peter no doubt thought he was being magnanimous. He doubled the rabbinical prescription, then rounded the number up to a perfect 7, possibly thinking the Lord might commend him for his generosity.

Jesus' reply undoubtedly stunned Peter and all the other disciples.

JESUS' ANSWER

Jesus said to him, "I do not say to you, up to seven times, but up to seventy times seven" (vv. 22).

The fleshly mind immediately protests what seems an unreasonable standard. Doesn't forgiveness have a limit? Common sense would seem to suggest that repeat offenders should not be granted pardon indefinitely. At what point does grace become gullibility? Seventy times seven is 490! No one can possibly even keep count of such a high number of offenses!

But that is precisely the point! Keeping count has nothing to do with true forgiveness. If an offense is sincerely forgiven, it cannot be held against the offender. The rabbinical system in effect required the offended party to remember and record supposedly forgiven offenses and stop forgiving after the third time. Jesus' teaching on forgiveness permits no such score-keeping. "Seventy times seven" set the standard so high that it would be pointless to keep an account of the injuries we have borne. But that is fitting, because the sort of love Christians are called to exemplify "does not take into account a wrong suffered" (1 Cor. 13:5).

The person who keeps track of wrongs, thinking he can stop forgiving when the tally reaches 490, has utterly missed the point of Jesus' words. Our Lord was not setting a numerical limit on forgiveness, but quite the opposite. He simply took Peter's number and multiplied it by seventy! For all practical purposes, He made it impossible to tabulate offenses the way Peter was thinking. In effect, He eliminated any limit on forgiveness whatsoever.

Jesus' words may contain an allusion to an Old Testament reference. Early in the book of Genesis, we encounter a man in Cain's lineage named Lamech. (This is a different Lamech from the man who was Noah's father.) Scripture says very little about Lamech, but what is recorded indicates that he was an angry man who loved vengeance. He killed someone, apparently in self-defense. Knowing that God had sworn to avenge Cain sevenfold, Lamech arrogantly believed he deserved seventy times as much vengeance. Scripture records that he devised a saying that, in Hebrew, reads like a song or a poem: "Hear my voice; ye wives of Lamech, hearken unto my speech: for I have slain a man to my wounding, and a young man to my hurt. If Cain shall be avenged sevenfold, truly Lamech seventy and sevenfold" (Gen. 4:23-24, KJV).

Lamech's boast typifies the tendency of sinful humanity. The sinful mind loves vengeance and thinks seventy times seven is a fitting ratio by which to measure revenge. Instead, Christ taught that seventy times seven is the measure by which we ought to forgive. In other words, we should always return good for evil in precisely the same abundant measure that we might otherwise be sinfully inclined to return evil for evil (cf. Rom. 12:17; 1 Thess. 5:15; 1 Pet. 3:9).

On another occasion Jesus said, "Be on your guard! If your brother sins, rebuke him; and if he repents, forgive him. And if he sins against you seven times a *day*, and returns to you seven times, saying, 'I repent,' forgive him" (Luke 17:3-4, emphasis added).[1] Again, the point is not to set a numerical limit, such as seven times in one day, but to underscore the freeness and frequency with which we are to forgive.

Someone might ask, Who in the world would commit the same offense seven times in one day and then profess repentance after each time? Here's the point: this sort of behavior is precisely how *we* sin against *God*. We sin; then we express sorrow for our sin and seek God's forgiveness; then we turn around and commit precisely the same sin again. Anyone who has ever been in bondage to a sinful habit knows precisely what the routine is like.

Does God forgive under such circumstances? Yes, He does. And since His forgiveness sets the criterion by which we are to forgive, the standard is set blessedly high. What may seem at first like an impossibly unfair and unattainable standard is in fact wonderful news for anyone who has ever needed to seek the forgiveness of God for repeat offenses. Jesus is teaching here that the forgiveness we extend to others should be as boundless as the mercy of God we desire for ourselves. That shatters all the limits anyone would try to place on human forgiveness.

All of this is underscored by the parable Jesus gave in reply to Peter's question. The main characters in the parable are a gracious king, a servant deeply in debt to the king, and another slave who owed the first servant a smaller debt.

THE KING'S FORGIVENESS

The parable begins by describing an incredible act of forgiveness on the part of the king:

> *"For this reason the kingdom of heaven may be compared to a king who wished to settle accounts with his slaves. And when he had begun to settle them, there was brought to him one who owed him ten thousand talents. But since he did not have the means to repay, his lord commanded him to be sold, along with his wife and children and all that he had, and repayment to be made. The slave therefore falling down, prostrated himself before him, saying, 'Have patience with me, and I will repay you everything.' And the lord of that slave felt compassion and released him and forgave him the debt."*
> — MATT. 18:23-27

This debtor to the king was very likely a man of high rank, even though he is referred to as a servant. Ancient kings employed provincial governors called satraps. One of the responsibilities of the satrap was to collect taxes. This indebted servant might have been one of these provincial governors, and the settling of accounts referred to in verses 23-24 was the time appointed for the satrap to bring the tax money from his region to the king.

This man was deeply in debt. Such a massive debt was no doubt because of some embezzlement or other dereliction of duty on the servant's part. Moreover, if he had taken all the tax money by theft or embezzlement, he had utterly squandered it, because he had no means by which to repay what he owed.

Ten thousand talents was an unbelievably large amount of money for one individual to owe. A talent was the largest measure of money in the Roman world. This refers to the Attic talent, in use at that time throughout the Empire. One such talent was worth 6,000 denarii, and a denarius was considered a fair wage for a day's work (cf. Matt. 20:2). In fact, a denarius was a soldier's wage for a day. So 6,000 denarii, one talent, was a considerable sum of money (about seventeen years' wages), and 10,000 talents were equal to seventeen years' wages for 10,000 men. This was an unfathomable amount of personal debt. In today's terms this would be millions, possibly billions, of dollars. To put it in perspective, records from the first century reveal that the total annual revenue collected by the Roman government from the entire land of Palestine averaged about 900 talents. Furthermore, Solomon's temple was world-renowned for the massive amounts of gold it contained. All that gold, according to the Old Testament, amounted to just over 8,000 talents (1 Chron. 29:4–7)—less than this one man owed!

The Greek expression translated "ten thousand" does not necessarily even signify a precise amount. This was the largest number expressible in the Greek language. It is the word from which we derive the English term *myriads*, and it was often used exactly the way we employ its English counterpart—to represent any uncountable number. In the *New American Standard Bible* translation the same word is translated "myriads" in Revelation 5:11; in 1 Corinthians 4:15 it is rendered "countless."

So this man owed the king a debt that, for all practical purposes, was unpayable. Since he had no means by which to finance such a massive liability, the king commanded that he, his family, and all his possessions be sold, with the proceeds to be paid against the debt.

Obviously, this debt was so large that the sale of the man and his family would not have covered even the smallest fraction of what was owed. Nonetheless, it was the king's right to demand such a penalty for this man's misdeeds.

The servant's state was utterly hopeless. His only hope lay in the king's goodness. So he began to plead for mercy. Jesus said, "falling down, [he] prostrated himself" before the king (v. 26). This was far more than the usual homage given a king. It signified the man's utter, abject despair. He was literally throwing himself before the king in a plea for mercy. He offered no defense because he had none. He fully admitted his guilt and simply petitioned for mercy.

"Have patience with me, and I will repay you everything," he cried (v. 26). The promise was no doubt sincere, but the burden of such a debt was more than a hundred men could ever repay, and the monarch knew it.

At this point the average monarch might be expected to deal mercilessly with the slave. The gross abuse of his position, the waste of a fortune, the size of the deficit, combined with the servant's foolish pledge to pay it back, is the stuff that would exasperate a typical king. The servant certainly deserved no mercy.

But this was no typical sovereign. In an incredible gesture of pardon, he freely forgave the man's debt. No repayment plan was instituted; the king was willing to absorb the loss himself, simply for the sake of showing mercy to a helpless servant. This is an amazing, unearthly compassion. It is the very picture of what God does on behalf of every sinner who repents.

The servant perfectly symbolizes the lost sinner, saddled with a monstrous, unpayable debt—the overwhelming burden of sin's guilt. The debtor's prison pictures hell, where condemned sinners will spend eternity paying for the unpayable. And the king pictures a loving and compassionate heavenly Father, a God of unfathomable mercy and grace who is always willing and eager to forgive.

This king's forgiveness is astonishingly generous. Consider all that his pardon involved. In order to forgive this massive amount of money, he had to regard it as a legitimate loan, though the facts make clear that this was a case of embezzlement and waste. Even in the best case, the debt resulted from unconscionable malfeasance combined with inconceivable extravagance. In fact, the man may well have been guilty on all counts. Yet the king graciously forgave not only the debt, but also whatever wickedness had helped accrue such monstrous debt. He did not chide the man or punish him for his crookedness. He simply, compassionately forgave him.

One wonders how any king could be so compassionate with such a wicked subject. But remember, this is precisely the picture of what God does for the repentant sinner. He not only forgives sin's guilt, but He elevates the sinner to a position of incomprehensible, utterly undeserved favor!

THE SERVANT'S UNFORGIVINGNESS

You would think that someone so freely forgiven would appreciate the importance of showing compassion to others. But the behavior exhibited by the forgiven slave is shocking: "That slave went out and found one of his fellow-slaves who owed him a hundred denarii; and he seized him and began to choke him, saying, 'Pay back what you owe'" (v. 28).

A hundred denarii represented about 100 days' wages. That is not an insignificant sum considered by itself, but compared to the amount the first servant had been forgiven, it was nothing. Jesus' wording indicates that the forgiven servant went out immediately from his encounter with the gracious king, and practically the first thing he did was find this other servant who owed him money. He then began to demand immediate repayment, punctuating his demands with the harshest conceivable threats, and even physical brutality.

Think for a moment about the situation this parable presents. The debt owed to this man by his fellow servant was a legitimate debt. From a legal standpoint, he did have a rightful claim on what was owed to him. Technically, he was completely within his rights to demand repayment. But do not our moral senses naturally and rightfully recoil at his behavior?

We see his act as morally repugnant, because it is. The first servant's very existence depended on an incomprehensible act of mercy that had been shown to him. Did he not therefore have a duty to love mercy and to extend it to others as well?

The totally undeserved forgiveness he had received from the king should have made him profoundly grateful, and also profoundly merciful. His unmerciful actions toward his fellow slave were therefore an insult to the king who had forgiven him. The extraordinary mercy he had received ought to have been the thing that filled his heart and mind. Instead, he was obsessed with regaining the paltry sum owed him by a fellow servant. His actions betrayed a lack of gratitude. It was as if he had already forgotten the great mercy that had been shown to him.

The slave's behavior is grotesque. It reads like a caricature of the worst kind of villainy. It seems unreal, inhuman. Who could ever behave this way?

That was exactly the point Jesus wanted to make with the disciples. He purposely portrayed the servant in a way that would shock them. If the slave's behavior seems unreasonable and totally irrational, it is supposed to. Our Lord was underscoring the absurdity of an unforgiving Christian. This is bizarre, unconscionable behavior. No sensible person could ever be expected to act this way.

But it is exactly what occurs every time a Christian is unforgiving.

Notice that the servant who owed the lesser debt made precisely the same plea the original servant had made to the king: "Have patience with me and I will repay you" (v. 29). The forgiven servant *should* have been moved by this echo of his own despair. After all, only a very short time before he had been in a far worse predicament, and those were his very words! If anyone in the world should have understood the plight of the second servant, it was this man who had already been forgiven for so much.

But he turned a deaf ear to his fellow servant's plea. With astonishing coldheartedness, he "threw him in prison until he should pay back what was owed" (v. 30).

Debtors' prisons were common in that time. The debtor was imprisoned and given some menial labor to do, for which he was paid a pittance. Those wages went toward the payment of the debt, and the prisoner was not released until the debt was paid. It was a questionable way to deal with debtors, however, because imprisoning them cut their earning power, imposed further hardships on their families, and in many cases made repayment practically impossible. The creditor therefore often came out on the losing end. So imprisonment was usually a last resort used for only the most recalcitrant debtors.

It was for those reasons extremely unwise and unduly severe to have a debtor thrown in prison who was willing to repay. Even if the first servant had decided to insist on repayment of what was owed to him, he did not need to have the second servant imprisoned. Such punishment was unreasonable, overly harsh, and irrational. It perfectly pictures the absurdity of a Christian with a vengeful heart.

THE OTHER SERVANTS' OUTRAGE

Notice who was most offended by the servant's harsh treatment of the debtor: his fellow servants. "When his fellow-slaves saw what had happened, they were deeply grieved and came and reported to their lord all that had happened" (v. 31).

These servants obviously knew about the great debt the first man had been forgiven. And they were rightfully indignant when they saw his response to a fellow servant in need. In effect, the unforgiving servant had placed himself above the king. His actions suggested that he believed he had a right to extract vengeance in a situation identical to the one in which he had asked the king to show him mercy. This was unspeakably wicked. It is no wonder that his fellow servants were outraged.

The other servants' involvement pictures how the sin of one individual affects the entire body. One unforgiving person in the church can cause offense to the entire flock, and it is right that Christians should get involved in dealing with such an obvious offense. In fact, the broader context of Matthew 18 includes Jesus' instructions on how discipline is to be handled in the church (see chapter 7 for a fuller discussion of the process of church discipline).

THE KING'S ANGER

Understandably, the king also was outraged when he heard the report of what had happened:

> *"Then summoning him, his lord said to him, 'You wicked slave, I forgave you all that debt because you entreated with me. Should you*

not also have had mercy on your fellow-slave, even as I had mercy on you?' And his lord, moved with anger, handed him over to the torturers until he should repay all that was owed him."

– vv. 32-34

The king's response was so severe that it causes many people to conclude that the unforgiving servant in this parable cannot possibly represent a true believer. They assume punishment this harsh must represent hell; and since no genuine believer is ever subject to the threat of hell, this man must represent an unregenerate person.

Others cite the parable as an argument in favor of the view that disobedient Christians can lose their salvation.

This is admittedly a difficult passage. It is possible to read verse 34 ("handed him over to the torturers until he should repay all that was owed him") to mean that the unforgiving servant was saddled with the same debt that had already been forgiven. But that introduces some obvious difficulties into the imagery of the parable. Does this suggest that God will withdraw His judicial forgiveness—justification—from those who fail to forgive others? Certainly not. That would ultimately make justification hinge on the sinner's own works. It would also suggest that God Himself is vacillating—granting "forgiveness" but withdrawing it later. Scripture plainly says He will not do that. When God forgives us, He removes our sins as far from us as the east is from the west (Ps. 103:12). He blots out our sins and promises to remember them no more (Isa. 43:25; Jer. 31:34; Heb. 8:12). He does not forgive and then rescind His forgiveness.

Could it be that the unforgiving servant represents a professing believer who was actually never regenerate to begin with? This is a popular view. Those who advocate this interpretation say the unforgiving servant pictures someone who hears the Gospel and embraces it externally, but who never really receives the forgiveness offered in the Gospel. That is a more viable interpretation, but it still suggests that the servant's response, rather than the king's decree, is the key issue in justification. It makes forgiveness conditional on the sinner's subsequent behavior.

An important rule of thumb when interpreting parables is to look for the parable's central meaning and to resist the temptation to try to press too much meaning out of peripheral details. The meaning of this parable is expressed plainly by Christ in verse 35: "So shall My heavenly Father also do to you, if each of you does not forgive his brother from your heart." This whole parable is virtually a commentary on Jesus' earlier words in Matthew 6:14-15: "For if you forgive men for their transgressions, your heavenly Father will also forgive you. But if you do not forgive men, then your Father will not forgive your transgressions."

Remember also that this parable is a lesson for Peter and the other disciples. Jesus did not aim the message of the parable at interested but uncommitted hearers. He clearly made it a warning to those in the innermost circle of His followers (v. 35). The lesson it contains is for already-regenerate people—believers, not merely pretenders.

Therefore, the first servant must represent a truly regenerate, yet unforgiving believer. The severity of the king's punishment here is actually illustrative of how God will discipline unforgiving believers. It is sometimes necessary for a parent to deal harshly with a persistently rebellious child; and God Himself will employ harsh measures when necessary to correct a disobedient Christian. The harshness of His discipline is a measure of His love for His people and His concern for their purity. As we saw in chapter 3, it is not true that God's discipline is always mild and friendly; often it is prompted by the severest kind of fatherly displeasure. And some of His most severe discipline is given to believers who refuse to show mercy to others.

Notice how the king addressed the unforgiving servant: "You wicked slave." Would God refer to one of His own children as "wicked"? He certainly is not blind to their wickedness (cf. 2 Chron. 7:14). And this slave was behaving in a way that was undeniably wicked. Sin is wicked, whether committed by a believer or unbeliever. In fact, unforgivingness is *more* wicked in a believer because the believer's refusal to forgive is a slight against the very grace on which he depends for redemption. In a case like this, it would not be any more inappropriate for God to call a believer "wicked" than it was for Christ to address Peter as "Satan" (Matt. 16:23).

Notice also that the punishment administered, though extremely severe, seems to picture only the harshest kind of discipline, not eternal condemnation. The king "handed him over to the torturers"—not the executioners—"until he should repay all that was owed him" (v. 34).

Look at that verse closely. What was now owed to the king? Since the earlier debt was already legally forgiven, the remaining debt was primarily this man's duty to show the same kind of mercy to others. The "torturers" represent the rod of God's discipline. The lesson of the parable is this: Christians who refuse to forgive others will be subject to the severest kind of discipline until they learn to forgive as they have been forgiven.

"All that was owed him" also represents the temporal consequences of sin. Again, justification erases the guilt of our sin in the eternal court of God, but it does not necessarily guarantee an escape from sin's consequences in this life. This parable seems to suggest that as a means of His loving discipline, God might actually magnify the temporal consequences of sin. Though the *guilt* of sin is forgiven so that it will never be an issue in eternal judgment, God may permit the *consequences* of sin to be even more severe, in order to motivate a sinning believer to obey. Because unforgivingness is so completely foreign to what Christians should be, Christ applies this threat particularly to that sin: "So shall My heavenly Father also do to you, if each of you does not forgive his brother from your heart" (v. 35).

Christians *ought* to be the most forgiving people on earth, because they have been forgiven as no one else has. Therefore, those who refuse to forgive are worthy of the most severe kind of discipline from the hand of a loving Father.

James 2:13 gives an inexorable principle of divine justice: "Judgment will be merciless to one who has shown no mercy." For the unsaved, the prospects of this principle are fearsome indeed. Those who have been merciless will have no mercy in the eternal court of God. They will suffer eternal torment entirely without mercy.

But there is an application of this principle for the believer as well. Christians who fail to show mercy will be subject to divine chastisement without much mercy. That is the whole message of this parable. I am convinced that multitudes of Christians who suffer from stress, depression, discouragement, relationship problems, and all sorts of other hardships experience these things because of a refusal to forgive. Forgiveness from the heart would liberate the person immediately from such "torturers"—and glorify God in the process.

In fact, the corollary of the James 2:13 principle is one of the Beatitudes: "Blessed are the merciful, for they shall receive mercy" (Matt. 5:7). Divine mercy is promised to those who show mercy. On this subject, Scripture speaks with extraordinary clarity.

Notice that Jesus speaks of forgiveness "from your heart" (Matt. 18:35). Genuine forgiveness is not feigned or grudging, but is given as freely as we ourselves desire to be forgiven. It involves a deliberate refusal to hold the guilt over the head of the offender. It means ending the bitterness, laying aside anger, and refusing to dwell on the offense that has been forgiven. It is a complete letting go of any thought of retaliation or reprisal. It is, as nearly as possible, the human equivalent of what God promises—to remember the sin no more (cf. Jer. 31:34).

Such forgiveness does not come easy, particularly when it deals with the kinds of sins that destroy lives and relationships. When we're talking about a personal slight or an unkind word, it's relatively easy to forgive. But what if the offense is more serious? Where do people find the strength to forgive when they discover a spouse has cheated, or when a drunk driver causes the death of a loved one? Is it humanly possible to forgive such offenses?

It may not *seem* humanly possible, and it certainly does not lie within the power of fallen human nature alone to forgive such things from the heart. But it certainly is possible for redeemed people, under the influence of the Holy Spirit's power, to forgive even the most serious offenses. In the chapter that follows we will look more intently at some of these issues and will delve into some of the most important practical issues regarding how we should forgive one another.

SIX

Just As God Has Forgiven You

Forgiving each other,
just as God in Christ also has forgiven you.

EPH. 4:32

It was Monday, December 1, 1997. About a dozen students were huddled to pray—as they did every morning—in the hallway outside the administration office at Heath High School in Paducah, Kentucky. Classes would start in a few minutes, so someone closed in prayer.

The final amen still hung in the air. Students had not yet begun to move away to their classes. Suddenly the sound of gunshots shattered the peace of the moment. A fourteen-year-old freshman had walked up to the group with a .22 caliber automatic pistol and was firing into the prayer circle, calmly shooting students one at a time.

When it was over, three students were dead and five others seriously wounded. The story made headlines for weeks. What was so astonishing was that by all accounts, the students in the prayer circle had done nothing to provoke the boy who did the shooting. In fact, several of them had previously befriended him. The secular media were at a loss to explain how anyone so young could commit such a heinous act of pure evil.

Another aspect of the story also caught the media's eye—the amazing forgiveness immediately extended by the survivors and their loved ones. Many relatives of the victims were interviewed by the press in the days and weeks following the shooting. Despite the utter senselessness of the crime, no one spoke with bitterness or a desire for vengeance. Churches in Paducah, while ministering to the victims and their loved ones, also reached out to the shooter and his family. One of the injured girls was fifteen-year-old Melissa Jenkins. As she lay in the hospital less than a week after the shootings, fully aware that the damage to her spinal cord was so severe she would be a paraplegic for the rest of her life, she sent a message through a friend to the boy who had deliberately shot her: "Tell him I forgive him."

How can someone who has been so grievously wounded forgive so freely and so quickly? Apart from Christ, it is well nigh impossible. "But we have the mind of Christ" (1 Cor. 2:16). The Holy Spirit indwells and empowers us. Therefore, Christians are capable of superhuman acts of forgiveness.

My own brother-in-law went to a jail to express his forgiveness and offer the forgiveness of God to the drug addict who had murdered his son in a market holdup.

One of the earliest examples of this sort of forgiveness is Stephen, the first martyr. While he was being stoned, with large rocks battering his body, breaking his bones, causing him to bleed and ultimately die—in the midst of all that trauma he found strength to pray for his killers. "Falling on his knees, he cried out with a loud voice, 'Lord, do not hold this sin against them!' And having said this, he fell asleep" (Acts 7:60). Despite the violence of the moment, his death was so peaceful that Scripture portrays him as simply drifting into a tranquil slumber.

The natural tendency in such situations is to pray for vengeance. In fact, the death of the Old Testament prophet Zechariah makes an interesting contrast with that of Stephen. Like Stephen, Zechariah was stoned, but notice the marked difference in his dying prayer:

> *So they conspired against him and at the command of the king they*
> *stoned him to death in the court of the house of the LORD. Thus*
> *Joash the king did not remember the kindness which his father*

Jehoiada had shown him, but he murdered his son. And as he died he said, "May the LORD see and avenge!"

— 2 CHRON. 24:21-22

We cannot fault Zechariah for praying for vengeance. He recognized, of course, that vengeance belonged to God, and he properly left the matter with God. His praying this way should not be regarded as a sin.

In fact, there's a legitimate sense in which all martyrs are entitled to plead for vengeance against their persecutors. Revelation 6:10 gives us a look behind the curtains of the cosmic drama. There we learn that the perpetual cry of the martyrs of all ages is, "How long, O Lord, holy and true, will You refrain from judging and avenging our blood on those who dwell on the earth?"

There is certainly no sin in crying for justice like that. God *will* avenge His people, and when His vengeance is finally administered, no one will be able to complain that it is unjust. In fact, we will simply marvel at the long-suffering of God that restrained vengeance for so long.

But for now, in the bright light of the New Covenant, while the fullness of divine vengeance is restrained and the Gospel is being proclaimed to the world, there is a higher cause than vengeance to plead for—forgiveness and reconciliation with those who persecute us. Jesus said, "Love your enemies, do good to those who hate you, bless those who curse you, pray for those who mistreat you" (Luke 6:27-28). Christ Himself gave us the example to follow when, as He died at the hands of evil men, He prayed for their forgiveness. Stephen obviously got the message.

What about justice? It is natural, and even right, to want to see justice fulfilled and divine vengeance administered. But for the Christian there is another priority. Justice will come, but in the meantime our thoughts and actions toward others are to be driven by mercy. As Christians, we should be obsessed with forgiveness, not vengeance.

THE VOICE OF THE BLOOD

There is a clear illustration of this in the book of Hebrews. The writer of that Bible book makes several references to Abel, Adam's second-born, who was killed unjustly by his own elder brother. Abel is listed in Hebrews 11 as the first member of the famous "Hall of Faith" found in that chapter. Hebrews 11:4 says this about Abel: "By faith Abel offered unto God a more excellent sacrifice than Cain, by which he obtained witness that he was righteous, God testifying of his gifts: and by it he being dead yet speaketh" (KJV).

That phrase "he being dead yet speaketh" is a familiar one, but have you ever realized what it refers to? It is an allusion to Genesis 4:10, where God said to Cain, "What have you done? The voice of your brother's blood is crying to Me from the ground." Though Abel was dead, he still spoke through his innocent blood, crying out for vengeance.

Those were figurative terms, of course. Abel's blood did not literally cry out. But the violent and unjust manner of his death—brutal murder at his own brother's wicked hand—fairly screamed for vengeance. Justice needed to be done. A crime had been committed for which severe punishment was in order. Abel's blood, spilled on the ground, was a testimony against Cain. In metaphorical terms, Abel's blood was crying for retribution against Cain.

Abel was the first martyr, and the blood of every martyr since then has joined the cry for justice against the persecutors of God's people. In that sense, they *all* still speak, though they are dead. They are the very ones pictured in Revelation 6:10, under the altar, calling for God to glorify Himself in the accomplishment of justice.

But Hebrews 12:24 makes an interesting contrast. There the writer mentions *Jesus'* blood, "which speaks better than the blood of Abel." The meaning is clear: whereas Abel's blood (and the blood of other martyrs) screams for vengeance, Christ's blood pleads for mercy.

Jesus' blood, shed as an atonement for sins, appeals for *forgiveness* on behalf of sinners. This is a remarkable truth. All the blood of all the martyrs of all time cries out for justice and vengeance and retribution. But Christ's blood "speaks better."

Again, there is nothing wrong with desiring justice. Justice honors God. It is certainly legitimate to want to see wrongs made right and evildoers recompensed for their wickedness. But the longing for forgiveness is better still. Christians are to be characterized by a desire for mercy, compassion, and forgiveness—even for their enemies.

How do we develop such a state of mind? How can a Christian, badly hurt by the offenses of another, learn to forgive "from [the] heart" the way Jesus commanded (Matt. 18:35)? What about the commands in Scripture to confront those who sin against us? How do we know when to confront and when to overlook an offense?

Furthermore, how can we forgive those who have not repented? Doesn't God himself withhold forgiveness from the unrepentant? If we are to forgive in the same way we have been forgiven, don't we first need to require the repentance of the offender?

Those are all essential questions. Does the Bible offer answers? I believe it does. Let's begin by exploring what Scripture means when it commands us to forgive in the same way God forgives.

GOD'S FORGIVENESS/OUR FORGIVENESS

How can forgiveness between fellow sinners be compared to the forgiveness of an offended deity? There must be some similarities, because Scripture instructs us to forgive in the same manner as we have been forgiven. This idea occurs in two verses we have quoted repeatedly: Ephesians 4:32 ("forgiv[e] each other, just as God in Christ also has forgiven you") and Colossians 3:13 ("just as the Lord forgave you").

Some take the position that this teaches forgiveness should always be conditional. Their rationale goes like this: God forgives only those who repent. Therefore, if we are going to forgive in the same manner as we have been forgiven, we should withhold forgiveness from all who are unrepentant. Some fine teachers hold this view. For example, Jay Adams writes:

> It should go without saying that since our forgiveness is modeled after God's (Eph. 4:32), it must be conditional.

> Forgiveness by God rests on clear, unmistakable conditions. The apostles did not merely announce that God had forgiven men. . . . Paul and the apostles turned away from those who refused to meet the conditions, just as John and Jesus did earlier when the scribes and the Pharisees would not repent.[1]

There is some merit in Adams's position. There are times when forgiveness must be conditional, and we shall discuss that issue before the close of this chapter. I have great respect for Adams and have recommended his book on forgiveness as a helpful study of the subject. On this issue, however, I must disagree with the position he takes.

To make conditionality the gist of Christlike forgiving seems to miss the whole point of what Scripture is saying. When Scripture instructs us to forgive in the manner we have been forgiven, what is in view is not the idea of *withholding* forgiveness until the offender expresses repentance.

Listen carefully to what these verses are saying:

• *Matthew 6:12, 14-15*: "And forgive us our debts, as we forgive our debtors. . . . For if ye forgive men their trespasses, your heavenly Father will also forgive you: but if ye forgive not men their trespasses, neither will your Father forgive your trespasses" (KJV).

• *James 2:13*: "For judgment will be merciless to one who has shown no mercy; mercy triumphs over judgment."

• *Matthew 18:35*: "So likewise shall my heavenly Father do also unto you, if ye from your hearts forgive not every one his brother their trespasses" (KJV).

• *Luke 6:36-38*: "Be merciful, just as your Father is merciful. And do not pass judgment and you will not be judged; and do not condemn, and you shall not be condemned; pardon, and you will be pardoned. Give, and it will be given to you; good measure, pressed down, shaken together, running over, they will pour into your lap. For whatever measure you deal out to others, it will be dealt to you in return."

The emphasis is on forgiving freely, generously, willingly, eagerly, speedily—and from the heart. The attitude of the forgiver is where the focus of Scripture lies, not the terms of forgiveness.

Most of those who hold that all forgiveness is conditional portray forgiveness as a formal transaction in which the forgiven one must repent and the offended party promises in return never to bring up the sin again. If this transaction has not occurred, they say, real forgiveness has not yet taken place. In some cases the offender may repent and ask forgiveness without prompting, and forgiveness should be granted on the spot. But in most cases, particularly when the offender is ignorant of having committed a wrong, the offended party must first confront the offender and formally solicit repentance before he or she can forgive. In short, no act of forgiveness can occur until the offender asks for forgiveness.

Sadly, I have seen people who hold this opinion become obsessive confronters and ultimately make themselves odious to friend and foe alike. Others nurse grudges, refuse to relinquish bitterness, and even sever friendships over relatively petty offenses, justifying such attitudes because they are convinced they have no duty to forgive until the offender repents.

While it is often true that forgiveness involves a two-way transaction, it is not true of *all* forgiveness. There are times when forgiveness should be unconditional and unilateral, and there are other times when forgiveness must be withheld until the offender repents. The biblical principles governing these different kinds of forgiveness are clear.

CONDITIONAL FORGIVENESS/ UNCONDITIONAL FORGIVENESS

It is obvious from Scripture that sometimes forgiveness must be conditional. For example, in certain cases the offender is to be confronted and ultimately even excommunicated from the church if he or she refuses to repent (Luke 17:3; Matt. 18:15-17). We will closely examine the biblical process for church discipline in chapter 7.

But does *every* offense call for confrontation, possibly leading to formal church discipline? Is there no place for simply granting unilateral forgiveness for petty offenses? Is there no time when the offended party should simply overlook a transgression, choosing to suffer wrong and forgive without being asked or without formally confronting the offender?

Obviously, these questions have important practical ramifications. If you had a friend who scrupulously tried to confront you every time you committed a petty offense, wouldn't the friendship grow tedious pretty quickly? And if marriage partners saw it as their solemn duty to confront each other for every offense, wouldn't such a mind-set make the marriage relationship practically impossible to endure?

It is a mistake to assume that verses like Luke 17:3 ("If your brother sins, rebuke him") and Matthew 18:15 ("If your brother sins against you, go and show him his fault," NIV) are absolute prescriptions for every kind of transgression. If we were obligated to confront one another for every paltry misdeed, we would be doing little else.

Indeed, Scripture gives us another principle for dealing with the vast majority of petty infractions: overlook the offense. Forgive unilaterally, unconditionally. Grant pardon freely and unceremoniously. Love demands this. "Keep fervent in your love for one another, because love covers a multitude of sins" (1 Pet. 4:8). "Hatred stirs up strife, but love covers all transgressions" (Prov. 10:12). "He who covers a transgression seeks love" (Prov. 17:9). Love "does not take into account a wrong suffered . . . [but] bears all things, believes all things, hopes all things, endures all things" (1 Cor. 13:5-7). The *New International Version* renders 1 Corinthians 13:5 this way: "[Love] keeps no record of wrongs."

Jay Adams recognizes the Christian's duty to overlook petty offenses, citing some of these same texts. "But," he writes, "it is not . . . forgiveness."[2] Having defined forgiveness as a two-way transaction, he has no room in his system for unilateral or unconditional forgiveness. So he draws a distinction between forgiveness and overlooking another's transgression. If true, that would mean all the

petty offenses we choose to overlook (or "cover," in biblical terminology) are not really to be regarded as forgiven.

But the Bible itself makes no such distinction. Covering
another's transgression is the very essence of forgiveness. Speaking
of God's forgiveness, Psalm 32:1 equates the concepts of forgiveness
and the covering of sin: "How blessed is he whose transgression is
forgiven, whose sin is covered!" This is a Hebrew parallelism,
employing two different expressions to designate the same concept.
To cover someone else's sin is the very essence of forgiveness.

Psalm 85:2 draws the same parallel: "You forgave the iniquity of
Your people; You covered all their sin."

James 5:20 also equates forgiveness with the covering of sin:
"He who turns a sinner from the error of his way will save his soul
from death, and will cover a multitude of sins."

So when 1 Peter 4:8 says, "Love covers a multitude of sins," it is
describing forgiveness.

Furthermore, Scripture also teaches that forgiveness can be
unilateral and unconditional. Mark 11:25-26 clearly speaks of this
kind of forgiveness and even makes it a condition for receiving
God's forgiveness:

> *"Whenever you stand praying, forgive, if you have anything against
> anyone; so that your Father also who is in heaven may forgive you
> your transgressions. But if you do not forgive, neither will your
> Father who is in heaven forgive your transgressions."*

That describes an immediate forgiveness granted to the offender
with no formal meeting or transaction required. It necessarily refers
to a pardon that is wholly unilateral, because this forgiveness takes
place *while the forgiver stands praying*.[3] "Forgive" is the clear command
of that verse, and it is to take place on the spot. There is no mention
of confrontation. There is no command to seek the offender's
repentance. The forgiveness of Mark 11:25 is therefore different
from the forgiveness of Luke 17:3. *This* forgiveness is to be granted
unconditionally and unilaterally.

UNCONDITIONAL FORGIVENESS: WHAT DOES IT MEAN?

What does unilateral forgiveness entail? If there's no transaction, no seeking of forgiveness, no formal granting of pardon, no words exchanged between the two parties, then what exactly is accomplished by this sort of forgiveness?

Its chief effects are wrought in the heart of the forgiver. This kind of forgiveness involves a deliberate decision to cover the other person's offense. "Forgive" in Mark 11:25 is an imperative, a command. The forgiveness called for here is necessarily a volitional matter. In other words, it is a choice, not a feeling or an involuntary response.

It is, as Matthew 18:35 suggests, *from the heart*; but even that does not place forgiveness primarily in the realm of feeling. "Heart" in Scripture normally designates the seat of the intellect (cf. Prov. 23:7; Luke 9:47). So this speaks of a deliberate and rational decision. It is a choice made by the offended party to set aside the other person's transgression and not permit the offense to cause a breach in the relationship or fester in bitterness.

In effect, the person who chooses to forgive resolves not to remember the offense, refuses to hold a grudge, relinquishes any claim on recompense, and resists the temptation to brood or retaliate. The offended party simply bears the insult. The offense is set aside, lovingly covered for Christ's sake. For petty and unintentional offenses, this is the proper and loving way to forgive—unilaterally, without confrontation and without stirring any strife.

This, I believe, is what Scripture refers to most often when it calls us to forgive one another. The heavy emphasis on forgiveness in Scripture is not meant to make us more confrontational, but quite the opposite. When Scripture calls us to have an attitude of forgiveness, the emphasis is always on long-suffering, patience, benevolence, forbearance, kindness, and mercy—not confrontation.

To deny that forgiveness can ever be unilateral is in my view a potentially serious mistake. It places too much stress on confrontation. And that tends to produce more conflict than it avoids. People who insist on confronting every wrong often simply stir strife—the antithesis of what Jesus' teaching on forgiveness was intended to produce. Real love should *cover* the vast majority of transgressions, not constantly haul them out in the open for dissection (1 Pet. 4:8).

TO CONFRONT OR NOT TO CONFRONT?

All of this calls for some careful distinctions. Obviously there are times when confrontation is essential. How do we identify those situations? Are there clear biblical principles that teach us when to confront and when to forgive unilaterally?

I believe there are. Here are some guidelines to help you in drawing the distinction:

Whenever possible, especially if the offense is petty or unintentional, it is best to forgive unilaterally. This is the very essence of a gracious spirit. It is the Christlike attitude called for in Ephesians 4:1-3:

> *Therefore I, the prisoner of the Lord, entreat you to walk in a manner worthy of the calling with which you have been called, with all humility and gentleness, with patience, showing forbearance for one another in love, being diligent to preserve the unity of the Spirit in the bond of peace.*

That calls for a gracious tolerance ("forbearance ") of others' faults. This is necessary for the sake of maintaining peace.

In other words, believers are supposed to have a sort of mutual immunity to petty offenses. Love "is not easily angered" (1 Cor. 13:5, NIV). If every fault required formal confrontation, the whole of our church life would be spent confronting and resolving conflicts over petty annoyances. So for the sake of peace, to preserve the unity of the Spirit, we are to show tolerance whenever possible.

This, then, is the governing rule: Unless an offense *requires* confrontation, unconditional, unilateral forgiveness should cover the transgression. The offended party, in suffering the offense, is following in the footsteps of Christ (1 Pet. 2:21-25). This is the very attitude Christ called for in Matthew 5:39-40: "Whoever slaps you on your right cheek, turn the other to him also. If anyone wants to sue you and take your shirt, let him have your coat also."

If you are the only *injured party, even if the offense was public and flagrant, you may choose to forgive unilaterally.* Examples of this abound in Scripture. Joseph, for example, was the victim of a grievous wrong at the hands of his brothers. They plotted to kill him, then sold him into slavery.

But he held no grudge. Years later, when famine drove the wicked brothers to Egypt in search of food, Joseph recognized them and freely forgave them, without any expression of repentance on their part. Before they even realized who he was, he was moved to tears with compassion for them. Finally revealing his true identity to them, he said, "I am your brother Joseph, whom you sold into Egypt. And now do not be grieved or angry with yourselves, because you sold me here, for God sent me before you to preserve life" (Gen. 45:4-5). His forgiveness was unconditional, unilateral, not predicated on any expression of remorse from them.

In fact, as far as we know from Scripture, the closest these brothers ever came to formally declaring their repentance was after Jacob died. Once their father was no longer there to stay Joseph's hand, they imagined their offended brother might unleash vengeance against them. The brothers, knowing the gravity of their sin, were evidently unable to believe that his charity toward them was well-meant. They feared he might still secretly harbor a wish for vengeance. So they told Joseph that it was *their father's* wish that he grant them forgiveness (Gen. 50:16-17). They did not formally admit their wrong and express repentance, though it is quite clear that they were humbled men by now.

But all their pleading was wholly unnecessary. Joseph had forgiven them long before. Having seen undeniable evidence that the hand of Divine Providence was working good in his life through the evil that was done to him, Joseph had long since forgiven his brothers fully, freely, and unconditionally. His perspective? "You meant evil against me, but God meant it for good" (Gen. 50:20). The knowledge that God had a good purpose for his sufferings made it impossible for Joseph to harbor a grudge.

There are also other examples of unilateral forgiveness in Scripture, even when the offense was public and pronounced. For example, on at least one significant occasion David unilaterally and unconditionally forgave the most humiliating kind of public insult.

It occurred during Absalom's rebellion against David. David was forced to flee Jerusalem so that his defiant son would not destroy the city in his zeal to overthrow David's throne. During that agonizing and painful exodus from Jerusalem, a worthless character named Shimei publicly taunted the already heartbroken David, trying to humiliate him further. Second Samuel 16:5-8 records what happened:

> *[Shimei] came out cursing continually as he came. And he threw stones at David and at all the servants of King David; and all the people and all the mighty men were at his right hand and at his left. Thus Shimei said when he cursed, "Get out, get out, you man of bloodshed, and worthless fellow! The LORD has returned upon you all the bloodshed of the house of Saul, in whose place you have reigned; and the LORD has given the kingdom into the hand of your son Absalom. And behold, you are taken in your own evil, for you are a man of bloodshed!"*

Abishai, one of David's companions, wanted justice on the spot: "Why should this dead dog curse my lord the king? Let me go over now, and cut off his head" (v. 9).

But David's response was a godly forbearance:

> *"If he curses, and if the LORD has told him, 'Curse David,' then who shall say, 'Why have you done so?' . . . Behold, my son who came out from me seeks my life; how much more now this Benjamite? Let him alone and let him curse, for the LORD has told him. Perhaps the LORD will look on my affliction and return good to me instead of his cursing this day."*

Shimei continued to run along the hillside next to David, cursing and throwing rocks and dirt at the king, but David bore the insults with grace and forbearance—though under the circumstances it would have been perfectly appropriate for David, a sitting king, to demand that the mocker be punished.

Later, after David was victorious over the rebels, Shimei made a show of remorse, begging David's mercy. David, still over the protest of his men, reaffirmed his forgiveness to Shimei (2 Sam. 19:18-23). Having already forgiven the initial offense unilaterally, David now forgave Shimei formally.

Stephen's prayers for those who stoned him are another example of unilateral, unconditional forgiveness. The fact that Stephen prayed for God's mercy for his murderers shows that he had already forgiven them. It is true that *God's* forgiveness was not to be granted apart from their repentance; but Stephen himself had already made a deliberate, conscious choice to relinquish the right to retribution. He had forgiven them in his heart.

This brings up an important point. Even after we have forgiven offenders for their transgressions against us, God Himself may exact justice for their sins against *Him*. We can forgive an offense against us. But we cannot grant forgiveness for sin against God. "Who can forgive sins, but God alone?" (Luke 5:21). To forgive someone does not convey some priestly absolution, clearing them of sin before God. Those whom we forgive must still give account to God.

For example, Stephen's forgiving his killers did not assure that their sins would go unpunished if they did not also seek *God's* forgiveness. In the case of Saul of Tarsus (who stood by the garments of Stephen's killers, consenting to the martyr's death, Acts 7:58; 8:1), his offense was completely blotted out when he fully repented. We are never told what became of those who threw the stones, but if they never embraced Christ as Lord and Savior, they will suffer the wrath of God for the sin of killing Stephen. Stephen forgave the offense against him; the sin against God still had to be reckoned with.

Shimei is another case in point. David kept his promise not to kill Shimei, but Shimei remained an unregenerate and worthless man to the end of his life. Knowing this, on his deathbed David instructed Solomon how to deal with Shimei: "Do not let him go unpunished, for you are a wise man; and you will know what you ought to do to him, and you will bring his gray hair down to Sheol with blood" (1 Kings 2:9).

This is a difficult command to explain, until we realize that David, as the divinely appointed king, was responsible to see that God's glory was not besmirched in Israel. He had kept his promise to Shimei: he did not kill him for his insult. As far as David was concerned, the personal offense against him was forgiven. But Shimei's act also involved the most wretched kind of blasphemy against God. And since Shimei remained in wanton rebellion against God, divine justice still had a claim on him. For the sake of the nation's purity, this needed to be dealt with. It was now time for the account to be settled—for the sake of *God's* glory, not David's. David could overlook a personal transgression against him; he could not ultimately overlook a public act of overt hostility to God. As Puritan commentator Matthew Henry wrote, David's instructions to Solomon "proceeded not from personal revenge, but a prudent zeal for the honour of the government and the covenant God had made with his family, the contempt of which ought not to go unpunished."[4] Surely that is why David waited until he was on his deathbed to order that Shimei be punished. This way, no one could say that David did it to preserve his own honor.

And Solomon wisely honored David's forgiveness of Shimei's insult. Instead of summarily executing him for that past offense, Solomon imposed a restriction on Shimei, forbidding him ever to set foot outside the city of Jerusalem. As long as he stayed in the city, under the king's supervision, he could move about freely in perfect safety. But the day he set foot across the Kidron Valley, he would be killed. Shimei agreed to the terms, which were gracious (1 Kings 2:36-38). But because he was a wicked man, Shimei broke his word. He left the city in search of some runaway slaves, and when Solomon found out, he summoned him and said:

"Did I not make you swear by the LORD and solemnly warn you, saying, 'You will know for certain that on the day you depart and go anywhere, you shall surely die'? And you said to me, 'The word which I have heard is good.' Why then have you not kept the oath of the LORD, and the command which I have laid on you? . . . You know all the evil which you acknowledge in your heart, which you did to my father David; therefore the LORD shall return your evil on your own head."

— vv. 42-44, *emphasis added*

In other words, Shimei's death was the Lord's, not David's, reprisal for Shimei's sin. David forgave the man and kept his promise not to retaliate. But in the end, given Shimei's refusal to repent, God Himself demanded justice.

Our forgiving an offense does not guarantee that the offender will receive judicial forgiveness from God. God, who knows the heart, always judges righteously. Our part is to be gracious, bear the wrong, and pray for the offender's full repentance. God Himself will see to it that justice is done if the offender fails to seek divine forgiveness.

WHEN UNCONDITIONAL FORGIVENESS IS NOT AN OPTION

There are times when it is necessary to confront an offender. In such cases, unconditional forgiveness is not an option. These generally involve more serious sins—not petty or picayune complaints, but soul-threatening sins or transgressions that endanger the fellowship of saints. In such situations Luke 17:3 applies: "If your brother sins, rebuke him; and if he repents, forgive him." In such cases, if a brother or sister in Christ refuses to repent, the discipline process outlined in Matthew 18 applies (see chapter 7).

Here are some guidelines for determining when such confrontation is necessary:

If you observe a serious offense that is a sin against someone other than you, confront the offender. Justice does not permit a Christian to cover a sin against someone else. I can unilaterally and unconditionally forgive a personal offense when I am the victim, because it is I who then bears the wrong. But when I see that someone else has been sinned against, it is my duty to seek justice. (The only exception to this would be when the offended person himself chooses to ignore a personal slight or insult. This was the case when David forbade Abishai to wreak vengeance against Shimei.)

While we are entitled, and even encouraged, to overlook wrongs committed against us, Scripture everywhere forbids us to overlook wrongs committed against another.

- *Exodus 23:6*: "You shall not pervert the justice due to your needy brother in his dispute."
- *Deuteronomy 16:20*: "Justice, and only justice, you shall pursue."
- *Isaiah 1:17*: "Learn to do good; seek justice, reprove the ruthless, defend the orphan, plead for the widow."
- *Isaiah 59:15-16*: "Yes, truth is lacking; and he who turns aside from evil makes himself a prey. Now the LORD saw, and it was displeasing in His sight that there was no justice. And He saw that there was no man, and was astonished that there was no one to intercede."
- *Jeremiah 22:3*: "Thus says the LORD, 'Do justice and righteousness, and deliver the one who has been robbed from the power of his oppressor. Also do not mistreat or do violence to the stranger, the orphan, or the widow; and do not shed innocent blood in this place.'"
- *Lamentations 3:35-36*: "To deprive a man of justice in the presence of the Most High, to defraud a man in his lawsuit—of these things the LORD does not approve."

It is not our prerogative to "forgive" someone for an offense against another. Therefore, those who witness such an offense have a duty to confront the offender with his or her transgression.

When ignoring an offense might hurt the offender, confrontation is required. Sometimes choosing to overlook an offense might actually injure the offender. In such cases it is our duty to confront in love.

Galatians 6:1-2 says, "Brethren, if a man be overtaken in a fault, ye which are spiritual, restore such a one in the spirit of meekness; considering thyself, lest thou also be tempted. Bear ye one another's burdens, and so fulfil the law of Christ" (KJV).

The word translated "overtaken" in that passage literally means "caught." It can signify two things. It might mean that the person was discovered in some secret transgression. Or it could mean that the person is ensnared in some sinful habit. Either way, confrontation is necessary. Overlooking the sin is not an option. Love for the sinning brother requires that you confront and seek to restore. This is an essential part of bearing one another's burdens (v. 2).

Sins that require confrontation because of their potential for harm to the sinning person include serious doctrinal error, moral failure, repeated instances of the same offense, sinful habits or destructive tendencies, or any other transgression that poses a serious danger to the offender's spiritual well-being.

In all such cases, confrontation should be motivated by love and a desire for the offender's good. Such confrontation should never be used to gratify a thirst for personal vengeance, to punish the offender, or to fulfill any other self-aggrandizing purposes. That is why Galatians 6:1 expressly says those who are "spiritual" should deal with the sinning individual.

Ironically, these are the circumstances in which confrontation is the hardest. We are easily tempted to confront the sins we should overlook and to overlook the ones we should confront. But whether the situation calls for forbearance or confrontation, the primary motivation should always be love for the offender (as well as for the offended).

When a sin is scandalous or otherwise potentially damaging to the body of Christ, confrontation is essential. Some sins have the potential to defile many people. Hebrews 12:15 warns of such dangers: "See to it that no one comes short of the grace of God; that no root of bitterness springing up causes trouble, and by it many be defiled."

The responsibility is incumbent on every member of the body not only to "stimulate one another to love and good deeds" (Heb.

10:24), but also to exhort one another, so that no one becomes hardened through "the deceitfulness of sin" (Heb. 3:13).

The apostle Paul rebuked the Corinthians for their failure to confront and deal with scandalous sin within the flock. One of their members was having sexual relations with "his father's wife" (1 Cor. 5:1)—probably his stepmother; the sin carried such a stigma in the culture that it was tantamount to incest. Such sins did "not exist even among the Gentiles." Even the rankest pagans in Corinth were scandalized by the sin in that church.

Paul rebuked them: "Ye are puffed up, and have not rather mourned" (v. 2, KJV). "Puffed up" is from a Greek expression that literally means "inflated." It speaks of pride. Perhaps, as is true of many today, the Corinthians' pride was in their tolerance. They may have been boasting in the very fact that they were not so "narrowminded" as to make an issue out of this man's misdeeds.

Paul rebuked them harshly: "Your boasting is not good. Do you not know that a little leaven leavens the whole lump of dough?" (v. 6). He ordered them to excommunicate the offender, who, he said, needed to be "removed from [their] midst" (v. 2).

I, on my part, though absent in body but present in spirit, have already judged him who has so committed this, as though I were present. In the name of our Lord Jesus, when you are assembled, and I with you in spirit, with the power of our Lord Jesus, I have decided to deliver such a one to Satan for the destruction of his flesh, so that his spirit may be saved in the day of the Lord Jesus.

—vv. 3-5

Open sin is *always* a scandal in the church and must be dealt with. It is not our prerogative to "forgive" those intent on living lives of flagrant disobedience. The entire church suffers when this sort of sin is permitted to exist. Such sin is like leaven, working its way through a lump of dough. Covering such sins, overlooking the evil, is never the right thing in such situations. This sort of sin must be rebuked, and in chapter 7 we will carefully examine the process by which this is to be done.

Any time an offense results in a broken relationship, formal forgiveness is an essential step toward reconciliation. Any sort of offense that causes a breach in relationships simply cannot be overlooked. Both the offense and the breach must be confronted, and reconciliation must be sought.

Reconciliation is always the goal when we confront someone about a wrong done. Once again, if your confronting aims at punishing the offender, or if it is simply a means of castigation and censure, you are confronting with the wrong aim in mind. The goal of all righteous confrontation is the repair of a broken relationship and the restoration of the offender.

Whenever there is a broken relationship between Christians, *both* parties have a responsibility to seek reconciliation. If you are the offended party, Luke 17:3 applies: "If your brother sins, rebuke him." You are the one who must go to him. If you are the offender, Matthew 5:23-24 applies: "If . . . you are presenting your offering at the altar, and there remember that your brother has something against you, leave your offering there before the altar, and go your way; first be reconciled to your brother, and then come and present your offering."

A rift in the relationship between Christians rules out the possibility of the kind of forgiveness that simply overlooks a fault. Whether harsh words have been exchanged or an icy silence prevails, if both sides know that a breach exists, the only way to resolve matters is by the formal granting of forgiveness. Sometimes the wrong is one-sided. Other times it involves admission of wrong and the seeking of forgiveness on both sides.

In any case, reconciliation is essential. If you have committed the offense, it is sinful not to make it right. If you are the offended party, you also have a duty to seek reconciliation—to try to win your brother. There is never any excuse for a Christian on either side of a broken relationship to refuse to pursue reconciliation. The only instance where such a conflict should remain unresolved is if all the steps of discipline in Matthew 18 have been exhausted and the guilty party still refuses to repent.

But even then, you are to hold no bitterness in your heart, and you are to love that offender as you love your enemies, with a longing for their spiritual well-being and restoration to fellowhship. "Yet do not regard him as an enemy, but admonish him as a brother" (2 Thess. 3:15). Though no formal transaction of forgiveness is possible, the heart holds no ill will, and reconciliation remains the goal.

Furthermore, if you are the guilty party, you have a responsibility to pursue reconciliation *quickly*. This is repeatedly emphasized in Scripture. For example, Matthew 5:23-24 (cited above) suggests that if you are in the middle of an act of worship and you remember that you have offended a brother, you are to leave your gift at the altar, and *"first* be reconciled to your brother." In such a case reconciliation of a broken relationship takes precedence over worship!

That makes reconciliation a very high priority indeed, for it even takes precedence over worship offered to the Lord. My book on the subject of worship was titled *The Ultimate Priority* because worship is normally the supreme priority in the Christian's life. But there is this one exception: when you know you have offended a brother or sister. *Then* the first priority is the reconciling of the broken relationship.

Matthew 5 continues:

> *"Make friends quickly with your opponent at law while you are with him on the way, in order that your opponent may not deliver you to the judge, and the judge to the officer, and you be thrown into prison. Truly I say to you, you shall not come out of there, until you have paid up the last cent."*
>
> —vv. 25-26

In such cases, especially if you have committed a wrong, your duty is to seek reconciliation without delay. Those who delay or impede the reconciliation process will reap additional punishment. The allusion is to divine chastisement, and the verse implies that God

Himself will enforce the penalty due to those who defer such an urgent duty.

SUFFERING WRONG RATHER THAN CAUSING REPROACH

The presumption in Matthew 5:22-26 seems to be that the party who is being handed over to the judge is the guilty party. Since he has committed the wrong, it is therefore incumbent on him more than on anyone else to seek to remedy the wrong speedily.

But sometimes it may be even appropriate for the one who has been wronged simply to suffer the wrong, especially if necessary to avoid the dishonor of bringing a dispute before a secular court.

In the church at Corinth, for example, there were believers who, refusing to settle their differences among themselves, were suing one another in pagan courts (1 Cor. 6:1). Paul reminded them that it is better to suffer wrong or be defrauded than to bring a lawsuit against another believer before a pagan judge. That is the most-notable example of Christian forgiveness, even when there is not reconciliation.

Sadly, I have known of several Christians who were willing to violate that clear command. They always seem convinced that somehow *their* case is the exception to Paul's rule. Give them an opportunity to explain why they feel they are within their rights to sue a fellow Christian and inevitably they will explain how they are about to be wronged through some great injustice that only a court can remedy. Surely God does not countenance such gross injustices, they typically plead, saying He cannot wish that *this* wrong be overlooked, and so on.

Paul recognizes that the other person may be wrong. But he plainly says it is better to be defrauded than to sue another Christian (1 Cor. 6:7). Lawsuits where a Christian takes another Christian before a secular judge are never justifiable.

But what if the offender stubbornly and deliberately refuses to acknowledge the wrong? The church, rather than a secular court, should act as arbiter. Ultimately in such cases, the church may need to institute discipline against the offending member (1 Cor. 6:2).

I'm convinced that if church discipline were more consistently practiced, there would be fewer such conflicts between Christians, and genuine love and harmony would prevail more in the church.

An appalling number of churches refuse to obey the biblical instructions to discipline sinning members. What should someone do who has exhausted every avenue of appeal in the church and still feels an injustice has been done? In such cases, 1 Corinthians 6:7 applies: suffer the wrong for the sake of Christ. If the church you attend is wantonly disobeying Christ's clear instructions about how to deal with sin within the fellowship, you may need to seek a church where Scripture is more faithfully obeyed.

But some injustices will never be made right this side of eternity. It is clear that the Christian's duty in such cases is to suffer the wrong gracefully, magnanimously, and willingly for the sake of Christ. God Himself will ultimately right all such wrongs. Meanwhile, we must refuse to harbor a grudge. We must never allow a spirit of resentment to stain our character. We must seek to be like Joseph, willing to see the hand of God working good, even in the most unjust circumstances.

WHEN IT IS HARD TO FORGIVE

Forgiveness certainly does not come naturally to fallen creatures. We tend to be driven too much by our feelings. Those who indulge themselves in bitter feelings will find forgiveness does not easily germinate in such soil. Instead, the root that springs up is a defiling influence. It is hurtful not only to the bitter person, but to many others as well (Heb. 12:15).

Forgiveness is often frustrated by negative emotions, lingering resentment, and unquenched anger. Some imagine, wrongly, that they cannot forgive if they do not "feel" like forgiving.

But as we already noted briefly, forgiveness is not a feeling. Those who insist on being driven by passion will find forgiveness very hard indeed, because forgiveness often involves a deliberate choice that runs contrary to our feelings. Bitter emotions tell us to dwell on an offense. In contrast, forgiveness is a voluntary, rational decision to set the offense aside and desire only the best for the offender.

"But I cannot do that," someone says. "I *try* to set it aside, but everywhere I go, something reminds me, and I find myself thinking about it and getting upset all over again."

Such thoughts are temptations to sin. Brooding over an offense is no less a sin than lust or covetousness or any other heart-sin. A willful choice must be made to turn away from that kind of thinking. Instead we must deliberately cover the offense and refuse to succumb to angry and vengeful thinking, whether we feel like it or not.

Those who forgive even when it's hard invariably find that the proper emotions will follow. "Love your enemies, do good to those who hate you, bless those who curse you, pray for those who mistreat you" (Luke 6:27-28)—those are all willful, deliberate, rational acts, not emotional reflexes. Obey Christ's commands to do such things, and your anger will eventually give way to meekness, frustration will be overcome by peace, and anxiety will succumb to calm.

Forgiveness results in the lifting of many burdens. To grant someone forgiveness when he or she repents is to lift the burden of guilt from that person. But to forgive when forgiveness is unilateral and unconditional liberates the forgiver to enjoy the even greater mercies given in return by a generous heavenly Father, who promises to pour into our laps a "good measure, pressed down, shaken together, running over" (Luke 6:38).

SEVEN

If Your
Brother Sins

If your brother sins, rebuke him;
and if he repents, forgive him.

LUKE 17:3

There are times when sin has to be dealt with through confrontation.
And if the guilty party refuses to repent, the ultimate result may
mean excommunication from the church. This is true chiefly when
the offender's sin has a potential to continue working injury, or when
the offense brings a public reproach on the name of Christ.

The process Scripture outlines for dealing with sin in the flock
is called "church discipline." That's a fitting name for it, because as
with parental discipline, the main goal is correction. Church discipline is successful when it brings about repentance and reconciliation. When it is unsuccessful, it ends in excommunication. But
excommunication is never the desired goal; restoration is.

The mere subject of church discipline is enough to stir strong feelings among Christians. Not long ago we dealt with the subject on our
radio broadcast. I was amazed at the letters we received from people who
strongly felt that all forms of church discipline are inherently unloving.
One listener, who admitted she heard only part of a broadcast, wrote:

> The whole process of church discipline sounds incredibly
> controlling and uncharitable. I cannot believe that any church

would ever threaten to excommunicate its own members for what they do in their private lives. And I cannot imagine a church making a public pronouncement about someone's sin! What people do on their own time is their business, not the whole church's. And the church is supposed to be where people can come to learn how to overcome sin. How can they do that if they have been excommunicated? If we shun our own members, we're no better than the cults. I cannot imagine that Christ would ever excommunicate someone from His church. Didn't he seek out sinners and avoid those who were holier-than-thou? After all, it's not the people who are whole that need a physician. I'm glad my church does not excommunicate members who sin. There'd be none of us left! I thought the gospel was all about forgiveness!

Those comments reflect several common and widespread misunderstandings about the subject.

First of all, church discipline is not antithetical to forgiveness. In fact, Jesus' instructions for the discipline process outline exactly *how* forgiveness should work when a believer's sin has implications for the whole flock.

Second, biblical discipline is not about micromanaging people's lives. As we saw in the previous chapter, the kind of offenses that require confrontation and biblical discipline are not unintentional transgressions, minor peccadilloes, petty annoyances, or matters of simple preference, but serious violations of clear biblical principles—sins that hurt other believers, destroy the unity of the flock, or otherwise sully the purity of the church. In such cases, sin *must* be dealt with. Such sins cannot be covered up. They are like leaven, and left alone their evil effects will eventually permeate the whole church (1 Cor. 5:6).

Third, proper discipline is not out of harmony with the Spirit of Christ. Christ Himself prescribed this method of dealing with sin in the flock. If your opinion of Christ is that He would never countenance the excommunication of a sinning church member, you have a distorted understanding of Christ.

Fourth, correctly applied discipline is not incompatible with love. In fact, just the opposite is true. In earlier chapters we discussed the fact that God lovingly disciplines believers who sin. The Matthew 18 process recognizes the legitimate role of the church as an instrument of both loving exhortation and, on occasion, divine chastening. Properly applied church discipline therefore pictures God's love for His children (cf. Heb. 12:7-11).

Fifth, the public aspect of discipline is a final resort, not the first step. The point of reporting a person's offense to the church is not to get church members to "shun" the sinning individual, but precisely the opposite: to encourage them to pursue that person in love, with the aim of restoration.

The permissiveness that results when discipline is neglected inevitably leads to chaos. This is as true in the church as it is in a family. No adult enjoys being around children who are never disciplined. In the same way, a church that is lax on dealing with sin in the body ultimately becomes intolerable to all but the most immature believers. Failing to practice church discipline therefore insures that the flock will be spiritually stunted. It is also a sure way to incur God's displeasure (Rev. 2:14, 20).

Jesus' instructions about church discipline in Matthew 18 are clear and unequivocal. This issue is therefore a good test of whether a church is serious about obedience to Christ. People often ask me what to look for in a church. Consistent, proper discipline is near the top of my list. One thing is certain: a church that does not discipline sinning members is going to have perpetual and serious problems.

THE PLACE

Matthew 18 begins with a long discourse from Christ about the childlikeness of the believer. At the start of His discourse, He took a child and set him in the midst of the disciples as an object lesson. The discourse that ensued includes numerous references to "little ones"—by which He means *believers*, not literal children (cf. vv. 6, 10, 14). He was comparing believers to children because of their simple trust, their loving obedience, their need for protection, and their need for discipline.

The section outlining the discipline process covers only three verses:

> *"If your brother sins, go and reprove him in private; if he listens to you, you have won your brother. But if he does not listen to you, take one or two more with you, so that by the mouth of two or three witnesses every fact may be confirmed. If he refuses to listen to them, tell it to the church; and if he refuses to listen even to the church, let him be to you as a Gentile and a tax-gatherer."*
>
> —vv. 15-17

Notice that He uses the expression "the church" twice in verse 17. The Greek word is *ekklesia*, literally meaning "called-out ones." The word is sometimes employed to speak of any assembly of people. An example of this would be Acts 7:38, which refers to the congregation of Israel during the Exodus as "the church in the wilderness" (KJV). Some argue that since the discourse in Matthew 18 preceded Pentecost, Christ could not have been speaking of the New Testament church. But Christ had already introduced the concept of the church to his disciples, ("I will build my church; and the gates of Hades shall not overpower it," Matt. 16:18). So the instructions in Matthew 18 were given in anticipation of the New Testament body. It is hard to see how anyone could exempt the New Testament church from the principle set forth in this passage.

In fact, our Lord's whole point was that the assembly of God's redeemed people is the proper arena in which matters of dispute or discipline should be handled. There is no external court or higher authority on earth to which sin issues may be appealed (1 Cor. 6:2-3).

It is by divine design that discipline should take place in the church. True believers are motivated by a genuine love for one another (1 John 3:14). In such a context, discipline may be administered in love, by loving fellow believers, for the genuine good and edification of the whole body.

THE PURPOSE

Discipline, properly administered, is always motivated by love. Its first purpose is the restoration of the sinning brother: "If he listens to you, you have won your brother" (v. 15). It will also purify the church in that believers will watch their lives to that they'll not have to be confronted.

The goal of church discipline is not to throw people out, shun them, embarrass them, or to be self-righteous, play God, or exercise authority in an abusive or dictatorial manner. The purpose of discipline is to bring people back into a right relationship with God and with the rest of the body. Proper discipline is never administered as retaliation for someone's sin. Restoration, not retribution, is always the goal.

This is obvious from the text of Matthew 18. The Greek word translated "won" in verse 15 is *"kerdaino,"* a word often used to speak of financial gain. (The expression is translated "gained thy brother" in the *King James Version*.) Christ thus portrayed the errant brother as a valuable treasure to be won back. That should be the perspective of every Christian who ever confronts a brother or sister about sin.

That is, in fact, the expression of God's own heart with regard to discipline: He sees each soul as a treasure to be recovered. That is the whole context in which Christ spoke these words. The verses immediately preceding these instructions for discipline compare God to a loving shepherd, concerned for each lamb in the flock:

> *"What do you think? If any man has a hundred sheep, and one of them has gone astray, does he not leave the ninety-nine on the mountains and go and search for the one that is straying? If it turns out that he finds it, truly I say to you, he rejoices over it more than over the ninety-nine which have not gone astray. Thus it is not the will of your Father who is in heaven that one of these little ones perish."*
> – vv. 12-14

Every Christian must have that same sense of concern. It's tempting sometimes to take the path of least resistance and avoid confrontation—especially when sin is already drawing a brother or sister away from the fellowship. But that is the very time when we *most* need to get involved. That is the heart of a true shepherd, who will go to any length to recover a missing or wounded sheep and restore him or her to the flock.

Confrontation is not easy, nor should it be. We're not to be busybodies, constantly intruding into others' business. But when we become aware that someone has sinned, we have a duty before God to lovingly confront that person. We cannot protest by saying it is none of our business. Once we become aware of a soul-threatening sin in a fellow believer's life, it is our business to exhort, confront, and labor for purity in the fellowship of the church and victory in the life of the sinning one. These are noble and necessary concerns.

Nonetheless, we must be on guard against abuses and must keep the loving purposes of proper discipline in view at all times. There is a real danger of becoming too fond of chiding one another. Pride can poison the discipline process, just as it pollutes every virtue. That is why Jesus cautioned those who confront to examine themselves before trying to remove the speck from a brother's eye. We must be sure we don't have a log protruding from our own eye (Matt. 7:3-5)!

One person who had seen some discipline cases handled poorly wrote, "If I ever fall into a sin, I will pray that I don't fall into the hands of those censorious, critical, self-righteous judges in the church. I'd rather fall into the hands of the barkeepers, streetwalkers, dope peddlers, because the church people tend to tear each other apart with their gossipy tongues." That is a sad testimony on the reputation of the church.

On the other hand, a person under discipline who refuses to repent is likely to feel abused and mistreated, just as disobedient children sometimes despise the discipline of their parents. It is not at all unusual for an unrepentant person to accuse those who have confronted him of being unloving, unfair, unkind, or otherwise abusive. That is all the more reason for those administering the discipline to take great care to act in love, with careful self-examination and great long-suffering.

THE PERSON

Notice that the discipline process begins at the individual level. "If your brother sins, go and reprove him in private" (v. 15). Discipline is not instituted by a committee. If the offender repents, there is no need to involve others at all. Discipline, if successful, therefore both suppresses the effects of sin and limits the circle of knowledge. Far from broadcasting knowledge of someone's sin unnecessarily, the discipline process confines knowledge of the offense as much as possible. In most cases, if repentance occurs early enough in the process, no one but the offender and the person who confronts ever needs to know about the offense.

The personal, private confrontation prescribed in Matthew 18 also means that church discipline is the responsibility of every believer in the church. It is not something to be delegated to church officials. In fact, if you see a brother in sin, the *wrong* first response is to report his sin to church leaders, or to anyone else. "Go and reprove him in private" (v. 15).

Too many Christians regard discipline as the exclusive domain of church elders. It is not. The purity of the church is every Christian's concern. The responsibility to confront sin that defiles the church lies with the first person to become aware of the sin. Don't defer to someone else. Don't spread the circle of knowledge further than necessary. Above all, don't just say, "Well, I'll pray that my brother will see the light." That may not be enough. You have the light—go and shine it in his eyes!

THE PROVOCATION

What sins are grounds for discipline? Any offense that cannot be safely overlooked without harm to the offender or to the body of Christ (see our discussion in chapter 6).

Matthew 18:15 has been rendered in various English Bible translations with two slightly different senses. Most modern versions read, "If your brother sins, go and reprove him" or something similar. The *King James Version* says, "If thy brother shall trespass *against thee* . . . " (emphasis added). Ancient manuscripts differ on this point. Some include the expression "against thee"; others simply say, "If your brother sins," implying that we should confront one another whether or not we are directly victimized by the sin.

The textual variation turns out to be relatively unimportant, however, when we realize that all disciplinable sins are sins against the entire body of Christ. So whether the other person's sin is *directly* "against thee" or only *indirectly* (because it is a sin that brings a reproach on the whole body), go and show him his fault in private. Suppose you observe a brother in Christ in a morally compromising situation. Should you confront him? By all means. It would be wrong, and ultimately hurtful to the whole body, to reason that since you are not directly victimized by the offense, you have no obligation to confront your brother's sin. That is precisely the sort of situation Paul rebuked the Corinthians for tolerating in their midst (1 Cor. 5).

Some examples of sins committed directly against you include: if someone attacks you physically in anger, steals from you, deceives you, slanders you, or commits a crime of immorality against you. The wrong response in such cases is to retaliate in kind, to return evil for evil, to hold a grudge, or to report the sin to others without having first gone to your brother. Love for him demands that your immediate response be private confrontation.

Indirect offenses against you include any sin that brings a reproach on the church. This includes sins that tend to draw the sinner away from the fellowship of believers—such as habitual worldliness, sloth, negligence of one's spiritual duties, or even doctrinal error. When a brother or sister is drawn away from our fellowship, the loss affects the whole body. So any sin that has the potential of causing such a loss is a sin that should be confronted. Any pattern of disobedience to Christ—or any other sin that brings a reproach on the name of Christ—also is an indirect sin against us, because as Christ's ambassadors we bear His reproach.

Even sins against non-Christians are subject to church discipline, because those sins dishonor Christ in the world's eyes and thus bring a reproach that stains the entire fellowship. So *any* sin you observe is grounds for instituting the discipline—not just those sins by which you are directly victimized. In all such cases, your duty is the same: you must privately confront the offender.

THE PROCESS

But what if the sinning brother refuses to heed your admonition? Then private confrontation is only the first step. Three other steps are very clearly delineated in the passage. Let's examine the whole process, starting with private confrontation.

Step One:
Confront Him with His Sin in Private

"If your brother sins, go and reprove him in private" (v. 15). The verb translated "go" is a present imperative, meaning that this is a command, not a suggestion, not merely an option. If you see your brother in sin, you *must* go.

And go privately first of all. There is no need to involve others at this point. Don't gossip about the offense with others, even under the guise of seeking prayer support. Just go quietly to your brother; tell him his fault between you and him *alone*.

Discipline is difficult with close friends because so much is at stake. Moreover, those who know you best may respond by pointing out some sin of yours. But discipline is also difficult with people we don't know well. We tend to think, *Who am I to intrude into this person's life?* Thus we are intimidated by the thought of confronting friends, and we tend to be indifferent toward people we aren't close to. Either way we must see that what Christ commands here is a solemn duty and is not to be rationalized away for convenience's sake.

What if you are just as guilty as your brother? Did not Jesus suggest that the log in your own eye ought to stop you from dealing with the speck in your brother's? Not at all. "*First* take the log out of your own eye, and *then* you will see clearly enough to take the speck out of your brother's eye" (Matt. 7:5, emphasis added). But if you truly love your brother, you cannot ignore his sin. Having dealt with your own sin, you will then be in a *better* position to confront your brother with a proper spirit of humility. Never is it right to confront a sinning brother with a pious, pontificating attitude, as if to make yourself look good and him look bad. You must go with a loving, humble desire to restore him.

The Greek verb in the phrase "reprove him" (or "show him his fault") is a word that conveys the idea of light exposing something that is hidden. It calls for a clear, precise divulging of the brother's offense. "Reprove him" does not necessarily imply that he is heretofore unaware of his sin. This process is not limited to sins of ignorance. Rather, the phrase means that you should disclose what you know about his sin, so that he will realize his offense is known, thus establishing his accountability for the offense. If he thought his sin was secret, he must realize it has been uncovered. If he thought he could sin without consequence, he must now give an answer.

If the first step of discipline is successful, his answer will be repentance. That will be the end of the process, in which case, "you have won your brother." You will have a bond of intimacy with him that nothing will be able to break.

If he repents, in most cases, nothing more needs to be done. Of course, you will want to encourage him to demonstrate the genuineness of his repentance by doing whatever is necessary to make things right. If any kind of restitution is called for, urge him to follow through. If others have been directly hurt by his sin, he should go to them and seek reconciliation (Matt. 5:23-24). But assuming he demonstrates real repentance, that should end the matter. Uninvolved parties have no need to be told. No further discipline needs to be imposed. You may rejoice in having won your brother. Ideally, this is the final step in the majority of discipline cases.

Step Two:
Take Some Witnesses

Unfortunately, however, that is sometimes *not* the end of the matter. "If he does not listen to you, take one or two more with you, so that by the mouth of two or three witnesses every fact may be confirmed" (v. 16). Sometimes the sinning brother refuses to hear the rebuke. He may deny his guilt; he may deliberately continue in sin; he may try to cover up what he has done. Whatever his response, if it is not repentance—and assuming you are *certain* of his guilt—you must now take one or two other believers with you and confront him again.

The presence of one or two others serves several purposes. First, and most pragmatically, it turns up the pressure. The people you take with you represent the beginning of the whole church's involvement in the matter. The offender is thus put on notice that if he or she continues in sin, the consequences will only grow more severe. Again, however, the proper objective is nothing less than gaining back your brother. Step one is repeated; you must carefully, patiently, lovingly show him his sin again. But this time it is done in the presence of one or two witnesses.

This is another reason for bringing one or two others in step two: they serve as witnesses. The two-witness principle was established in Moses' law (Deut. 19:15) to ascertain guilt beyond reasonable doubt before any verdict could be made—especially in court cases. Therefore, having witnesses in this second step of discipline also suggests that the end of the process will be a form of judgment if the offender does not repent.

The question is sometimes raised whether the "witnesses" must be witnesses to the original offense. Are they brought only to establish the offender's guilt and only when he denies that any offense occurred?

Some do hold that view, but it cannot be the meaning in this context. First of all, if these witnesses were already aware of the offense, they *also* had a duty earlier to go privately and confront the offender, as mandated by verse 15.

Of course, it is also true that if the offender disputes whether the offense actually occurred, there needs to be a second witness or some other objective evidence to establish the offender's guilt. The Old Testament principle cited in verse 16 still applies: every fact must be established by the testimony of at least two or three witnesses. So if a dispute boils down to nothing more than the word of the accused against the word of the accuser, the mere accusation is an insufficient basis for pursuing discipline, and the matter should be dropped.

However, assuming the offender does not dispute the accusation itself and still refuses to repent or forsake the sin, witnesses must be brought in to establish the fact that the offender has been confronted and failed to repent. They are not necessarily witnesses to the original offense, but rather objective parties who will witness the confrontation. They will be able, if necessary, to confirm what was said privately in case the matter needs to be reported to the church (v. 17). They are witnesses to the fact that the discipline process itself has been properly followed. And their presence at this stage is as much a protection for the one being confronted as it is for the one doing the confronting. A person is not to be accused of impenitence before the whole church on the testimony of a single witness. In fact, the two or three others might become witnesses in favor of the accused, if it turns out the accuser is being overly harsh or unfair.

But if the accuser wasn't being too harsh, and if the process moves beyond step two, the fact of the offender's impenitence will need to be established by two or three witnesses.

In many cases the person confronted will respond to this second step with repentance. If so, the matter is settled. Assuming he demonstrates his repentance by forsaking the sin and making things right with any injured parties, this should be the end of the matter. It would be inappropriate at this point to broaden the circle of involvement beyond those who are already witnesses. "My brethren, if any among you strays from the truth, and one turns him back, let him know that he who turns a sinner from the error of his way will save his soul from death, and will cover a multitude of sins" (Jas. 5:19-20). Covering the sin, not exposing it further, is the right response to the sinner's repentance.

Step Three:
Tell the Church

What happens if the offender still refuses to repent? Jesus' instructions are clear: "If he refuses to listen to them, tell it to the church" (v. 17).

This is where many churches balk. It is easy to think of reasons for *not* following this command: It's harsh. People will be offended. It's embarrassing for the person being disciplined. It will tarnish the public image of the church. What if the person being disciplined sues the church? The stark reality of the discipline process might drive unbelievers away. People's sin is best dealt with quietly, out of the limelight.

But in the face of all those arguments stands one powerful reason why the church cannot afford to ignore this important step of discipline: Christ commanded it, and it is therefore required for all who wish to honor Him as Lord.

Bear in mind that the overriding purpose of all discipline is to try to win the offender back. That is the goal of this step as well. The church is to be told about the person's sin not as a matter for gossip, but to enlist the help of the entire congregation in appealing to the sinning one.

The process has the same goal in each step. More people are involved at this point in order to pursue the sinning brother more effectively. In the first step, one individual confronts the sin. If there is no satisfactory response, two or three go, and the appeal is repeated. If there is still no repentance, the whole church is enlisted to appeal to the brother.

Again we see that discipline is the responsibility of the whole church. It is not delegated to an individual. It is not the responsibility of the pastor alone. It is a corporate duty. Once again, this can protect the church from abuses of power, such as that described by the apostle John:

> *I wrote something to the church; but Diotrephes, who loves to be first*
> *among them, does not accept what we say. For this reason, if I come,*
> *I will call attention to his deeds which he does, unjustly accusing us*

with wicked words; and not satisfied with this, neither does he him-
self receive the brethren, and he forbids those who desire to do so, and
puts them out of the church.
                                        — 3 JOHN 9-10, *emphasis added*

Diotrephes was evidently abusing his power and influence as a
leader in that church in order to turn people away and even excommunicate some singlehandedly. It is never the task of any one man
to make such a judgment. Church discipline is a corporate duty, and
that is why before anyone is excommunicated, the whole church
must be brought into the process. Only *after* everyone in the church
has had an opportunity to try to restore the sinning brother is he
eventually put out of the church.

After all, the entire church is affected by the offender's sin. If,
after all this, the offender repents, it will be the duty of all to reaffirm their love and forgiveness. In 2 Corinthians 2:5-8 Paul gave
precisely those instructions:

> *But if any has caused sorrow, he has caused sorrow not to me, but in*
> *some degree—in order not to say too much—to all of you. Sufficient*
> *for such a one is this punishment which was inflicted by the major-*
> *ity, so that on the contrary you should rather forgive and comfort him,*
> *lest somehow such a one be overwhelmed by excessive sorrow.*
> *Wherefore I urge you to reaffirm your love for him.*

The whole church ultimately became involved in pursuing this sinning person. Apparently he finally responded with repentance. So
Paul in essence said, "Now that he has responded, don't hold him
at arm's length and browbeat him. Rather, embrace him and forgive
him in love." They had won their brother back.

Dietrich Bonhoeffer was a German theologian who suffered
under the Nazi government during World War II. His overall theology we would by no means endorse, but he nonetheless offered
some profound insight about why the entire church must be told
about an unrepentant brother's sin. Bonhoeffer wrote:

Sin demands to have a man by himself. It withdraws him from the community. The more isolated a person is, the more destructive will be the power of sin over him, and the more deeply he becomes involved in it, the more disastrous is his isolation. Sin wants to remain unknown. It shuns the light. In the darkness of the unexpressed it poisons the whole being of a person. This can happen even in the midst of a pious community. In confession the light of the gospel breaks into the darkness and seclusion of the heart. The sin must be brought into the light. The unexpressed must be openly spoken and acknowledged. All that is secret and hidden is made manifest. It is a hard struggle until the sin is openly admitted, but God breaks gates of brass and bars of iron (Ps. 107:16).

Since the confession of sin is made in the presence of a Christian brother, the last stronghold of self-justification is abandoned. The sinner surrenders; he gives up all his evil. He gives his heart to God, and he finds the forgiveness of all his sin in the fellowship of Jesus Christ and his brother. The expressed, acknowledged sin has lost all its power. It has been revealed and judged as sin. It can no longer tear the fellowship asunder. Now the fellowship bears the sin of the brother. He is no longer alone with his evil for he has cast off his sin in confession and handed it over to God. It has been taken away from him. Now he stands in the fellowship of sinners who live by the grace of God and the cross of Jesus Christ. . . . The sin concealed separated him from the fellowship, made all his apparent fellowship a sham; the sin confessed has helped him define true fellowship with the brethren in Jesus Christ.[1]

But suppose the offender does not repent. How long should the church wait before going to step four? Until it becomes obvious that the offender is simply hardening his heart. No objective time limits are given in Scripture. But I am inclined to think it should be a fairly short time, at most a few weeks, rather than months or years. God Himself demands a response, and a delay only signifies the hardening of the heart (cf. Heb. 4:7).

Step Four:
Regard Him as an Unbeliever

The final step in the discipline process involves excommunication: "If he refuses to listen even to the church, let him be to you as a Gentile and a tax-gatherer" (Matt. 18:17). This does not call for heaping scorn on the person. It is not a command to treat the person badly. It means that the person is to be regarded as an unbeliever. The repeated hardening of his heart calls the reality of his faith into question. From henceforth he should be regarded as an evangelistic prospect rather than a brother in the Lord.

Implicit in this is the revocation of his membership. He is no longer to be deemed a member of the body. Rather, he should be regarded as an unbeliever, and therefore he should not be permitted to participate in the blessings and the benefits of the Christian assembly. In particular, he should not be welcomed as a communicant in the celebration of the Lord's Table. That is precisely what the term *excommunication* means.

But as far as the treatment extended to him by church members is concerned, this is no license for hostility or contempt. In fact, Christ's treatment of heathens and tax collectors is notable chiefly because of how He reached out to them in love. A similar kind of compassionate evangelistic pursuit should characterize our treatment of those who have been excommunicated in this manner, with one significant difference: as long as the "so-called brother" (1 Cor. 5:11) remains unrepentant, believers must not carry on a relationship with that person as if nothing were wrong. In order to send clear signals both to the sinning individual and the watching world, even fellowship in everyday social settings is to be suspended. Paul wrote in 1 Corinthians 5:9-11:

> *I wrote you in my letter not to associate with immoral people; I did not at all mean with the immoral people of this world, or with the covetous and swindlers, or with idolaters, for then you would have to go out of the world. But actually, I wrote to you not to associate*

with any so-called brother if he should be an immoral person, or cov-etous, or an idolater, or a reviler, or a drunkard, or a swindler—not even to eat with such a one.

In 2 Thessalonians 3:6 Paul underscored this distinction between everyday unbelievers and professing Christians who live like unbelievers: "Now we command you, brethren, in the name of our Lord Jesus Christ, that you keep aloof from every brother who leads an unruly life and not according to the tradition which you received from us." Likewise, in Romans 16:17-18 he wrote, "Now I urge you, brethren, keep your eye on those [in the church] who cause dissensions and hindrances contrary to the teaching which you learned, and turn away from them. For such men are slaves not of our Lord Christ but of their own appetites; and by their smooth and flattering speech they deceive the hearts of the unsuspecting." In other words, because of the strong tendency for people to be deceived by someone who *professes* faith in Christ and yet lives a dis-obedient life, the lines must be drawn as clearly as possible. We are supposed to have as little association as possible with such people.

Again, the point is not to be antagonistic or malevolent toward them, but to make clear that willful sin is incompatible with Christian fellowship. Since this person has identified with Christ and is a "so-called brother," it becomes vitally important for the fellow-ship as a whole to demonstrate that this person's deliberate rebellion against Christ is incompatible with a profession of faith in Him.

Even at this point, however, the primary goal with regard to the offender is to win him back. Second Thessalonians 3:15 says, "And yet do not regard him as an enemy, but admonish him as a brother." There is a sense in which you never really let him go; though you put him out of the church and out of your sphere of social fellow-ship, you keep calling him back. If the offender at any time demon-strates genuine repentance, he is to be welcomed back into the fellowship. But until that point, he is to be regarded as an outsider.

Paul, for example, instructed the Corinthian assembly to excommunicate the incestuous man from their midst. He wrote:

It is actually reported that there is immorality among you, and immorality of such a kind as does not exist even among the Gentiles, that someone has his father's wife. And you have become arrogant, and have not mourned instead, in order that the one who had done this deed might be removed from your midst.

— 1 COR. 5:1-2, emphasis added

Details of what, if anything, had been done to pursue this man's repentance are not recorded. But his sin was already known to all, and he was continuing impenitently in the grossest kind of immorality. The time for excommunicating him was long past. So Paul exercised his apostolic prerogative and ordered the man excommunicated immediately:

For I, on my part, though absent in body but present in spirit, have already judged him who has so committed this, as though I were present. In the name of our Lord Jesus, when you are assembled, and I with you in spirit, with the power of our Lord Jesus, I have decided to deliver such a one to Satan for the destruction of his flesh, so that his spirit may be saved in the day of the Lord Jesus.

— vv. 3-5

Paul's words are harsh, but they give insight into what excommunication is about. The sinning person is "deliver[ed] . . . to Satan for the destruction of his flesh." In other words, he is given over to the Satan-controlled system of sin and dissipation that he has chosen, where he will reap the full consequences of his sin. The excommunicated person may descend to the very depths of sin before repenting. If he or she is a genuine believer, this should be a further motivation to repent, and the person will be ultimately saved, though by fire (cf. 1 Cor. 3:15). Again, the primary objective is the repentance and restoration of the offender.

A secondary objective at this point, however, is the purity of the larger fellowship. Willful sin is like leaven. If tolerated, it will eventually permeate the entire body. "Do you not know that a little leaven leavens the whole lump of dough? Clean out the old leaven, that you may be a new lump, just as you are in fact unleavened" (1 Cor. 5:6-7). The unrepentant believer must be put out of the assembly.

Notice that Paul characterizes the consequences of the offender's persistent rebellion and subsequent excommunication as "the destruction of his flesh" (v. 5). Sin, especially the deliberate and wanton varieties, often takes a physical toll on the sinner. Sin's natural consequences may include illness, or in extreme cases, even death (1 Cor. 11:30). In the discipline process, the church in essence hands the sinner over to the consequences of his sin.

There's a punitive element in this. In 2 Corinthians 2:6 (quoted above), Paul refers to it as "punishment."

There's also a remedial element, however. In 1 Timothy 1 Paul speaks of "Hymenaeus and Alexander, whom I have handed over to Satan, so that they may be taught not to blaspheme" (v. 20). Suffering the consequences of their own sin would be a learning experience. Paul's hope was no doubt that this would provoke them to repentance.

THE PRESENCE

Jesus went on in Matthew 18 to teach an incredible truth about church discipline: it is one of the instruments by which God Himself mediates His discipline over His people. He is at work in the discipline process. Jesus said:

> *"Truly I say to you, whatever you bind on earth shall have been bound in heaven; and whatever you loose on earth shall have been loosed in heaven. Again I say to you, that if two of you agree on earth about anything that they may ask, it shall be done for them by My Father who is in heaven."*
>
> *–vv. 18-19*

Those verses are often taken out of context and applied to prayer requests of every kind. But they actually apply specifically to the subject of church discipline. "Whatever you bind" and "whatever you loose" refers to the church's verdict in a discipline case. *Binding* and *loosing* were rabbinical terms undoubtedly familiar to the disciples. They referred to the bondage of sin and to liberation from the guilt of it. Jesus was saying that heaven is in agreement with the church's verdict in a properly handled discipline case.

The verb tenses in the previous quotation of Matthew 18:18 are literal renderings. The idea is not that heaven follows the church's lead, but that when discipline is correctly administered, whatever is done on earth has *already* been done in heaven. This is one of the requests in the Lord's Prayer, isn't it? "Your will be done, on earth as it is in heaven" (Matt. 6:10). If God's will is to be done on earth as it is in heaven, the church must practice the proper discipline of sinning members.

This promise is meant as a comfort and encouragement. Too many people think that if the church confronts sin, that is unloving. But the truth is, when a church practices discipline as Christ commanded, that church is simply doing heaven's work on earth.

Verse 19 is also often misunderstood. The Greek word translated "agree" is the same word from which the English word *symphony* is derived. It literally means "to produce a sound together." Whether the verdict involves binding or loosing, when the church is in harmony—and especially the "two or three witnesses" who establish the fact that the sinning individual is unrepentant—the Father is also in agreement. This verse does not mean that anytime you can get two people to agree on something, God has to honor their prayer request. The "two" in verse 19 are two witnesses whose testimony is in agreement. If they are also in agreement with God's will when they impose discipline on a sinning brother, they can be certain that God Himself is working in their midst and on their behalf.

Verse 20 reiterates a similar promise from Christ: "For where two or three have gathered together in My name, there I am in their midst." Not only is the Father acting in accord with us (v. 19), but the Son is participating as well (v. 20).

Although verse 20 is often cited to invoke Christ's presence at prayer meetings, that is a misinterpretation of the intent. God is omnipresent, of course; so He is present whether only one person is praying or fifty. But in this context the "two or three" refers back to the "two or three witnesses" of verse 16. And the verse speaks not merely of Christ's *presence*, but of His *participation* in the discipline process. He joins in the discipline carried out by the church, a fearsome reality for the individual who refuses to repent, but a rich comfort to those who must administer the discipline.

THE PRIORITY

As we have seen throughout the process, the primary goal of all church discipline is to restore the sinning brother or sister. This goal is never abandoned, even after the individual has been excommunicated. And if at any time he repents, he is to be restored and welcomed with great love and compassion. Another passage of Scripture, Galatians 6, outlines three important steps for restoring the brother or sister who has fallen into sin.

Pick Them Up

Galatians 6:1 says, "If a man is caught in any trespass, you who are spiritual, restore such a one in a spirit of gentleness; looking to yourselves, lest you too be tempted." The word translated "trespass" literally means "a side-slip." It refers to a stumble, a blunder, or a fall. The *King James Version* renders it "fault," and some interpreters take it to mean something less than a sin. But it is the very same word translated "transgressions" in Matthew 6:15 ("If you do not forgive men, then your Father will not forgive your transgressions"). The same word is also used in Romans 4:25 ("He who was delivered up because of our transgressions, and was raised because of our justification"). It clearly has reference to sins.

Paul expressly calls for the restoration of the one caught in sin to be handled by "you who are spiritual." That is Paul's term for those who are discerning: "He who is spiritual appraises all things" (1 Cor. 2:15). This is the Spirit-filled believer (Eph. 5:18), in whom the Word dwells richly (Col. 3:16).

The word translated "restore" literally means "repair, mend, or refurbish." It conveys the idea of bringing something damaged back to its former condition. It is the same word used in Matthew 4:21 to speak of James and John mending their nets. It also appears in 1 Corinthians 1:10, where it speaks of reuniting two factions, like the setting of a broken bone. In that verse, the *King James Version* translates the word with the expression "perfectly joined together."

The person who would restore a fallen brother must do so with an attitude of deep humility, "looking to yourselves, lest you too be tempted." That echoes 1 Corinthians 10:12: "Let him who thinks he stands take heed lest he fall." No Christian is invincible. None of us is sin-free; so we are in no position to have a haughty attitude toward those who need restoration. Love for them, and simple humility, demands that we not try to do eye therapy to remove a bit of sawdust from their eye until we have checked to make sure there's no lumber in our own eye.

The role of restorer therefore calls for a mature, discerning, humble believer who is willing to lift up and encourage a brother in need. Don't think, *Well, the job is best left to someone besides me.* This passage is describing the kind of Christian we are *all* supposed to be.

Hold Them Up

There's more. The restorer must also be willing to help shoulder the fallen brother's burden. Verse 2 continues: "Bear one another's burdens, and thus fulfill the law of Christ."

What burden is to be borne? Notice that in this context, Paul's subject is the Christian's *walk.* "Walk by the Spirit" (Gal. 5:16, 25). The picture here is of two travelers. One overtakes the other, who is carrying a load too heavy to bear, which has caused him to stumble ("side-slip," v. 1). So he helps the fallen brother to his feet and shoulders part of the burden.

The word "burdens" represents spiritual weaknesses that can cause a fall. We can help bear such burdens through encouragement, exhortation, and accountability. Something as simple as developing a friendship can have a wonderfully strengthening effect on a weak Christian.

Once a young man came to see me, distraught over his moral failure. He had lived a totally immoral life before becoming a Christian, and he found the memories of his sin were a constant temptation. He had in fact fallen back into immoral relationships on several occasions. He claimed he had tried everything he knew to overcome temptation but was not able to avoid dwelling on evil thoughts, and the evil thoughts sometimes gave way to acts of sin. Trying to help him, I said, "I want you to keep a record of these sins. I'm not interested in the details of your sin, but I do want you to make a record of the incidents. Every time you cultivate ungodly thoughts or commit an immoral act, I want you to record the fact that it occurred. I also want you to note what you were doing at the time that might have sparked the evil thought. And then think it through and record what you *should* have done to flee from the temptation, because Scripture teaches in 1 Corinthians 10:13 that there is always a way of escape." I was hoping to make him review his behavior so he could clearly see patterns of behavior that led him into temptation.

But two weeks later we met again, and when I asked him for his list, he smiled and told me there was no list. "I didn't have anything to record because I didn't fall into those sins. I was so afraid to have to tell you about it that I carefully avoided situations that might cause me to be tempted." It turned out that he knew how to avoid those sins all along. All he needed was some accountability. And that accountability helped lighten his load.

There are many ways to carry someone's load. I often tell people struggling with the bondage of sin to pick up the phone and call me whenever they feel vulnerable to temptation. Praying with someone for victory over a certain sin lifts part of the burden. Sometimes simply having a friend who knows about their struggle can strengthen them and lighten the load.

In every case, however, helping bear the burden entails getting involved in the other person's life. It involves much more than merely saying, "Go in peace, be warmed and be filled" (Jas. 2:16). We have to be mutual burden-bearers.

Build Them Up

Skipping down to verse 6 of Galatians 6, we read, "Let the one who is taught the word share all good things with him who teaches." Paul is still speaking in the context of restoring the sinning brother. At first glance, this verse might seem to have little to do with the restoration process. But here's what Paul is saying: "The one who is taught" refers to the person being restored, and "him who teaches" is the person doing the restoring. The one being taught and the one teaching are supposed to have a ministry of mutual edification with one another.

So this is the process for restoration: *Pick* up your brothers and sisters who have fallen, *hold* them up, and then *build* them up.

I'm convinced that the biblical discipline process, properly observed, would utterly revitalize the church of our generation. Many who have become acclimated to the spirit of our age will no doubt protest that church discipline is not "user-friendly" enough. Years ago when I began to teach on the subject of church discipline in our church, a chorus of voices warned me that if we instituted these principles we would open the doors for a mass exodus from our flock. But the actual results were exactly the opposite. By making clear that we were serious about purity in our fellowship, we not only saw remarkable spiritual growth and maturity among our people, but we also began and continue to experience significant numerical growth as well. People who are committed to Christ are drawn to a fellowship where His word is obeyed.

Church discipline, properly observed, is an ongoing object lesson about how God's own love and forgiveness works. As Hebrews 12:11 suggests, God's discipline may at times seem to serve only negative purposes, but its long-term fruit is always eternal righteousness. Likewise with church discipline. It may sometimes appear harsh and punitive, but its real purpose is ultimately the outworking of forgiveness and mutual encouragement in the visible body of Christ.

EIGHT

The Blessings
of Forgiveness

If I have forgiven anything, I did it for your sakes
in the presence of Christ, in order that no advantage be taken
of us by Satan; for we are not ignorant of his schemes.

2 COR. 2:10-11

Unforgivingness is a toxin. It poisons the heart and mind with bitterness, distorting one's whole perspective on life. Anger, resentment, and sorrow begin to overshadow and overwhelm the
unforgiving person—a kind of soul-pollution that enflames evil
appetites and evil emotions. Such bitterness can even spread from
person to person, ultimately defiling many (Heb. 12:15).

Forgiveness is the only antidote. Forgiveness is a healthy, wholesome, virtuous, liberating act. Forgiveness unleashes joy. It brings
peace. It washes the slate clean. It sets all the highest virtues of love
in motion.

In a sense, forgiveness is Christianity at its highest level.

Second Corinthians 2 contains a vignette on forgiveness that
makes a fitting addendum to our study of church discipline and a
good concluding summary of the virtues of forgiveness. There the
apostle Paul urges the Corinthians to forgive a man who had been
under their discipline but had repented of his sin. Paul beseeches
them to receive the repentant brother back into their fellowship and

to stop punishing him for his offense. In the process, the apostle highlights some of the vast blessings of forgiveness.

Details of the incident that forms the backdrop for Paul's comments are sketchy. We don't know who the individual was whose forgiveness Paul sought. We don't know for certain what he had done. The context seems to suggest that the man's offense involved some sort of personal affront to the apostle. If that is the case, Paul was not merely instructing the Corinthians about forgiveness; he was himself exemplifying Christian forgiveness.

Some commentators surmise that the man referred to in 2 Corinthians 2 is the same person Paul ordered disciplined for incest in 1 Corinthians 5. But what we know about the historical background and timing of the two epistles makes that unlikely. Much had occurred in the interval between 1 and 2 Corinthians. A mutiny had evidently been fomented by someone in the Corinthian assembly. Paul's apostolic credentials had even come into question. That is why a significant portion of 2 Corinthians is devoted to a defense of Paul's apostleship (e.g., 3:1-3; 6:4-10; 10:7-18; 11:5-33; 12:11-13).

It was not surprising that this church gave rise to such a rebellion. Problems at Corinth were rife, despite an auspicious beginning. The apostle Paul himself had founded the church at Corinth (Acts 18) and then spent eighteen months of his life establishing the saints in sound doctrine. But almost as soon as the apostle left Corinth, the church there began to struggle.

The fact that a church existed at all in Corinth was somewhat remarkable. The city was known throughout the Roman Empire for its gross perversion and wickedness. Corinth was filled with brothels. In its pagan temples acts of fornication were thought of as high liturgy, and lasciviousness was regarded as an intense spiritual experience. The young Corinthian church, situated amid so many evil influences, was continually beset with serious problems. The pollution of fleshly paganism began to seep into the church. Word soon came to Paul that abuses and scandals were disrupting the fellowship at Corinth. Some of the brethren had turned the communion service into an occasion for wanton self-indulgence. Worship services at Corinth had become frenzied contests to see who could display the most extraordinary spiritual gifts. Meanwhile, gross sin was being tolerated by people in the fellowship—to such an extreme that even unbelievers in that debauched culture were appalled. Paul's first epistle to the Corinthians addressed those and other serious problems in the church.

Sometime after Paul wrote 1 Corinthians, a rebellion against him broke out in the Corinthian church. Some false teachers (men evidently posing as apostles) came into the church and found a ready audience for their lies and heresies (2 Cor. 11:13-15). Naturally, the false apostles sought to discredit the reigning authority in the Corinthian church—namely, Paul. They made an all-out assault on his character, his life, and his teaching. They did everything they could to disparage him, to impugn his integrity, and to undermine the Corinthians' confidence in his apostolic authority.

Despite the wonderful love Paul had shown the Corinthian church, even though he was the human instrument by whom they had first heard the Gospel, although they owed him their very lives, many in the Corinthian assembly were duped by the lies of the false apostles. They began to question Paul's authority openly. They denigrated his appearance and his speech (2 Cor. 10:10). They questioned his motives and his integrity (1:12). They accused him of vacillating (1:17) and openly voiced doubts about his sincerity (2:17).

To deal with the mutiny, Paul wrote the Corinthians a letter, referred to in 2 Corinthians 7:8. Paul's comments about that letter and the circumstances surrounding it suggest that the epistle to which he refers is not 1 Corinthians, but a different, undoubtedly later epistle—one not preserved as a part of the New Testament canon. (Before 1 Corinthians Paul had also written the Corinthians a letter, mentioned in 1 Corinthians 5:9. The absence of these letters from the canon would indicate that they were never intended to be regarded as Scripture. Had they been God-breathed epistles, they would have been preserved; see 1 Peter 1:25).

In the interim after 1 Corinthians was written, Paul seems to have made a brief visit to Corinth, because twice in 2 Corinthians he speaks of his plans to visit them a "third time" (12:14; 13:1). That visit between 1 and 2 Corinthians was probably a brief fact-finding visit as Paul was en route to somewhere else. The visit evidently did not put a stop to the mutiny. In fact, it may be the case that while in Corinth Paul was assaulted verbally, publicly, and to his face. Paul apparently left Corinth heartsick, heartbroken, and grieved over what he saw and experienced (cf. 2 Cor. 12:20-21). He also gave the Corinthians a stern warning before he left (13:2).

Either during his visit, or (perhaps more likely) in the letter, which was written afterward, Paul instructed the Corinthians to discipline the man referred to in 2 Corinthians 2. This man was obviously a member of the Corinthian church. Perhaps he had also become a ringleader in the rebellion. It may be that his sin involved a personal and public attack on the apostle Paul. All of that would fit well with the context of Paul's remarks.

Whatever the circumstances, sometime after his own visit Paul sent Titus to Corinth to get a firsthand update on the state of things in the church there. Titus went with the express purpose of reporting back to Paul about how the Corinthians had responded to the epistle he had written. One of Paul's concerns was how this man was being dealt with.

So here is the setting for 2 Corinthians: Titus had returned and had given Paul an encouraging report about the Corinthians' repentance (7:6-16). Titus also informed Paul that the Corinthians longed to restore their relationship with him. They were repentant (7:9). They were even mourning over how they had treated Paul (7:7). Best of all, they were indignant about the mutiny that had been fomented in their midst, and they were now zealous to avenge the wrong (7:11).

And the focus of their avenging zeal was evidently this man who had somehow wronged the apostle Paul. They had already pursued him with the discipline process. In fact, the man himself had already repented.

But avenging zeal is not always quenched by the repentance of an offender, and it seems that some in Corinth still wanted to punish this man. They were not satisfied with his repentance. They wanted a measure of vengeance for all the trouble and confusion the man had caused in their fellowship.

One group in particular would have been zealous to avenge any wrongs committed against the apostle Paul. Paul mentioned them in 1 Corinthians 1:12 and 3:4, where he confronted some factious tendencies in the Corinthian fellowship. There he alluded to a group who identified strongly with him—the Paul coalition ("I am of Paul"). It is possible that some of these people who felt such a strong affection for the apostle Paul were the main ones who were still seeking vengeance against this guilty but repentant man.

But not Paul himself. He was more than eager to forgive. Far from siding with those who wanted to inflict more punishment against the offender, he instructed them to forgive and restore the man immediately:

> But if any has caused sorrow, he has caused sorrow not to me, but in some degree—in order not to say too much—to all of you. Sufficient for such a one is this punishment which was inflicted by the major-ity, so that on the contrary you should rather forgive and comfort him, lest somehow such a one be overwhelmed by excessive sorrow. Wherefore I urge you to reaffirm your love for him. For to this end also I wrote that I might put you to the test, whether you are obedi-ent in all things. But whom you forgive anything, I forgive also; for indeed what I have forgiven, if I have forgiven anything, I did it for your sakes in the presence of Christ, in order that no advantage be taken of us by Satan; for we are not ignorant of his schemes.
>
> —2 COR. 2:5-11

Paul had the heart of a tender pastor. Though he himself had caused the Corinthians sorrow with his earlier letter of rebuke, caus-ing sorrow was not his goal (vv. 1-4). Motivated only by love for them (v. 4), he had written them through his own tears with no desire to punish them, but only seeking their repentance and the restoration of the broken relationship. He had never used his author-ity as an apostle to lord it over them but had always sought their joy

(1:24). The sorrow he had aimed to provoke with his letter was sorrow of a godly sort, designed only to secure their repentance in order to liberate them from their sin and unleash the joy again.

That is a good summary of how forgiveness works. It reverses the sorrowful aftermath of an offense and sets right a host of things made wrong by sin.

And in order to make his point, Paul employs this repentant individual as an object lesson for the Corinthians. He instructs them to forgive and restore the man, subjecting him to no further punishment. The apostle's instructions highlight seven blessings of forgiveness.

FORGIVENESS DEFLECTS PRIDE

There is little doubt that Paul himself had instructed the Corinthians to discipline this man until he repented—just as he had instructed them in the case of the incestuous man in 1 Corinthians 5.

But now that the man had repented, it was time to forgive him. And Paul, though probably the target of the man's original offense, took the lead in seeking his forgiveness.

This is a refreshing and godly example. Often the offended party feels justified in withholding forgiveness. Not Paul. He demanded no personal apology. He sought no act of penance. Anyone else might have demanded that the man's case be held open until he could come to Corinth and personally assess the genuineness of the man's contrition. But Paul did not. He was eager to forgive.

This illustrates the absence of pride in Paul's heart. Pride, I am convinced, is the primary reason most people refuse to forgive. They nurse self-pity (which is nothing but a form of pride). Their ego is wounded, and they will not stand for that. Prideful reactions to an offense can run the gamut from those who simply wallow in self-pity to those who retaliate with an even worse offense. All such responses are wrong because they are motivated by pride.

Paul would have none of it. Self-glory, self-protection, ego, pride, vengeance, and retaliation had no place in his heart at all. He did not want pity. He did not encourage those who wanted to take up his offense and see to it that the offender paid in full. Paul did not bask in sympathy offered by others who were angry at the offense against him.

Those are all natural inclinations prompted by sinful pride. When we are offended and someone else expresses outrage at our hurt, our tendency is to lap it up with a selfish delight. Someone says, "You poor thing! Oh, how much you have endured! Oh, how you have suffered! You have made yourself praiseworthy by enduring such excruciating pain!" And we love every word of it.

Paul wanted nothing to do with that. He refused to magnify the offense. "But if any has caused sorrow, he has caused sorrow not to me . . ." (v. 5). In other words, although the man's offense seemed to have involved a personal, perhaps public slight against Paul, the apostle declined to hold it against the man. He waived the personal aspect of the offense completely.

That would defuse anyone who believed that the offender needed additional punishment for Paul's sake. It would take the sword out of their hand. Paul simply minimized his own personal hurt. He refused to take the offense personally. He would not wallow in self-pity. He did not invite commiserating people to join in his despondency. He did not foster bitter resentment. He declined to pursue a personal vendetta. Whatever personal grief and public embarrassment the man's offense might have caused Paul were not important. As far as Paul was concerned, the offense against him was nothing.

And so Paul, by personally forgiving the man, softened the charge against him. The church could deal with the offender with no thought of making him pay for the grief he had caused the apostle. The Corinthian believers did not need to carry out some personal agenda on Paul's behalf. They were not to inflict extra punishment against the offender for Paul's sake. As far as Paul was concerned, no personal score needed to be settled between him and the offender. Paul knew how to be abased and how to abound (Phil.

4:12). He was "well content with weaknesses, with insults, with distresses, with persecutions, with difficulties, for Christ's sake" (2 Cor. 12:10).

Paul did not take this man's offense personally, any more than Jesus took personally the sin of those who nailed him to the cross. Stephen, under the bloody stones, set a similar example (Acts 7:60).

Here is virtue at its noblest. Paul simply rose above the offense and above the offender and took himself out of a victim status.

Modern psychology pushes people in the opposite direction, often teaching them to see themselves as victims and to magnify blame against others. I recently saw a book by one psychologist with a chapter entitled, "You Don't Have to Forgive." That's bad advice. Self-pity is an act of sinful pride. The wounded ego that cannot rise above an offense is the very antithesis of Christlikeness.

Paul was a godly man. He was too humble to seek vengeance when his pride was dented. Personal slights and personal sorrows were not his concern.

He makes a qualifying statement in verse 5: "He has caused sorrow not to me, but in some degree—in order not to say too much—to all of you." Paul was intent on minimizing the man's offense—and not only the offense against him personally. Paul also wanted the Corinthians to downplay their own hurt for the sake of restoring the man. "In some degree" suggests that the sorrow the man had caused the Corinthians was limited in extent. And "in order not to say too much" means "not to exaggerate the point." In other words, "He has caused sorrow to a limited extent, but let's not exaggerate it." It was time to move on, bury the penitent man's offense, and not make it an ongoing crusade in the church.

So Paul utterly dismissed any personal sorrow the man's offense had caused him, and he discouraged the Corinthians from overstating or embellishing the amount of sorrow it had caused *them*. Now that the man had repented, they were not to make more out of the offense than was absolutely necessary. They were particularly forbidden to overdo the significance of the offense against Paul. But they were also cautioned not to overstate the offense against the rest of the fellowship or blow out of proportion the hurt they had suffered. The man had repented. The Corinthians were not to seek vengeance on Paul's behalf. And whatever grief he had caused them should be graciously forgiven too. They were to forgive the man and move on.

Our sinful pride inclines us to respond exactly the opposite way. Pride always wants to demand eye-for-an-eye justice. We want to prolong punishment as long as possible and extract every ounce of suffering in return.

Forgiveness is not like that. It buries the offense as quickly as possible, even at the cost of personal pride. That is the attitude Paul exemplifies in this passage. Paul was a very hard man to offend, simply because he would not take offense. That is a wonderful virtue. It is true godliness and genuine love in action: "[Love] does not take into account a wrong suffered" (1 Cor. 13:5).

Paul had nothing in his heart but love and forgiveness for the offender. He had already forgiven him from the heart. The discipline process needed to be followed until there was repentance. But in his heart Paul harbored no bitterness. And now that the discipline process had borne the desired fruit, Paul was eager to forgive and restore the offender.

True forgiveness sets aside the wounded ego. One of the most beautiful biblical illustrations of this is Joseph. Joseph's own brothers sold him into Egyptian slavery. In Egypt Joseph was falsely accused by Potiphar's wife and then imprisoned for many years. For many people those would have been years of festering resentment and time spent plotting revenge. Not Joseph. When he finally encountered his brothers again, he was in a position to save them from famine. He told his brothers, "Do not be grieved or angry with yourselves, because you sold me here; for God sent me before you to preserve life" (Gen. 45:5).

All Joseph saw was the divine providence that placed him where he was so he could feed his brothers when famine ravaged the land. "For the famine has been in the land these two years, and there are still five years in which there will be neither plowing nor harvesting.

And God sent me before you to preserve for you a remnant in the earth, and to keep you alive by a great deliverance" (vv. 6-7). Where's the ego in that? Where's the "poor me"? Where's the coddled misery? Where's the self-pity? Where's the longing for vengeance?

There isn't any. Forgiveness erases all such evil influences. Forgiveness frees us from the bitter chains of pride and self-pity.

FORGIVENESS SHOWS MERCY

Paul also admonished the Corinthians to show mercy to the repentant offender: "Sufficient for such a one is this punishment which was inflicted by the majority" (2 Cor. 2:6). The discipline the man had already suffered was enough. He had confessed his sin and repented. Paul wanted the Corinthians to back off. Now it was time to show mercy.

The word translated "punishment" in verse 6 is *epitimia*, a Greek word that refers to a legal penalty or a formal censure. It does not refer to personal vengeance or punishment discharged by an individual. Instead it speaks of an official sanction, a corporate reprimand issued "by the majority." It is clear that this speaks of an official, formal act of discipline. The man's offense had been brought before the church, and "the majority" had approved his punishment—which, if the Matthew 18 process was followed, may have gone all the way to formal excommunication.

As we saw in chapter 7, church discipline is not a form of vengeance. It is a biblically mandated formal response from the church with regard to open sin. But the church's action against sinning people in the fellowship is never supposed to be vindictive. Rather, its proper aim is to draw the offender back.

As long as this man remained unrepentant, it was right for the Corinthians to keep away from him. Paul wrote in 2 Thessalonians 3:6, "Now we command you, brethren, in the name of our Lord Jesus Christ, that you keep aloof from every brother who leads an unruly life and not according to the tradition which you received from us." Later he wrote that same church and underscored those instructions: "If anyone does not obey our instruction in this letter, take special note of that man and do not associate with him, so that he will be put to shame. Yet do not regard him as an enemy, but admonish him as a brother" (2 Thess. 3:14-15). He told the church at Rome, "Keep your eye on those who cause dissensions and hindrances contrary to the teaching which you learned, and turn away from them" (Rom. 16:17). Jesus' instructions were similar: "If he refuses to listen to them, tell it to the church; and if he refuses to listen even to the church, let him be to you as a Gentile and a tax-gatherer" (Matt. 18:17). And Paul had already instructed the Corinthian church "not to associate with any so-called brother if he should be an immoral person, or covetous, or an idolater, or a reviler, or a drunkard, or a swindler—not even to eat with such a one" (1 Cor. 5:11).

The Corinthians were simply doing what the rabbis called "binding" (cf. Matt. 16:19; 18:18). The man's sin was bound to him as long as he would not repent, and their discipline was just. As Paul had instructed in the case of the incestuous brother in 1 Corinthians 5:5, they were to "deliver such a one to Satan for the destruction of his flesh." "Remove the wicked man from among yourselves," Paul had told them in that instance (v. 13). The discipline was to be administered publicly, "when you are assembled" (v. 4).

But this man had responded to the church's discipline, and now it was time to show him mercy. The binding had been done, but the loosing was equally important. The binding had been done publicly by the whole body; the loosing should be equally public.

Christians should be more eager to loose than to bind, because forgiveness, not condemnation, epitomizes the heart of our Lord (Luke 9:56, margin; John 3:17). Furthermore, we who live only by the mercy of God should be eager to show mercy to others. When an offender repents, we should restore him in a spirit of gentleness, realizing we too could be in the same situation (Gal. 6:1). We are not to be harsh. We are not to browbeat the repentant brother. We don't put him under a lifetime of penance. We don't make him do something to atone for his sin. We accept his repentance. That should be the end of the issue. That's the whole gist of Ephesians 4:32 and Colossians 3:13, which tell us we should forgive in the same manner Christ forgave us—generously, eagerly, magnanimously, and abundantly. How does God treat a repentant sinner? With total, complete instantaneous forgiveness. He holds forgiveness and love in His heart as He waits for the penitent sinner to come and seek that forgiveness. And then He bestows His mercy with the greatest joy and liberality.

FORGIVENESS RESTORES JOY

Paul, modeling the forgiveness he wanted the Corinthians to show to the offender, was eager to restore the man's joy: "You should rather forgive and comfort him, lest somehow such a one be overwhelmed by excessive sorrow" (2 Cor. 2:7).

Sin destroys joy. David noted this in his great confession of sin in Psalm 51: "Restore to me the joy of Your salvation" (v. 12). Sin always shatters the sinner's joy. But forgiveness restores the joy. Two verses later David wrote, "Deliver me from bloodguiltiness, O God, [the] God of my salvation; then my tongue will joyfully sing of Your righteousness" (v. 14).

So Paul instructs the Corinthians to forgive their brother and end his sorrow. The sorrow of discipline had brought him to repentance; now it was time for joy. The believers in the Corinthian fellowship needed to be more eager to bring the man joy than they were to cause him sorrow.

That is the heart of God. He is always tenderhearted toward repentant sinners. He takes no pleasure in the punishment of the wicked but delights when the wicked repent (Ezek. 18:23, 32; 33:11). "He does not afflict willingly or grieve the sons of men" (Lam. 3:33). God is like the prodigal son's father, who ran to meet his son and embraced and received him "while he was still a long way off" (Luke 15:20).

That is the heart of Christ as well. The prophet Isaiah said of Him, "A bruised reed He will not break, and a dimly burning wick He will not extinguish" (Isa. 42:3; cf. Matt. 12:20). The reed was a shepherd's flute constructed from a soft, hollow, bamboo-like plant. In time the little flutes would become weathered and soft— "bruised." They would lose their fine tone and become difficult to play. The typical shepherd would then simply snap the bruised reed, discard it, and make a new one.

Isaiah said the Messiah would be so tender a shepherd that He would not throw away the little flute that did not play the perfect tune. Instead He would restore the melody and bring back the song.

"Dimly burning wick" refers to a lamp-wick that was old and well-burned or for some other reason smoldered or smoked while it burned, producing an imperfect light and annoying smoke. The common practice was to extinguish the smoking wick and replace it. But the heart of Christ is to use even the smoldering wick, not to throw it away. Instead, He cleanses and trims the wick so that it burns more brightly.

God delights to revive and uplift the heart of the contrite. Elsewhere Isaiah wrote:

> *For thus says the high and exalted One Who lives forever, whose name is Holy, "I dwell on a high and holy place, And also with the contrite and lowly of spirit in order to revive the spirit of the lowly and to revive the heart of the contrite. For I will not contend forever, neither will I always be angry; for the spirit would grow faint before Me, and the breath of those whom I have made. Because of the iniquity of his unjust gain I was angry and struck him; I hid My face and was angry, and he went on turning away, in the way of his heart. I have seen his ways, but I will heal him; I will lead him and restore comfort to him and to his mourners, creating the praise of the lips. Peace, peace to him who is far and to him who is near," says the Lord, "and I will heal him."*
>
> *– ISA. 57:15-19*

God desires His people to have fullness of joy. The apostle John wrote, "These things we write, so that our joy may be made complete" (1 John 1:4). Joy is a fruit of the Spirit (Gal. 5:22). And when a Christian under God's discipline repents, God glorifies Himself by restoring that person's joy.

Paul therefore writes to the Corinthians, "so that on the contrary you should rather forgive and comfort him" (2 Cor. 2:7). They were not to hold back their forgiveness; rather they needed to comfort him actively and earnestly, seeking to restore his joy. Hebrews 12:12-13 describes the process: "Strengthen the hands that are weak and the knees that are feeble, and make straight paths for your feet, so that the limb which is lame may not be put out of joint, but rather be healed."

The church cannot set false borders on grace. There are no limits on divine mercy toward penitent people. There are no boundaries on forgiveness. The church must discipline sin in its midst, but we cannot deny a penitent person, no matter how serious his sin may have been.

Someone might protest, "But we want to make sure he will never do it again." We cannot have that assurance. If he sins seventy times seven, we must forgive him that many times.

Refusing to forgive is a sin. And it is a sin that is doubly destructive to Christian joy, because it not only steals the original offender's joy, but it also diminishes the joy of the one who is refusing to forgive. As we have seen repeatedly, failure to forgive brings the unforgiving person under God's discipline. It hinders worship and creates disunity in the fellowship. It is an extremely destructive kind of sin.

Forgiveness reverses all those effects. It restores joy on both sides. It heals the breach caused by sin. It salves the sorrow of both offender and forgiver.

And this should all take place the moment the sinning one repents. As soon as there is repentance, the offender should be restored and strengthened, "lest somehow such a one be overwhelmed by excessive sorrow" (v. 7).

Notice the anonymity of Paul's expression: "such a one." There was no reason to name the man, because he had repented. There was no further need to inform the church of his sin, but only to encourage them to restore him. As soon as the offender acknowledged his own sin and was willing to confess and repent, God wanted him to know joy.

God finds no pleasure in an unending or excessive despair. He seeks our joy, not our sorrow. He does not require sinners to spend a lifetime in pain and despair. A morose obsession with one's own guilt is not a godly virtue. It is actually a kind of self-righteousness. When you see someone who is preoccupied with mourning over sin, refusing to enter into the joy of the Lord, what you're seeing is an artificial spirituality. It is tantamount to refusing God's forgiveness, because forgiveness always brings joy.

FORGIVENESS AFFIRMS LOVE

Paul's instructions for restoring the sinning brother continue: "Wherefore I urge you to reaffirm your love for him" (v. 8). Forgiveness necessarily involves an affirmation of love to the offender. In fact, to withhold forgiveness is to withhold love. Love is the new commandment given to the church by Christ (John 13:34). Love is also called "the royal law" (Jas. 2:8). Therefore, unforgivingness is a very grave sin indeed.

The Greek word translated "reaffirm" in 2 Corinthians 2:8 is significant; it is a technical term that speaks of legally validating a document or a contract. It is the same word used in Galatians 3:15 to speak of the formal ratification of a covenant. Here in 2 Corinthians 2 it undoubtedly refers to a formal, public announcement. As we noted, verse 6 implies that the man had been formally and publicly disciplined. Here Paul suggests that the matter should be concluded with a formal and public reaffirmation of love toward the man. The discipline was announced formally to the whole church; the restoration should likewise be broadcast.

Paul told Timothy that an elder who sins should be rebuked before all, so that others may fear (1 Tim. 5:20). If the purpose of dealing with sin publicly is so that everyone understands how serious sin is, then restoration must also be dealt with publicly so that everyone understands how important forgiveness is. Grace is, if anything, a higher principle than law. Loosing is even better than binding. Since all heaven rejoices when a sinner repents (Luke 15:7), surely the saints on earth should participate in that joy. And so the matter was to be handled publicly.

However, the public affirmation of love should be only a prelude to the display of love that should pour forth from the saints on an individual level toward the restored brother. The Greek word for "love" is *agape*—the love of choice, the love of will, the love of serving with humility. Paul expected something more than a mere formal announcement. The saints were to demonstrate their love to this brother in practical ways.

This is the very character by which a church should be known: "By this all men will know that you are My disciples, if you have love for one another" (John 13:35). How does the world know Christians love one another? What about our love for one another is remarkable, and visible, to a watching world? Is it because we socialize? No. Non-Christians socialize too. It's not our potluck meals or group activities that best display our love toward one another, but our *forgiveness*. Love is best manifested in forgiveness. And the real test of love is how eagerly we forgive when we are offended.

Almost nothing can fracture a church where forgiveness is practiced, because unresolved issues are never left to fester. Offenses are dealt with. They are forgiven. Transgressions are covered. That is why it is so crucial for churches to practice discipline. The discipline process seeks to bring about the forgiveness and reconciliation that keep the unity and love of the church intact.

And when repentance takes place, the affirmation of love to the repentant one should be even more ceremonious than the discipline. Like the father who dressed the prodigal son in the finest clothing, killed the fatted calf, and called his neighbors together for a celebration (Luke 15), we should be lavish with our forgiveness. True forgiveness delights to affirm the sinner's repentance with munificent expressions of love.

FORGIVENESS PROVES OBEDIENCE

We have seen so far that forgiveness is inextricably tied to humility, mercy, joy, and love. Those are all noble virtues—fruit of the Spirit (cf. Galatians 5:22-23). Forgiveness prompts and nurtures all those virtues. But if forgiveness were entirely unrelated to those crucial Christian character qualities, if forgiveness did nothing to cultivate the fruit of the Spirit, it would still be right to forgive.

Why? Because God has commanded that we forgive.

Forgiveness is a simple matter of obedience. That is what Paul means in 2 Corinthians 2:9: "To this end also I wrote that I might put you to the test, whether you are obedient in all things." Their earlier discipline of the offender was one step of obedience. Now they needed to continue showing themselves obedient by restoring their repentant brother.

It is relatively easy to be obedient in some things. Scripture commands us to sing songs of praise to the Lord (Col. 3:16). That is not a difficult thing. The Bible says we're to pray (Luke 18:1). That comes fairly easy, though faithfulness in the task is sometimes a challenge. But of all the commandments Christ gave, it seems one of the hardest things is dealing with sin in the church. That is why many churches avoid discipline altogether. Everything about dealing with sin is difficult. Confronting the sinner privately is hard. Bringing an unrepentant brother's sin before the church is harder still. Pursuing an unrepentant person who has turned his back on the church is one of the most difficult things of all. The further into the process we go, the harder it is to obey.

But the restoration process can also be extremely hard. Picking up the pieces after the offender has repented, restoring him to the fellowship, strengthening him, and affirming love is not easy. Such forgiveness does not come naturally. But it is nonetheless an essential aspect of obedience to the Lord.

The contemporary church has failed in virtually all areas related to dealing with sin. Many churches practice no discipline whatsoever. They do not confront sin. They do not go after the sinner. And ultimately they also forfeit many opportunities to obey in the matter of forgiveness. Their disobedience with regard to disciplining sinners nullifies any opportunity to forgive those who repent.

The converse is also true. Those who do the hard work of confronting and disciplining sin inevitably have more opportunities and a greater willingness to forgive and show love to repentant offenders. Discipline and forgiveness often go hand in hand. And both are equally necessary to maintain the purity and soundness of the church.

Rooting out sin in the church through the discipline process does not necessarily guarantee a pure church. The sin of an offender may be eliminated, but the attitudes and responses of the rest of the flock must also be right (cf. Gal. 6:1). Paul alludes to this in 2 Corinthians 7:12, where he tells the believers, "So although I wrote to you it was not for the sake of the offender, nor for the sake of the one offended." In other words, throughout this episode in Corinth, Paul's chief concern was never merely for the one person who had committed the offense. Nor did he seek this man's discipline in order to vindicate himself (as the offended person). Rather, Paul was mostly concerned with the response of the Corinthian church. He longed to see them demonstrate complete obedience.

The Corinthian church, despite their many shortcomings, were beginning to show signs of the obedience Paul longed to see. The report Titus brought back from Corinth comforted and encouraged him, because they had so far responded exactly as Paul hoped (7:13). All Paul's highest expectations had so far been met, and Titus's own affection for the Corinthians was made to abound (7:14–15). They had obeyed in the matter of the man's discipline. But now they also needed to obey in the matter of his restoration. The same church that had once shown such a wanton neglect of discipline (1 Cor. 5) now was called to prove their obedience in the restoration of a repentant brother. Their discipline had had the desired effect. Now one further test was necessary: they needed to demonstrate forgiveness to the man and thereby prove their obedience in all things.

FORGIVENESS REVITALIZES FELLOWSHIP

Paul further writes, "But whom you forgive anything, I forgive also; for indeed what I have forgiven, if I have forgiven anything, I did it for your sakes in the presence of Christ" (2 Cor. 2:10).

Again we see Paul's humility. He wants to deflect those who might desire to withhold fellowship from the offender for Paul's sake. So Paul is eager to affirm his own personal forgiveness to the offender.

And again he minimizes the offense: "What I have forgiven, if I have forgiven anything, I did it for your sakes"—as if from Paul's perspective the offense was hardly worth noticing in the first place. But he wants to state his forgiveness formally and explicitly for the sake of the Corinthians. No one could say, "We can't receive this man back because of our loyalty to Paul. After all, Paul was the one offended."

Paul, in essence, tells them, "No, it's done. If you have forgiven, I forgive. I want the fellowship restored, for your sakes." He was concerned that unity in the church be reestablished, and complete forgiveness was the only way that would occur. The Corinthians were to hold nothing back for Paul's sake. He wanted the church's fellowship renewed and revitalized. He was eager for the rest of the church to be rejoined with the repentant one. He desired unity in the church. Whatever fracture had been caused by the man's offense must be repaired. Any discord and disharmony must be resolved. Bitterness and vengeance needed to be set aside. The rejuvenation and revitalization of the fellowship took priority over all that. And forgiveness made it all possible.

FORGIVENESS THWARTS SATAN

Finally, Paul urged the Corinthians to forgive, "[so] that no advantage be taken of us by Satan, for we are not ignorant of his schemes" (2 Cor. 2:11).

Satan's whole agenda is undermined by forgiveness. If forgiveness deflects pride, shows mercy, restores joy, affirms mercy, proves obedience, and revitalizes fellowship, imagine how Satan must hate it! Therefore, forgiveness is an essential part of undoing Satan's schemes.

To refuse forgiveness is to fall into Satan's trap. Unforgivingness has all the opposite effects of forgiveness: it hinders humility, mercy, joy, love, obedience, and fellowship—and therefore it is as destructive of individual character as it is of harmony in the church.

First Peter 5:8 says Satan "prowls around like a roaring lion, seeking someone to devour." And one of the ways he devours people is by taking advantage of an unforgiving spirit. Unforgivingness gives him a tremendous advantage.

However, Paul says, "we are not ignorant of his schemes." It is sheer folly to promote Satan's agenda by refusing to forgive. Where unforgivingness reigns, Satan rules. He has his way in a church that refuses to forgive.

But where forgiveness flows freely, Satan's schemes are thwarted.

Forgiveness, then, is the soil in which numerous spiritual fruits and divine blessings are cultivated. Tending and nurturing the soil of forgiveness is one of the surest ways to develop spiritual health and maturity.

On the other hand, as we have seen throughout this book, refusing to forgive is spiritually debilitating. It provokes divine discipline and inflames a host of evils.

Why, then would any Christian ever deliberately withhold forgiveness? We whose very existence depends on the inestimable mercy shown to us in Christ ought to foster a similar mercy in our dealings with one another, and we ought to model forgiveness before a watching world whose greatest need is God's forgiveness.

Think about it like this: Forgiveness is both a blessing and a means to further blessings. Those who refuse to forgive forfeit the multiple blessings of forgiveness. But those who forgive unleash multiple divine blessings, not only on those whom they forgive, but also on themselves. This is the very thing to which we are called.

To sum up, let all be harmonious, sympathetic, brotherly, kind-hearted, and humble in spirit; not returning evil for evil, or insult for insult, but giving a blessing instead; for you were called for the very purpose that you might inherit a blessing.

—1 PET. 3:8-9

NINE

Answering
the Hard Questions
About Forgiveness

For You, Lord, are good, and ready to forgive,
and abundant in lovingkindness to all who call upon You.

Ps. 86:5

I know a young man (we'll call him Jim) who believes he was mistreated by a fellow Christian several years ago. There was a dispute
about who was wrong in the incident. Jim brought the matter to the
elders of his church for resolution. The elders attempted to inves-
tigate the matter but ultimately concluded there was insufficient
evidence to determine who was at fault. It was one person's word
against the other's, with no other witnesses. The elders finally
advised both Jim and the other party to forgive one another and put
the dispute behind them.

Jim refused to do that. He had read a popular Christian book on
forgiveness, and the book taught that forgiveness can never be
granted until the other party repents and seeks forgiveness. Jim now
believes he is justified in withholding forgiveness from his brother
as long as the other man refuses to admit he was wrong. Jim is determined to see that he gets justice, and he has already spent several

years seeking someone who will take up his cause. But almost everyone has given him the same advice: "The issue is petty. It's your word against the other fellow's. This might not be resolved until Christ Himself sorts it out and you lay your differences aside in heaven. Give it up and move on. It is beginning to dominate your life and rob you of opportunities to bear the fruit of the Spirit."

Jim refuses to heed that advice. He believes that God, who hates injustice, would *never* want him to suffer an injury and simply forgive the offender unconditionally. Although numerous Christians have shown him 1 Peter 2:20-23, Jim has somehow managed to explain it away in his own mind. For years he has gone from counselor to counselor, desperately seeking someone who will agree with him and help him pursue justice against this other Christian who Jim says sinned against him. He believes he is obeying the biblical injunction of Colossians 3:13 ("Just as the Lord forgave you, so also should you") because, after all, God does not forgive apart from the repentance of the offender. Thus he has twisted a commandment to forgive into an excuse for withholding forgiveness. (See chapter 6 for a thorough discussion on the question of whether forgiveness is always conditional.)

I don't know whether Jim or the other fellow was at fault in the original dispute. It may well be that both of them were partly wrong. But even if the other fellow was totally at fault, I believe Jim is clearly wrong to hang on to his bitterness and justify his refusal to forgive on the ground that the offender has not repented. This is precisely the kind of situation in which we are supposed to turn the other cheek (Matt. 5:39). Those who keep account of such wrongs, constantly demanding redress of personal affronts, are violating the very spirit of Christ.

As I said at the outset of this book, I am convinced that many, if not most, of the personal problems Christians see counselors for have to do with forgiveness. And there are some difficult questions surrounding this subject of forgiveness.

In this chapter I want to address some of those issues. These are some of the hardest questions about forgiveness that have come my way in thirty years of ministry.

WHAT IS THE DIFFERENCE BETWEEN TRUE REPENTANCE AND A MERE APOLOGY?

Genuine repentance always involves a confession of wrongdoing and a willingness to make things right. An apology often takes the form of an excuse.

The word *apology* comes from the Greek *apologia*, which literally means "a speech in defense of." Apologies are often nothing more than self-defense: "I'm sorry if you took offense, but . . ." Genuine repentance is properly expressed in an admission of wrongdoing and a plea for forgiveness: "It was unthoughtful of me to say that. Will you forgive me?"

Be wary of using merely apologetic language in place of genuine repentance.

TO WHOM SHOULD WE CONFESS OUR SINS?

Confession of guilt must *always* be made to God. Confession is also owed to whomever our sin has injured. The arena of confession should be as large as the audience of the original offense. Public transgressions call for public confession; private sins should be confessed to God alone.

WHAT IF I SIN WITH MY THOUGHTS AGAINST ANOTHER PERSON?

Only actual injuries require confession of a wrong. It would be inappropriate for a man who had a lustful thought to confess that thought to the woman who was the object of his lust. Confession in such cases should be made only to God.

That does not, however, rule out confession in *every* case where the victim is unaware of the offense. If you have quietly slandered someone, that person may be unaware of the offense. Nonetheless, the offense is real. It needs to be made right not only with those who received the original slander, but also with the person who was slandered, even if that person is not yet aware of the offense.

SHOULD I CONFESS MY UNFAITHFULNESS TO MY WIFE, EVEN IF TELLING HER ABOUT IT MAY HURT HER MORE THAN KEEPING IT A SECRET WOULD?

There is no doubt that in some cases confessing a sin may cause as much hurt as the offense itself. Nonetheless, I believe that in all cases the unfaithful party in a marriage relationship broken by adultery should confess the sin to his or her spouse.

Why? For one thing, it takes two people to commit adultery. The other party in the sin already knows about the offense. It compounds your unfaithfulness to share a secret with your cohort in sin but keep your spouse in the dark. The lack of total openness—the need to hide things and keep secrets—will continue to be a barrier to the proper unity of the marriage. Something as serious as a breach in the marital union cannot be repaired if the truth must be kept from your marriage partner. Failure to confess simply compounds lying and cover-ups. That sort of thing will eventually destroy the relationship, whether or not the adultery is repeated.

As difficult as it may be for both you and your spouse, you must deal honestly with a sin like this. If the offended spouse discovers the sin through other means, the hurt that is then caused will be drastically increased. You owe it to him or her to confess.

HOW SHOULD WE HANDLE REPEAT OFFENSES?

Jesus answered this question expressly in Luke 17:3-4: "If your brother sins, rebuke him; and if he repents, forgive him. And if he sins against you seven times a day, and returns to you seven times, saying, 'I repent,' forgive him." Again, our forgiveness is supposed to be lavish, enthusiastic, eager, freely offered, and unconstrained—even for repeat offenders. After all, we are all repeat offenders against God.

BUT WHAT IF THERE IS REASON TO THINK THAT THE OFFENDER'S "REPENTANCE" IS A SHAM?

In normal circumstances, love obliges us to assume the best about those who profess repentance (1 Cor. 13:7). Scripture does suggest, however, that there are certain times when it is legitimate to demand fruits of repentance before assuming that someone's profession of repentance is genuine (Matt. 3:8; Luke 3:8).

One author paints a hypothetical scenario where an offender intentionally punches an innocent person in the nose. After the first offense, the offender asks for, and receives, forgiveness. Moments later, in another unprovoked attack, he punches the same person in the nose a second time. The cycle is repeated a third time, and a fourth, and so on, with the bully professing repentance each time and the victim granting forgiveness each time. That author suggests this is how Jesus' words are to be interpreted: "If he . . . returns to you seven times, *saying*, 'I repent,' forgive him." All the offender needs to do is to say he repents, and the offended person is obliged to forgive.

But that is far too wooden an interpretation of Jesus' words. Our Lord was not suggesting that the disciples should throw discernment out the window when it comes to evaluating a person's repentance. Nothing in the context of Luke 17:3-4 suggests that the offense Jesus had in mind was deliberate or that the repentance was feigned.

In fact, it is important to be wary of feigned repentance in cases like the hypothetical one just described. Such deliberately repeated offenses, especially when accompanied by phony repentance, are evidence of a profoundly evil character and a cynical hatred of the truth. John the Baptist was justified in refusing baptism to the Pharisees until they showed the reality of their profession of repentance (Matt. 3:8).

So there are times when it is sheer folly to accept a mere profession of repentance, especially in the wake of several deliberate repeat offenses.

Nonetheless, even after multiple offenses, the offended person must be prepared to forgive—*eager* to forgive—unless there remains some very compelling reason to doubt the offender's profession of repentance. Even the hardest and most deliberate offender should never be permanently written off; rather, complete forgiveness and reconciliation should remain the offended person's goal.

WHEN IS RESTITUTION APPROPRIATE?

Whenever an actual loss has been caused by a wrong, restitution is certainly appropriate. The granting of forgiveness for the guilt of the offense does not automatically nullify the need to make reparations, especially when the injured party's loss is quantifiable. Whether the loss was caused deliberately (as in a theft) or accidentally (through some form of negligence), restitution should be made.

Under the Old Testament law, most restitution was as nearly as possible matched to the actual loss (Lev. 24:18-21). If your negligence caused you neighbor's ox to die, you had to pay him the value of the ox (Exod. 21:33-34). Deliberate thievery was punished with additional restitution. Someone who stole money had to repay an additional 20 percent (Lev. 6:4-5; Num. 5:6-7). Certain thefts of animals (especially if the stolen animals were killed) required four- and fivefold restitution (Exod. 22:1).

Zaccheus offered fourfold restitution to those he had defrauded, more than the law required (Luke 19:8). That spirit of willingness to make restitution should accompany all true confession of wrongdoing.

Restitution should never be regarded as a meritorious act of penance. The purpose of restitution is simply to restore the value of the damages. Under Moses' law, when restitution was required over and above the actual amount of the loss, the purpose of the restitution was both to punish and to deter.

The one forgiving is free, of course, to forego restitution and to choose to suffer the wrong without demanding repayment. But that is the offended person's option. The offender, if truly repentant, must be willing to right the wrong as much as is possible (cf. Matt. 18:26, 29).

WHAT RESTITUTION CAN BE MADE IF THE OFFENSE WAS A SIN LIKE LYING, SLANDER, DISHONORING ONE'S PARENTS, OR OTHER SINS WHERE NO ACTUAL VALUE CAN BE ATTACHED TO THE DAMAGE?

In some cases tangible restitution is impossible, and yet reparations need to be made. Lies should be confessed and the truth communicated at least as widely as the lie was. Slander needs to be corrected by a sincere effort to restore the offended person's reputation and honor.

Restitution in all such instances begins with a humble confession of the wrongdoing and a willingness to do whatever is reasonable to right the wrong.

IS THE FORGIVER OBLIGATED TO FORGET THE OFFENSE?

"Forgive and forget." The expression has attained the status of a cliché. When we grant forgiveness, does that entail a promise to forget the offense completely?

Yes and no. There is obviously no way to purge the memory of an offense. And the more severe the offense, the more difficult it may be to keep the memory from coming to mind.

I've heard people suggest that God forgets our sins when He forgives. They usually cite Hebrews 8:12 and 10:17: "Their sins and their lawless deeds I will remember no more." Or Isaiah 43:25: "I, even I, am the one who wipes out your transgressions for My own sake, and I will not remember your sins."

But those verses don't say God forgets our sins. They say *He will not remember them.* What's the difference? To forget something is to have no memory of it. Obviously God, who is omniscient, has not lost His memory of our transgressions. Rather, He refuses to call them to mind. He promises not to bring them up.

And that is exactly what is involved in forgiveness. It is a promise not to remind the person of the offense. Jay Adams characterizes this as a threefold promise: "You promise not to remember his sin by bringing it up to him, to others, or to yourself. The sin is buried."[1]

WHAT IF I CANNOT FORGIVE MYSELF?

I realize there are some who teach that a kind of self-forgiveness is necessary. I find this nowhere in Scripture. I've met many people who *claim* to be unable to forgive themselves, but on careful examination this usually turns out to be a kind of sinful pride exacerbated by modern self-esteem philosophy. The person who complains about not being self-forgiving is often simply looking for flattering or consoling words from others as a way of salving the hurt that guilt has caused to their pride.

Jay Adams offers good insight into this question. He writes:

The problem is not self-forgiveness. Their expressed agony stems from the very fact that, in the worst way, they want to forgive themselves. They want to put it all behind them, they want to bury it once and for all. . . .

The problem is that people who talk this way recognize something more needs to be done. Forgiveness is just the beginning; it clears away the guilt. They also recognize that they are still the same persons who did the wrong—that though they are forgiven, they have not changed. Without being able to articulate it, and using instead the jargon they have heard all around them, they are crying out for the change that will assure them they will never do anything like it again. When, as a counselor, I help them to deal with the problems in their lives that led to the wrong, in such a way that they lead a more biblical lifestyle, I then ask, "Are you still having trouble forgiving yourself?" Invariably, they say no.[2]

WHAT IF THE OFFENSE WAS A GRAVE ONE AND I AM STILL HURTING? SHOULDN'T I WAIT TO FORGIVE UNTIL I CAN BE HONEST ABOUT IT? WOULDN'T IT BE HYPOCRITICAL TO DO OTHERWISE?

Some transgressions, particularly offenses involving marital infidelity, can cause pain so intense that the offended person imagines it is okay to withhold forgiveness in *this* case. They rationalize that Jesus' teaching on forgiveness might be all right for dealing with petty offenses, but a *serious* offense surely justifies a cooling-off period or a time of "emotional healing."

Normally, however, those who take that approach merely allow themselves to seethe, and thus the negative emotions are only fed, and the breach caused by the original offense is made worse by a heart-hardening resentment.

Much of Jesus' teaching on forgiveness was given to teach us *not* to be driven by our passions in such matters. Allowing emotions to take over and control us so that we violate what we know rationally is our duty is the very essence of sensuality. And sensuality is sinful, whether it is the kind of sensuality that leads to sins of lust like adultery, or the kind of sensuality that allows emotions to become a roadblock to forgiveness.

Forgiveness is first of all an act of the will. It is not hypocrisy to will forgiveness when the emotions are screaming for vengeance. Be obedient to the Lord regardless of how you feel. If you refuse to harbor spite or dwell on the offense, evil emotions will be starved. Moreover, the Lord Himself will set your heart right. Right emotions will eventually come if you surrender to Him.

And ultimately a conscious, deliberate, willful choice to forgive is the *only* thing that can free a heart from the bondage of such emotions.

APPENDIX ONE

How Are We to Understand theAtonement?

He had to be made like His brethren in all things, so that He might become a merciful and faithful high priest in things pertaining to God, to make propitiation for the sins of the people.

HEB. 2:17

There is no way to deal adequately with the subject of God's forgiveness without discussing the doctrine of the Atonement.

It is at the very heart of the Gospel of forgiveness. The Gospel we proclaim is ultimately determined by our view of the Atonement. And no one is truly preaching Christ who is not declaring the true meaning of His death (cf. 1 Cor. 1:23; 2:2; Gal. 3:1). When we take up the subject of the Gospel, we are immediately brought face to face with the doctrine of the Atonement.

We introduced this topic briefly in chapter 1, but because the subject is so crucial, we return to it here for a closer look. As noted in chapter 1, various theories of the Atonement have been set forth historically. And the undeniable reality is that one's view of the Atonement has ramifications for all of one's understanding of the truth revealed by God. A defective view of the Atonement can be utterly disastrous. The annals of church history are filled with examples of people who, having gone astray on this matter, have utterly made shipwreck of the faith.

The doctrine of the Atonement has often been a battleground between Christians and heretics. Many of the primary differences between the true church and the major cults arise directly from the cultists' erroneous views of the Atonement. So these are extremely fundamental issues, and for that very reason they are best *not* left to experts. Rank and file Christians need to have a basic grasp of the doctrine of the Atonement, so they can be on guard against these deadly errors.

The very worst kinds of heresy are often set forth in innocuous-sounding language. Many of these erroneous views of the Atonement contain kernels of truth that sound good, and even biblical. And in recent years virtually all of them have surfaced wearing sheep's clothing. These old, once-discredited errors are now clamoring for acceptance again among evangelicals. Worst of all, a broadening doctrinal tolerance in the evangelical movement has left most believers poorly equipped to identify, much less refute, errors on matters like this.

My aim in this appendix is to outline the major views of the Atonement and explain *why* the erroneous ones are so deadly. If you keep alert for these errors, you will be able to spot some subtle dangers and refute them before they gain a foothold. More important, understanding these issues will strengthen your grasp of the Gospel and make you a better witness for the truth.

CHRIST'S DEATH AS A RANSOM PAID TO SATAN

One of the earliest faulty views of the Atonement was the notion that Christ's death was a payment rendered to Satan. Mark 10:45 says, "The Son of Man [came] . . . to give His life a ransom for many." And 1 Timothy 2:6 teaches that Christ "gave Himself as a ransom for all." According to the view we are now discussing, the "ransom" spoken of in those verses was a fee paid to Satan to purchase the release of sinners from the devil, who supposedly had a claim on their souls. Many of the early Church Fathers seemed to lean toward this notion of the Atonement (often referred to as "the ransom theory" of the Atonement). This view was more assumed than argued, however. In the early centuries terms such as *atonement* and *ransom* were often employed without careful definition.

The early church was consumed with controversies about the person of Christ. The Gnostic heretics denied the humanity of Christ, and the Arians attacked His deity. Church apologists in the first four centuries were kept busy making defenses against such heresies, and the doctrine of the Atonement simply did not receive intense scrutiny in those centuries. Consequently, for the most part the Church Fathers' comments about the ransom of Christ should not be regarded as studied, conscientious doctrinal statements, but rather as childlike expressions of an unformed and inadequate doctrine of the Atonement.

A. A. Hodge pointed out that all the elements of a *sound* doctrine of the Atonement were implicit in the Church Fathers' writings, though never clearly systematized. Hodge wrote that the Fathers' more orthodox views on the Atonement, while present, were nonetheless "often left to a remarkable degree in the background, and mixed up confusedly with other elements of truth or superstition."[1] Therefore, it is a mistake to read too much significance into selected Church Fathers' remarks regarding the payment of a ransom to Satan.

The ransom theory in recent years has been revived in a crude form by various charismatic teachers, especially Kenneth Copeland, Kenneth Hagin, and others who have been influenced by an early-twentieth-century charismatic evangelist named E. W. Keynon.[2] These men teach that Christ purchased ransom for sinners by literally suffering in hell (rather than atoning for sin through His death on the cross). They surmise that when He died He descended into hell and suffered there in order to render a payment for sin to Satan.

But nothing in Scripture implies that Satan has any legitimate claim on sinners. Satan is not the one who must be propitiated, or satisfied, before sinners can be redeemed. The biblical word *ransom* alone simply means "redemption-price." There is no biblical warrant to conclude that Satan has any authority to demand such a price for the salvation of sinners. In fact, to think in such terms is to open one's theology to sheer superstition. Satan himself is under God's condemnation (Matt. 25:41); so he is in no position to demand any payment for the souls of sinners.

Furthermore, Scripture clearly teaches that Christ's atonement was a sacrifice *to God*: "Christ . . . loved you, and gave Himself up for us, an offering and a sacrifice to God as a fragrant aroma" (Eph. 5:2). Speaking prophetically of the death of Christ, the prophet Isaiah wrote, "The LORD was pleased to crush Him, putting Him to grief . . . He would render Himself as a guilt offering" (53:10). The guilt offering was an offering given to God, and as this verse suggests, the purpose of Christ's dying was to satisfy the claims of *God's justice*, not to compensate the devil.

CHRIST'S DEATH AS AN EXAMPLE OF RIGHTEOUSNESS

Another faulty view of the Atonement is the notion that Christ's death serves primarily as a moral example. This opinion (sometimes called "the moral influence theory" of the Atonement) has surfaced throughout church history in various incarnations. It was propounded by Peter Abelard in the early twelfth century, in reaction to Anselm's views (see below). Abelard denied that God's justice demanded any payment for sin and asserted that the redeeming value of Christ's death consisted mostly in the example He left for sinners to follow.

A nearly identical theory was set forth during the Reformation by a heretical group known as the Socinians. The forerunners of modern liberalism, the Socinians insisted that God's predominant attribute is His love, which virtually cancels out His wrath. They therefore believed that God is inclined to pardon sinners without demanding any payment.

The Socinians argued that sins can be forgiven, or they can be atoned for, but not both. If sins are forgiven, no payment is necessary. Whatever is paid for is not really forgiven. We know from

Scripture that God forgives generously, gladly (Neh. 9:17; Isa. 55:7; Mic. 7:18). Therefore, said the Socinians, the death of Christ could not have been any kind of *payment* for sins. Rather, Christ's death served as an example of obedience and love to believers, pointing the way to life.

Multitudes have evidently found that subtle argument persuasive—to the utter detriment of the church. The tragic legacy of this view of the Atonement can be seen in the effects of liberal theology on all the mainline denominations.

Furthermore, the argument itself is patently unbiblical. Remember, the gist of the Socinian argument is this: divine forgiveness is so lavish that it renders a payment for sin unnecessary; sins are freely remitted without any payment to satisfy divine justice. In particular, the idea that a blood sacrifice is required to buy forgiveness is regarded as barbaric by most who hold this view of the Atonement.

But what does Scripture say? "Without shedding of blood there is no forgiveness" (Heb. 9:22). Scripture teaches that divine forgiveness is rooted and grounded in a blood atonement. Far from making a payment for sins unnecessary, divine love was expressed in God's willingness to pay for sins with His Son's blood.

Furthermore, once you embrace the notion that Christ's death is nothing but an example, you have boxed yourself into the purest kind of works-salvation. It becomes the sinner's responsibility to rescue and reform himself.

If Christ's redemptive work is only an example to us, it accomplishes nothing objective on our behalf. Redemption from sin becomes a subjective matter of each sinner's following His example. Again, the inevitable result is some sort of works-salvation.

CHRIST'S DEATH AS A DEMONSTRATION OF GOD'S JUSTICE

Another erroneous view of the Atonement is the one we mentioned briefly in chapter 1—"the governmental theory." This is a compromise position between the orthodox view (below) and the moral influence theory of the Socinians and modern liberals. The governmental theory takes the position that Christ's death was a *demonstration* of God's wrath against sin, but not an actual payment on behalf of sinners. According to this view the cross displays both God's wrath against sin (seen in the severity of Christ's sufferings) and God's love (seen in Christ's willingness to endure those sufferings). However, according to this view, the sufferings were not a vicarious payment for anyone's sins. Christ's death was merely a public display of what God's wrath against sin would look like—not a real substitution that actually paid sinners' debt. So rather than satisfying divine justice on our behalf, Christ's death serves to move sinners to repentance by revealing both the goodness and the severity of God. Like the Socinians, advocates of the governmental theory believe God forgives sin without a payment, simply setting aside sin's penalty on behalf of those who repent.

The governmental theory approaches the Atonement from a legal standpoint. God's law and His moral government have been challenged by sin. Christ's death reveals to sinners the severity of God's law against sin. Thus the dignity and standard of the law are thereby maintained, so God can be just in forgiving, even though He simply waives sin's penalty.

In this view, Christ did not actually pay the price of sin on anyone's behalf. Like the Socinian view, this theory suggests that the Atonement accomplished nothing objective on the sinner's behalf; it was merely a symbolic gesture. Redemption therefore is primarily a subjective issue hinging completely on the sinner's response. The governmental theory necessarily leads to an extreme form of Arminianism (a doctrine that emphasizes human responsibility at the expense of divine sovereignty) or even Pelagianism (a denial that man's fallen condition renders him unable to save himself).

The earliest advocate of the governmental theory was Hugh Grotius, a Dutch theologian in the early seventeenth century. Grotius's theory was embraced by several New England theologians in the seventeenth and eighteenth centuries, including Charles Finney. The governmental theory is once again enjoying a revival through the influence of groups like Youth With A Mission (YWAM) and several popular Christian authors and youth speakers.

Its tendency, however, is deadly. The governmental theory alters the Gospel so that rather than being a message about what God has done for sinners, the emphasis is on what the sinner must do. Carried to its logical end it often involves a denial of the crucial doctrine of justification by faith. Like the Socinian theory of the Atonement, the governmental theory leaves the sinner ultimately responsible to reform and redeem himself.

George Otis, a modern advocate of the governmental theory, describes the moral dilemma his view aims to solve:

> God loves man, He loves him so much, He wants this intimate fellowship with him. But He also recognizes that sin is a horrible, powerful thing and He doesn't want it to start spreading out of control in the universe. And to allow man, to help man to understand how He viewed sin and how terrible sin really was, He attached a sanction to it and that sanction was death.
>
> So what is God going to do? Is He going to, in effect, condone sin? And say "Okay, I know I said, 'The soul that sinneth it shall surely die'—but in this case, the soul that sinneth it shall live, because I really like you and I really don't want you to die"?
>
> But then what's going to happen when the next person sins? God really likes him too. And the same with the next one and pretty soon nobody's going to die for their sin. But the other alternative, of course, is that everybody dies. And that's not too hot an alternative either. So this is God's government problem. How can God, as the righteous moral governor of the universe, whose responsibility it is to uphold the law of the universe and to uphold righteousness and to protect society. How is He going to get out of this dilemma? This is God's governmental problem.[3]

According to Otis, God met the "dilemma" by making a dramatic display of divine justice in the death of Christ. Otis quotes Romans

3:24: "God *displayed* [Christ] publicly as a propitiation in His blood through faith. *This was to demonstrate His righteousness*, because in the forbearance of God He passed over the sins previously committed" (emphasis added).

Passing over the crucial concept of propitiation (which necessarily speaks of satisfying God's wrath), Otis homes in on the word *demonstrate* and insists that Christ's dying was *only a demonstration* of divine justice, not an actual payment for sin. He says:

> Christ did not pay the debt or literally suffer the penalty of the law for His people. He prepared the way for our debt to be remitted. Or in plain language, dispensing with all metaphor, He made it consistent and proper and honorable for sin to be forgiven according to the prescribed terms of the Gospel.
>   The truth is Christ paid no man's debt.[4]

Echoing the historic view of both the Socinians and the governmental theorists, Otis also claims that the forgiveness of sins requires no payment:

> On a personal basis God could say the second after a sin is committed, "hey, I forgive you." He doesn't hold any grudges or bitterness. He doesn't need to be paid back before He can forgive. There are no strings attached to His love. But He's got to be careful in His role, not as our father, but in His role as righteous, moral governor of the universe, that He's not careless in extending forgiveness so that it encourages others to sin. He can't do that.[5]

So according to the governmental theory, the Atonement was necessary only to salvage God's reputation, not as an actual substitution on sinners' behalf.

Charles Finney embraced this view of the Atonement because he began with the assumption that neither sin nor righteousness could be imputed from one person's account to another. Finney insisted that the idea of imputation, transferring guilt from the sinner to Christ, was inherently unjust.[6] Therefore he also ruled out the transfer of Christ's righteousness to the sinner (despite Rom. 4:5; Phil. 3:9). This led him to deny several vital evangelical doctrines, such as justification by faith and the doctrine of original sin.

Regarding justification by faith, Finney denied that God justifies the ungodly (cf. Rom. 4:5). Instead, he taught that in order to be justified, sinners must actually *become* perfectly righteous. He wrote:

> There can be no justification in a legal or forensic sense, but upon the ground of universal, perfect, and uninterrupted obedience to law. This is of course denied by those who hold that gospel justification, or the justification of penitent sinners, is of the nature of a forensic or judicial justification. They hold to the legal maxim, that what a man does by another he does by himself, and therefore the law regards Christ's obedience as ours, on the ground that he obeyed for us. To this I reply: . . . His obedience could no more than justify Himself. It can never be imputed to us. . . . It was naturally impossible, then, for Him to obey on our behalf.[7]

On what ground did Finney believe Christians were to be justified? Only their own obedience to the law could possibly justify them. Finney's whole argument was that a sinner cannot be justified by the imputation of another's righteousness. Therefore, he was left with one option: he had to embrace a theology of self-justification. It was, any way you look at it, a doctrine of salvation by works. In other words, it was a different gospel, and not true Christianity.

The legacy of Finney's own theological journey shows in microcosm where the governmental theory of the Atonement inevitably leads. Finney saw clearly the consequences of his doctrine of the Atonement. He plainly stated that not only justification, but also regeneration, must be the sinner's own work, not God's. He wrote:

> [Sinners] are under the necessity of first changing their hearts, or their choice of an end, before they can put forth any volitions to secure any other than a selfish end. And this is plainly

the everywhere assumed philosophy of the Bible. That uniformly represents the unregenerate as totally depraved [a purely voluntary condition, not a constitutional depravity, according to Finney], and calls upon them to repent, to make themselves a new heart.[8]

All of these errant views grew out of Finney's commitment to the governmental model of the Atonement. They are the inevitable result of a consistent application of that view.

The governmental view is often found alongside a strong emphasis on revivalism. I mentioned in chapter 1 that a major Web site advocating this theology is called "Revival Theology Resources."

But the revivalism you'll find linked with the governmental theory of the Atonement inevitably has a strongly man-centered emphasis. They insist that revival is the result of human choices and human actions, not a sovereign work of God. In fact, the whole emphasis of this theology is not on what God does on our behalf, but on what we must do to better ourselves.

That is the inevitable result of a theology that portrays the Atonement as anything other than an objective work God does on behalf of those whom He redeems. Deny that the Atonement means Christ paid for sin on sinners' behalf, and you must inevitably define salvation in terms of what the *sinner* must do.

This also forces a redefinition of the significance of the Cross. Rather than emphasizing what Christ accomplished there, governmental theorists must define the Cross in terms of how it can change the human heart. Rather than seeing the atoning work of Christ as an objective, finished work, this theory defines the Atonement as a subjective potential. George Otis, whose messages on the Atonement are quoted above, provides a classic example of this. He says: "The power of the cross does not lie in some vague, abstract, ethereal cosmic transaction. The power of the cross, the power of the blood of Christ, lies in its ability to literally, literally, literally, literally subdue the human heart."[9]

By characterizing substitutionary atonement as "some vague, abstract, ethereal cosmic transaction," Otis denigrates the idea of an objective, finished work. He is left only with the subjective elements of salvation. This is the inevitable result of the governmental theory of the Atonement. And as we see in the legacies of Charles Finney and numerous other advocates of this view, the results are ultimately fatal to the true Gospel.

THE TRUTH: CHRIST'S DEATH AS A PENAL SUBSTITUTION

Here is the true doctrine of the Atonement as taught in Scripture: Christ's death was a substitution for sinners. God imputed the guilt of their transgressions to Christ and then punished Him for it. Christ's righteousness is also imputed to those who believe. This we established in chapter 1, but allow me to review some biblical texts that underscore these truths:

• *Isaiah 53:5-6*: "He was pierced through for our transgressions, He was crushed for our iniquities; the chastening for our well-being fell upon Him, and by His scourging we are healed. All of us like sheep have gone astray, each of us has turned to his own way; but the LORD has caused the iniquity of us all to fall on Him."
• *2 Corinthians 5:21*: "He made Him who knew no sin to be sin on our behalf, so that we might become the righteousness of God in Him."
• *Galatians 3:13*: "Christ redeemed us from the curse of the Law, having become a curse for us."
• *1 Peter 2:24*: "He Himself bore our sins in His body on the cross, that we might die to sin and live to righteousness."
• *1 Peter 3:18*: "Christ also died for sins once for all, the just for the unjust."
• *1 John 2:2*: "He Himself is the propitiation for our sins."

The Atonement was a full payment of the price of sins, to satisfy both the wrath and the righteousness of God, so that He could forgive sins without compromising His own holy standard.

As noted above, A. A. Hodge argues that all the elements of this view have been an essential part of Christian doctrine from the beginning. "With few exceptions," Hodge wrote, "the whole church from the beginning has held the doctrine of Redemption in the sense of a literal propitiation of God by means of the expiation of sin."[10] Hodge also pointed out that the clearer the church's conception of the Atonement has been, the more true vitality and strength the church has enjoyed. The decline of understanding of the doctrine of the Atonement has always been accompanied by a corresponding decline in the spiritual health of the visible church.

As we noted, however, in the early centuries, sound views on the Atonement were mixed with much confusion and were often all but obscured by superstition generated by the ransom theory.

A fuller understanding of the Atonement finally began to come clearly into focus with the work of Anselm of Canterbury (1033-1109). Anselm was the first great theologian to focus his energies on trying to understand the Atonement as a doctrine. The ground he laid in defining the Atonement ultimately became the foundation on which the Protestant Reformation was built.

Subsequent church history reveals that when the penal-substitution aspects of the Atonement have been emphasized and understood, the church has prospered. When these doctrines have been challenged or obscured, the church has fallen into serious decline.

What Is the Unforgivable Sin?

*"Any sin and blasphemy shall be forgiven people,
but blasphemy against the Spirit shall not be forgiven. And whoever
shall speak a word against the Son of Man, it shall be forgiven
him; but whoever shall speak against the Holy Spirit,
it shall not be forgiven him, either in this age,
or in the age to come."*

MATT. 12:31-32

We have seen repeatedly that God is by nature forgiving. The theme of forgiveness runs through Scripture from beginning to end. Even as Moses descended from Sinai with the tablets of the law, God emphasized His willingness to forgive: "Then the LORD passed by in front of him and proclaimed, 'The LORD, the LORD God, compassionate and gracious, slow to anger, and abounding in lovingkindness and truth; who keeps lovingkindness for thousands, who forgives iniquity, transgression and sin" (Exod. 34:6-7). One could say that both law and Gospel are designed to teach us about forgiveness—the law by underscoring our need of forgiveness, and the Gospel by actually offering forgiveness to sinners who have seen that need.

Forgiveness therefore is an integral part of what defines the moral character of God. God is an eager forgiver. Anyone who turns to Him in genuine repentance—even the worst of sinners—will find mercy granted abundantly, lavishly, generously.

But there is a sinful tendency in most unbelievers to doubt whether God will truly forgive *their* sins. I often encounter people who seem positive that certain sins they commit are unforgivable. Is that true? Is there any sin that God won't forgive? Does the severity and the amount of sin put one beyond forgiveness?

I'm sure you would agree that the worst conceivable sin would be to kill Jesus Christ. I can't imagine any sin being more wicked than that. Of course, that's exactly what men did to the Son of God. Yet while our Lord was hanging on the cross and about to die, He prayed for His executioners: "Father, forgive them; for they do not know what they are doing" (Luke 23:34). If killing God's Son is forgivable, certainly the *degree* of sin will not forfeit forgiveness.

What about the *amount* of sin? When anyone—whether he is a seventy-year-old profligate who has lived a life steeped in immorality or a seven-year-old child whose worst sin was being naughty—turns to God in confession and repentance, God will forgive him.

Finally, is there any *kind* of sin that God won't forgive? A survey of Scripture will show that God forgives idolatry, murder, gluttony, fornication, adultery, cheating, lying, homosexuality, blasphemy, drunkenness, extortion, and every other kind of sin imaginable, including self-righteousness. He even forgives those who reject Christ. If He didn't, then no one could ever be saved. Everyone, to one degree or another, rejected Christ before they were saved.

Yet there was one group of people who rejected Christ and discovered that there is indeed one sin God will not forgive. The Pharisees hounded Jesus throughout His ministry, rejecting both His works and His words. The epitome of their rejection resulted in these scathing words of our Lord: "Any sin and blasphemy shall be forgiven people, but blasphemy against the Spirit shall not be forgiven. And whoever shall speak a word against the Son of Man, it shall be forgiven him; but whoever shall speak against the Holy Spirit, it shall not be forgiven him, either in this age, or in the age to come" (Matt. 12:31-32). What is blasphemy against the Spirit, and what led the Pharisees to sin in such a way? Let's back up in

Matthew to establish the context and discover the nature of the unpardonable sin.

HOW A HEALING LED TO REJECTION

During Jesus' ministry in Galilee, on one occasion "there was brought to Him a demon-possessed man who was blind and dumb, and He healed him, so that the dumb man spoke and saw" (v. 22). Christ's ministry was filled with many such events. Both the people and religious leaders already had been exposed to scores of instantaneous, total, permanent, and verifiable healings performed by the Lord (vv. 9-15; cf. 4:23-25; 8:2-4; 9:1-8). The source of His supernatural powers was no longer open to scrutiny, either by the multitudes or the religious leaders.

Yet most of the people were ambivalent about Jesus' identity and the source of His power. The scribes and Pharisees, however, were far beyond ambivalence. They were no longer skeptical and resentful of Jesus; they considered Him a threat to their power and had become adamantly hostile.

It appears that Jesus performed this particular healing to force the Pharisees to make their animosity public. This man, who was demon-possessed, blind, and unable to speak (possibly associated with deafness), suddenly and miraculously began to speak and see. And he did so to such a degree that "all the multitudes were amazed, and began to say, 'This man cannot be the Son of David, can he?'" (v. 23).

Apparently, this particular miracle proved to be unusually overwhelming, since "the multitudes were amazed." The Greek verb indicates that the people were totally astounded, filled with amazement and wonder. Such a response reveals that Jesus purposely intensified the supernatural character of this miracle.

The reaction of the people revealed that they recognized this miracle as a possible messianic sign: "This man cannot be the Son of David, can he?" "Son of David" was one of the many scriptural titles for the Messiah (2 Sam. 7:12-16; Ps. 89:3; Isa. 9:6-7). That the people were seriously considering the possibility that Jesus was the Messiah put the Pharisees under intense pressure to disprove such a notion.

THE EPITOME OF REJECTION

In their rush to counter the reaction of the multitudes, the Pharisees unwittingly walked into the trap Jesus had set for them: "When the Pharisees heard it, they said, 'This man casts out demons only by Beelzebul the ruler of the demons" (v. 24). The Pharisees in effect were claiming that Jesus wasn't the Messiah, but was rather the very antithesis of the Son of David—the servant of "Beelzebul the ruler of demons." "Beelzebul" was the pagan deity considered to be the prince of demons, Satan himself.

The Pharisees had put themselves in quite a quandary. Jesus' power was obviously supernatural, and it could only come from one of two possible sources: God or Satan. Since the Pharisees had already refused to recognize that Jesus was from God, they were forced to claim that He was an agent of Satan.

While the Pharisees were attempting to attract the crowd to their position, Jesus was keenly aware of what they were doing. He then proceeded to confront their accusation on all its illogical points.

The Absurdity of the Accusation

First, Jesus attacked the logical absurdity of their charge: "Any kingdom divided against itself is laid waste; and any city or house divided against itself shall not stand. And if Satan casts out Satan, he is divided against himself; how then shall his kingdom stand?" (vv. 25-26). It is logical that any kingdom, city, or house that is divided against itself would destroy itself. The same would thus be true of the spirit world. Satan is far too shrewd to order his minions to fight against each other and destroy his plans to work in the lives of people.

It is true, however, that evil is destructive by nature, and often evil agents are self-destructive (Mark 5:13). Demonic forces may occasionally fight with each other. But satanic forces would never wage outright war against one another. It was absurd to accuse Jesus of casting out demons by the power of Satan.

The Prejudice of the Accusation

Jesus next proceeded to reveal the corrupt, wicked bias of the Pharisees' hearts: "And if I by Beelzebul cast out demons, by whom do your sons cast them out? Consequently they shall be your judges" (v. 27). "Sons" was often used as an epithet for disciples or followers (see 2 Kings 2:3). The Pharisees revealed their prejudice by approving of the exorcisms performed by their followers. Such activity they would never claim as ungodly, and certainly not satanic. Yet when Jesus cast out demons *and* every kind of disease, they attributed His works to Satan.

The basic reason people reject Christ is not lack of evidence but personal bias. Those who are steeped in evil works avoid at all costs exposure to the righteousness of Christ. The Pharisees represent all children of darkness, who cannot and will not tolerate His light (John 3:19). They look instead for ways to justify their own wickedness and to destroy anyone who dares to expose them.

Since the Pharisees supported the exorcisms of their followers, Jesus was justified in suggesting that those followers judge the logic of the Pharisees' accusation of Christ. Who was the source of the sons' exorcisms? If it was Satan, they would condemn themselves and any of the religious leaders who supported them. If it was God, that would refute the Pharisees' accusation of Jesus.

The Rebelliousness of the Accusation

The third and basic reason behind the Pharisees' accusation was their rebellion against God, which Jesus exposed in this manner: "But if I cast out demons by the Spirit of God, then the kingdom of God has come upon you. Or how can anyone enter the strong man's house and carry off his property, unless he first binds the strong man? And then he will plunder his house. He who is not with Me is against Me; and he who does not gather with Me scatters" (vv. 28-30).

The only remaining possibility was that Jesus performed His miracles by the power of God, and thus He had to be the Messiah. Any Jew familiar with the Scriptures knew that all the miracles Jesus performed were prophesied as accompanying the Messiah (Isa. 29:18; 35:5-6). Since the Messiah was to be Israel's eternal King, the logical extension was that the kingdom of God (represented as the sphere of Christ's rule in any place or age) had arrived as well.

The proof of Jesus' claim was in all the miracles He did. He used the picture of a thief breaking into a strong man's house. A thief could not begin to carry out any loot unless he tied up the strong man first. Likewise, Jesus could not cast out Satan's demons unless He already had bound him. And only God could enter the house of Satan, successfully bind him, and carry off his property. Only God could have such power and authority.

Jesus then established the Pharisees' relationship to Him: if they were not for Him, they were against Him. Those are the only two possible relationships; there can be no neutral ground. The Pharisees' accusation revealed their rebellion and their status as enemies of God.

EXAMINING THE UNPARDONABLE SIN

How far men can proceed in sin and lose the opportunity to be saved is the basis for what Jesus then said to the Pharisees: "Therefore I say to you, any sin and blasphemy shall be forgiven men, but blasphemy against the Spirit shall not be forgiven. And whoever shall speak a word against the Son of Man, it shall be forgiven him; but whoever shall speak against the Holy Spirit, it shall not be forgiven him; either in this age, or in the age to come" (vv. 31-32).

Blasphemy is a form of sin, but here Jesus treats the two separately, emphasizing blasphemy as the most extreme form of sin. Jesus uses "sin" to describe all ungodly thoughts and actions, and he uses "blasphemy" to represent any conscious condemnation and rejection of God. Those who blaspheme God are guilty of defiantly defaming or mocking Him (cf. Mark 2:7). The Old Testament penalty for it was death by stoning (Lev. 24:16).

Yet Jesus even says that God will forgive blasphemy when it is confessed and repented of. The apostle Paul experienced such forgiveness: "I was formerly a blasphemer and a persecutor and a violent aggressor. And yet I was shown mercy, because I acted ignorantly in unbelief; and the grace of our Lord was more than abundant, with the faith and love which are found in Christ Jesus" (1 Tim. 1:13-14). Peter blasphemed Christ (Mark 14:71), but the Lord forgave and restored him. Any believer can blaspheme, since any thought or word that defames the Lord's name is blasphemy.

Even blasphemy against Jesus will be forgiven: "Whoever shall speak a word against the Son of Man, it shall be forgiven him" (Matt. 12:32). "Son of Man" refers to the Lord's humanity, and thus to His life on earth in His incarnation. If people misjudge Jesus and sin against Him with less than full exposure to the evidence of His deity, forgiveness is still possible if they believe once they have received full knowledge. Paul's conversion certainly attests to that; prior to his salvation he "acted ignorantly in unbelief" (1 Tim. 1:13).

There is one form of blasphemy, however, that God will not forgive, and that is "blasphemy against the Spirit" (Matt. 12:31-32). This is a deliberate rejection of Christ in full light of the Holy Spirit's testimony. These men had spurned the Spirit-wrought conviction that Christ's claims were all true and rejected Him for politcal reasons (John 11:47-48). When people have been exposed to the evidence that proves the source of all the Lord's words and works, and still reject Jesus as the Messiah, they are beyond forgiveness and are settled in their unbelief. It is inconceivable for those of us who know and love the Lord to understand how anyone who is given such full revelation could reject and condemn Him.

Those who refuse to believe in Christ lose the opportunity ever to "be forgiven . . . either in this age, or in the age to come" (Matt. 12:32). "This age" refers to all human history, and "the age to come" speaks of eternity. Forgiveness is forever unavailable for those who blaspheme the Holy Spirit.

The people in view in this passage heard Jesus teach and preach God's truth, yet refused to believe. They saw the divine power of the Holy Spirit working in and through Him, healing every kind of disease, casting out every kind of demon, and forgiving every kind of sin; yet they accused Him of deceit, falsehood, and demonism, attributing His power to Satan. God can do nothing for those who reject Christ as God in that manner and in the face of such overwhelming evidence. Commentator William Hendriksen says of such people:

> Their sin is unpardonable because they are unwilling to tread the path that leads to pardon. For a thief, an adulterer, and a murderer there is hope. The message of the gospel may cause him to cry out, "O God be merciful to me, the sinner." But when a man has become hardened, so that he has made up his mind not to pay attention to the . . . Spirit . . . he has placed himself on the road that leads to perdition.[1]

During Jesus' earthly ministry, the Pharisees and all others who blasphemed the Spirit cut themselves off from God's mercy. God had offered them His mercy in Christ, yet they rejected and ridiculed Him as satanic. The writer of Hebrews offers a stern warning to all who follow in the footsteps of the Pharisees and reject Christ in spite of exposure to the truth and the biblical record of His supernatural works:

> *How shall we escape if we neglect so great a salvation? After it was at the first spoken through the Lord, it was confirmed to us by those who heard [the apostles], God also bearing witness with them, both by signs and wonders and by various miracles and by gifts of the Holy Spirit according to His own will. . . . For in the case of those who have once been enlightened and have tasted the heavenly gift and have been made partakers of the Holy Spirit, and have tasted the good word of God and the powers of the age to come, and then have*

fallen away, it is impossible to renew them again to repentance, since
they again crucify to themselves the Son of God, and put Him to
open shame.

— HEB. 2:3-4; 6:4-6

During World War II action in the North Atlantic, an American naval force was engaged in battle on a particularly dark night. In the midst of the battle, one of the aircraft carriers was exposed to attack from the enemy, so a blackout was ordered. Yet six planes were heading back to the carrier from a mission and could not land without runway lights. Their request for the ship to turn on the lights just long enough so they could land was denied because to do so would jeopardize the lives of thousands of men. When the planes ran out of fuel, the pilots were forced to ditch in the freezing water, and all the crew of those six planes died.

God also reaches a point when He turns out the lights, and the opportunity for salvation is then gone forever. The one who rejects the full light of salvation will have no more light. He has lost forever his opportunity for forgiveness.

Two Classic Sermons on Forgiveness

Therefore let it be known to you, brethren,
that through Him forgiveness of sins is proclaimed to you, and through
Him everyone who believes is freed from all things, from which
you could not be freed through the Law of Moses.

ACTS 13:38-39

C.H. Spurgeon
Forgiveness Made Easy

Forgiving one another, even as
God for Christ's sake hath forgiven you.[1]

EPH. 4:32

The heathen moralists, when they wished to teach virtue, could not point to the example of their gods, for, according to their mythologists, the gods were a compound of every imaginable and, I had almost said, unimaginable vice. Many of the classic deities surpassed the worst of men in their crimes: they were as much greater in iniquity as they were supposed to be superior in power. It is an ill day for a people when their gods are worse than themselves. The blessed purity of our holy faith is conspicuous, not only in its precepts, but in the character of the God whom it reveals. There is no excellency that we can propose but we can see it brightly shining in the Lord our God; there is no line of conduct in which a believer should excel but we can point to Christ Jesus our Lord and Master as the pattern of it. In the highest places of the Christian faith you have the highest virtue, and unto God our Father and the Lord Jesus be the highest praise.

We can urge you to the tenderest spirit of forgiveness by pointing to God who for Christ's sake has forgiven you. What nobler motive can you require for forgiving one another? With such high examples, brethren, what manner of people ought we to be? We have sometimes heard of men who were better than their religion, but that is quite impossible with us; we can never, in spirit or in act, rise to the sublime elevation of our divine religion. We should constantly be rising above ourselves, and above the most gracious of our fellow Christians, and yet above us we shall still behold our God and Saviour. We may go from strength to strength in thoughts of goodness and duties of piety, but Jesus is higher still, and evermore we must be looking up to Him as we climb the sacred hill of grace.

At this time we wish to speak a little concerning the duties of love and forgiveness; and here we note, at once, that the apostle sets before us the example of God Himself. Upon that bright example we shall spend most of our time, but I hope not quite so much as to forget the practical part, which is so much needed in these days by certain unforgiving spirits who nevertheless assume the Christian name. The theme of God's forgiving love is so fascinating that we may linger awhile, and a long while too, upon that bright example of forgiveness that God has set before us; but from it all I hope we shall be gathering grace by which to forgive others even to seventy times seven.

We shall take the text word by word, and so we shall obtain the clearest divisions.

I. The first word to think about is *"for Christ's sake."* We use these words very often; but probably we have never thought of their meaning. Let us touch thereon with thoughtfulness, praying the good Spirit to instruct us. *"For Christ's sake"*; all the good things that God has bestowed upon us have come to us "for Christ's sake," but especially the forgiveness of our sins has come "for Christ's sake." This is the plain assertion of the text. What does it mean? It means, surely, first, *for the sake of the great atonement that Christ has offered.* The great God can, as a just Lawgiver and King, readily pass by our offenses because of the expiation for sin that Christ has offered. If sin were merely a personal affront toward God, we have abundant evidence that He would be ready enough to pass it by without exacting vengeance; but it is a great deal more than that. Those who view it as a mere personal affront against God are but very shallow thinkers. Sin is an attack upon the moral government of God; it undermines the foundations of society, and were it permitted to have its way it would reduce everything to anarchy and even destroy the governing power and the Ruler himself.

God has a great realm to govern, not merely of men that dwell on the face of the earth, but beneath his sway there are angels and principalities and powers, and we do not know how many worlds of intelligent beings. It would certainly be a monstrous thing to suppose that God has made yonder myriads of worlds that we see sparkling in the sky at night without having placed some living creatures in them; it is far more reasonable to suppose that this earth is an altogether insignificant speck in the divine dominion, a mere province in the boundless empire of the King of kings. Now, this world having rebelled against God high-handedly, as it has done, unless there were a satisfaction demanded for its rebellion, it would be a tolerated assault upon the dominion of the great Judge of all, and a lowering of His royal influence over all His domain. If sin in man's case were left unpunished, it would soon be known through myriads of worlds, and in fact by ten thousand times ten thousand races of creatures, that they might sin with impunity; if one race had done so, why not all the rest? This would be a proclamation of universal license to rebel. It would probably be the worst calamity that could happen—that any sin should go unpunished by the supreme Judge.

Sometimes in a state, unless the lawgiver executes the law

against the murderer, life will be in peril, and everything will become insecure, and therefore it becomes a mercy to write the death-warrant. So is it with God in reference to this world of sinners. It is His very love as well as His holiness and His justice that, if I may use such a term, compels Him to severity of judgment; and so sin cannot and must not be blotted out until atonement has been presented. There must first of all be a sacrifice for sin, which, mark you, the great Father, to show His love, Himself supplies, for it is His own Son who is given to die, and so the Father Himself supplies the ransom through His Son, that Son being also one with Himself by bonds of essential unity, mysterious but most intense. If God demands the penalty in justice, He Himself supplies it in love. 'Tis a wondrous mystery, this mystery of the way of salvation by an atoning sacrifice; but this much is clear, that now God for Christ's sake has forgiven us, because satisfaction has been made to the injured honor of the divine government, and justice is satisfied.

I want you to consider for a moment how readily God may now blot out sin since Christ has died. The blotting out of sin seems hard until we see the cross, and then it appears easy enough. I have looked at sin until it seemed to blind me with its horror, and I said within myself, "This damned spot can never be washed out; no fuller's soap can change its hue; sooner might the Ethiopian change his skin or the leopard his spots. O sin, thou deep, eternal evil, what can remove thee?" And then I have seen the Son of God dying on the cross, and read the anguish of His soul, and heard the cries that showed the torment of His spirit when God His Father had forsaken Him, and it has seemed to me as if the blotting out of sin were the easiest thing under heaven. When I have seen Jesus die, I have not been able to understand how any sin could be difficult to remove. Let a man stand on Calvary and look on Him whom he has pierced, and believe and accept the atonement made, and it becomes the simplest thing possible that his debt should be discharged now that it is paid, that his freedom should be given now that the ransom is found, and that he should be no longer under condemnation since the guilt that condemned him has been carried away by his great Substitute and Lord. It is then because of what Jesus Christ has suffered in our stead that God for Christ's sake has forgiven us.

The second rendering of the text would be this, that God has forgiven us *because of the representative character of Christ*. It should never be forgotten that we originally fell by a representative. Adam stood for us, and he was our federal head. We did not fall personally at the first, but in our representative. Had he kept the conditions of the covenant, we would have stood through him; but inasmuch as he fell, we fell in him. I pray you cavil not at the arrangement, because there lay the hope of our race. The angels probably fell individually, one by one, and hence they fell irretrievably; there was no restoring them. But as we fell in one Adam, there remained the possibility of our rising in another Adam; and therefore in the fullness of time God sent forth His Son, Jesus Christ, born of a woman, made under the law, to become the second Adam. He undertook to remove our burdens and to fulfil the conditions of our restoration. According to God's covenant He had to appear in our nature, and that nature in the fullness of time He assumed. He had to bear the penalty; that He has done in His personal suffering and death. He had to obey the law; that He has done to the utmost.

And now Christ Jesus, having borne the penalty and fulfilled the law, is Himself justified before God and stands before God as the representative of all who are in Him. God for Christ's sake has accepted us in Him, has forgiven us in Him, and looks upon us with infinite and changeless love in Him. This is how all our blessings come to us—in and through Christ Jesus; and if we are indeed in Him, the Lord not only forgives us our sin, but He bestows upon us the boundless riches of His grace in Him. In fact, He treats us as He would treat His Son; He deals with us as He would deal with Jesus. Oh, how pleasant to think that when the just God looks upon us, it is through the reconciling medium—He views us through the Mediator. We sometimes sing a hymn that says:

> *Him and then the sinner see,*
> *Look through Jesus' wounds on me.*

And this is just what the Lord does. He counts us just for the sake of our Saviour's atonement and because of His representative character.

Now go a little further. When we read "for Christ's sake" it surely means *for the deep love that the Father bears Him*. My brethren, can you guess a little of the love that the Father has toward the Only-begotten? We cannot pry into the wondrous mystery of the eternal filial relationship of the Son of God lest we be blinded by an excess of light; but this we know, that they are one God—Father, Son, and Holy Spirit; and the union that exists between them is intense beyond conception. "The Father loves the Son" was always true, and it is true now; but how deeply, how intensely He loves the Son no mind can conceive. Now, brethren, the Lord will do great things for the sake of a son whom He loves as He loves Jesus, for in addition to the fact of His eternally loving Him, as being one with Him by nature and essence, there is now the superadded cause of love arising out of what the Lord Jesus has done as the servant of the Father. Remember that our Lord Jesus has been obedient to His Father's will—obedient to death, even to the death of the cross; wherefore God has highly exalted Him and has given Him a name that is above every name. One of the sweetest thoughts, to my mind, that I sometimes feed on when I am alone is this—that *God the Father will do anything for Christ*. Here is another piece of a honeycomb— *when I can plead Christ's name, I am sure to be heard*. "For Christ's sake" is a plea that always touches the heart of the great God. Show that your receiving such and such a blessing will glorify Christ, and the Father cannot withhold it, for it is His delight to honor Jesus.

We speak after the manner of men, of course, and on such a theme as this we must be careful; but still we can only speak as men, being only men. It is the joy of the Father to express His love to His Son. Throughout all ages They have had fellowship one with another; They have always been one in all their designs; They have never differed upon any points and cannot differ. And you notice that when our Lord says, "Father, glorify thy Son," He is so knit with the Father that He adds, "that thy Son also may glorify thee." Their mutual love is inconceivably great, and therefore, brethren, God will do anything for Jesus. God will forgive us for Christ's sake; yea, He has done so in the case of thousands around me. And thou, great sinner, if you will go to God at this moment and say, "Lord, I cannot ask You to forgive me for my own sake, but do it out of love for Your dear Son," He will do it, for He will do anything for the sake of Jesus. If you are at this time conscious of sin so as to despair of yourself, it is well that you should be so, for self-despair is only common sense, since there is nothing in yourself upon which you can rely. But do catch at this hope—it is not a straw, it is a good, substantial life-buoy—ask forgiveness for the sake of Jesus, for God will do anything for Jesus, and He will do anything for you for His dear Son's sake.

So we read our text once more in the light of a truth that grows out of the love of God; namely, that *God does forgive sin for the sake of glorifying Christ*. Christ took the shame so that He might magnify His Father, and now His Father delights to magnify Him by blotting out men's sin. If you can prove that any gift to you would reflect glory upon Christ, you may depend upon the fact you will have it. If there is anything under heaven that would make Christ more illustrious, the Father would not spare it for a moment. If you see that for you to have your sin forgiven would raise the fame of the Saviour, go and plead that argument with God, and you shall surely prevail. Will it not make Christ glad if He saves such a sinner as you are? Then go with this argument in your mouth: "Father, glorify Your Son by exalting Him as a glorious Saviour in saving me." I find this often a great lever to move a heavy load, to say unto God, "Lord, You know the straits I am in. You knowest how undeserving I am. You know what a poor, undone creature I am before You. But if Your dear Son shall help and save me, the very angels will stand and wonder at His mighty grace, and so *it will bring glory to Him*, and therefore I entreat You, be gracious unto me."

You are certain to prevail if you can plead that it will glorify Christ, and surely you would not wish to have a thing that would not glorify Him. Your prayer shall always be answered if your heart is in such a state that you are willing to have or not to have, according as it will honor your Lord. If it will not glorify Christ, be more than content to do without the choicest earthly good; but be doubly grateful when the boon that is granted tends to bring honor to the ever dear and worshipful name of Jesus. "For Christ's sake." It is a precious word; dwell upon it, and lay up this sentence in the archives of your memory—the Father will do anything for the sake of Jesus Christ, His Son.

II. Now, secondly, we pass on to observe what it is that we are told in the text has been done for us, and to us, for Christ's sake. "God for Christ's sake *hath forgiven you*."

First notice, that He has done this *certainly*. The apostle does not say he hopes so, but he says, "God . . . for Christ's sake *hath* forgiven you." Are you in the number of the forgiven, my dear hearer? Have you believed in the Lord Jesus Christ? Then, as surely as you have believed, God for Christ's sake *has* forgiven you. Have you put your trust in the atoning sacrifice? Then God for Christ's sake *has* forgiven you. You have not begun to be a Christian, I hope, with the idea that one day, at some future period, you may obtain forgiveness. No. "God . . . for Christ's sake *hath* forgiven you." Pardon is not a prize to be run for, but a blessing received at the first step of the race. If you have believed in Jesus, your sin is all gone; all your sin has been erased from the records of the past, never to be accounted against you again ever. The moment a sinner looks to Christ, the burden of his sin rolls off his shoulders, never to return. If Christ has washed you (and He has if you have believed in Him), then you are clean every whit, and before the Lord you stand delivered from every trace of guilt.

Pardon is not a matter of hope, but a matter of fact. Expectation looks for many a blessing, but pardon is a realized favor that faith holds in her hand even now. If Christ took your load, your load cannot remain on your own back; if Christ paid your debts, then they do not stand in God's books against you. How can they? It stands to reason that if your Substitute has taken your sin and put it away, your sin lies no more on you. God for Christ's sake has forgiven you. Get hold of that grand truth, and hold it, though all the devils in hell roar at you. Grasp it as with a hand of steel: "God for Christ's sake has forgiven me." May each one of us be able to say that. We will not feel the divine sweetness and force of the text unless we can make a personal matter of it by the Holy Ghost.

Then notice that God has forgiven us *continuously*. He not only forgave all our sins at the first, but He continues daily to forgive, for the act of forgiveness is a continuous one. I have sometimes heard it said that we were so forgiven when we first believed that there is no need to ask for further forgiveness; to which I reply: We were so completely forgiven when we first believed that we ought continually to ask for the perpetuity of that one far-reaching act, that the Lord may continue to exert toward us that fullness of forgiving grace that absolved us perfectly at the first, that we may continue to walk before Him with a sense of that complete forgiveness, clear and unquestioned. I know I was forgiven when first I believed in Christ; and I am equally sure of it now. The one absolution continues to ring in my ears like joy bells that never cease. Pardon once given continues to be given. When through doubt and anxiety I was not sure of my pardon, it was still true, for he that believes on Him is not condemned, even though he may write bitter things against himself. Beloved friend, catch hold of that, and do not let it go. Divine pardon is a continuous act.

And this forgiveness on God's part was *most free*. We did nothing to obtain it by merit, and we brought nothing wherewith to purchase it. He forgave us for Christ's sake, not for aught that we had done. True, we did repent, and we did believe, but He gave us repentance and faith, so that He did not forgive us for the sake of them, but purely because of His own dear love, because He delights in mercy and is never more like Himself than when He forgives transgression, iniquity, and sin.

Remember, also, that He forgave us *fully*. It was not here and there a sin that He blotted out, but the whole horrible list and catalog of our offenses He destroyed at once. The substitution of our Lord has finished that matter even to perfection.

Because the sinless Saviour died,
My sinful soul is counted free;
For God, the Just, is satisfied
To look on Him and pardon me.

All our transgressions are swept away at once, carried off as by a flood, and so completely removed from us that no guilty trace of them remains. They are all gone! O believers, think of this, for *all* is no little thing: sins against a holy God, sins against His loving Son, sins against the Gospel as well as against the law, sins against man as well as against God, sins of the body as well as sins of the mind, sins as numerous as the sands on the seashore and as great as the sea itself—all, *all* are removed from us as far as the east is from the west. All this evil was rolled into one great mass and laid upon Jesus; and having borne it all, He has made an end of it forever. When the Lord forgave us, He forgave us the whole debt. He did not take the bill and say, "I strike out this item and that," but the pen went through it all: *PAID*. It was a receipt in full for all demands, Jesus took the handwriting that was against us and nailed it to His cross, to show before the entire universe that its power to condemn us had ceased forever. We have in Him a full forgiveness.

And let it be remembered that this forgiveness that God has given us for Christ's sake is an *eternal* forgiveness. He will never bring up our past offenses and a second time impute them. He will not find us on an evil day and say, "I have had great patience with you, but now I will deal with you according to your sins." Far otherwise; he who believes in Jesus has everlasting life and will never come into condemnation. Irreversible is the pardon of heaven. "The gifts and calling of God are without repentance." He never repents what he has given, or forgiven. 'Tis done, 'tis done forever: Jehovah absolves, and the sentence stands fast forever. "There is therefore now no condemnation to them which are in Christ Jesus." "Who shall lay any thing to the charge of God's elect? It is God that justifieth. Who is he that condemneth?" Blessed be God for His eternal pardon!

And since I could not find a word to finish with but this one, I will use it: he has *divinely* pardoned us. There is a truth, reality, and emphasis in this, for though a man should forgive all you have done against him, if you have treated him very badly, it is more than you could expect that he should quite *forget* it. But the Lord says, "Their sins and iniquities will I remember no more forever." If a man has played you false, although you have forgiven him, you are not likely to trust him again. An old proverb says, "Never ride a broken-kneed horse," and it is not a bad proverb either. But see how the Lord deals with His people. When Peter was set on his legs again he was a broken-kneed horse, and yet see how gloriously the Lord rode that charger on the day of Pentecost. Did he not go forth conquering and to conquer? The Lord lets bygones be bygones so completely that He trusts pardoned souls with his secrets, for "the secret of the Lord is with them that fear him"; and He entrusts some of us with his choicest treasures, for Paul said, "He hath put me in trust with the gospel, though I was a blasphemer." He commits to our keeping that priceless casket that encloses the best hope of men, namely, the Gospel of Jesus. "We have this treasure in earthen vessels."

This shows how perfect is our forgiveness—nay, I must put it, how *divine* is the forgiveness that we have received. Let us rejoice in that grand promise that comes to us by the mouth of Jeremiah of old: "In those days, and in that time, saith the Lord, the iniquity of Israel shall be sought for, and there shall be none; and the sins of Judah, and they shall not be found: for I will pardon them whom I reserve." Here is annihilation—the only annihilation I know of— the absolute annihilation of sin through the pardon that the Lord gives to His people. Let us sing it as though it were a choice hymn: "The iniquity of Israel shall be sought for, and there shall be none."

III. Now, if you have drunk into the spirit of our subject you will be strengthened to hear what I have to say to you upon a point of practice: "*Forgiving one another*, even as God for Christ's sake hath forgiven you."

"Forgiving one another, even as God for Christ's sake hath forgiven you." Now observe how the apostle puts it. Does he say "forgiving another"? No, that is not the text. It is "forgiving *one another*."

One another! Ah, then that means that if you have to forgive today, it is very likely that you will yourself need to be forgiven tomorrow, for it reads, "forgiving *one another*." It is turn and turnabout, a mutual operation, a cooperative service. In fact, it is a joint-stock business of mutual forgiveness, and members of Christian churches should take large shares in this concern. "Forgiving one another." You forgive me, and I forgive you, and we forgive them, and they forgive us, and so a circle of unlimited forbearance and love goes around the world. There is something wrong about me that needs to be forgiven by my brother, but there is also something wrong about my brother that needs to be forgiven by me, and this is what the apostle means—that all of us are to be mutually exercising the sacred art and mystery of forgiving one another.

If we always did this, we would not endure those who have a special faculty for spying out faults. There are some who, whatever church they are in, always bring an ill report of it. I have heard this sort of thing from many—"There is no love among Christians at all." I will tell you the character of the gentleman who makes that observation; he is both unloving and unlovely, and so he is off the track of the pilgrims of love. Another cries, "There is no sincerity in the world now." That man is a hypocrite; you can be quite sure of that. Judge a bird by its song, and a man by his utterance. The censorious measure our corn, but they use their own bushels. You can know very well what a man is by what he says about others. Judging other men by their own judgment of their fellows—that is a gauge of character that very seldom will deceive you. Their speech betrays their heart. "Show me your tongue, sir! Now I know whether you are sick or well." He who speaks with an ill tongue about his neighbor has an ill heart; rest assured of that. Let us engage in our Christian career with the full assurance that we will have a great deal to forgive in other people, but there will be a great deal more to be forgiven in ourselves. Let us count on having to exercise gentleness, and needing its exercise from others. "Forgiving one another, even as God for Christ's sake hath forgiven you."

Note again: when we forgive, it is a poor and humble business compared with God's forgiving us, because we are only forgiving one another—that is, forgiving fellow servants—whereas when God forgives us, the Judge of all the earth is forgiving, not his fellows, but his rebel subjects, guilty of treason against His Majesty. For God to forgive is something great; for us to forgive, though some think it great, should be regarded as a very small matter.

Then reflect upon the matter to be forgiven. Our Lord in His parable tells us that the fellow servant owed a few pence, but the servant himself was debtor to his master for many talents. What we owe to God is infinite, but what our fellow creature owes to us is a very small sum. What did he do who has so much offended you? "He said a very shameful thing about me." That was very bad of him, no doubt. "Then he played me a very nasty trick and acted very ungraciously; in fact, he behaved scandalously, and if you hear the story you will be quite indignant." Well, I am indignant. He is a bad fellow, there is no doubt about it; and so are you. So were you certainly when you first came to God; bad as he was to you, you have been much worse to the Lord. I will warrant that his blacks toward you are whites compared with your blacks in the presence of God. "Oh, but you would not believe how basely he acted." No, and I dare say I should hardly believe it if I heard how base you have been to the Lord. At any rate, it should make our eyes fill with tears to think how we have grieved our God and vexed His Spirit. Some of us have had so much manifest forgiveness, so much outward sin forgiven, that for us to forgive ought to be as natural as to open our hands. After such forgiveness as the Lord has bestowed on some of us, we should be wicked servants indeed if we were to take our brother by the throat and say, "Pay me what thou owest." We should deserve to be given over to the tormentors by our angry Master if we did not count it joy to pass by a brother's fault.

If anyone here who is a Christian finds it difficult to forgive, I am going to give him three words that will help him wonderfully. I would put them into the good man's mouth. I gave them to you just now and prayed you to get the sweetness of them. Here they are again: *"For Christ's sake."* Cannot you forgive an offender on that ground? Ah, the girl has acted very shamefully, and you, her father, have said some strong things, but I beg you to forgive her for Christ's sake. Cannot you do it with that motive? It is true that your son has behaved very wrongly, and nothing hurts a father's heart more than the wicked conduct of a son. You did in a fit of anger say a very stern thing and deny him your house forever. I entreat you to eat your words up for Christ's sake. Sometimes when I have been pleading a case like that, the person I have been persuading has kindly said, "I will do it for you, sir." I have said, "I will thank you if you will do it at all, but I would rather you would have said you would do it for my Master, for what a blessed Master He has been to you! Do it for His sake."

I may be speaking very directly to some of you. I hope I am. If there be any of you who have gotten into a bad state of heart and have said you never will forgive a rebellious son, do not say so again until you have looked at the matter for Christ's sake. Not for the boy's sake, not for your neighbor's sake who has offended you, not for any other reason do I urge you to mercy, but for Christ's sake. Come, you two brothers who have fallen out, love each other for Christ's sake. Come, you two sisters; come, you two friends who have been alienated—get together and end all your ill feeling, for Christ's sake. You must not keep a drop of malice in your soul, for Christ's sake. Oh how this charming word melts us, and as it melts it seems to leave no trace of anger behind it. For Christ's sake our love suffers long and never fails.

I do not know how to put this next word I am going to say. It is a paradox. You must forgive or you cannot be saved; at the same time, you must not do it from compulsion—you must do it freely. There is a way of carrying this into practice, though I cannot explain it in words. You must forgive not because you are forced to, but because you heartily do it. Remember, it is of no use for you to put your money into that offering box as you go out unless you remember first to forgive your brother. God will not accept the gifts, prayers, or praises of an unrelenting heart. Though you leave all your substance to His cause, He will not accept a penny of it if you die in an unforgiving temper. There is no grace where there is no willingness to overlook faults. John said, "He that loveth not his brother whom he hath seen, how can he love God whom he hath not seen?" The very prayer that teaches you to ask for mercy bids you say, "Forgive us our debts, as we forgive our debtors." Unless you have forgiven others, you read your own death-warrant when you repeat the Lord's Prayer.

Finally, I want to say to you all, brethren, that as brothers and sisters in Christ Jesus, if we are to forgive one another, there must also be some other things that we ought to do. And the first is, do not let us provoke each other to offend. If I know that a man does not like a certain thing, I will not thrust it in his way. Do not say, "Well, if he is short-tempered, I cannot help it; he should not be so ready to take offense. I cannot be always paying deference to his absurd sensitiveness." No, but, brother, your friend is very ready to take offense, and you know that he is; have respect, then, to his infirmity of temper, such as you would have if he were afflicted in body. If you have rheumatism or gout, your friends do not go stamping across the room and saying, "He ought not to mind that; he ought not to feel it." Kindhearted people step across the floor with a light step, for fear they should hurt the poor suffering limb. If a man has a diseased mind and is very irritable, treat him gently, pity his infirmity, and do not irritate him.

A friend wrote me a short while ago a letter of serious complaint against a brother who had been very angry with him and had spoken very sharply while irritated. I felt bound to hear the other side of the story, and I was obliged to say, "Now, you two brothers are both wrong. You, my brother, lost your temper. But you, my other brother, irritated him, so that I do not wonder he did lose his temper. And when you saw he had lost his temper, why did you not go away or do something to quiet him? No, but you remained to increase the wrath, and then wrote to expose him." I blame the wood for burning, but what shall I say of the bellows? It was wrong to blaze, but was it right to fan the flame? Very often when a man is angry, he may not be the only one to blame. Therefore, brothers and sisters, if we are to forgive each other, do not let us provoke each other to the point of offense.

In the next place, do not see offenses where they do not exist. Oftentimes a man has been offended at another for no reason at all. One person has said of another as he passed him in the street, "He will not even nod to me. He is too proud to acknowledge me because I am a poor man." Now, that beloved friend who was thus blamed could not see much further than his hand, for he was short-sighted. Another has been censured for not hearing, though he was deaf, and another for not shaking hands when his arm was crippled. Do not imagine offenses where they are not intended.

Next, do not take offenses where they *are* intended. It is a splendid thing if you will not be offended. Nothing makes a man feel so small as when you accept what he intended for an insult as if it were a compliment and thank him for it. Can you master yourself to that point? Remember, when you have conquered yourself, you have conquered the world. You have overcome everybody when you have so fully overcome your own spirit that you remain content with that which naturally would excite your wrath.

Then, if you must be offended, dear brother, do not exaggerate an offense. Some good women, and *men* also, when they come as tale-bearers, make a great many flourishes and additions. They go a long way around, and they bring innumerable beliefs and suggestions and hints and hearsays into the business, until a fly's egg becomes as huge as ever was laid by an ostrich. I begin coolly to strip off the feathers and the paint, and I say, "Now, I do not see what that point had to do with it, or what that remark has in it. All I can see when I come to look at the bare fact is so-and-so, and that was not much, was it ?" "Oh, but there was more intended." Do not believe that, dear brother, dear sister. If there must be something wrong, let it be as little as you can. If you have a telescope, look through the large hole and minify instead of magnifying, or better still, do not look at it at all.

A blind eye is often the best eye a man can have, and a deaf ear is better by far than one that hears too much. "Also take no heed," says Solomon, "unto all words that are spoken, lest thou hear thy servant curse thee." Something you have done may irritate a servant, and he may make remarks that are unbecoming and impertinent. Don't hear what he is muttering. Keep out of hearing; he will be sorry tomorrow, and if he thinks you did not hear him, he will continue in your service and be faithful to you. What would *you* do if *your* master held you accountable for every word and if he scrutinized every sentence that you uttered? How would you live at all if he reckoned sharply with you? No, dear friends, as you are to forgive one another, do not take offense; and when offense is given, do not exaggerate it, and if you can, do not even observe it.

Then again, do not publish offenses. There has been something very offensive said. What now? Do not repeat it. Do not go first to one, and then to another and say, "Now this is quite private, and mind you keep it a secret—So-and-so has spoken shamefully." Better that you should let your heart break than go up and down with a firebrand in this fashion. If a brother has done wrong, why should you do wrong also? And you will be doing wrong if you publish his fault. Remember how the curse came upon Noah's son for exposing his father. How much better it is for us all when there is anything wrong to go backward and cover it, without even looking at it ourselves, if we can help it. Cover it up! Charity covers a multitude of sins. Not only one, two, three sins will charity cover, but she carries a cloak that covers a whole host of faults.

Above all, my brethren, and with this I close, never in any way, directly or indirectly, avenge yourselves. For any fault that is ever done to you, the Master says unto you, "Resist not evil." In all things bend, bow, yield, submit. "If you tread on a worm, it will turn on you," some say. Is a worm your example? Christ will be mine. It is a shocking thing when a Christian man forgets his Lord and finds an excuse for himself among the poor creatures under his feet. But if it must be so, what does a worm do when it turns? When you have trodden on a worm, does it bite? Does the worm hurt anyone? Ah, no. It has turned, but it has turned in its agony and writhed before you, that is all. You may do that, if you must. Brother, the most splendid vengeance you can ever have is to do good to them who do you evil, and to speak well of them who speak ill of you. They will be ashamed to look at you; they will never hurt you again if they see that you cannot be provoked except to greater love and larger kindness.

This ought to be the mark of Christians. Not "I will bring the law against you," or "I will avenge myself," but "I will bear and forbear even to the end." "Vengeance is mine; I will repay, saith the Lord." Do not take into your hand that which God says belongs to Him. Rather, as He for Christ's sake has forgiven you, so also forgive all those who do you wrong. "How long am I to do that?" says one. "I would not mind doing it three or four times." There was one of old who would go the length of six or seven, but Jesus Christ said, "Seventy times seven." That is a very considerable number. You may count whether you have yet reached that amount, and if you have, you will now be glad to begin again, still forgiving, even as God for Christ's sake has forgiven you.

May God help us to be patient to the end. Christ Jesus must be the object of our imitation. This is the kind of doctrine that Christ Himself preached, and therefore, since He preached continually this love to our neighbor, and also forgiveness of our enemies, we ought both to preach and to practice it. Go and believe in Him, and be imitators of Him, remembering that He forgave His murderers upon the cross on which He accomplished our redemption. May His Spirit rest upon you evermore. Amen.

Alexander MacLaren
the Forgiving Son of Man

But that ye may know that the Son of Man hath power
on earth to forgive sins, (then saith he to the sick of the palsy,)
Arise, take up thy bed, and go unto thine house.

MATT. 9:6

The great example of our Lord's teaching, which we call the Sermon on the Mount, is followed in this and the preceding chapter by a similar collection of His works. These are arranged by the evangelist with some care in three groups, each consisting of three miracles, and separated from each other by other matter. The miracle to which our text refers is the last member of the second triad, of which the others are the stilling of the tempest and the casting out of demons from the two men in the country of the Gergesenes (Gadarenes).

One can discern a certain likeness in these three incidents. In all of them our Lord appears as the Peace-bringer. But the spheres in which He works are different in each. The calm that was breathed over the stormy lake was peace, but of a lower kind than that which filled the souls of the demoniacs when the power that agitated them and made discord within had been cast out. Even that peace was lower in kind than that which brought repose by assurance of pardon to the poor paralytic. Forgiveness is a loftier blessing than even the casting out of demons. The manifestation of power and love rises steadily to a climax.

The text subordinates the mere miracle to the authoritative assurance of pardon and thus teaches us that the most important part of the incident is not the healing of disease, but the accompanying forgiveness of sins. Here we have noteworthy instruction given by our Lord Himself as to the relation between His miracles and that perpetual work of His, which He is doing through the ages and today, and will do for us if we will let Him. It towers high above the miracle, and the miracle is honored by being its attestation. We deal, then, with this narrative as suggesting great principles over and above the miraculous fact.

MAN'S DEEPEST NEED IS FORGIVENESS

How strangely irrelevant and wide of the mark seems Christ's response to the eager zeal of the bearers and the pleading silence of the sufferer! "Son," or as the original might more accurately and tenderly be rendered, "Child," "be of good cheer; thy sins be forgiven thee." That sounded far away from their want. It was far away from their wish; but it was the direct answer to the man's true need. Possibly in this case the disease was the result of early profligacy—

A sin of flesh avenged in kind.

Probably, too, the paralytic felt, whatever his four kindly neighbors may have done, that what he needed most was pardon, for Christ casts not His pearls before eyes that cannot see their luster, nor offers His gift of pardon to hearts unwounded by the consciousness of sin. The long hours of compelled inactivity may have been not unvisited by remorseful memories, and the conscience may have stirred in proportion as the limbs stiffened. Be that as it may, it is to be observed that our Lord points to the miracle as a proof of His power to pardon, given not to the palsied man, but to the cavillers standing by, as if the former needed no proof, but had grasped the assurance while it was yet unverified. Thus both Christ's declaration and the swift acceptance of it seem to imply that in that motionless form stretched on its pallet an inward tempest of penitence and longing raged, which could only be stilled by something far deeper than any bodily healing.

At all events, the plain lesson from Christ's treatment of the case is that our deepest need is pardon. Is not our relation to God the most important and deep-reaching relation that we sustain? If that be right, will not everything else come right? As long as that is wrong, will not everything be wrong? And is it not true that whatever may be our surface diversities, we all have this in common, that we are sinners? King and clown, philosopher and fool, cultured and ignorant are alike in this, that "all have sinned, and come short of the glory of God." Royal robes and linen jackets cover the same human heart, which in all is gone astray, and which in all writhes more or less consciously under the same unrest, the consequence and token of separation from God.

Hence is seen the wisdom of Christ and the adaptation of His Gospel to all men, in that it does not trifle with symptoms, but goes direct to the deep-lying and often latent disease. It is wasted time and energy to dally with surface and consequential evils. The only way of making the fruit good is to make the tree good, and then it will bring forth according to its kind. Cooling draughts are alleviations for the sick, but the cure must be something more potent. The source of all sorrow is sin, for even to the most superficial observation, the greater part of every man's misery comes either from his own wrongdoing or from that of others; and for the rest of it, the judgment of faith that accepts the declaration of God regards it as needed because of sin, in order to discipline and purify.

The first thing to do in order to stanch men's wounds and redress their misery is to make them pure, and the first thing to do in order to make them pure is to assure them of God's forgiveness for their past impurity. So the sarcasms that are often launched at religious men for "taking tracts to people when they want bread" and the like are excessively shallow and simply indicate that the critic has but superficially diagnosed the disease and is therefore woefully wrong about the needed medicine. God forbid that we should say a word that even seemed to depreciate the value of other forms of philanthropic effort, or to be lacking in sympathy and admiration for the enthusiasm that fills and guides many self-sacrificing and earnest workers amid the squalor and vice of our complex and half-barbarous "civilization." It is the plain duty of

Christian people heartily to rejoice in and to help all such work and to recognize it as good and blessed, being as it is a direct consequence of the Christian view of the solidarity of humanity and of the stewardship of possession.

But we must go a great deal deeper than aesthetic or intellectual or political or economic reforms can reach before we touch the real reason why men are miserable. The black fountainhead must be stanched, or it is useless trying to drain the bog and make its quaking morass solid, fertile soil. We shall effectually and certainly cure the misery only when we begin where the misery begins, where Christ began, and deal first with sin. The true "saviour of society" is he who can go to his paralyzed and wretched brother and, as a minister declaring God's heart, say to him, "Be of good cheer; thy sins be forgiven thee." Then the palsy will go out of the shrunken limbs, and a new energy will come into them, and the sufferer will rise, take up his bed, and walk.

FORGIVENESS IS EXCLUSIVELY A DIVINE ACT

We read that there were sitting by, with jealous and therefore blind eyes, a company of learned men, religious formalists of the highest order, gathered, as one of the other evangelists tells us, out of every corner of the land, as a kind of ecclesiastical inquisition or board of judges to report on this young Galilean teacher, whom His disciples unauthorizedly called Rabbi. They were as unmoved by the dewy pity in Christ's gaze as by the newborn hope beginning to swim up into the paralytic's dim eyes. But they had a keen scent for heresy, and so they fastened with sure instinct on the one questionable point: "Why doth this man speak blasphemies? who can forgive sins but God only?" (Mark 2:7). Formalists, whose religion is mainly a bundle of red tape tied around men's limbs to keep them from getting at things that they would like, are blind as bats to the radiant beauty of lofty goodness and insensible as rocks to the wants of sad humanity.

But still these scribes and doctors were perfectly right in the principle that they conceived Jesus to be violating. Forgiveness is an exclusively divine act. Of course that is so. Sin is the perversion of our relation to God. The word *sin* is meaningless unless the deed be thought of in reference to God. The same act may be regarded as being sin or crime or vice. As sin, it has to do with God; as crime, it has to do with public law and with other men; as vice, it has to do with a standard of morality and may affect myself alone. The representatives of national law can pardon crime. The impersonal tribunal of morals is silent as to the forgiveness of vice. God alone has to do with vice or crime considered as sin, and He alone against whom only we have sinned can pardon our transgression.

God only can forgive sins, because the essential in forgiveness is not the remission of external penalty, but the unrestrained flow of love from the offended heart of Him who has been sinned against. When you fathers and mothers forgive your children, does the pardon consist simply in sparing the rod? Does it not much rather consist in this, that your love is neither deflected nor embittered anymore by reason of your child's wrongdoing, but pours on the little rebel, just as before the fault? So God's forgiveness is at bottom, "Child, there is nothing in My heart to you but pure and perfect love." Our sins fill the sky with mists, through which the sun itself cannot but appear a red ball of lurid fire. But it shines on the upper side of the mists all the same and all the time, and thins them away and scatters them utterly, and shines forth in its own brightness on the rejoicing heart. Pardon is God's love, unchecked and unembittered, granted to the wrongdoer. That is a divine act exclusively. The carping doctors were quite right: "who can forgive sins but God only?"

Such forgiveness may coexist with the retention of some penalties for the forgiven sin. "Thou wast a God that forgavest them, and Thou tookest vengeance on their inventions." When sins are crimes, they are generally punished. The penalties of sins considered as vices or breaches of the standard of morality are always left, for the evil thing done has entered into the complex whole of the doer's past, and its "natural issues" are not averted, though their character is modified when they are borne in consciousness of God's forgiveness. Then they become merciful chastisement, and therefore tokens of the Father's love. The true penalty of evil, considered as sin, is wholly abolished for the man whom God forgives, for that penalty is separation from God, which is the only real death, and he who is pardoned and knows that he is, knows also that he is joined to God by the pouring on him, though unworthy, of that infinitely placable and patient love. Pardon is love rising above the dark dam that we have piled up between us and God and flooding our hearts with its glad waters.

We might add here, though it be somewhat apart from our direct purpose, that the forgiveness of sin is a possibility, in spite of modern declarations that it is not. When we venture to ask, with the humility that becomes a mere believer in Christianity when addressing our modern wise men, why forgiveness is impossible, we are referred to the iron links of necessary connection between a man's present and his past, and are assured that in such a universe as we live in, neither God nor man can prevent the seed sown from springing, and the sower from reaping what he has sown. But we may take heart to answer that we, too, believe that "whatsoever a man soweth, that shall he also reap" and then may ask what that has to do with the scriptural doctrine of forgiveness, which leaves that solemn law quite untampered with insofar as the iron links that the objectors contemplate are concerned, and proclaims this as the very heart of God's pardon, that the sinful man, who forsakes his sin and trusts in Christ's sacrifice, will be treated as if his sin were nonexistent, insofar as it could interfere with the flow of the full tide of God's love.

But we need a definite conveyance of this divine forgiveness to ourselves. If we have ever been down into the cellars of our own hearts and seen the ugly things that creep and sting there, a vague trust in a vague mercy from a half-hidden God will not be enough for us. The mere peradventure that God is merciful is too shadowy to grasp and too flimsy for a troubled conscience to lean on. Nothing short of the King's own pardon, sealed with His own seal, is valid; and unless we can come into actual contact with God and hear, somehow, with infallible certitude from His own lips His assurance of forgiveness, we shall not have enough for our soul's needs.

CHRIST CLAIMS AND EXERCISES THIS DIVINE PREROGATIVE OF FORGIVENESS

The fact that Jesus answered the muttered thought of these critics might have convinced them that He exercised other divine prerogatives and read men's hearts with a clearer eye than ours. *He* must be rightly addressed as "Lord" of whom it can be said, "There is not a word in my tongue, but, lo, O LORD, thou knowest it altogether." If He possess the divine faculty of reading hearts, He is entitled to exercise the divine power of forgiving what He discerns there.

But mark His answer to the objectors. He admits their premises completely. They said, "No man can forgive sins, but God only." Now, if Jesus were only a man like the rest of us, standing in the same relation to God as other saints, prophets, and teachers, and having nothing more to do with God's forgiveness than simply to say to a troubled heart, as any of us might do, "Brother, cheer up; I tell you that God forgives you and all who seek His pardon," if His words to the paralytic were, in His intention, only ministerial and declaratory, then He was bound, by all the obligations of a religious teacher, to turn to the objectors and tell them that they had misapprehended His meaning. Why did He not say to them in effect, "I speak blasphemies? No, I do not mean that. I know that God alone forgives, and I am only telling our poor brother here, as you might also do, that He does. The blasphemy exists only in your misunderstanding of My meaning"?

But Christ's answer was not in the least like this, though every sane and devout teacher of religion would certainly have answered so. In effect He says, "You are quite right. No man can forgive sins, but God only. I forgive sins. Then who do you think that I, the Son of man, am? I claim to forgive sins. It is easy to make such a claim, easier than to claim power to raise this sick man from his bed, because you can see whether his rising follows the word, whereas the other claim cannot be visibly substantiated. Both sentences are equally easy to say, both things equally impossible for a man to do; but the doing of the one is visible, and the other is not. I will do the visible impossibility, and then you can judge whether I have the right, as I allege, to do the invisible one."

Clearly there is in this answer of Jesus a distinct claim to forgive sins as God does. The objection that He meets and the manner of meeting it alike forbid us to take the power to "forgive sins" in this context in any but the highest divine sense. Now, this claim seems to bring us face to face with a very distinct alternative, which I venture to urge on your consideration. To offer the choice of being impaled on one or other horn of a dilemma is not the best way of convincing hesitating minds of the truth; but still it is fair, and to some it may be cogent, to say that a very weighty "either/or" is here forced on us. Either the Pharisees were right, and Jesus Christ, the meek, the humble, the religious sage, the pattern of all self-abnegation, the sweet reasonableness of whose teaching eighteen centuries have not exhausted nor obeyed, was an audacious blasphemer, or He was God manifest in the flesh. The whole incident compels us, in all honest interpretation, to take His words to the sick man as the Pharisees took them, as being the claim to exercise an exclusively divine prerogative. He assumed power to blot out a man's transgressions and vindicated the assumption, not on the ground that He was declaring or bringing the divine forgiveness, but on the ground that He could do what no mere man could.

If Jesus Christ said and did anything like what this narrative ascribes to Him—and if we know anything at all about Him, we know that He did so—there is no hypothesis concerning Him that can save His character for the reverence of mankind, but that which sees in Him the Word made flesh, the world's Judge, from whom the world may receive, and from whom alone it can *certainly* receive, divine forgiveness.

JESUS CHRIST BRINGS VISIBLE WITNESSES
OF HIS INVISIBLE POWER TO FORGIVE SINS

Of course, the miracle of healing the paralytic was evidence in very complete and special form, inasmuch as it and the forgiveness that it was wrought to attest were equally divine acts, beyond the reach of man's power. We may note, too, that our Lord here teaches us the relative importance of these two, subordinating the miraculous healing to the higher work of giving pardon. But we may permissibly extend the principle and point to the subsidiary external effects of Christianity in the material and visible sphere of things as attestations of its inward power, which only he who feels his burden of sin falling from his shoulders at the cross knows as a matter of experience. The manifest effects of the Christian faith on individuals, and of the less complete Christian faith that is diffused through society, do stand as strong proofs of the reality of Christ's claim to exercise the power to forgive. The visible results of every earnest effort to carry the Gospel to men, and the effects produced in the lives of the recipients, do create an immense presumption in favor of the reality of the power that the Gospel proclaims that Jesus exercises. We may admit the extravagance, the coarseness, the narrowness, that too often deforms such efforts and dwarfs the spiritual stature of their converts. But when the bitterest criticism has blown away as froth, is there not left in the cup a great deal that looks and tastes very like the new wine of the kingdom? Passions tamed, hopes hallowed, new and noble direction given to aspirations, self subdued, the charities of life springing like flowers where there were briers and thorns or waste barrenness, homes made Bethels, houses of God, that were pandemoniums—these and the like are the witnesses that Jesus Christ advanced no rash claims, nor raised hopes which He could not fulfill, when He said, "Thy sins be forgiven thee."

Whenever Christ's forgiving power enters a heart, life is beautified, purified, and ennobled, and secondary material benefits follows in its train. We have a right to claim the difference between so-called Christian and non-Christian lands as attestations of the reality of Christ's saving work. It is a valid answer to much of the doubt of today. If you wish to see His credentials, look around. His own answer to John's messengers still remains applicable: "Go and tell John the things that ye see and hear." There are miracles, palpable and visible, still wrought by Jesus Christ, more convincing than were those to which the forerunner was directed when his faith faltered. It is still true that "His name, through faith in His name, makes men whole," and that in the presence of unbelievers, who may test the cure. The dead are still raised, deaf ears are opened, dormant faculties are quickened, and, in a thousand channels, the quick spirit of life flows from Jesus, and "everything lives whithersoever that river cometh." Let any system of belief or of no-belief do the like if it can. This rod has budded. Let the modern successors of Jannes and Jambres do the same with their enchantments.

These thoughts yield two very plain lessons. One is addressed to professing followers of Jesus Christ. You say that you have received in the depths of your spirit the touch of His forgiving hand, blotting out your sins. Nobody can tell whether you have or not except by observing your life. Does it look as if your profession were true? The world takes its notions of Christianity a great deal more from you, its professors, than it does from preachers or apologists. You are the books of evidences that most men read. See to it that your lives worthily represent the redeeming power of your Lord, and that men, looking at your beautiful, holy, and gentle life, may be constrained to say, "There must be something in that religion that makes him such a man."

The other lesson is for us all. Since we are all alike in that forgiveness is our deepest need, let us seek to have that prime and fundamental necessity supplied first of all; and since Jesus Christ assures us that He exercises the divine prerogative of forgiveness and gives us materials for verifying His claim by the visible results of His power, let us all go to Him for the pardon that we need most among all our needs, and which He and only He can give us. Do not waste your time trying to purify the stream of your lives miles down from its source; let Him heal it and make the bitter waters sweet at the Fountainhead. Do not fancy, friend, that your palsy or your fever, your paralysis of will toward good, or the diseased ardor with which you follow evil and the consequent restless misery, can be healed anywhere besides. Go to Christ, the forgiving Christ, and let Him lay His hand upon you. Listen to the blessed words from His own sweet and infallible lips, words that will work like a charm upon all your nature: "Son, be of good cheer; thy sins be forgiven thee." "Daughter, thy faith hath made thee whole; depart in peace." Then shall the eyes of the blind be opened, then shall the lame man leap as a hart, and the tongue of the dumb sing. Then limitations, sorrows, and the diseases of the spirit shall pass away, and forgiveness will bear fruit in joy and power, in holiness, health, and peace.

Notes

Chapter 3:
If We Confess Our Sins . . .

1. Bob George, *Growing in Grace* (Eugene, OR: Harvest House, 1990), 67.

2. Bob George, *Classic Christianity* (Eugene, OR: Harvest House, 1989), 193-194.

3. Ibid., 195.

4. Ibid., 193.

5. Ibid., 194 (emphasis in original).

6. For a thorough discussion on the security of salvation, see John MacArthur, *Saved Without a Doubt* (Wheaton, IL: Victor, 1992).

7. Matthew Henry, *Matthew Henry's Commentary on the Bible*, 4 vols. (Old Tappan, NJ: Revell, n.d.), 4:page unknown.

Chapter 5:
Forgiving One Another

1. See Appendix 3 for a further discussion of this passage.

Chapter 6:
Just As God Has Forgiven You

1. Jay Adams, *From Forgiven to Forgiving* (Amityville, NY: Calvary, 1994), 34.

2. Ibid.

3. Jay Adams cites this verse but argues that it calls only for the preparation of the heart for forgiveness. He suggests that the command "forgive" in this verse merely means that the one praying should be "ready to forgive" (ibid., p. 30). But Adams believes actual forgiveness does not occur until the offender asks for forgiveness. The person who has "forgiven" in this manner therefore cannot regard the forgiveness as complete until he confronts the offender, obtains that person's repentance, and formally grants forgiveness.

4. Matthew Henry, *Matthew Henry's Commentary* (Old Tappan, NJ: Revell, n.d.), page unknown.

Chapter 7:
If Your Brother Sins

1. Dietrich Bonhoeffer, *Life Together* (New York: Harper & Row, 1954), 112-113.

Chapter 8:
Answering the Hard Questions About Forgiveness

1. Jay Adams, *From Forgiven to Forgiving* (Amityville, NY: Calvary, 1994), 25.

2. Ibid., 64.

Appendix 1:
How Are We to Understand the Atonement?

1. A. A. Hodge, *The Atonement* (Memphis: Footstool, n.d.), 267.

2. See John MacArthur, *Charismatic Chaos* (Grand Rapids, MI: Zondervan, 1994), 278ff.

3. George Otis, Jr., "The Atonement" (transcribed from a message delivered at a series of YWAM meetings in Tacoma, Washington, autumn 1981). Transcripts of these messages are available on the World Wide Web at: http://www.concentric.net/~for1/otisa.htm.

4. Ibid.

5. Ibid.

6. Finney spends a considerable amount of time in his *Autobiography* arguing against "that theological fiction of imputation" (Old Tappan, NJ: Revell, 1908), 56ff.

7. Ibid., 362.

8. Charles Finney, *Systematic Theology* (Minneapolis: Bethany House, 1994), 249.

9. Otis, ibid.

10. Hodge, 269.

Appendix 2:
What Is the Unforgivable Sin?

1. William Hendricksen, *The Exposition of the Gospel According to Matthew* (Grand Rapids, Mich.: Baker, 1973), 529.

Appendix 3:
Two Classic Sermons on Forgiveness

1. All Scripture references in these classic sermons are from the *King James Version*.

Scripture Index

General Index